The Penumbra of Ethics

The Penumbra of Ethics

The Gifford Lectures of V. A. Demant
with Critical Commentary and Assessment

V. A. DEMANT
Edited and with critical introduction and commentary
by Ian S. Markham and Christine Faulstich

CASCADE Books • Eugene, Oregon

THE PENUMBRA OF ETHICS
The Gifford Lectures of V. A. Demant with Critical Commentary and Assessment

Gifford Lectures Series

Copyright © 2018 V. A. Demant. All rights reserved. Except for brief quotations in critical publications or reviews, no part of this book may be reproduced in any manner without prior written permission from the publisher. Write: Permissions, Wipf and Stock Publishers, 199 W. 8th Ave., Suite 3, Eugene, OR 97401.

Cascade Books
An Imprint of Wipf and Stock Publishers
199 W. 8th Ave., Suite 3
Eugene, OR 97401

www.wipfandstock.com

PAPERBACK ISBN: 978-1-4982-9778-3
HARDCOVER ISBN: 978-1-4982-9780-6
EBOOK ISBN: 978-1-4982-9779-0

Cataloguing-in-Publication data:

Names: Demant, V. A. (Vigo Auguste), 1893–1983 | Markham, Ian S., editor | Faulstich, Christine, editor

Title: The penumbra of ethics : the Gifford Lectures of V. A. Demant with critical commentary and assessment / V. A. Demant, edited and with critical introduction and commentary by Ian S. Markham and Christine Faulstich.

Description: Eugene, OR: Cascade Books, 2018 | Series: Gifford Lectures | Includes bibliographical references and index.

Identifiers: ISBN 978-1-4982-9778-3 (paperback) | ISBN 978-1-4982-9780-6 (hardcover) | ISBN 978-1-4982-9779-0 (ebook)

Subjects: LCSH: Christian ethics | Church and social problems | Civilization, Western | Christian civilization | Christian sociology

Classification: BV4639 D25 2018 (paperback) | BV4639 (ebook)

Manufactured in the U.S.A.   04/17/18

Contents

Preface | vii
Acknowledgments | ix
   From Ian Markham and Christine Faulstich

SECTION ONE: V. A. DEMANT IN CONTEXT
Chapter One: Setting V. A. Demant in Context | 3
Chapter Two: Social Credit and Christian Sociology | 20
Chapter Three: Christians and Pre-War Europe | 34
Chapter Four: Demant's Christian Background | 41

SECTION TWO: THE GIFFORDS
Introduction | 75

SERIES I: THE RELIGIOUS CLIMATE
Series I, Lecture I: *Ethos and Logos* | 105
Series I, Lecture II: *God, Man, and the World* | 122
Series I, Lecture III: *Moral Goodness and Blessedness* | 134
Series I, Lecture IV: *The Mystery of the Will* | 142
Series I, Lecture V: *Spirituality: Cultivation of the Inner Life* | 154
Series I, Lecture VI: *Secularization* | 157
Series I, Lecture VII: *Being and Becoming* | 167
Series I, Chapter VIII: *Gender* | 174
Series I, Lecture IX: *Eastern and Western Religion* | 191
Series I, Lecture X: *The Christian Revolution* | 194

SERIES II: THE MORAL CAREER OF CHRISTENDOM
Series II, Lecture I: *The Place of Ethics in Our Culture* | 199
Series II, Lecture II: *Not of This World* | 217
Series II, Lecture III: *The Field is the World* | 229
Series II, Lecture IV: *Natural Law Doctrine* | 239
Series II, Lecture V: *Is Man a "Real Kind"?* | 249

Series II, Lecture VI: *Society* | 257
Series II, Lecture VII: *Work* | 269
Series II, Lecture IX: *Enterprise and Establishment* | 281
Series II, Lecture X: *How Adaptable is Christian Ethics?* | 291

SECTION THREE: ASSESSMENT AND CRITIQUE
Assessment and Critique | 303
Bibliography for Section Two, The Giffords | 319
Bibliography for Sections One and Three | 325
Bibliography of the Writings of V. A. Demant | 331

Index of Names | 339
Index of Subjects | 345

Preface

INSIDE THE ACKNOWLEDGMENTS OF John Milbank's magisterial *Theology and Social Theory*, you will find a certain V. C. Demant given some credit. Leaving to one side that Vigo Auguste Demant is known as V. A. Demant, it is fascinating that this mid-twentieth-century theologian and ethicist gets this attention from our postmodern advocate of Augustinian orthodoxy. The reason for this is that Milbank was from 1983–1991 the holder of the Maurice Reckitt Teaching Fellow at Lancaster University. Milbank took seriously the responsibilities of the post. The endowment obligated him to listen afresh to the ideas that shaped the Christendom group, which in turn birthed "Christian Sociology." Although Demant had been writing in a different time and place, Milbank was struck by the concept that the Christian narrative is so all-embracing that it creates a set of assumptions that contrasts markedly with the secular foundations of contemporary social sciences. It was this key idea that shaped Milbank's *Theology and Social Theory*.

Milbank had a capacity to see beyond the time bound production of Demant's work—the ubiquitous use of "man" to describe all people; the enthusiasm for a misguided view of economics known as "Social Credit"; and nostalgia for the medieval age that often failed to confront the difficulties. Milbank could see an intriguing metaphysic that became the basis for the movement known as "Radical Orthodoxy."

In other areas, Demant can now be read with fresh eyes. His *Religion and the Decline of Capitalism* makes much more sense after the trauma of 2008 and the rise of contemporary populist movements that challenge the god of globalization. His affection for Christendom had a green dimension, after all, it included a desire for meaningful work, a simpler life style, and more care for the environment. And his Natural Law account remains one of the clearest restatements of the doctrine, which is appropriately disentangled from Aristotelian assumptions.

The Gifford Lectures are the most prestigious set of lectures in religion in the world. Both Reinhold Niebuhr and Karl Barth delivered the Giffords. Therefore, any set which has not been published leaves a significant gap. The selectors of the Giffords get it right. They are good at identifying a key voice or position that deserves appropriate attention. And V. A. Demant was a key voice in UK theology throughout the war years into the early 1960s.

These are the Gifford Lectures as delivered by V. A. Demant. He never finished the manuscript. He wrote long hand in exercise books—jotting down notes, alluding to books, suggesting possible trajectories of argument that he might develop. Yet as we read this incomplete manuscript, it does provide the fullest, clearest statement of his worldview. This is the mature Demant. All the great Demantian themes are developed in the Giffords.

As the co-editors worked on the manuscript, Ian Markham was responsible for the initial scene setting. The purpose was to provide a survey of writings of Demant, sufficient to make the Giffords intelligible. Like many theologians and philosophers, the Giffords are the culminating of a career. Many of the themes that emerged in a person's work are developed in greater detail in the Giffords. This introduction was necessary to make the partial Giffords intelligible. Christine Faulstich was responsible for reproducing the long hand of Demant and creating a readable text from Demant's notes and incomplete sentences. This process had many puzzles and mysteries. So in many cases the footnote reveals the precise nature of the text available from which the suggested interpretation emerged. Our goal was an intelligible and readable set of Giffords, even where the actual Demant was very limited.

These lectures serve a variety of roles. This book is both a contribution to the history of ideas and an invitation to explore afresh some of the key insights of Demant's projects. Within the history of ideas, it affords an opportunity to understand a particular and distinctive approach of Christian ethics as it emerged in England in the early to mid-twentieth century. And in respect to Demant's key insights, we can understand Milbank's project even more and appreciate this anti-globalization, green, prophet who was just eighty years before his time.

Acknowledgments
From Ian Markham and Christine Faulstich

WE ARE BOTH GRATEFUL to Professor Andrew Louth, the Literary Executor of V. A. Demant, for permission to create this set of the Gifford Lectures. We were pleased with the editorial staff at Cascade Books, particularly Robin Parry, who saw the potential in publishing this book; Brian Palmer, who provided careful guidance around submission; Sallie Vandagrift, the copy editor; and Ian Creeger, the typesetter.

FROM IAN MARKHAM

This has been a project that has taken 27 years to come to fruition. The family of V. A. Demant were so helpful to this young graduate student at the University of Cambridge. They gave me access to the handwritten manuscript of Demant. I was working at the time with Brian Hebblethwaite, who must remain one of the gracious and generous theologians of his generation. Leslie Houlden took an extraordinary interest in my work. The handwritten manuscript was typed up by my sister-in-law Elaine Croft. Elaine is one of the most important people in my life. She and her husband (also called Ian) are a gift, and one of the true delights of living.

I am grateful to a Conant grant that helped provide some space to work on this book. My senior team at the Seminary understand and appreciate the importance of writing for me. So thanks are due to my Board Chair, Dr. David Charlton, and to the Senior Team, Rev. Dr. Melody Knowles, Ms. Jacqui Ballou, Ms. Linda Dienno, and Ms. Katie Glover. And as always, I am grateful to the Rev. Katherine Malloy. This project would not have been realized except for the interest shown in Demant by the Rev. Christine Faulstich. Christine was a delight to teach and has been a delight to work with on this project. David Goldberg and Maurice Dyer both helped in the closing stages with the book manuscript.

Finally, my time at Cambridge was a special time for my wife and me. Lesley and I started our married life in this extraordinary setting. For Cambridge and the many blessed memories, I am forever grateful.

FROM CHRISTINE FAULSTICH

While working on this book, Flannery O'Connor's words kept ringing in my ears, "The Catholic novelist believes that you destroy your freedom by sin; the modern reader believes, I think, that you gain it in that way." I can hear Demant saying that he believes one gains freedom by having a foundation like Christendom and the modern person believes you do so by rejecting it. It has been fascinating to ponder his reflections on the idea of human freedom and how it has changed in the last hundred years.

I am forever grateful to the Very Rev. Dr. Ian Markham for inviting me to participate in this project. His support and kindness toward me have been unflagging. I am also grateful to Lesley Markham for welcoming me on so many occasions over the course of this work.

I also offer thanks to my parents, Lynne and John Faulstich, for raising me in a home in which reading and intellectual inquiry were always valued. To my fiancé, David, for all he has done, thank you.

Finally, I would extend my gratitude to the Episcopal Church of the Epiphany in Houston, Texas. It is an honor to serve as their rector and I am grateful for the time and opportunity to do this sort of work as well.

SECTION ONE

V. A. Demant in Context

Chapter One

Setting V. A. Demant in Context

TO UNDERSTAND VIGO AUGUSTE Demant it is necessary to place him in his historical context. This will be done under two headings. We start with a biographical survey before moving to a more historical and contextual survey. This will provide a brief outline of Christian social concern since the Tractarians and F. D. Maurice's Christian Socialists. It will describe the various splinter groups including the rise of the Christendom Group and its subsequent fall. Demant's intellectual agenda is inevitably set by his church and academic setting. With the ecumenical developments, this proved to be a creative time for Christian ethics.

OUTLINE OF THE LIFE

Born: 8th November 1893. Newcastle upon Tyne
Parents: T. and E. Demant. Early Education: Tournan France

1913:	BS in Engineering. Armstrong College, Durham University.
1916:	Manchester College, Oxford, to train for the Unitarian ministry.
1918:	Received into the Church of England.
1919:	Ely Theological College; made Deacon.
1920:	Ordained Priest.
1919–1923:	Assistant Curate, St. Thomas, Oxford.
1921:	Exeter College, Oxford, Diploma in Anthropology.

1924:	BLitt, Oxford, for Book on Images and Idols.
1924–1926:	Curate St. Nicholas, Plumstead.
1925:	Married to Majorie Tickners.
1926–1929:	Curate All Saints, Highgate.
1929–1933:	Curate St. Silas, Kentish Town.
1933–1942:	Vicar of St. John the Divine, Richmond.
1942–1949:	Canon of St. Paul's Cathedral, London.
	—Chancellor 1942–1948
	—Treasurer 1948–1949
1949–1971:	Canon of Christ Church, Oxford, and Regius Professor of Moral and Pastoral Theology.
1957–1958:	Gifford Lecturer, University of St. Andrews.
1961:	Appointed Select Preacher, University of Oxford.
1971:	Retired to Headington.
Died:	March 3rd, 1983.

DEMANT'S BACKGROUND

Vigo Auguste Demant was born in 1893 of Danish descent. His father named his son "Auguste" after Comte, which reflected his father's Positivist views.[1] It was also from his father that Vigo derived his ability for learning languages. His father was an extremely competent linguist, who spoke most of the continental languages and provided a translation service for various governments and industrial companies. Therefore Vigo could speak French, Danish, German, and of course English, fluently. His father's work meant that Vigo spent much of his time on the continent; and his early education was in France.

V. A. Demant's initial interest was in engineering. In 1913 he went to Armstrong College, Durham, where he studied for a BS in engineering. It was while he was studying Engineering that he decided to train for the Unitarian ministry. In 1916, he left the north of England and moved to Oxford, which was to figure prominently in his life. At Manchester College he was influenced by Bishop Gore and rejected Unitarianism. He became an Anglican and was sent to Ely Theological College to train for the Anglican ministry. This was a crucial stage in Demant's life. Gore introduced him to Christian social concern; and Ely Theological College was Demant's introduction to the Anglo-Catholic tradition. His rejection of Unitarianism

---

1. See Peter Mayhew, "The Christendom Group," 73.

explains his fear of much theological liberalism: Demant felt that the two had much in common. Anglo-Catholicism, social concern and opposition to liberal theology proved to be the dominating influences in his life. He was almost 25 when he finally decided to become ordained. The striking feature of Demant's education was the almost accidental way he became a professional theologian. He was an extremely capable person who was able to turn his hand to almost anything, and once a subject was engaged, he rapidly achieved competence.

In 1919, he became a curate attached to St. Thomas Church, Oxford; while he was there, he wrote a book in Anthropology for which he was awarded a B.Litt. degree. In 1923 he went to St. Michael's Summertown Oxford; then in 1924, he moved on to All Saints Highgate, staying there for three years. Demant married in 1925 and his commitment to his wife and family were apparent throughout his life.

Throughout the 1920s Demant maintained an interest in social ethics. He was a reader of *The New Age*, and through that became interested in Major Douglas's social credit proposals. The General Strike of 1926 and the plight of the coal miners disturbed him greatly. In 1929 he was made Assistant Priest of St. Silas, Kentish Town, and for the first time became a public figure through his appointment as Director of Research to the Christian Social Council, working on such issues as unemployment and the miners. Demant was responsible for the sensitive and disturbing research into the plight of the miners, which made his *Miners' Distress and the Coal Problem* such a good book. Maurice Reckitt "discovered" him; he described his initial impressions of Demant when he toasted him on his 80th birthday: "I believe it was as long ago as May 1926 that we met for the first time. I was very soon made aware of what was said as long ago as the 18th century of some great figure (was it Burke?) that anyone who had stood for shelter for ten minutes under a tree in a thunder storm shall have realized in that very period that 'here was a remarkable man.'"[2] A very deep friendship developed between the two men. Each admired the other immensely, so that some scholars have suggested that it was a mutual admiration society! In 1933 Demant became Vicar of St. John the Divine, Richmond, and in the same year joined Maurice Reckitt on the editorial board of *Christendom*, a journal devoted to the promotion of Christian Sociology. He was involved with it until its demise in 1952. It was his involvement with *Christendom* which bought him in contact with the Chandos Group.[3]

---

2. V. A. Demant, Unpublished Papers. Speech made by Reckitt on Demant's 80th birthday 6th November 1973. A second copy can be found in the Reckitt Papers held at the University of Sussex.

3. Ibid., Chandos Group. See also Mayhew, "The Christendom Group," and Roger

The Chandos Group was so called because their meetings were held in the Chandos Restaurant which was at the lower end of St. Martin's Lane in London. These meetings became the hub around which much was planned and organized. The group was a most important part of Demant's life; he never missed their fortnightly meetings. The organizer and leading light was Maurice Reckitt, and the initial members were D. Mitrinovic, Travers Symons, Philip Mairet, and Alan Porter. They were all supporters of Major Douglas's social credit proposals. It was this group that provided the inspiration for several publications, namely, *Coal: A Challenge to the Nation's Conscience*; *The Miners Distress and the Coal Problem*; and finally, *Politics: A Discussion of Realities*. As time passed the membership changed. Egerton Swann, J. V. Delahaye, Bernard Boothroyd, Reginald Ronds, and T. M. Heron all became regular members. Probably the most significant person to join the group was T. S. Eliot, with whom Demant formed a deep and intimate friendship. He received several signed copies of Eliot's books each with a special word of thanks for times spent together. For several years Demant was confessor to Eliot, and it is very clear that Eliot held Demant in high regard. The Chandos Group were very active in several journals. *Christendom* was the best known, but others included *The New English Weekly* and *The New Age*. They entertained Lewis Mumford and Reinhold Niebuhr when they were in Britain. In 1942, Demant was appointed a Canon of St. Paul's Cathedral. During the second World War his duties included fire watching. John Betjeman used to watch with him, and both men remembered their conversations with considerable affection.[4]

Demant was at his most influential from 1929 to 1945. This was apparent in three ways. First, as a leading member of the Christendom group. Maurice Reckitt claims that Demant "came into the field of Christian Sociology with an equipment unrivalled before or since, and the directions in which it has developed since 1930 in this country, at any rate in Anglican circles, are primarily dependent upon his thinking."[5] This is rather excessive; however, amongst its members he was considered the thinker, the philosopher, and the intellect of the group. Secondly, he was an important exponent of social credit. He generated more interest in social credit than the theory deserved. This is the element of Demant's work which has received the most criticism, from Ronald Preston, Denys Munby, and Peter Mayhew.[6] Thirdly,

Kojecky, *Social Criticism*, 79ff.
   4. Interview with Henry Chadwick, 11.1.88.
   5. Maurice Reckitt, *As It Happened*, 270.
   6. See especially Ronald Preston, *Religion and the Persistence*; and D. Munby, *Christianity and Economic Problems*.

Demant was very highly regarded as an interpreter of the crisis which was afflicting civilization as the second World War approached. His *Religious Prospect* was very widely read. This is the element of his thought which will be the focus of the second section of this book.

It is ironic that as Demant's influence started to fade, along with that of a whole host of pre-war British theologians, he was offered a Professorship at Oxford. In 1949, he was offered the post of Canon of Christ Church and Regius Professor of Moral and Pastoral Theology in the University. As Ronald Preston accurately observed, there is a problem every time this chair is available, because there is a shortage of Anglican clergy interested in Christian ethics.[7] In fact Demant was the only person suitable, so he settled into Oxford life, continuing to lecture and write. In 1957–58 he delivered the Gifford Lectures at the University of St. Andrews, and subsequently began to prepare them for publication. On 16th May 1977, he wrote to Maurice Reckitt, "We are both old men now, but I have still five years to go before reaching your age, though I am doubtful whether I shall retain the intellectual vitality you still display. After two hours at my desk I want to sleep or do something with my hands. But I continue writing the long delayed Gifford Lectures, and hope to finish the job before I expire."[8] He never actually managed it. He was always very conscientious as a writer, and as he felt that verbally delivered lectures would be completely unsuitable for publication, he undertook the major task of rewriting them. Part of the problem was that Demant always found other more interesting things to do. He sat on the Wolfenden Committee, and supported the majority recommendation for the limited legalisation of homosexuality. Demant retired from academia in 1971, and moved into a small cottage in Headington, Oxford to enjoy his retirement. He died there, on 3rd March 1983.

It is a common criticism of Demant that the main reason for his ultimate irrelevance was that he was an academic with little genuine knowledge of anything beyond the immediate confines of Oxford and the Christendom Group. This attitude certainly lies behind Peter Mayhew's observation that, "The Group was composed of educated persons who delighted in discussion of principles. The people of the Church (and of the nation) were concerned more with the doing (or not doing) of what was right than with the reasons for declaring its rightness. Christendom thought hard concerning the good which ought to be, not hard enough concerning how the good should

---

7. Interview with Ronald Preston. 16.2.88.

8. See M. B. Reckitt archives held at the University of Sussex. The letter is written two days before Reckitt's 89th birthday

be brought about."⁹ One must be very careful with this type of criticism. Each and every one of us will find our perspective limited and ultimately inadequate. This is as true of Demant as it is of anyone. However, as will be pointed out in due course, it is true that for Demant there is no equivalent of Niebuhr's "Detroit" experience. It is difficult to decide to what extent Demant's errors of judgement can be blamed on his situation. For example, his disastrous economic judgments cannot be blamed on Oxford. When he was at St. Paul's and mixing with those actually involved with finance, he took up economic themes. In Oxford surrounded only by academic theorizers, he was intimidated by their expertise into silence.[10] This problem relates to the theme of the book. It will be argued that Demant did not succeed in relating his enterprising cultural analysis to any concrete proposals, partly because of the magnitude and difficulty of that task.

Any survey of Demant's life would be incomplete without mentioning the fact that everybody I have spoken to remembers him with great warmth and affection. Henry Chadwick remarked that Demant was liked by everyone at Christ Church: "he was the sort of person everyone looked forward to sitting next to in the Senior Common Room."[11] Bishop Michael Ramsey described Demant as "a very genuine and authentic thinker,"[12] and Leslie Houlden found "Demant a very thoughtful, generous man."[13] One of the reasons why he was so popular is that he rarely held conventional opinions, and he could defend his unconventional views with some success; for example, anyone discussing Shakespeare with Demant would soon discover that they are talking to a member of the Shakespearean Authorship Society, and that he tended to think that De Vere was the most likely author of many of "Shakespeare's" plays. The other reason always cited for Demant's popularity was his sermons. They were never rhetorical, indeed they were often difficult, but they were always informed and well thought out. Henry Chadwick recalls the tragic suicide of Michael Foster, Student of Christ Church and a philosopher, and recalls that there was only one person who could bring words of healing to the distraught community of Christ Church. Demant proceeded to preach a very sensitive yet positive sermon, which helped to place the tragedy in some sort of context.[14] As a preacher

9. Mayhew, *Christendom Group*, 52. He subsequently confirmed this interpretation in an interview 16.3.88.

10. Interview with Andrew Louth. 19.7.88.

11. Interview with Henry Chadwick, 11.1.88.

12. Interview with Bishop Michael Ramsey, 16.3.88.

13. Interview with Leslie Houlden, 10.11.87.

14. Interview with Henry Chadwick, 11.1.88. See also Demant's Unpublished Papers. A collection of his unpublished sermons.

and a friend Demant has never been forgotten, even if his scholarship has been neglected.

It is certainly a remarkable and interesting life. He became an academic almost by accident and he was surprised when other people found his thoughts helpful. His family tend to think that he always thought of himself as, first and foremost, a parish priest, and an academic second. As a younger man he was certainly very significant and highly regarded. This makes him a difficult subject for a study, for two reasons. First, he raises an important question regarding the significance of the second World War for British Theology. Bishop Ramsey observed that Demant was listened to when Britain was in the middle of a depression, and as Hitler took control of continental Europe; yet was forgotten when it came to a welfare state and the self-confident sixties.[15] Secondly, one has to try to disentangle some of Demant's perceptive ideas from a whole host of less happy aspects, such as the social credit proposals, his medieval sentimentality, and his interpretation of Martin Luther

Moving away from the biographical, it is now necessary to examine the intellectual trajectories that are acting on Demant.

ANGLO-CATHOLICISM AND THE RISE OF THE CHRISTENDOM GROUP

Demant's conversion to Anglo-Catholicism in the early 1920s came at a time when many people were finding Anglo-Catholicism attractive. The High Church movement was growing dramatically. In February, 1920 the first Anglo-Catholic Congress was held with 1300 people present, and it received considerable attention in the press. It was very wide-ranging, with papers delivered on subjects as diverse as the nature of the sacraments and relations with the Orthodox and Free Churches. One of the topics dealt with was called "The Church and Social and Industrial Problems," and the speakers were Bishop Gore, G. K. Chesterton, A. Moore and E. K. Talbot.[16] This shows that some Anglo-Catholics, at least, were interested in social issues and their relation to the church.

The roots lie in two quite separate movements which developed in the nineteenth century. The idea of the Church of England's catholicity was one developed by the Tractarians, notably Newman, Keble, and Pusey. The concern with social justice was developed by the "Christian Socialists," notably Maurice, Kingsley, and Ludlow. It is somewhat ironic

15. Interview with Bishop Michael Ramsey. 16.3.88.
16. See Report of the First Anglo-Catholic Congress 1920.

that these two movements became so intertwined, considering the initial conflict between Maurice and the Tractarians. However, the period from 1890–1920 is marked by two chief factors. First, almost all Christian social concern, which incorporated a political dimension, was being undertaken by the Anglo-Catholic wing of the church. Secondly, while their efforts were considerable, their success was limited. On the first factor Adrian Hastings writes:

> While much of the Anglo-Catholic movement was spikily unconcerned with anything other than highly ecclesiastical matters, it remains true that almost all Christian socialism from the late-nineteenth century on, was more or less Anglo-Catholic in inspiration. It is not surprising. Just as the conservative Evangelical tradition—pure Protestantism as it had come to seem—tends to stress individual salvation in religion and the importance of individual initiative in social and economic life, so a Catholic stress upon the corporate aspects of the Christian faith tends to go with a belief in the value of collective responsibility.[17]

The second factor is not surprising, in that there are always many people in every age who do not feel that change is necessary, and therefore are "conservative" in outlook. Maurice Reckitt writes, "For all the stir they made, the Guild of St. Matthew, the Christian Social Union and Christian Socialist League always remained very small societies. The Guild never numbered more than 400; the Union, for all its moderation, had only 6000 members when it was at its height in 1910; the League about the same time boasted 1200. When one considers not only the number of practicing church people at this period, but the wide and excited interest in social issues which characterized the years before the 1914 war, these figures appear almost microscopic."[18] Reckitt brings out the significance of the first World War. Before 1914, there was a ground swell of sympathy for the poor, which enabled William Temple to declare in 1908: "The alternative stands before us—Socialism or Heresy; we are involved in one or the other." It can be argued that before the war there was considerable sympathy for such sentiments. However after the war there was a different attitude. Hastings identifies three reasons for this change: First, the reforms of Lloyd George actually meant an increase in taxation, and this put a different perspective on the idea of reform! Secondly, the Labour Party was attracting more and more support, yet it was an unknown quantity with a socialist message.

17. Hastings, *English Christianity*, 174. In agreeing with Hastings, I am disagreeing with Oliver; see Oliver, *Church and Social Order*, 121.

18. M. B. Reckitt, *Maurice to Temple*, 190.

Third, the socialist revolution in Russia was violently atheistic, and deeply unattractive.[19]

The Guild of St. Matthew came to an end in 1910. Those within it, who supported the thirty-nine Labour MPs who were elected in 1906, left the Guild to form the Church Socialist League. The League included many of the later Christendom group such as P. E. T. Widdrington and N. Egerton Swann. The Christian Social Union had a similar split in 1918, when Conrad Noel, Vicar of Thaxted, formed the Catholic Crusade and Sunday after Sunday preached a solid socialist message to his congregation. The Church Socialist League soon ran into problems as there were two contradictory elements in the movement. One element wanted to build an overtly Christian basis for Christian social action, and this was the forerunner of *Christendom*. The other element remained committed to the Labour Party. When the League ceased in 1923, the first element formed the League of the Kingdom of God, which became known as Christendom, because of the volume of essays they produced called *The Return to Christendom*. The second element formed the Society of Socialist Christians, an interdenomenational body, which later became the Christian Socialist League. It is with the League of the Kingdom of God that Demant comes in.

THE RISE OF THE CHRISTENDOM GROUP

In 1897, Scott Holland had founded a journal for the Christian Social Union called *The Commonwealth*. During the early 1920s the editorial committee included three of the four future editors of the *Christendom* journal, namely, P. E. T. Widdrington, Ruth Kenyon, and Maurice Reckitt. When the League of the Kingdom of God was formed, they took space in *The Commonwealth* for articles and to promote their events. The leader of the League was Widdrington, a charismatic, stimulating, yet practical parish priest. The origin of the Christendom group is hard to date, as no membership list ever existed, but the group formed a distinct identity in 1922 when *The Return of Christendom* was published. The book was introduced by Bishop Gore and rounded off with an epilogue by G. K. Chesterton, while Widdrington and Reckitt were both contributors. Its book was that our age has come adrift from its religious moorings, and the dominance of the economic, the lack of community and the lack of culture are all consequences of the Enlightenment. There is some dispute as to the extent to which the authors were suggesting a return to the medieval period, but some of the essays implied this quite crudely. One example is L. S. Thornton's essay, "The Necessity of

---

19. Hastings, *English Christianity*, 173.

Catholic Dogma," which, having attacked modern individualism, states explicity that "it is a situation which calls loudly for a return to Catholic Christendom. Protestantism is helpless: for its distortion of both religion and morality is largely responsible for the actual state of things. It destroyed the only world-wide fellowship man has ever known, and broke up that unity of belief upon which it rested."[20]

Bishop Gore's introduction is interesting. It identifies tentatively with the themes of the book, describing the contributors as all "socialists in a general sense, that is to say, they are all at one in believing that no stable or healthy industrial or social fabric can be built upon the principle of Individualism, or is consistent with the assertion of an almost unrestricted Right of Private Property."[21] Gore's major criticism of the volume is that some of the contributors are advocating Guild Socialism, and Gore feels that "the advocates of Guild Socialism seem to me to have yet a great deal of thinking to do before they can claim that Guild Socialism is a working proposal."[22] Reckitt was a foremost advocate of Guild Socialism, seeing it as the alternative to Capitalism and State Socialism, and he hoped the Trade Unions would take it up. In general, John Oliver is correct in his judgement on this volume: "*The Return of Christendom* is a muddled and ill-balanced book, but it is important for its embryonic expression of the ideas of the Christendom Group."[23] It also describes the embryonic ideas of the Distributist League, especially in G. K. Chesterton's epilogue. In 1926, Chesterton became president of the Distributist League, which was basically the Roman Catholic equivalent of the Christendom Group.[24] For both groups, *The Return of Christendom* articulated their desire to find a genuine alternative to the current political options, and to ground it firmly in the resources of the Christian tradition.

The Christendom Group developed slowly: there were annual conferences on Christian Sociology and the League continued to publish in *The Commonwealth*, and slowly their ideas began to develop. They discussed contemporary issues, and the one which provoked most discussion was the General Strike of 1926.

The General Strike provided the impetus for Christendom's identification with such ideas as Guild Socialism and Social Credit. The Chandos

---

20. L. S. Thornton, in Gore, introduced *The Return of Christendom*.
21. Ibid., 9.
22. Ibid., 39.
23. Oliver, *Church and Social Order*, 123.
24. For a description of the Distributist League see J. S. Peart-Binns, *Maurice B. Reckitt. A Life*, 77ff.

Group[25] started work on a volume called *Coal: A Challenge to the Nations Conscience*; it was edited by Alan Porter, and the other contributors were Reckitt, Swann, Symons, Newsome, Mairet, and Demant. It was published in 1927, and is written with considerable passion and feeling. It is an attempt to stand back and assess the implications of the strike. It identifies a social problem, the division in society and the lack of community. It identifies also a political problem, in that because the political parties lacked the necessary vision to tackle these major problems. And it identifies a religious problem, which demands a rediscovery of the spiritual dimension in society. Finally, it identifies an economic problem, and here the Major Douglas Social Credit analysis comes to the fore. These four themes were to figure prominently in the Christendom Group's discussions and evaluation. One of the unfair features of much discussion of Christendom is that all their work is judged by the last factor, the mistaken Social Credit analysis. This ignores the other, quite independent, themes completely.[26]

In the book, the activities of Davidson and the Kirk committee intervention are interpreted favorably. It succeeds in showing the mistake in interpreting the strike as primarily about constitutional government. "A slight illegality committed by the Trade Unionists (known as leaving without notice) was magnified into an anti-constitutional act of the most awful dimensions. The few real revolutionaries in the whole Labour movement were flattered, by the inexhaustible bogeyman prattle of Sir William Joynson-Hicks. In fact, the Red Flag was hoisted by Mr. Churchill, and waved by Sir William Joynson-Hicks, while the Trade Union Council tried to pull it down."[27] This is perceptive and true. As a constitutional crisis the General Strike never amounted to much, and yet that is how the vast majority of people perceived it. The major problem with the book is the rather odd demands they made of the Government. It asks, first, that individuals ought to understand the ideas put forward in the book; secondly, that these individuals "form self-appointed councils to . . . make every effort to bring the new social synergy into consciousness, using every means to persuade the nation to act upon it"; and finally "we demand the creation of national

---

25. See earlier discussion.

26. See J. Oliver *The Church and Social Order*. He takes this as the predominant aspect of their work. Both Ronald Preston and Peter Mayhew, who are both trained as Economists, cannot find much else in the Christendom group, and are very critical of this aspect. For P. Mayhew, *The Christendom Group: A History and an Assessment*; R. Preston, *Religion and the Persistence of Capitalism*, 15ff. It is largely due to P. Mayhew's overemphasis on this theme that J. Peart-Binns has made the same mistake in his biography of Reckitt. See J. S. Peart-Binns, *Maurice B. Reckitt. A Life*.

27. Porter, *Challenge to the National Conscience*, 18.

inquires to deal with these questions as though no opinions had previously been accepted, with total disregard for private interests and prejudices; and with freedom also to make any recommendations they judge necessary; even involving great changes in the existing system of government and administration. The findings of these commissions, we finally insist, should be made the basis of immediate action."[28] This is quite clearly ridiculous; governments do not set up commissions promising to implement the recommendations before knowing what they will be. Furthermore, the topics they wanted to place on the agenda would have been very difficult for any government; one cannot have commissions on such abstractions as the spiritual and the community life of nation.

One other article of the time warrants a mention. Maurice Reckitt wrote in *The Commonwealth* an article called "Some Reflections on the strike." This is characteristic Reckitt, showing sensitivity for the miners. He tries to stand back from the details of the dispute, and evaluate the major themes. Reckitt cannot understand why anyone need take a pay cut in an age of plenty, and therefore writes, "It is this belief which has prompted our demand for an inquiry into 'the relation between banking and the issue of credit on the one hand, and the needs of the community, both as producer and consumer, on the other'—a demand which we are glad to note has now been made the subject of a petition to Parliament which is being extensively signed."[29] This is part of the Social Credit analysis, and Reckitt makes this explicit in his concluding paragraph:

> The "servile state" analysis of Mr. Belloc and the Distributism he and Mr. Chesterton present as an alternative to freedom; the Guild idea which has suffered so much from the doctrinairism of its most brilliant advocates, but which contains a large element of truth; the proposals for agricultural revival put forward by such men as Mr. Fordham; the proposals for democratic control of credit now being widely discussed, and linked by Major Douglas to striking and original ideas of price regulation and a "social dividend for all":—these three, taken together, constitute a new category of social thinking, and if they can be woven into a harmony will give us a new social outlook as distinct from Collectivism as it would be from capitalist Individualism."[30]

This is very revealing. Reckitt cites these various movements—all of which had different, incompatible and inadequately thought out ideas—and

---

28. Ibid., 11.
29. Reckitt, *Some Thoughts After the Strike*, 170.
30. Ibid., 172.

is hoping that a viable alternative to capitalism and socialism will come from it. Although it is unrealistic, it is also understandable. The Christendom Group took this as their main objective into the 1930s. They were living in the world of the Wall Street Crash, the Great Depression, and the rise of the anti-religious Stalin. They saw the quest for an alternative as essential, indeed as their duty as Christians.

SOURCES FOR DEMANT'S THOUGHT

Demant was an eclectic thinker. Inevitably, an Anglo-Catholic supporter of Christendom will be attracted by neo-Thomism, and this is the place to start this brief survey of Demant's intellectual antecedents. A neo-Thomist is inevitably going to draw upon the new Thomist thought which was developing on the continent at this time, especially that of Jacques Maritain, whose influence on Demant was considerable.

Jacques Maritain, a convert to Catholicism, became a major interpreter of St. Thomas Aquinas, and applied his insights to a variety of philosophical, moral, and political problems. Demant simply presupposed the major themes of his work. However, it was Maritain's political analysis that Demant chiefly drew upon. Maritain distinguished between the medieval world and the secular world in their social and political impact. The former was dominated by a sense of God which places politics below the spiritual, whilst the latter sees the temporal order as dominant, with freedom and human dignity realizable within the temporal sphere.[31] In *True Humanism* Maritain suggested that the world was now on the verge of a new Christendom—"a new Christian social order."[32] Demant agreed with this analysis. How exactly might this new order be realized? Like the Christendom Group, Maritain was, in his early years, an advocate of Guild Socialism. He was also searching for a compromise between socialism and capitalism. His influence on the Christendom Group was considerable. Demant, however, did not really grasp what was the central problem for Maritain: the problem of justifying human freedom. Maritain saw great value in the development of thought about freedom and toleration in the period of the Enlightenment and subsequently. There is for Demant, as for T. S. Eliot, a problem with regard to toleration. However, Demant preferred the work of Christopher Dawson on this question.

---

31. For an excellent discussion of Maritain's social ethics see Cooper, *Theology of Freedom*.
32. Maritain, *True Humanism*, 156.

Christopher Dawson made his impact on Demant before he went to the States and took a Harvard Professorship. Dawson was an exceptional historian partly because of the perspective from which he was writing. Glenn Olsen observes that, instead of simply tracing the development of certain theological ideas, "Dawson saw himself as an historian of culture, which he defined as the world-view of a people with a shared historical experience."[33] It was this perspective which so impressed Demant: "(Dawson) makes perhaps his most valuable contribution by resetting the problem of Europe in terms of much deeper import than is reached by the current propaganda thinking in terms of Democracy versus Dictatorship, Capitalism or Socialism, Communism or Fascism. Such antitheses arise out of division, in one and the same sociological ethos, of tendencies striving to achieve some human values in a mass society which has lost the meaning of human life as a whole."[34] Demant liked the perspective from which Dawson was writing. It transcended the petty divisions and exposed the ultimate similarity behind many contemporary disagreements. Dawson makes the following claims. First, religion is an indispensable element in any civilization. This is illustrated by the development of western culture. Second, there is a rise and fall with regard to the fortunes of Christendom, as his division of it into six major phases[35] clearly implies. He believes that the fourth age (medieval Christendom) was the most mature cultural form, with its balance and creativity. It is for this reason that the journal *Christendom* and the movement surrounding it found Dawson so congenial. One other similarity between Demant and Dawson is intriguing. In *Beyond Politics* Dawson attempted to suggest a possible practical step which Christians in agreement with his analysis might want to take. Demant was impressed: "The one definite proposal to which his book leads is that there should be a voluntary non-political organ for the preservation and enhancement of the cultural life of the community."[36] Demant suggested that such a movement ought to be called "Friends of Civilization." His only criticism was that Dawson had

---

33. Olsen "The Maturity of Christian Culture: Some Reflections on the Views of Christopher Dawson" in Cataldo, *Dynamic Character*, 99.

34. Demant, *Christian Roots*, 189.

35. Dawson believed that there were six ages of the church. They were:
1. Primitive Christianity. (Jesus— 300 AD)
2. Patristic Christianity. (4th—6th AD)
3. Formation of Western Christendom (5th—11th AD)
4. Medieval Christendom (11th—15th AD)
5. Divided Christendom (16th—18th AD)
6. Secularized Christendom (18th—to present)
See Dawson, *Historic Reality of Christian Culture*, 1961.

36. Demant, *Theology of Society*, 194. And Dawson, *Beyond Politics*, 24.

not appreciated the destructive effect that financial capitalism was having on our culture. Therefore, he suggested that this movement should have the responsibility for overseeing all economic activity.[37] This was all hopelessly impractical. Neither Dawson nor Demant really had any practical suggestions to make as a result of their cultural analysis. This problem of arriving at practical applications was to remain with Demant throughout his work.

Two philosophers are important for an understanding of Demant's work. John Macquarrie rightly links Dawson with Collingwood.[38] For Collingwood, eventually Professor of Philosophy at Oxford University from 1935–1941, emphasized the importance of history over science in cultural developments. Demant's "penumbra" which, it will become apparent, is his main contribution in the Giffords, can be seen in part in the work of Collingwood. Collingwood argued that all thinking is historically conditioned. Our answers are determined by the questions, and the questions are determined by certain presuppositions. These "absolute presuppositions" are not to be judged true or false, they simply express a certain particular historical and cultural situation. This applies even to the natural sciences by which he means more than just the physical sciences, appearing to include in the term almost any area of human thought and action.[39] As with any strongly historicist position, Collingwood has a problem in conceptualizing movements and changes in underlying cultural presuppositions. His explanation suggested in "An Essay on Metaphysics," is that within a single culture there are incompatible sets of absolute presuppositions, so "one phase changes into another because the first phase was in unstable equilibrium and had in itself the seeds of change, and indeed of that change."[40]

Demant was unhappy with this historicism (and therefore relativism), but accepted the importance of "absolute presupposition." However, as we shall see later, he attempted to analyze the conflicts he discerned between these basic presuppositions and the conscious ideals present in a given culture. Demant also felt that much more could be said about these ultimate presuppositions than Collingwood had thought possible.

A final important influence on Demant was Nicolas Berdyaev. In some respects Berdyaev, a Russian emigre, living and working in Paris, is a rather surprising influence on the neo-Thomist Demant. He is best known as a "Christian existentialist" "philosopher of freedom," and in these areas, there are significant differences between Demant and Berdyaev, of which two

---

37. Ibid., 197.
38. Macquarrie, *Religious Thought*, 132.
39. For helpful clarification see Mink, *Mind, History, and Dialectic*, 139.
40. Collingwood, *Metaphysics*, 74.

are especially important. First, Demant would not have shared Berdyaev's epistemology. Berdyaev believed that all knowledge must be appropriated subjectively. He thought in terms of a unity between the knower and the known, and believed that discursive reasoning has a very limited function. Demant would strongly disagree with these loosely "existential" elements in Berdyaev's thought. Secondly, Berdyaev was opposed to the Thomist system in that he strongly distrusted all systems of rational theology. So what exactly did attract Demant to Berdyaev?

Demant was primarily impressed with Berdyaev's analysis of the modern world. He shared Berdyaev's anxieties about the reduction of the human person which rather ironically is found in humanism. Berdyaev has a strong doctrine of man as made in the image of God, thereby giving humanity almost the status of co-creator with God. Humanism lost sight of this creative status of humanity. In this Berdyaev was quite distinctive, as Eugueny Lampert summarizes:

> Berdyaev wants to overcome humanism, not against man, in order to degrade him, but in the name of the God-man, and hence in the name of man. Most of the anti-humanistic tendencies of to-day, on the other hand, imply derogation of man and dehumanization of life and thought. So-called dialectical theology (Karl Barth, E. Brunner and others) is particularly interesting in this respect. It has shown not only an acute and just reaction against humanism, but also a revolt, an almost demonic revolt, against any link and vital relation between the creature and his Creator: hence a revolt against the eternal mystery of God-manhood, which is revealed in Christ and must be revealed in Christ's humanity.[41]

In the debate between Barth and Berdyaev, Demant was clearly on the side of Berdyaev.

Two further links need to be noted. Berdyaev believed that the crisis of our time is a result of technology. In an intriguing essay called "Man and the Machine," Berdyaev argued that the technological success story is in fact the cause of our social disruption. He contrasts the organic, settled world before technology with the isolation and alienation after the rise of technology. Technology—a result of human creativity—now destroys that very creativity.[42] The second link, which Demant found very congenial, was Berdyaev's belief that we need a "new Middle Ages." This would provide the solution to our contemporary technological crisis, and would lead to the much-needed

---

41. Lampert, *New Middle Ages*, 49.
42. N. Berdyaev, "Man and the Machine" in Berdyaev, *Bourgeois Mind*, 31.

unity between the aristocratic and democratic elements which any healthy civilization needs. This "new Middle Ages" would recover those organic, natural elements which our modern culture has lost.

DEMANT'S APPROACH

We are now in a position to understand the various strands in Demant's approach. He can rightly be described as a broad minded neo-Thomist; he is deeply committed to Catholicism and convinced it has many resources to help us make sense of a changing world. From Maritain, Dawson, Collingwood, and Berdyaev, Demant took various strands. The synergy which he formulated emphasizes the historical dimensions, the need for depth in understanding our contemporary crisis, and the resources which the Christian tradition can provide.

It is strange that these strands are not the ones highlighted by most scholars who discuss Demant's work. Instead, they are preoccupied with Guild Socialism and Social Credit. To these elements of Demant's thought we now turn.

Chapter Two

Social Credit and Christian Sociology

THE CHRISTENDOM GROUP WAS so called because its members felt that the Middle Ages had a unified Christian culture and an appropriate balance of various social, political, and economic forces which their age had lost. Our age was off balance, and as a result was in real danger of destroying itself. However, they never lost hope, and were constantly trying to generate ideas which could enable their country and world to regain the appropriate balance. Two such movements captured the support of the Christendom Group—the Guild movement, and Social Credit. This chapter will briefly explore these two movements.

Reckitt admits that the primary reason why Guild socialism was so attractive was that he believed it was a viable alternative to conventional socialism. Capitalism was clearly destructive, and socialism was clearly unsatisfactory. An alternative was needed. A. J. Penty, who was to have much to do with the Christendom Group, was responsible for the idea. Its model was the guilds of medieval cities. A. R. Orage took the idea up and started to propagate it in *The New Age*. The most significant recruit was G. D. H. Cole, a young Oxford don, who in 1913 produced a volume called *The World of Labour*. Briefly, the idea was that the country needed a method of organizing industry, which did not depend on the wage system, whereby profits are taken by the managers, and which enabled the Trade Unions to play a positive role. So a "National Guild would be a democratically self-governing association which, consisting of all the workers engaged in any main industry, would be responsible for carrying it on in conjunction with the State."[1] Both managers and manual workers were to have equal status. They would

---

1. Reckitt, *National Guilds*, 1.

elect a self-governing body to run every aspect of the industry, without outside interference. Reckitt felt that this was the way the Trade Unions should go, the alternative being a collectivism "which excluded them from a responsible partnership," and which would "perpetuate the servile status of their members." Reckitt envisaged "the State . . . which ought to become the trustee of the national assets of production, distribution, and exchange; but it was the trade unions developing into responsible guilds by the incorporation of salaried and professional grades, which must become the agents of administration."[2] Despite the efforts of the Guildsmen (as they became known), the Trade Unions did not take up these ideas. However, Reckitt continued to believe throughout his life that the Guilds concept should be part of the Christendom proposal for our society.

When Reckitt and Bechhofer revised their *The Meaning of National Guilds* in 1920, they added a section on Social Credit. Major Douglas—the founder of Social Credit—was given space to publish his ideas in *The New Age* after A. R. Orage had been converted by him in 1919. Reckitt and Bechhofer argued that Major Douglas's analysis would achieve for finance, what the Guilds proposal would achieve for property, that is, both proposals challenged important symbols in the respective ideologies of capitalism and socialism. They felt that the two were quite compatible. "It seems to us that the proposals made by *The New Age* for the development of an encroaching economic control by the mobilisation of the credit inherent in labour-monopoly and for the simultaneous socialisation of the machinery of price-fixing, offer a vast and immediate opportunity to enlarge the effective scope of the Guild programme."[3] In fact the only common ground between these two movements was that they were both unconventional; in detail they were incompatible.

Social Credit is the aspect of Christendom which has attracted most criticism. Edward Norman writes, "The attraction and pervasiveness of Social Credit to church radical thinkers is an unhappy testimony to their economic gullibility, and their ability to fall for almost any social panacea dressed up in moralistic language."[4] Denys Munby castigates the entire Christendom Group and sums them up thus, "What characterized the writings of this group was a brilliance of intellect and imaginative grasp of problems unhampered by any solid knowledge of the realities of the issues with which they tried to grapple, and any willingness to learn from experts. As a result, they naturally failed to say anything of significance on economic

2. Reckitt, *As it Happened*, 117.
3. Reckitt, *National Guilds*, 268.
4. Norman, *Church and Society*, 323.

matters."⁵ And John Oliver, who tries to be fair, is harsh when it comes to Social Credit: "It was a serious misfortune of the Christian social movement in the Church of England that many of its most active and influential leaders . . . were persuaded to advocate this fallacious panacea, rather than the economic measures which Keynes and his associates were propounding from 1923 onwards. In doing so, they were not only throwing away an opportunity of making a constructive contribution to the solution of the country's economic problems, but also bringing all Christian involvement in economics into discredit."⁶ These three quotations are representative of scholarly evaluation of the Christendom Group, and the judgement is severe. However, we shall argue that although Social Credit is clearly fallacious, and to identify closely with such an eccentric analysis was an appalling mistake, there were understandable and good reasons for this mistake, which have not been given sufficient attention. We shall now outline the main features of Social Credit, and then try and establish its main attractions.

Major C. H. Douglas was an engineer by training and had never studied economics. The Christendom Group was introduced to Douglas's ideas by A. R. Orage through his journal, *The New Age*. This was how Demant met them; while still a young man who knew nothing about economics, he was an avid reader of *The New Age*. It is worth noting that in June and July 1926, Demant contributed a series of articles to *The New Age* under the title "Anthropological Economics." Here, Demant links up Social Credit with a variety of anthropological judgements. He claims that other cultures do not have the paradox of the 'curse of plenty' because they do not have such elaborate financial controls. These articles are an interesting mixture of cultural analysis and an attempt at political recommendations.⁷ It is this mixture which generates Demant's difficulty. This is a point I will return to.

Douglas was in the habit of starting his meetings by asking questions like, "Would a maggot starve because the apple was too big?"; "There is a surplus of machines and an over production of commodities. Why can't some of the people who are short of everything have some of the surplus or make some of the things they need?"⁸ These were good questions. The paradox of the "curse of plenty" was puzzling everybody, and Douglas claimed to have the answer. Basically, Douglas believed that the problem was that the economy had a deficiency of purchasing power. This was because the

5. Munby, *God and The Rich*, 158.
6. Oliver, *Church and Social Order*, 124.
7. Mayhew, *Christendom Group*, 73.
8. Quoted by Lewis, *Critique of Social Credit*, 7.

price of a product is made up of a whole host of component costs, of which the wage is only a small part. The other costs included bank charges, raw materials, and overheads. Therefore, Douglas argued, the purchasing power of a community (i.e., wages) is always less than the price of the goods on the market. This meant that either goods are not made, or goods are made but not sold, or each country would try to sell its goods abroad, and obtain a balance of payments surplus thereby increasing the purchasing power of the community at home. Of course, not every nation can do this, a fact which leads to a destabilized world, as nations scramble for export markets. This was a constant danger to world peace.

Two qualifications are needed at this stage. First, the account just given is the popular account. It is almost certainly the one which Demant believed. Hugh Gaitskell identifies five different interpretations of Social Credit, and the obscurity and vagueness of the theory was one of the reasons for its success. "For each supporter there is an interpretation which suits his intelligence and his knowledge. For the critics there is not one but a collection of heads to cut off."[9] Second, this is also the way the theory was presented in the early years. As Douglas became frustrated by the complete neglect of his ideas by established economists, so his ideas developed in complexity and paranoia.

Douglas had a "painless" solution to the problem—simply increase the purchasing power of the community. This, he felt, should be done by a social dividend, that is, by an automatic reduction of 25% in the price of all goods, and the difference to be made up by a dividend to the employer. Furthermore, the banks, who control the scarce purchasing power of the community and make a profit from it, must have this power taken from them and the responsibility for credit placed under government control. There are two main fallacies in this theory. First, the model of the economy which Douglas is using is completely static. He concentrates on the end product, completely ignoring the many stages beforehand which although forming part of the retailer's costs, also distribute purchasing power into the economy. Secondly, Douglas does not understand how credit and saving operate in the economy. As John Oliver usefully summarizes, "Douglas was wrong to suppose that bank loans, because they are not usually fully covered by cash deposits, are imaginary creations, the repayment of which is bound to create economic disequilibrium. In fact a bank loan is always a form of saving."[10] Social Credit was tried once, in Alberta, Canada. In 1935 a Social Credit Provincial Government led by William Aberhart was

---

9. H. Gaitshell in Cole, *What Everyone Wants to Know About Money*, 389.
10. Oliver, *Church and Social Order*, 125.

elected. His problem was that almost all of Douglas's proposals were illegal, and "by March 1942, nine of Alberta's laws, mostly aimed at achieving social credit had been disallowed."[11] Both in theory and practice Social Credit was proved to be completely mistaken.

In many respects, Social Credit was an odd theory for Christendom to espouse. Douglas was a committed advocate of capitalism. He saw his proposals as the method of freeing capitalism to produce more and therefore benefit more people. He had no qualms about industrialization and technology. The Christendom Group was aware of some of the difficulties with the theory, primarily because A. J. Penty made them aware of them. Penty was a ferocious opponent of Social Credit. He was the original advocate of Guild Socialism, and always retained a conviction that a return to the rural life was essential for the survival of our society. Penty shared Christendom's admiration for the medieval period, and was convinced that Social Credit was wholly inconsistent with this ideal. He did succeed in persuading his colleagues that there were problems with Social Credit, problems which they saw as their task to overcome.[12] Many of his criticisms of Social Credit were quite pointed; for example, he attacked the manner in which it had become so all embracing. He likened it to the socialist critique, where "it was customary to connect every social evil with the institution of private property. . . . Nowadays the pendulum has swung to the opposite extreme, and money is called upon to explain everything."[13] It was this all-embracing character which led to disastrous political judgements. The best example was the Christendom Group's judgement on the League of Nations between the wars. The objection ran thus: the League, amongst its many functions was required to encourage international trade. However, international trade is only essential because of the lack of purchasing power within each nation state. The frantic efforts to trade and generate a balance of payments surplus will leave the other nation with less purchasing power within its economy, which will make it less stable. So, for the good of international relations, it is essential to oppose international trade. Reckitt saw a finance conspiracy in the League: "We feel that all these activities are apt to—and ought to—provoke our suspicion, since they are the opportunity for secret and centralised finance to advance its own ends."[14] This is a straight social credit analysis. As the international position continued to deteriorate, some in the group felt

---

11. See Encyclopedia Britannica. *10 Eventful Years. 1937-1946*. Under Alberta.
12. See for example Reckitt, *As it Happened*, 115. Reckitt's interesting analysis of Penty.
13. A. J. Penty, "Has Machinery Causal Importance?"
14. M. B. Reckitt, "A Report of the Anglo-Catholic Summer School," 248.

that this position should be modified. At the Christendom Conference, in 1936, Widdrington insisted that the League must be supported. The main opposition came, sadly, from Demant, as the report of his speech shows:

> Father Demant next took the Conference back behind even these comparatively evident dangers to the whole perverted structure of the economic basis of the twentieth century society. Our problem, he said, is to discover why there are wars—what makes people embark on what it declares with truth that it does not want to do? It is a problem of a divided will, of something behind our conscious and rational intentions, some fundamental conflict of interests between nations which must be brought into consciousness before it can be resolved. If it is not resolved it breaks out, not in pursuit of a deliberate aim, but as a way of escape from experienced frustration. This conflict of interests arises out of that god of the nineteenth century economists, the large-scale division of labour. When that arrived at the division of labour between nations, so that nations were no longer self-sufficient, the basis was laid, not as was claimed for an internationalism which united, but an interdependence which divides. For so long as consumption is made dependent upon employment, and employment upon exports, and the economies of large-scale production drive every enterprise to produce more and more of everything, national economic organizations are struggling against one another for export markets, for a "favourable balance of trade," which it is not possible for all of them to achieve. The thirst for full employment of capital and labour within each nation becomes a most dangerous thing even economically and politically, let alone its obvious cultural and ethical and social dangers. A stage on the way to the resolution of this dangerous situation is the dissociation of employment from export. Hence the fact that Economic Nationalism is at present a genuine hope for Internationalism. But ultimately to solve our problem it is necessary also to dissociate livelihood from employment.
>
> Father Demant was of the opinion that the League of Nations, as a quack promise to heal the diseases of the world-order with no attempt first to diagnose them, had better crash, and so draw attention to the consequences of neglect of truth and reality. The Church, at all events, could not back it, because a primary duty of the Church is to bear witness to the truth,

which a world involved in sin—in this case of interests—cannot by itself perceive.[15]

This reveals much about Demant. First, there is the element of stubbornness. Demant was in a minority, but he refuses to alter his message and analysis. Secondly, it demonstrates the context in which Demant was operating. He was not concerned with the perspective of newspapers, concerned about the immediate past and immediate future, but operated from the perspective of centuries. Thirdly, it exposes the central problem for Demant, that of making concrete political proposals from the perspective of cultural analysis, which was with him throughout his life. If one operates from such a perspective, it is very difficult to make current policy prescriptions. In 1937, he wrongly opposed the League of Nations; in 1947, he wrongly thought that capitalism was in decline. Yet his actual analysis could still contain certain insights. Demant's mistake was confusion of two different types of analysis. The first, which is immediate, must accept the given limitations of culture and society and can then make certain limited policy proposals. Such detailed policies require an awareness of the debates amongst the experts and of political realities. The other is "the judgement of History" where it is a matter of discerning general trends and their implications. When operating from the latter perspective, it is likely that mistakes will be made if one tries to make detailed policy proposals, and this is true of Demant. However, because of the sweepingly generalized nature of the analysis, no particular historical event can in itself falsify it. Thus Demant manages to accommodate the particular errors of judgement in his general scheme.

The reasons why Social Credit was so attractive need to be outlined. The main reason was that Social Credit was perceived as an alternative to the evils of both Capitalism and Communism. Reckitt is representative, and tells the story with some candor. In 1913, he admits that he called himself a socialist because there was no alternative, but when the Guild movement started to develop he became an enthusiastic supporter. However this did not take off, and this was the start of his attraction towards Social Credit. He summarizes thus,

> By 1921, then, I had said goodbye for ever to Socialism in any sort of dogmatic sense, but a new orientation was preparing to fill the vacuum which nature abhors, one must suppose, as much in political thought as everywhere else. This could not be other than an eclectic faith since, with the deliquescence of guild socialism, there was no movement to which I could any longer

15. See the "Report of the Christendom Conference," 131.

look for a true and sufficient social synergy. But the new element in my outlook, the skeleton which gave shape and strength to the whole was provided by that claim to be a new economics which christened itself social credit.[16]

Reckitt admits that he is searching around for a substitute. This is understandable enough in the 1920s and 1930s.

The second reason was that it purported to explain "the paradox of plenty." Why was it in a world of such wealth, technological advance, and manufacturing success, that there was so much deprivation and poverty? The classical economists had no answer, a point which Keynes himself makes: "Since the war there has been a spate of heretical theories of under-consumption, of which those of Major Douglas are the most famous. The strength of Major Douglas's advocacy has, of course, largely depended on orthodoxy having no valid reply to much of his destructive criticism." Keynes then goes on to say that in detail Douglas was completely mistaken; however, he concludes, "Major Douglas is entitled to claim, as against some of his orthodox adversaries, that he at least has not been wholly oblivious of the outstanding problem of our economic system."[17] If the Christendom Group had been truly perceptive, they should have backed Keynes; however, at least they didn't back the orthodox, classical economists. As Keynes remarks, at least Douglas was on the right side of the main debate, and that obviously must be true of the Christendom Group. Although Social Credit adopted certain quite misguided positions, such as their opposition to the League of Nations, Social Credit was also the reason why the Christendom Group took up positions which were more appropriate. For example, Demant latches on to the "paradox of plenty" to attack those who in 1926 felt that the problem with our country was over-population. Demant writes, "Dean Inge, Bishop Barnes, Mr. Harold Cox and the rest, all hold before us a reduction in the birth-rate as the only alternative to the main evils which threaten the future of our civilization." And he responds, "While it is true that during the last hundred years the population of this country has risen from about 18 millions to 46 millions, an increase of 250%, it is estimated by experts that the general output of goods of all descriptions has increased by at least 3000 to 4000 per cent. On a conservative estimate, therefore, there ought to be twelve times as many goods per individual to-day as there were a century ago."[18] Here Demant's analysis is correct.

16. Reckitt, *As It Happened*, 164.
17. Keynes, *Theory of Employment*, 370.
18. Demant, *The Over-Population Hoax*, 242–45.

Social Credit was given an enormous boost in 1929, with the Stock Market crash. Throughout the 1930s, Social Credit remained to the fore of the Christendom's analysis. One volume in particular warrants mention, Demant's *This Unemployment: Disaster or Opportunity*. Demant was writing as a member of the Research Committee of the Christian Social Council, and he writes with considerable feeling. "The Christian Church, has, therefore, a vital concern in squarely grappling with this problem, first, because the situation is inherently wrong and absurd—what the church fathers would call contrary to reason; secondly, on ethical grounds, because of the problem's human results in suffering and despair; and thirdly, as a warrant of her own claim to embody the truest view of human life known to men."[19] Once again, the theme of the book is the "paradox of plenty," and the solution is Social Credit. Apparently this side of the book caused a prominent official in the Bank of England to throw up his hands in horror at the ignorance of a good man who "knew no economics."[20] This is Demant's most explicit support for Social Credit, and he is intensely critical of everybody who does not share Douglas's analysis, including Keynes.[21] In all his later works, he is much more tentative in his opinions and mostly his commitment to Social Credit is implied, rather than explicit. *This Unemployment* was fairly influential: W. G. Peck describes a discussion with William Temple, "I asked if he had read Dr. V. A. Demant's book *This Unemployment* and he replied that he was just about to do so. The book made a great impression on him and not many days later he expounded its book to his Diocesan Conference at York."[22] It justified Christian involvement in economics: it just failed—rather ironically—to get involved with the experts in economics.

CHRISTENDOM, THEOLOGY, AND CHRISTIAN SOCIOLOGY

We now proceed to explore the theological presuppositions of the group, concluding with Demant's description of the Group's task as Christian Sociology.

The term "Christendom" is a reference to a perception of medieval Europe, where society was as a whole imbued with Christian values. Every aspect of life was affected, including the legal, cultural and economic aspects. The Christendom Group believed that modern society, having rejected its

19. Demant, *Disaster or Opportunity*, 13.
20. Mayhew, *Christendom Group*, 113.
21. Demant, *Disaster or Opportunity*, 83.
22. Matthews et al., *An Estimate and an Appreciation*, 68.

Christian foundations at the Enlightenment, had lost a great deal. The modern world lacked a true and valid perspective; for example, the economic life of the community did not have any over-riding end; and the state acknowledged no higher authority than itself, which made totalitarianism a constant threat. The rise of Hitler in the 1930s made this analysis plausible, for Hitler was linked with the Enlightenment, and the Enlightenment with the Reformation, which meant that Martin Luther was responsible for Hitler.

The most explicit example of this view is found in P. F. Weiner's *Martin Luther: Hitler's Spiritual Ancestor*, published in 1945, which enjoyed considerable popularity. At about the same time Jacques Maritain had his *Three Reformers: Luther, Descartes and Rousseau* translated into English. Maritain says of these three men that they "each for very different reasons, dominate the modern world and govern all the problems which torment it."[23] Maritain, taking Denifle and Grisor as authoritative, describes Luther as an uncontrollable drunkard, who constantly swore and slept with women. Maritain argues that this selfish immoral Luther explains the doctrine of Lutheranism. So, for example, the "justification by faith alone" doctrine elevates the self and eliminates any moral obligation. Basically, this doctrine of Lutheranism was an unrestrained individualism, and its result is that "it has inflamed everything and healed nothing. It leaves us hopeless in the face of the great problems which Christ and his Doctors solved for redeemed humanity so long as it was faithful. Problems which, nearly four centuries ago, once more began to rack the human heart like angelic instruments of torture."[24] Here Maritain is setting the damaging consequences of the Reformation against the successes of the medieval period. In slightly more restrained language, Demant takes the same line when he writes "By Luther's utter separation between the Natural Law and the Gospel the way was paved for interpreting the Law of Nature in a sense of pure expediency and utilitarianism." Then the dominoes start to fall. Demant goes on, "it is not a far step from this to abolishing all higher law by which the powers that be may be checked. Machiavelli took this step. For him the State is an end in itself, and in Hegel it takes the place of God as the end of man . . . By seeking a subjective liberty—in origin a freedom from ecclesiasticism—Luther began a trail that ended in political absolutism."[25] This connection between Luther and Hitler was so widely accepted in England that even Archbishop

---

23. Maritain, *True Humanism*, 4.

24. Ibid., 50.

25. Demant, *Christian Polity*, 84–85.

Temple was able to remark at Malvern that "it is easy to see how Luther prepared the way for Hitler."[26]

Gordon Rupp devoted most of his life to refuting this interpretation of history. In 1945 he published a reply to Weiner taking his argument systematically apart and exposing him as a propagandist rather than a scholar. Rupp also argued that whatever the causes which gave rise to Hitler, they were a good deal more complicated than simply the tracing of a line between Luther, the Enlightenment and National Socialism. Elsewhere, Rupp attacks Maritain's essay on Luther. "In this kind of essay, with which our time abounds, history is used much as the preacher uses sermon illustration: the facts have to fit a preconceived pattern of generalisation, in this case the theme 'metaphysical egocentrism.'"[27] This is an attack on the oversimplification of history. Rupp would agree that one of the consequences of the Reformation was the slow development of the notion of the modern secular state, and therefore the Reformation can be linked with the modern age; however, this does not begin to explain why Hitler came to power. In fact, Hitler himself was probably more influenced by his Roman Catholic upbringing than the limited contact he had with Luther's ideas.

Clearly the Christendom Group were guilty of an oversimplification of history and a sentimentality concerning the Middle Ages. However, this sentimentality for the concept of Christendom did have certain more constructive results. It provided a resource for specifically Christian analysis. After all, it was true that society had been dominated by Christian presuppositions. Unfortunately, too often exponents of "Christendom" sounded as if they were recommending a return to the Middle Ages, which is clearly an absurd proposition. Demant was the major exception, and his *God, Man and Society* was one of the most careful statements of what he termed "Christian Sociology."

He called it "Christian" because he claimed that he and his colleagues were seeking to discover, within the Christian tradition itself, the principles (chiefly medievally inspired) on which society should be constructed. It was called "Sociology" because it used the Christian dogmatic truth-claims about man and the world, to show how things actually are, not how they ought to be. The idea of a "Christian Sociology" was taken up with considerable enthusiasm. Reckitt is characteristic in his praise, when he writes, "Demant emerged at the opening of the thirties as a new voice in the Christian Social movement, demanding that it should advance 'from Ethics to

---

26. Temple, *Citizen and Churchman*, 13. Temple is following Maritain's argument which is a good example of this simplistic analysis.

27. Rupp, *Luther: The Catholic Caricature*, 202.

Sociology," from aspiration after what ought to be to proclamation of what essentially is."[28] This is a Demant slogan which recurs throughout his writings. In *God, Man and Society* he expresses this idea thus, "The Gospel is not good advice, but good news of deliverance from the obstacles which men have erected or found to the realisation of their deepest need."[29] Therefore this is a "Christian Sociology," because it provides an analysis of who and what men are, and "Sociology is the objective and dispassionate study of society,"[30] which means that a Christian Sociologist is one who judges, "in the light of Christian standards the quality of behaviour to which the social structure predisposes men and . . . elucidates and evaluates the forces which make up the structure in the light of the Christian doctrine of human nature and of the purposes of God . . ."[31] It is not a special method for doing sociology, instead it is the bringing of Christian insights into the ultimate nature of humanity to bear on society.

The only difference between Christian Sociology and Secular Sociology is the Christian has distinctive insights into the nature of humanity. The methods are the same. For Demant, these distinctive insights are partly derived from some of the achievements of the Middle Ages. One of the results of Demant's Christian Sociology is that the essential organic nature of human life is being undermined by the technological edifice of our modern world. This judgment illustrates the fact that Christian Sociology, for Demant, merges into an analysis of cultures. Christian Sociology, as an idea, did not necessarily have to make this move. For example, Reinhold Niebuhr believed that political and social judgments have to be made in the light of the insights about humanity derived from biblical religion, which in one sense could be described as an attempt at a Christian Sociology. Demant, of course, as a Natural Law theorist believes that there is a natural order for humanity and this leads to a more rigorous Christian Sociology. This also meant that the perspective required would in practise entail certain cultural judgements.

In *What is Happening To Us?* Demant links Christian Sociology with the task of a cultural historian. He starts: "As a sociologist and a historian of human cultures . . ."[32] And when giving a lecture to the Institute of Education, he uses the expression twice: "But I would ask you to consider some of the implications of this very curious and enigmatic achievement, speaking

28. Reckitt, *Maurice to Temple*, 176.
29. Demant, *God, Man, and Society*, 16.
30. Ibid., 58.
31. Demant, *Theology of Society*, 1.
32. Demant, *The School and the Churches*, 9.

as a theologian and student of the history of human cultures." And, later he writes, "When I look at this compromise with the eyes of an historian of human cultures I find it a unique and extraordinary achievement."[33] Christian Sociology collapses into Demant's primary task as a cultural historian.

There are four further aspects of *God, Man and Society*, that warrant discussion and bring out this cultural perspective. First, the basic argument is that certain human activities are playing a disproportionate and inappropriate role in our society because of a lost perspective on human life, resulting in a crisis at home and abroad. The crisis is two-fold; on the one hand, there is the rise of totalitarian regimes abroad, and on the other, the ever-deepening economic crisis with the dramatic rise in unemployment. These themes remained part of Demant's work throughout his life. Secondly, although he believes that Christianity was essential to our society, he is not so unrealistic as to expect everybody in that society to be Christian. He explains that a Christian world order, which is the aim of Christian Sociology, "is a world order of men, which is acceptable to Christians as a field in which the specifically Christian graces can be cultivated. It does not mean, for our purpose, a world order of redeemed and enlightened Christians."[34] Demant is rejecting the New Testament's sharp distinction between the church and the world advocated more recently by scholars like Emil Brunner, and opting for the Thomist view that church and world can and should be seen in tandem with each other, and that one can have a Christian society when—as a unified whole—it is recognizably Christian, that is, acknowledges Christian categories of thought and value. In practice, this meant for Demant that to change society's social structures requires a vocal and active Christian minority, and more broadly, a general acceptance of the Christian tradition. The church's duty is "to explain, as well as proclaim, that a religious climate is indispensable for the survival of the frail flower of civilization."[35]

The third aspect is that nowhere does Demant suggest a simple return to the Middle Ages. He is always sensitive to the dramatic changes of the last four hundred years. So he accepts, albeit reluctantly, that, "it is simply a fact that the modern state includes people of all religions and none, and with ethical assumptions of varying quality and intensity."[36] Demant also recognizes the difficulties involved in applying the tradition to any modern issue. Demant says with reference to politics, "whatever systematic Christian

---

33. Ibid., 59.

34. Ibid., 138. It is this defense of the Corpus Christianum approach which forms the basis of John Mack Stanley's doctoral book. See Stanley, *Church and the World*.

35. Demant, *God, Man, and Society*, 48.

36. Ibid., 97.

thought on politics has been developed in the past was worked out under conditions in which the State was something quite different from the modern secular state."[37] This sort of candor was completely missing from most of the essays in *The Return of Christendom*. Finally, Demant alludes to a Social Credit analysis and solution, and this is the weakest element of the book. The "paradox of plenty" takes up a substantial part of this economic discussion. The implication of this paradox is that economic activity has lost sight of its true purpose, namely to enable goods to be produced and then distributed to those who need. Too many scholars have focused on the Social Credit remarks, and do not concede sufficient validity to the analysis as a whole, which can stand independently of Social Credit theory.

As has been already noted this type of analysis is an attempt to make a sweeping historical and cultural judgment, which is bound to sit uneasily with immediate policy recommendations and comments on practical affairs. At times Demant perceives this, for example when he expresses his reservations over supporting a particular political party at an election. In an article written with Maurice Reckitt, he explains why a Christian may have a civic duty not to vote. They feel that one has a civic duty not to vote when all the political parties are failing to grapple with the serious problems facing the country. Behind all the parties' "Doctrine of Undated Salvation, which takes the form of believing that the evils of the modern world cannot be remedied by man, but only by time. . . . The gospel of 'the slow, gradual and painful' recovery is often a subtle form of fatalism, involving a denial of the Christian doctrine of man's responsibility for action here and now."[38] This is a cultural attack on an attitude which was a characteristic of the 1930s. However, the next two objections turn on a Social Credit analysis and are, in that respect at least, mistaken. The details of these objections need not concern us; suffice to say, there is a mixture of cultural insight combined with mistaken political policy, and the failure to distinguish these two was, as before, the ultimate mistake. In their attempt to analyze cultural forces, they were quite perceptive, and, to some extent, this justified their concluding remark: "And in so far we find ourselves outside politics, as ordinarily understood, we are so because we have thrust ahead of its bewildered armies, and in no sense because we have felt it possible to skulk behind."[39] It is Demant's cultural analysis which will occupy the rest of this book and is the theme of the Giffords.

37. Ibid., 95.
38. Reckitt and Demant. *Two Views of an Election*, 98.
39. Ibid., 98.

Chapter Three

Christians and Pre-War Europe

IN SEPTEMBER 1939 HITLER marched into Poland, and Britain was forced to declare war; later that month, on September 23rd, a group of friends known as the Moot met together. The group included T. S. Eliot, John Baillie, H. A. Hodges, Karl Mannheim, J. Middleton Murry, Reinhold Niebuhr, R. H. Tawney, and A. R. Vidler. There was a sense of profound confusion. Middleton Murry was deeply pessimistic and "associated the Christian message with the acceptance of suffering, and even defeat."[1] Others were less pessimistic. Mannheim was adamant that the Christian task was to start preparing for Hitler's defeat. Then the minutes of the meeting record an intervention by Eliot:

> It is strange that in 1914 we did not expect war and were not confused when it came. Now we have been expecting it for some time but are confused when it has come. We are involved in an enormous catastrophe which includes a war. (He mentioned Demant's *Religious Prospect* as a book which had enormously helped him in clarification of issues but was terrifying in the magnitude of the task of Christianization which it implied.) Where will people be found even to understand the basis of the task? A programme of publicity must recognize many levels, being addressed both to the many and the few.[2]

Here we have sensitive and intelligent men trying to understand what must have felt like the end of their world. Underlying their concern about

---

1. Kojecky, *Social Criticism*, 171.
2. Ibid.

the war and totalitarianism was the problem of how to be hopeful in a hopeless situation.

Christian attitudes to the crisis reached back to ideas developed between the wars. Ever since the first World War there were doubts about liberalism. Adamthwaite has an interesting passage where he cites Eliot and Tawney, both of whom had articulated a dissatisfaction with liberal, Protestant, western civilization. This created an ambivalence about totalitarianism, in that at least it was offering an alternative. Adamthwaite writes, "The world economic crisis increased foreboding about the future of western society. A profound pessimism pervades the politics and literature of the period. The resulting loss of confidence left opinion extremely vulnerable to ideological pressures."[3] This is a context in which one can place many Christians and churchmen. Eliot came closer than Demant to sympathizing with Germany, but both men felt that the reason for the crisis was not just Hitler; it was something much more fundamental. The real problem was western liberal and secular society.

The idea that the global crisis was a result of secularization was held by many Christian thinkers. When Pope Pius XII on October 20th 1939 issued the encyclical *Summi Pontificatus*, the press concentrated on his reference to Poland. However, the substance concerned a greater theme. Owen Chadwick summarizes, "He spoke of the anguish of his heart at human suffering through war; of the proof, given by war, that without Christian faith men cannot live in civilized society. He condemned the idea that the State has unlimited authority as a doctrine that brings death to the internal life of nations and to their prosperity, as well as the smashing of unity in international society, a unity which can only rest on agreement in the moral principles of the natural law."[4] This is the basic theme articulated by churchmen over and over again.

This chapter started with the Moot group. In many respects, this was just like the Chandos group—friends who shared a common concern and undertook many publications exploring this theme. The Moot group was the inspiration of J. H. Oldham, and he managed to bring together a most impressive array of people. The roots of the group can be traced back to the 1937 Oxford Conference, which attracted 400 delegates from forty different countries, on the subject of "Church, Community and State." Six months later, the Council on the Christian Faith and the Common Life (C.C.F.C.L.) was set up by William Temple, with the remit of following up the Oxford themes. Oldham was part of this Council and he suggested that an informal

3. Adamthwaite, *The Making of the Second World War*, 43.
4. Chadwick, *Britain and the Vatican*, 84.

grouping develop separately to discuss broader issues. Like the Chandos group, it played an important role in the lives of those who were part of it. Kojecky usefully summarizes, "It was not an official organization, although it inspired the Christian News-Letter and to some extent the C.C.F.C.L., but a group of friends, nearly all intellectuals and professional people, some of them well known in public life, who met two or three times a year from 1938 until 1947, the year of the death of one of the leading spirits, Karl Mannheim. Almost all the members shared a Christian commitment, or at least outlook, and this together with a desire to meet the challenge of the critical events of the times, united them."[5]

On the 3rd October 1938, J. H. Oldham expressed the feeling of the Group in a letter to *The Times*. He complained about the rather superficial analysis which had been propagated by the press, as to why Europe was now at war. Instead, Oldham argued,

> The basal truth is that the spiritual foundations of western civilization have been undermined. The systems which are in the ascendant on the continent may be regarded from one point of view as convulsive attempts to arrest the process of disintegration. What clear alternatives have we in this country? The mind of England is confused and uncertain. Is it possible that a simple question, an affirmative answer to which is for many a matter of course and for many others an idle dream or sheer lunacy, might in these circumstances become a live and serious issue? May our salvation lie in an attempt to recover our Christian heritage, not in the sense of going back to the past but of discovering in the central affirmations and insights of the Christian faith new spiritual energies to regenerate and vitalize our sick society? Does not the public repudiation of the whole Christian scheme of life in a large part of what was once known as Christendom force to the front the question whether the path of wisdom is not rather to attempt to work out a Christian doctrine of modern society and to order our national life in accordance with it?[6]

This is the same argument as that of the Pope, and it inspired T. S. Eliot to write *The Idea of a Christian Society*, 1939, one of its best known expressions.

The main public spokesman for this theme was William Temple, Archbishop of York from 1930 to 1942, and of Canterbury from 1942 to 1944. As Archbishop, and one of exceptional intellectual and moral authority, he

---

5. Kojecky, *Social Criticism*, 163.
6. Letter reprinted in T. S. Eliot, 1982, 97–98.

was expected to try and make some sense of war for the public. Temple was more aware than many of the developments in Europe. In 1935, in a lecture broadcast on Freedom, he argued that the English sentiment for liberty needed to be reconsidered. There are two possible roots for liberty, one in human selfhood, the other in divine sonship. If the former predominates, it expresses itself in an almost exclusively negative freedom, capable of producing certain political perversions. But the other liberty "is the principle of divine sonship. The man who believes himself to be a child of God can never allow that any earthly authority has an absolute claim to his allegiance or loyalty."[7] It is not self-centered like the first root; rather, it "will appear chiefly in demands for the emancipation of others—as in the abolition of slavery—rather than in demands for the concession of fuller freedom to those who make the demands."[8] Temple's message is clear: totalitarianism is much more likely on a secularized concept of freedom. This point he makes explicit when he writes, "If the citizen as he confronts the State is merely an episode in the passing stream of generations, if he is rooted only in transient history, then both in duration and in significance the State vastly surpasses him, and indeed his value to the State. On the other hand, if each man is a child of God created for eternal fellowship with his heavenly Father, the State is called upon to treat him according to that dignity and in preparation for that destiny."[9] This theme that totalitarianism is the logical consequence of secularization is one which also dominates Demant's writings. Temple returns to it time and time again. In *Citizen and Churchman* he writes, "The totalitarian States define justice as that treatment of the individual which most conduces to the welfare of the State. . ...None the less it is very hard to resist the Totalitarian claim on any humanist basis; if a man has no status or worth except his status as a citizen and his worth to an earthly community, he can have no rights against the State which acts for that community. There can be no Rights of Man except on the basis of faith in God."[10] He is stating in a popular way, ideas which Demant developed in a much more sustained and academic fashion.

Two further examples of this point of view can be seen in a series of radio talks, by J. H. Oldham, M. B. Reckitt, P. Mairet, D. Sayers, M. C. D'Arcy, V. A. Demant, and T. S. Eliot. All the speakers were convinced that the war

---

7. W. Temple, *Thoughts in War Time*, 119. These themes also occur in earlier writings, for example, Temple, *Essays on Christian Politics and Kindred subjects*.

8. Ibid., 121.

9. Ibid., 123ff.

10. Temple, *Malvern 1941*, 74.

was the result of secularization. E. L. Mascall, who wrote a preface for the book of the series, sums up:

> Winning the War may destroy Nazism, but if the vacuum thus created is left unfilled we may find it invaded by seven spirits more evil than Hitler and our last state may be worse than the first. Indeed, it may well be maintained that the rise of Nazism was possible only because we had allowed just such a vacuum to be formed at the heart of our civilization, because we had ceased to believe in the view of man, his nature, and his end upon which our Western civilization had originally been built, and because, in consequence, we had been living for generations upon spiritual capital which had been bequeathed to us by our Christian forefathers but which we ourselves had squandered to the point of bankruptcy.[11]

Dorothy Sayers concluded her talk with the same thought: "We must know what we are fighting about and what we are fighting for. And it will be well that we should begin by grasping this plain fact: that we can make no intelligent and whole-hearted fight for our 'European Culture' unless we are also ready to fight for the Christendom upon which that culture (whether we realize it or not) is founded."[12]

Two further themes were part of this analysis of the war. The first was the idea that the war was a judgment of God, because it was a result of human sin and disobedience over the last two hundred years. There are numerous examples of this kind of thinking, of which three will suffice. William Temple writes, "Now when by the operation of the law of God calamity comes upon us as a consequence of our neglect or defiance of His will, it is evident that this is properly called the judgement of God."[13] Maurice Reckitt in the already mentioned broadcast talks explains that the Christian, "must see the war not only as a just cause, and as a revelation of the failure of secularized Europe; he must see it as a judgement of God," and by that the Christian means, "that war is the logical consequence of the misuse of that free will and free thinking with which God has entrusted man."[14] The third witness is A. R. Vidler, who was drawing on his discussions in the Moot group when he produced a small volume actually entitled *God's Judgement*

---

11. Mascall in Oldham, *The Church Looks Ahead*, 10.
12. Ibid., 78.
13. W. Temple, *Thoughts in War Time*, 12.
14. M. B. Reckitt in J. H. Oldham, *The Churches Survey Their Task*, 46.

on Europe.[15] The influence of Demant is obvious, as the basic argument follows *The Religious Prospect*.

The second theme which was preoccupying these Christian thinkers was the hope and expectation that the war would signal the final demise of secularization and the return to Christendom, a society informed by Christian morals and values. This lay behind Reckitt's concluding remarks at the end of his broadcast: "Perhaps the whole future of a Europe which was once Christendom and must be Christendom again, will depend, more than we dare to think, on the degree to which those who claim to be 'the faithful' do in very truth believe, hope, love and understand."[16] The Moot group emphasized this theme. Society, they felt, needed a Christian vision, because the War was exposing the inadequacy of secular society. Middleton Murry circulated a paper before the second meeting, called "Towards a Christian Theory of Society." To the criticism that it is unrealistic that Britain will once again be dominated and informed by Christian values, Murry responded, "I regard it as no more inherently impossible that our society should be converted to Christianity, than for the Germans to be converted to Nazism."[17]

Temple, Demant, and the Moot group were all in sympathy with the same vision. The war was a result of a cultural drift away from God, and if there is a world to rebuild after the war, then secularism will have to go, and Christianity should reclaim its proper place. This was when Demant's influence was at its height, and it is ironic that as he moved to St Paul's and later to Oxford, so his influence faded. For, in the secular ebullience of the post-war period, he never stopped believing that our secular society is fatally flawed and that his pre-war analysis was fundamentally correct. He continued to believe that the effects of the Enlightenment constituted a major problem both for the church and the world. This was welcomed in the war-time period: it made sense of the confusion and provided hope—a hope that the church could rebuild society. The reconstruction after the second World War did not draw on this hope, instead it turned to the Labour Party and the welfare state was ushered in. Demant saw no salvation here. He continued to believe that this corporatist reaction was not the answer, and he foresaw many of the problems which produced the 1980s reaction. However he no longer had an audience, and it seemed that events were proving him wrong. Demant never believed this, and in his unpublished Gifford Lectures, he tried to show how events since the war have not proved his underlying pre-war analysis wrong, but have confirmed it. It is to this

---

15. Vidler, *God's Judgment on Europe*, 1940.
16. M. B. Reckitt in J. H. Oldham, *The Churches Survey Their Task*, 55.
17. Kojecky, *Social Criticism*, 166.

underlying analysis, found in essence also in Temple, and the Moot group, and developed and sustained in the Giffords as we will see later.

Kojecky reports Eliot at a meeting where he was explaining his role as a social thinker: "The distinctive contribution of men such as Reinhold Niebuhr, Christopher Dawson, Professor Demant, and hopefully himself, had been in this area of pre-political activity. Its importance was 'that it is the stratum down to which any sound political thinking must push its roots, and from which it must derive its nourishment. It is the domain of ethics—in the end, the domain of theology.'"[18] Demant would have agreed entirely. That was always his task, and it is in relation to that task that he must be judged.

---

18. Ibid., 217.

Chapter Four

Demant's Christian Background

DEMANT SAW HIMSELF AS an orthodox theologian, who believed in "catholicism." He was sensitive to more general questions, such as the nature of religious language; and that is where this chapter will start. However on many issues, he took much for granted. Nowhere does he explicitly provide a philosophical justification of his beliefs. Instead, he uses his beliefs to make sense of the world of human activity. The chapter will then elaborate Demant's conviction that the central claim of Christianity is that there are two worlds or planes. Demant believed that from this perspective one can then understand the purpose of such doctrines as the Trinity and Incarnation. This Christian insight, that humankind lives life on two planes and that denial of one leads to an unnatural life, is the basis of the Natural Law. The Natural Law is the basis of the Christian sociology. At this stage, three debates surrounding Demant will be examined. First, Michael Taylor and John Mack Stanley disagree about Demant's conception of the Natural Law. Secondly, some scholars feel that the claim to be formulating a "Christian Sociology" is not valid. And thirdly, Edward Norman claims that Demant in his post-war period became disillusioned with "Christian sociology."

Demant was a convert from Unitarianism, and like so many converts, he was completely opposed to that which he had left. He felt that a great deal of English Protestant Christianity was very similar to Unitarianism.[1] He was a campaigner against these elements, and argued that orthodox Christianity provided the only means to make sense of the world. Obviously, this meant that Demant was an objectivist. True religion, for Demant, consisted

---

1. Professor Henry Chadwick suggested this. Interview 11.1.88.

in cognitive propositions which affirm a reality that is not simply part of this world. He criticized a subjectivist approach. "A faith," writes Demant, "which makes the interior life a purely inward-looking thing, instead of a way back, up, and out to an objective spiritual world which is the common source of the inner and outer life, becomes a spiritual narcotic, which is what Marx called all religion."[2]

In *The Religious Prospect*, he sums up the main features of his understanding of Christianity thus:

> In brief, then, the configuration of Christian dogma which alone will enable modern man to give his historical existence any religious meaning will contain these elements of belief: God is absolute, unconditioned Being, transcendent to the world order as well as immanent in it. The world order, and all it contains, have a dependent, relative being. They also have an existence in the process of becoming which is relatively independent of the Creator. Becoming is of the nature of the Creation and therefore is not a fallen existence. But, without severance from its being, existence in the actual world is alienated from its true nature because the dependence of its being is denied by sinfulness. So existence in becoming splits up in oppositions pushing and pulling it round and across the centre of gravity of its being. Man is caught in the squirrel cage of these revolutions except in so far as he can establish a direct link with God transcendent. As redeemed, he finds that link established and sees the meaning of the oppositions. Thereby he discerns the working in them of God immanent, and finds direction for his own existence.[3]

There is much packed into this quotation. However, at this stage, it is essential to note the main feature of Demant's Christianity.

He focuses on the relation between God and the world. He believes that the important claim Christians make is that both eternity and history are real. Eternity is the transcendent world which is separate from, yet the foundation of, this temporal, historical world. Demant believes that the Bible is clearly opposed to the Platonic doctrine that the temporal world is a shadow of the eternal reality; or the Buddhist doctrine that the world is an illusion. "To adopt this attitude is to disbelieve that the Eternal God created a real world of things, of movements and of critical turning points, an insistence which the Bible makes by assuming that the created order is intended

---

2. Demant, *Religious Prospect*, 167. Demant would not have any sympathy with Cupitt, *Taking Leave of God*.

3. Ibid., 177.

and is not in itself a distorting panorama of eternity."[4] He holds that certain Protestants, in emphasizing the fallenness of the world, are undermining this conviction. The result is that "man can see nothing of God's hand in the historic order."[5] However, the greater problem in the West is not the belief that the temporal world is an illusion, but the opposite: the denial of the transcendent and the belief that the temporal world is all there is. Demant believes that Kant is responsible for this heresy. Kant took Descartes's idea that "the human mind contained in itself, prior to its relation to any external reality, the nature of truth," and created a system where, "the human being is practically the artificer of reality, and only by an act of will or faith can believe that the world is what the mind has prefigured it to be."[6] Man is placed at the center of all things. The only reality we can be confident of is the mind, and all else is inaccessible. Any meaning will be imposed by the mind on the world.

Demant holds that this belief is responsible for almost all the tragedies afflicting modern twentieth-century man. To take one example, which will be explored much more later on, Demant takes the German philosopher Fichte, who

> in his *Rede an die Deutsche Nation* said that man is made for an eternal end and is not inwardly content with a more limited one. But he used this truth to tell his compatriots that the individual person must therefore find his purpose and significance in the life of his Volk, for that, he averred, has an eternal life. You see what an easy but fatal mistake this can be. The race lasts much longer than the individual on earth, but the race still belongs to the temporal world; and if you give it the supreme value of the eternal you have to subordinate the person to the larger wave of temporal succession.[7]

In short, Nazism was a result of a denial of the reality of two worlds. God created both the Heavens and the Earth as realities. Orthodox Catholicism has always seen this, and this is the basis of Demant's understanding of Christianity.

---

4. V. A. Demant Unpublished Papers, Sermons. Sermon entitled "Not One World But Two," 2.

5. Demant, *Religious Prospect*, 13. Demant criticizes Barthian Protestantism for believing the world is totally alienated from the divine, and Liberal Protestantism for believing that there is nothing beyond the world. See also 170.

6. Demant, *God, Man, and Society*, 162.

7. V. A. Demant Unpublished Papers, Sermons. Sermon entitled "Not One World," 3.

ANTHROPOLOGY, NATURAL LAW AND CREATION

Demant believed that Christians have a distinctive insight into the nature of humankind. Armed with this insight, Christians are able to interpret the world and explain what happens. Demant presupposes a natural law theology, namely, that by reflecting on the nature of humankind and his needs, one can ascertain what is right and good. He writes, "The Christian religion provides such a criterion for placing the different activities of man in their instrumental order, for it has a doctrine of the essential nature of man."[8] Natural law theologies make much of the doctrine of creation, and Demant's is no exception. The creation reflects the mind of the creator, and this is seen supremely in humankind. Sin distorts, but does not destroy the image of God. All this is confirmed as we examine human society: "something of the essential nature of man is thus unfolded, and that nature appears to be the one assigned to him by the thought modes of the Christian tradition when it has held on to all the elements given in its revelation."[9] In other words, those in the Catholic natural law tradition will find their analysis of humankind confirmed when one looks at the difficulties facing western society. However, there is an interesting problem with Demant's conception which is exposed by the confusion which Michael Taylor finds himself in, when he discusses Demant's conception of natural law.[10] Taylor criticizes all Natural Law theories because of their emphasis on reason, and believes that there is "an inadequate understanding of the thoroughgoing effects of sin, leaving reason largely untouched."[11] But he then goes on to criticize Demant for his alleged Augustinian tendency to insist that because we are sinful we need the Christian revelation to show us the truth about humankind: for Demant thus loses the universal feature of the natural law theology which is one of its most attractive elements.[12] Demant cannot be guilty of both of these faults. Either Demant elevates the role of reason or sin has made reason part of the problem of man. John Mack Stanley argues that Taylor is wrong to suggest that Demant has elevated the role of reason, and rightly draws attention to Demant's repeated discussion of the perverted nature of reason.[13] Stanley, however, has oversimplified Demant's position. Demant

---

8. Demant, *God, Man, and Society*, 42.

9. Demant, *Religious Prospect*, 16.

10. See Taylor, *Christian Social Thinking*. We are indebted to much of his analysis.

11. Ibid., 91ff.

12. Ibid., 130f. Taylor writes, "It must be made clear that such revelation is necessary largely because sin has corrupted that which 'is' and the Gospel restores rather than creates something new."

13. Stanley, *Church and the World*, 210. For one example of Demant's view see

does not adopt the Reformation position that reason is fallen and therefore cannot be trusted. He explains his position very carefully: "Catholicism and Protestantism are agreed that there is an eternal world beyond the actual world, and that the actual world is perverted by sin. Protestantism seems to assert that man knows nothing of this eternal world except that it redeems him in the person of Christ. Catholicism holds that man as such can know something of what is eternally true about the created world, though he understands it not and his knowledge gives no power of any permanence. This knowledge of certain unchanging canons of a true order is knowledge of Natural Law."[14] Demant's view is complicated, but it appears to amount to the following. All humans, because of the fact that they are created in the image of God, are able to experience dissatisfaction with unnatural states and in so doing have a very limited knowledge of the natural law. Those who are redeemed have a vision which is much clearer, for "Redemption opens man's eyes to the real nature of things and their disorders."[15] The difficulty in interpreting Demant arises partly because there is a traditional problem in harmonizing the natural law approach with exclusive revelatory claims to those who are redeemed. We will now look at this problem in more depth.

THE TRINITY AND INCARNATION

According to Demant, the belief in the reality of two worlds lies behind the various doctrinal formulations. Doctrine, he argues, is not a result of arid logic denying the simplicity of Christian religious experience. Rather, it is intended to protect that experience. Demant cites Augustine's expression that the creeds are "fences around a mystery." They are intended to stop those who will explain the mystery away, usually in terms of some very limited philosophical world view. He writes, "The errors which doctrinal formulations forbid are the kinds of error to which the human mind is always liable—man being what he is, a creature of two worlds—at the intersection of time and eternity, and also a subject as well as part of the objective world. Therefore any mental picture of his existence, whereby the mind seeks to overcome mystery (as it should, for that is its job) is always liable to do it by just the kind of aberration that heresies represent in theology. The human intellect, hating the loose ends of mysterious being, wants either to separate or identify, what reality in the rough has connected but not fused."[16] The

---

Demant, *Christian Polity*, 98.

14. Demant, *Christian Polity*, 101.
15. Ibid., 98.
16. V. A. Demant Unpublished Papers, Sermons. Sermon entitled "The Holy

doctrines speak of the nature of all life: humankind lives in two worlds, and they represent the implications of that basic fact.

It is precisely because human life operates on the intersection between the two worlds that the Incarnation is so important. The life of Jesus is lived both within and yet beyond the temporal world. The Incarnation of God in Christ both confronts and shares the human problem. It is precisely this unique position which enables the Christian gospel to have the appropriate dogma which can transform the human situation. Demant believes it is entirely inappropriate for the Incarnation simply to be the fulfillment of God's original creative activity, because this does not affirm the dimension beyond the historical process. "The redemptive fact of Christ, in order to give him a foothold, must be understood as the act of God who is not exhausted by His relations with the creation . . . It provides the only Christian protection from tendencies which give an interpretation of man's significance in terms exclusively of the march of history."[17] Demant acknowledges an enormous debt to L. S. Thornton. Demant describes Thornton's "The Incarnate Lord" as a "profound essay on the historic Incarnation as the point of passage between the eternal and temporal order."[18]

For Demant, then, the doctrine of the Incarnation, coupled necessarily with the doctrine of the Trinity, provides both the power to attain a balanced life and the standard beyond history which judges all history. However, any natural law approach to Christian ethics will not make Christology primary. Those who want to make Christology central will find any Natural Law approach defective. Donald MacKinnon, who whilst a younger man was a critical member of the Christendom Group, found himself uneasy with the lack of overt Christological emphasis. Richard Roberts's analysis of MacKinnon's 1940s *God the Living and the True* rightly finds a mix of Barthian dialectical theology and neo-Thomism: "The rhetorical use of a conceptual vocabulary drawn from dialectical theology (in the first instance, as regards its extremity, Barthian, but later, with the increasing stress upon rationality, Brunnerian) coexists with scholastic conceptions flowing from the neo-Thomist revival. Overshadowing all is a massive commitment and adherence to the paradoxes of Crucifixion and Resurrection into which the dialectic of nature and grace is assumed."[19] MacKinnon's ultimate unhappi-

---

Trinity," 11.

17. Demant, *Religious Prospect*, 208.

18. Ibid. 209.

19. Richard Roberts, "Theological rhetoric and moral passion in the light of MacKinnon's Barth" in Surin, *Christ, Ethics, and Tragedy*, 4. Roberts explicitly acknowledges the significance of Demant as a representative of neo-Thomism later in the essay (p. 8). Donald MacKinnon directed me to this essay—Letter 15.2.90.

ness with the Christendom Group was partly due to the Group's neglect of Barth and partly due to the inadequate development of a *theologia crucis*. "Christian theology," writes MacKinnon, "is a theologia crucis simply in so far as it is the operation whereby the human intelligence adjusts its own appreciation of the human situation in the light of the impact upon it of the divine Word."[20] It is this book which Bonhoeffer must be referring too, when he writes: "With the Anglicans the connexion between natural theology and incarnational theology opens up the possibility of a peculiar natural-cum-Christian theory of the State. (Incidentally, the questionableness of this combination of natural and incarnational theology is now clearly perceived by the young Anglo-Catholics, who provide the corrective of a *theologia crucis*)."[21] In the end MacKinnon was not happy with Demant's Christology playing a secondary role within the wider theme of the significance of two worlds. It must be admitted that Demant, unlike MacKinnon, never really got to grips with Barth and these sorts of criticisms.

CHRISTIAN SOCIOLOGY

For Demant, Christianity makes sense of human life and the problems facing our culture. He claims that if we were more conscious of our tradition, "we should be able, much more than we do, to use our Christian understanding to interpret what goes on in the world . . . For it is a doctrine about the nature of things, and not only about the good life."[22] However, it is this idea that underlies the concept of Christian Sociology.

It is a Natural Law theology which forms the basis of Christian Sociology. The term "Christian Sociology" has provoked considerable disagreement. Ronald Preston feels that it is inappropriate because Demant had not studied sociology. It is yet another example of his disregard for the experts.[23] Denys Munby is particularly scathing when he says of the Christendom Group, "Nor . . . do the insights of Christian prophets afford any particular help to those whose task it is to help forward that painstaking progress of knowledge in the social sciences . . . it is in the barrenness of Christian sociology in contributing to this knowledge that the futility of its

20. MacKinnon, *God The Living and The True*, 63.

21. Bonhoeffer, *Ethics*, 298. This is the view of Donald MacKinnon himself—Letter 15.2.90. This might seem surprising given the circumstances facing Bonhoeffer in Germany at this time; but it is clear that he is referring to some Anglo-Catholics and MacKinnon must be a good contender.

22. Demant, *Religion and the Decline of Capitalism*, 119.

23. Ronald Preston Interview. 16.2.88.

short cuts must be seen."²⁴ In other words, the group contributed nothing to the discipline of sociology, thus showing how inadequate their Christian Sociology was. David Martin in rather more measured tones said that the Christendom Group was writing social philosophy and ethics rather than sociology.²⁵ Although it is true that not much sociology was actually written by the group, this is to misunderstand Demant's conception. He states his position with considerable care: "Sociology is the objective and dispassionate study of society. It includes not only an investigation of what exists in the way of social structure and change, but also of the forces at work which maintain or disturb the structure. In so far as our task is to undertake such an examination it can claim the title of Sociology. There is no specifically Christian method of doing this."²⁶ The argument, put simply, is that sociology is the study of society, and to understand society one needs an appropriate understanding of man. As the sociologist of religion Arnold Nash puts it, "Demant's insight is that sociology depends on an anthropology."²⁷ Demant emphasizes that it is not a different method, but a different set of presuppositions. This is a clearly fair comment. For example, when a Marxist comes to sociology, his anthropology will lead to a certain kind of result; the same is true of a Christian. It will be shown later on that Demant did make certain judgements which could be said to have a sociological character.

There is one last issue which must be discussed. Edward Norman believes that a shift can be identified in Demant's conception of Christianity, from his enthusiasm for Christian Sociology to his post-war realism. Norman cites the volume *Theology and Society*, and in particular the essay "The Mischief of Ideals." He believes that "Demant pointed to the absurdity of those Christians who spoke of politics as essentially concerned with the adjustment of 'a discrepancy between ideals and practice.' This, of course, was exactly what 'Christian Sociology' had done in the years between the wars, in its contrast between the economic order of medieval Christendom and modern competitive society. Demant now argued that 'the whole

24. Munby, *Anglican Self-Criticism*, 52.
25. David Martin cited by Mayhew, *Christendom Group*.
26. Demant, *God, Man, and Society*, 58.
27. Interview with Professor A. Nash. 18.7.88. It is interesting to note on this point how Christian anthropology is considered legitimate, whilst Christian sociology is not. Pannenberg describes such an anthropology as the study of humanity in a Christian framework. Demant does not talk about a different method; rather, it is the application of Christian insights regarding the facts about humanity to the study. This poses the difficulty of the relation between facts and interpretation. Perhaps some of the hostility is based upon a narrow empirical understanding of the nature of facts. Demant would want to claim that the transcendent elements of humanity are facts.

conception of a conflict between practice and ideals is misleading and even mischievous.' For Christianity is about man as he really is, man whose highest aspirations are alloyed with the ambiguities and corruptions germane to his fallen condition."[28] And later, Norman is able to conclude, "Demant's own disillusionment with earlier 'Christian Sociology' became evident."[29] At least, two errors are made by Norman here. First, Christian Sociology was never a comparison between the economic order of Christendom and modern competitive society. It was always grounded in the facts concerning human needs and wants (i.e., Natural Law) and the sort of society which meets these needs. Christian Sociology wanted to claim that the economic order of Christendom is a society whose order is more natural than that of modern society. Second, Demant believed that ideals were just verbal admonitions to improve, when what is needed is a Natural Law framework which grounds the analysis in the facts of the human situation, which, of course, always included sin. This point will be explored further later on. The opposite criticism, namely, that Demant is too static in his thinking, is more valid than Norman's conviction that Demant became disillusioned with Christian Sociology. Part of the reason why Demant appears so static is that he is operating from the perspective of the rise and fall of cultures and such long-term judgements are not falsified by the election of a Labour government in 1945. He never explicitly identified with a political party. Instead he did, as has been already pointed out, at one point advise people not to vote for any party, since each political program is as mistaken as the others.

The problem with Norman here is that he is assuming there are only two basic alternatives when it comes to the church and social action: on the one hand, the identification of the church with a political program, and on the other, the complete separation of the two. Demant does not fit into either account.[30] In 1952, at the time Norman thinks him disillusioned, Dem-

---

28. Norman, *Church and Society in England*, 380. Quotations from Demant, *Theology of Society*, 149 and 151. Norman's discussion of Demant is extraordinary. Preston, *Explorations in Theology*, 123, rightly identifies the fault. Norman always speaks of Demant with approval, and yet clearly has not understood him. For an example of the same sentiments in his pre-war period, see Demant, *Christian Polity*, 39, where Demant writes, "The characteristic Catholic outlook is always most deeply an outlook upon what things are, rather than upon what they do. . . .Tell men only what they must do, what price they must pay for existing at all, and you will numb them into despair; you will turn the Gospel into a shabby replica of the world's irreligious and nagging moralism, with its oceanfuls of good advice. But tell them what they are, of their dignity as made in the image of God, and that their sins are wicked perversions of their nature as spiritual beings . . ." Almost exactly the same sentiments as the article which so impresses Norman as evidence as Demant's later disillusionment with Christian Sociology.

29. Ibid., 149.

30. See especially Norman, *Christianity and the World Order*. This is the clearest

ant was a speaker at the Annual Conference of the Conservative Political Centre. The subject was "The Good Society" and Demant was speaking on "Religion and Modern Society." Towards the end of the lecture, Demant summarizes three possible approaches to the problem of religion in society. The first is the Protestant pietist approach (my name for it, not his), where the concern is with individuals: if the church concentrates on the conversion of individuals, then that will produce a better society. The second approach is to identify a certain party with the Kingdom of God, which is more a tendency of the Left than of the Right. This, Demant says uncompromisingly, "is incompatible with Christian theology."[31] The third approach he describes as follows:

> There are those who believe that the Christian Church has a message about the social order in addition to its message to individuals. It is concerned with the status of the human being as the doctrine of the Church expounds it. God gave man power over everything on earth. This power in man distinguishes him from other creatures like the fishes in the sea. Man has the power not simply to drift along, but to fashion the structure of his life. This power has dangerous as well as positive possibilities. It makes man arrogant, forgetting obedience to the laws of life. That is why the third view of the Church's responsibility, between the first two extremes, seems to me to be the right one. It was put clearly by T. S. Eliot, when he said that a society acceptable to Christian judgement would be "a society in which the natural end of man—virtue and well-being in community—is acknowledged for all, and the super-natural end—beatitude—for those who have eyes to see it."[32]

Demant was always a Christian theologian grounding his analysis of society in the Natural Law doctrine of the church. The fault with Norman's evaluation of Demant is that he has not understood him. He imagines that Christian Sociology was the attempt to find Christian reasons to support a certain political platform; when in fact, Demant always believed this to be wholly inappropriate. Norman latches on to the criticisms of the second position which occur throughout his work, and imagines that this must mean that Demant became disillusioned with Christian Sociology. Demant believed that a social message was possible precisely because the Christian

statement of Norman's crude outline of the two options. It is this attitude which pervades almost everything else he has written. Dr. A. Louth made this point in an interview 19.7.88.

31. Demant, *Religion and Modern Society*, 21.
32. Ibid., 21ff.

church had an insight into the truth about humanity. It was the task of Christian Sociology to bring this out.

Thus far we have examined the Christian background, Demant is presupposing in his ethics. The main emphasis is upon the reality of two worlds, both of which must be affirmed, if mankind is to live appropriately. Failure to do so leads to an unnatural and unbalanced life. Demant makes such a judgment because he is committed to a Natural Law theology. This Natural Law theology leads to a Christian anthropology which is the basis for a Christian Sociology.

DEMANT'S UNDERSTANDING OF HUMANITY

It has been shown that Demant's entire system of Christian Sociology rests upon his Natural Law belief. This section will explore four elements: first, his conception of humankind as a creature, made in the image of God with a relative independence; second, the sense in which humankind has fallen; third, the sense in which Christianity provides a message of power which can restore humankind back to his or her true nature; and finally, his conception of human life as a constant interaction between humankinds true selves and their sin.[33]

"Man is a part of Creation, a creature," writes Demant.[34] This means that man is part of the physical and biological processes of the world. There are clear physical constraints forced upon man as a species. We cannot walk through walls and if we fall it will hurt. We are also part of time and of a particular culture. None of this limitedness is sinful; it is simply a fact of the creation. This is a feature of our being which we share with the rest of creation, just as we have feelings such as hunger, sexual desire, and tiredness, in common with all other animals. However, man differs from the rest of the animals because he is created in the image of God. This means that man "embodies a measure of the nature of the Creator."[35] He or she is a spiritual being. This is the explanation for the capacity of choice, the ability to love, and the feelings of aspiration and despair. All these are expressions of the human spirit, and make humankind transcend the animal kingdom. Humankind has been given a certain relative independence both from the natural processes (e.g., humans can transcend some of the difficulties imposed by nature) and from the Creator who is the ground of his Being. In

---

33. Parts of this section are drawing on the work of Taylor, *Christian Social Thinking*, and Stanley, *Church and the World*.
34. Demant, *Religious Prospect*, 45.
35. Ibid., 45.

other words, humankind has a sphere of a genuine freedom. This freedom extends to the capacity to deny his or her very essence. Humanity has the ability to try to deny his or her creaturely dependence upon God.

It is this strange duality of being both a natural animal and a spiritual being which is responsible for the problems which can afflict humanity. "A mere creature, a fish," writes Demant, "has no problems. It does its job, is in complete accord with its environment, it has no doubts, scruples, hesitations, or summer schools. But man has a continual tension between these two aspects of his being." These problems arise because humankind is reluctant to recognize his or her dual dependence upon the world and God. However, this duality also has enormous potential. It is the civilizing force behind humankind. This civilizing impulse—as Demant likes to describe it—is "one activity of the spirit of man."[36] Of course, it requires a certain contingent set of historical factors to generate a civilization. But all humans everywhere have the impulse. The proof of that is human language itself. We are, potentially, very constructive—or very destructive. We create systems of remarkable power which can be used as forces for either good or evil.

There is a further complication: the human person divides into two elements, the inner or less conscious life and the outer or conscious life. These two elements of the human person are captured by St. Paul in Romans 7–8, where he describes his inner conflict between his will and his actual actions: the conflict between his aim to keep God's Law, and his discovery that he sees "in my members another law at war with the law of my mind and making me captive to the law of sin which dwells in my members."[37] Here, there is a conflict between his or her conscious mind and his or her unconscious life. To describe this distinction, Demant writes, "If we use the term 'soul' in its precise sense for this more hidden and formless part of our inner life, to distinguish it from the more conscious, deliberate part of our inner life, which is the spirit—and we do this when we talk about 'saving our souls'—then we can see an analogy between the soul of the individual and the culture of a community."[38] In *A Two-Way Religion*, Demant changes the terminology now using an image. He admits that each account is bound to be inadequate in at least some respects. He writes, "The structure of man's inner life is much like a set of circles inside one another." (One must note that the "inner life" describes any human thinking, both

---

36. Demant, *Theology of Society*, 32. The contingent circumstances in which a civilization arises are when men become consciously aware of the truth of this analysis, as of course happened in Christian Europe.

37. Romans 7:23 (RSV). See Demant, *Theology of Society*, 4, and *Religion and the Decline of Capitalism*, 72, for Demant's discussion of this chapter.

38. Demant, *Theology of Society*, 4.

conscious and unconscious.) He goes on, "The outer circle represents man's contact with the external world, inside it is a mixture of forces which make up the whole inner life—the feelings, the mind, the desires—what we might call the soul."[39] At the center of humankind, Demant says there is "the self or the human spirit, and the best way we can speak of its activity is to call it 'the will.' It is the principle of freedom in us. We have to think of it as a point, but it is not really in space at all, and it represents an opening to another dimension rather than a definite part of the soul's structure. Through that opening man is in contact with God and the eternal world by his very existence as man . . . this does not by itself make him religious. It just makes him human."[40] The image Demant has set out here is intended to show that where the natural life is centered on the divine, the rest of human activity takes its place around this center. Cultural and spiritual activities are nearest the center, whilst the economic and sexual activities are further out. In his discussion of Demant, John Mack Stanley seems to imply that the spirit is simply the central link with God, not something which pervades every aspect of human existence,[41] but Demant does not mean this at all. He writes, "The centrality of the spirit in man has to be understood not as the existence of a central point or force surrounded by non-spiritual layers, but as a penetrating operative reality which determines the character of human activity in all its layers. No human activity is non-spiritual."[42] Humanity can do nothing which is not in some sense spiritual, that is, linked with and dependent on God.

Despite the confusion with the terminology, the basic idea is clear. Humanity has a conscious and a less conscious element. I will use the terms inner and outer life. The outer life describes the conscious aims, outlooks, decisions, and the corresponding rational processes which accompany them. So, when a person gives a reason for doing anything, they provide you with an insight into their outer life. However, underlying the outer life is the inner life where unconscious forces which affect our behavior are operating. This is the arena of the factors which make up a world view: the rituals, and assumptions about the nature of reality. At the center of all this is the link

---

39. Demant, *A Two-Way Religion*, 40. The conception of God, developed by Demant in this largely devotional book, which underpins this conception of the nature of man, wins the approval of Professor Christopher Evans in a rather surprising place. He compares Demant's book with *Honest to God* and strongly implies that the task John Robinson set himself is one which Demant has done rather better. See Edwards, *The Honest to God Debate*, 110.

40. Ibid., 40.

41. J. M. Stanley, *Church and the World*, 204. Figure 4.

42. Demant, *Theology of Society*, 78.

with the Divine—the Image in which we were made. It is the opening on to the eternal.

When a person recognizes his dependence upon God, so every aspect of his life settles into an appropriate order and balance. The result is an internal unity, and as Demant writes in *A Two-Way Religion*, "in order to be at unity within myself I must be at one with God."[43] Demant does not actually list the order such a balanced life would take; although, as I have already said, he does make it clear that vitality is towards the edge, and reason is nearer the center.[44] The balanced life is achieved when the inner and outer life are in harmony with the spiritual link, recognizing the Divine ground of life. The order reflects an appropriate sense of priority and status. So, for example, the economic, although important, should not be overriding. For the person leading a natural, balanced life, the economic dimension of human life will function for certain specific and limited ends. It will never become an end in itself.[45] Unfortunately, the ideal, natural, balanced life is rarely realized, because humanity has fallen.

THE NATURE OF SIN

Animals cannot sin. Sin requires a certain set of conditions. It requires a creature with a degree of power. Demant writes that, "Sin is possible only to a being with that power over creation which on earth man distinctively possesses, the power to say No to God. Sin is the act of the creature, using that relative measure of freedom with which he is endowed to claim the absolute right of the Creator."[46] This privilege of freedom is not itself sinful; it is the "image of God in him, a kind of delegated replica of the freedom of God over His creation."[47] Sin is the assertion of human pride; it is a denial of the finitude and dependence of human life on the Creator. It is not something sub-human. It is not when humans act as animals; rather it is the elevation of the limited privilege of human transcendence into something absolute. Demant defines original sin in the following manner: "Original sin is that power by which, because we have in our specific nature a superiority to the temporal process, we claim the prerogatives of God's absolute and uncon-

---

43. Demant, *A Two-Way Religion*, 58.

44. See Demant, *Theology of Society*, 75.

45. A Demant theme throughout his life. See for example, Demant, *Religion and the Decline of Capitalism*, 185. "The economic sphere is one where the natural order is to-day most violently deranged."

46. Demant, *Theology of Society*, 17.

47. Demant, *Religion and the Decline of Capitalism*, 88.

ditioned Being."[48] Humanity is a child of eternity, of a second world; sin is the process by which we deny the true significance of the eternal world. In so doing some aspect of Becoming, of Time, is given an illegitimate and unnatural status. This has enormous tragic potential; it "gives him the power to become a devil."[49] It is the risk that God took with Creation.

Demant believes that the natural state for humanity is when humanity recognizes both his creaturely finitude and his dependence upon his Creator. Therefore, he sometimes talks about sin as a state of alienation away from this natural state. "The alienation is due . . . to the propensity in him to give some aspect of his relative and limited existence an absolute and infinite value."[50] Elsewhere, he uses his model of the balanced natural life of humanity as a state where the spirit of humanity is firmly rooted in the eternal world, and each layer of human existence is in its appropriate place, with the inner and outer life in harmony. On this model, sin is the ejection of the spirit away from its roots in the eternal world into one of the peripheral layers. Demant describes it thus: "the spirit—because it is spirit and not Nature—can deny its centrality and eject itself somewhere else—and the particular activity into which it is injected is treated as the human centrum."[51] When this happens the person becomes ex-centric.[52] He is off balance, unstable and unnatural. Demant makes the following list of layers which the human spirit is constantly tempted to make into the centrum, "It may be his mind or his spirit . . . it may be his possessions, or vital urges, . . . or it may be one valid part of his communal life—like his race, or state, or class or economic devices—that is assumed to give significance to all the rest."[53] It is the process of making eternal something that belongs to Becoming; it is taking that which is relative and making it absolute. When this happens, there is a complete loss of perspective. The ridiculous becomes serious. And the frustration becomes insurmountable.

To sum up, Demant conceives of sin in the following way: he starts with an understanding that the natural human state is one where both the creaturely limitations and Divine dependency are recognized. Sin is the exercise of a very limited human freedom which denies both the fact of human limitations and the need for Divine dependency. It is a state of alienation from a true, natural life. This happens when the spirit is ejected from

---

48. Demant, *Religious Prospect*, 227.
49. Demant, *Religion and the Decline of Capitalism*, 88.
50. Ibid., 88.
51. Demant, *Theology of Society*, 78.
52. Ibid., 82.
53. Demant, *Religion and the Decline of Capitalism*, 89.

its central position, rooted firmly in the Divine ground of our Being, in to one of the peripheral layers around the center. This could be anything from the vital urges to the economic. When this happens this becomes central, assuming a significance which the spiritual ought to have. It leads to an unbalanced and—in a literal, technical sense—an unnatural life. Although the spirit can eject itself into one of the outer layers, the link with the Divine ground of Being cannot actually be broken.

REDEMPTION IS ALWAYS A RESTORATION

"The Christian religion is primarily a religion of redemption, a gospel. It is good news, not a philosophy or good advice. The good news is that God, who is the source and end of the created world, is by an act of divine initiative restoring things to their true nature. . . . Redemption is always a restoration."[54] This summarizes Demant's conception of redemption exactly. Redemption is an act of restoration or recovery. It is not the "adding of something new to the world; it is the recovering for the world what it had in God's mind at the beginning."[55] It is the means by which God overcomes the sin of the world— the deformation of the natural order—and restores the world back to its original order. This claim is part of the Christian revelation and it has two component parts. First, humanity itself is unable to restore the natural balance after sin has distorted it. Second, God has created the means by which restoration can be effected; He has provided the power. Demant describes this as "a complication" when he writes, "The Christian Faith introduces a complication into this picture, for it asserts that the power by which man departs from his essential nature cannot effect the recovery without the action of Divine Grace which is supernatural."[56] It is a complication because Demant is constrained to hold that there is a limit to social improvement; ultimately humanity cannot do anything without the power exercised by God alone. It is for this reason that he describes the primary task of the church as to "bring men into the realm of grace."[57] Although the church can witness to the truth of a good social order, which is based upon the Christian understanding of the natural order, this function is secondary to the primary task of bringing the good news that God is providing the

---

54. Demant, *Religious Prospect*, 232. Incidentally, this is another example of the sort of sentiment which Edward Norman believes shows Demant's disillusionment with Christian Sociology: this was written in 1939.

55. Demant, "Man and Social Order," in *Christian Belief To-Day*, 117.

56. Demant, *Theology of Society*, 72.

57. Demant, "Man and Social Order," in *Christian Belief To-Day*, 124.

power to effect a restoration of our true nature. Here Demant is making an exclusive claim for Christianity, over against other religions, although, interestingly, he is very reluctant to explain how he justifies such a claim.

It was noted in the discussion of Demant's conception of Natural Law, that there was some confusion over whether redemption is essential to knowing the manner in which natural life should be ordered. It was concluded there that Demant believed that those who are not brought into the sphere of redemption do not see the natural order as clearly as those who are redeemed. Or rather, those who do not recognize their redemption are subject to the frustrations that an unnatural life generates, and thus have very limited insight into the natural order. But generally, Demant believes that "Man cannot know true nature (i.e., the purpose) of anything or activity by looking at its actual expression; but in the supernatural, eternal life in God he begins to know it."[58] This is the basis of his Christian Sociology claim.

There is no better way of summing up the argument so far than Demant's own words:

> The doctrine of the redemption of the world by God in Christ and His Church presupposes three dogmas. The first is that in the actual world things are not true to their own nature; there has been a fall. The second is that "the good" of any created thing is a recovery of its true nature, and that this recovery cannot be made by any self-improvement, but by the redeeming act of God. The third axiom is that, therefore, the true nature of any created thing is only sustained when it is kept to its true end by supernatural direction and power.[59]

THE FRUSTRATION OF SINFUL HUMANITY

Sin is the process of denying one's dependence upon God, thus ejecting the human spirit from its roots in God into one of the layers of human existence. In so doing, this layer assumes an all-embracing significance. It becomes the factor through which all of life is interpreted. Despite this sin, the link between God and humanity cannot be broken. The "alienation and contradiction . . . has not completely snapped the link."[60] But as a result of this link remaining together with the unnatural elevation of one area of human life

---

58. Demant, *Christian Polity*, 98ff.

59. Demant, "The Study of Sociology," in *The Priest As Student*, 348. Similar sentiments are expressed by Demant, *Religious Prospect*, 232ff.

60. Demant, "Man and Social Order" in *Christian Belief To-Day*, 119.

to an unwarranted status, there is a constant frustration. The human spirit is painful and uneasy and there is a constant tug back to the true order. However, as a result of human pride, it swings from one layer to another in quest for some ease from the discomfort, refusing to settle where it ought to settle, namely, in the life of God. "Existence," says Demant, "swings relentlessly from one form of maimed humanity to another."[61] So, for example, the tragic person who denies his spirit its true center, will perhaps, first concentrate on his career, sacrificing everything on this altar; then, disillusioned with this, will perhaps allow his life to become dominated by sexuality and discover this equally unsatisfying.

A further complication for the sinful humanity is that conscious aims are never enough. It is no good wishing to be better; nor do annual New Year's resolutions help. It is not a matter of the will deciding to improve. It is this mistaken attitude which lies behind much talk about a conflict between ideals and practice. The model which operates behind this language is one where a person has an idea of how life ought to be, tries to live it out, and then finds that it is difficult to achieve. Instead, says Demant, "it is the conflict between the inner and outer life that constitutes the problem which is misleadingly stated as a conflict of practice and ideals."[62] The difficulties that a person has in practice are not simply a result of "insufficient effort," but one of internal conflict between the conscious aims and unconscious assumptions. This Demant believes is a distinctive part of the Christian analysis. As has been already noted he cites St. Paul in Romans 7; and he also cites St. Augustine in the Confessions. "The Christian faith . . . knows nothing of a conflict of practice and ideals. It knows only a conflict of wills, or a divided will, or an imperfect will."[63] In other words, the inner and outer lives need to be harmonized; both need to recognize their dependence upon God before the human life can start reflecting the appropriate natural order. Demant believes that it is very common to find a person who consciously is seeking an appropriate balance and is dissatisfied with his life, whilst subconsciously is intent on the distortion. The liberal humanist is an example of one who suffers from just such a conflict: in the outer life, he has a conscious aim which acknowledges the rights of the human person not to be violated by anything however important; whilst in his inner life he believes that there is nothing more than this empirical world. This intellectual dilemma will

---

61. Demant, *Religious Prospect*, 236.

62. Demant, *Theology of Society*, 157. This is what Demant really meant by this article "The Mischief of Ideals," which misled Norman in his account of Demant's views.

63. Ibid., 151.

lead to a conflict between actions and justification. The assumptions that the liberal makes cannot sustain the conscious beliefs.

Demant describes this process of the constant tug towards the appropriate natural order and yet the alienation from it as "link-in-contradiction."[64] This seeming paradox is explained as follows: sin is the act of the human spirit turning in on itself and elevating some peripheral layer of human activity as primary. However, the link although strained is never broken. There is a struggle between the link and the human spirit. Demant believes that human life confirms this analysis; he writes that this "picture of these things, drawn from a Christian interpretation of existence, does . . . provide a more penetrating insight. The human situation at every point is the result of an interaction of two forces, man's link with the place of his origin and place of his fulfilment which Christians call God, and his alienation from it."[65]

So Demant's conception of humanity can be summed up as follows.

1. Humanity is both a creature limited by nature, and yet created in the Image of God. He is a spiritual being, linked inseparably to the supernatural ground of his being. When both the inner and outer life recognize this dependence then he is a spirit-centered creature, rooted in the Divine life, and with every aspect of his life in an appropriate balance.

2. Humanity has a limited freedom which gives him enormous potential for evil. Sin is the exercise of that freedom involving a denial of his dependence and the ejection of his spirit into an outer layer of his life.

3. Despite this condition humanity remains linked to God, and this link constantly attempts to tug him back to a natural life. The result in practice is a constant swing from one over-emphasized layer to another.

4. By surrendering to God's grace, humanity can be restored to the true natural order, and God will sustain the appropriate balance.

Demant took this anthropology and made it the basis of his Christian Sociology. His method was to draw an analogy between his doctrine of humanity and his theology of society. This is where we turn to next.

DEMANT'S SOCIAL PARALLEL

The idea that the nature of humanity can serve as a parallel for the nature of society can be traced back to Plato. In *The Republic*, Socrates says, "There are the same three elements in the personality of the individual as there are in the state."[66] So, as a methodology, it has a long and proud history

---

64. Demant, *Religious Prospect*, 249.
65. Demant, *Religion and the Decline of Capitalism*, 88.
66. Plato, *The Republic*, V.4, 441c.

though Plato's highly organic conception is only one form of it. There are two reasons why it is so attractive. The first is that a state is, in one sense, no more than the sum total of the individuals within its boundaries. The second is that the state is a human enterprise; it is a human achievement and, at the same time, is subjected to human problems. These two reasons seem to suggest that a parallel may be drawn between the nature of the individual and the state.

Demant, however, would not want to talk exclusively about the state because the state, as currently understood, is quite unlike any form of human community prior to the seventeenth century.[67] Rather, he prefers to refer to human community, regardless of what form its organization takes. Furthermore, Demant has a very sophisticated account of national identity. He rejects the liberal model because it is too individualistic, arguing that people are not born as individuals but into families. And each person within each family is a member of various associations, like trade unions, professional bodies, churches, and football supporters' clubs. It is these associations which give persons their identity. It is similar to Roger Scruton's organic conception of society, with one major difference. There are better and worse ways of organizing society and a judgment is made by comparing the actual society with the natural order of society.[68]

Demant believes that "man is always fundamentally a community fellow: that he belongs to a community by creation."[69] He talks about this sense of community as "human solidarity" and he quotes Augustine approvingly: "How should our celestial City have ever come to its origin, development or perfection, unless the saints all live in sociable union?"[70] Demant goes on to comment, "Solidarity as an aspect of the good life . . . Firstly, it is of the essence of reality. Social living is in the nature of things. Secondly, denials of it are not imperfect developments but positive disruptions. Disunion is sin. Thirdly, the re-creation of solidarity is a task of redemption. It is not a problem of creating union out of the materials of discord, but of combating the forces which disrupt solidarity, by the power inherent in a return to

---

67. Demant, *God, Man and Society,* 95ff. Demant writes, "For it happens that whatever systematic Christian thought on politics has been developed in the past was worked out under conditions in which the State was something quite different from the modern secular state." He then goes on to detail these differences.

68. For discussion of organic and liberal conceptions of the State, see R. Scruton, *The Meaning of Conservativism.* However, Demant would reject his implied relativist conclusions (see Scruton, 36); ie., one cannot make any judgements about a different social set of arrangements.

69. Demant, "Man and the Social Order," in *Christian Belief To-Day,* 120.

70. St. Augustine, *The City of God* xix, 5. Demant has a footnote to say that the whole of Book XIX is important for this point. See Demant, *Theology of Society,* 12.

the source of solidarity, namely God."[71] This is Demant's justification for the social parallel: it is valid because social living is part of being human; because the problem of sin has a social equivalent; and because the solution of restoration is available to the community.

SOCIAL EQUIVALENT TO THE HUMAN SPIRIT

The human person is made up both of the natural and of the spiritual.[72] It is the spirit which is responsible for language and the civilizing impulse. The social equivalent of the human spirit is primarily seen in the facts of history. When the spirit of society produces a civilization, then that is the start of history. "The advent of civilization is also the beginning of history," writes Demant. He goes on, "History means that man has learnt to stand somewhat out of the mere succession of generations; he can then trace a connection in the succession and make a pattern of living which is meant to last and to which the succession of generations is meant to minister. Civilization is then one of the attempts to express on earth his superiority to mere natural process."[73] It is a communal, rather than an individual, transcending of the natural processes. So, the social equivalent of the human spirit is civilization.

As the human spirit has a link with God which cannot be snapped, so "there is a link between the world and God that can never be broken."[74] The parallel with the individual is further maintained when Demant talks of a society being appropriately balanced and ordered; when it recognizes its dependence upon the Divine, its link with God. In his important essay, "The Idea of the Natural Order," Demant describes the nature of the balanced life for society in the following way: "The Natural Order of human life is there-

---

71. Demant, *Theology of Society*, 12.

72. Demant's use of the term "natural" and "nature" is confusing. There are, at least, two different meaning operating. Sometimes he means "nature" in the sense of the earth—the physical empirical world. Sometimes he means "nature" in terms of the appropriate balanced human life centered on God. In the latter sense, he talks of a human life as "unnatural." I will follow his usage and the context will make it clear as to which meaning is operating.

73. Demant, *Religion and the Decline of Capitalism*, 162. Much of this material is also found in Demant, *Theology of Society*, 32ff. John Mack Stanley fails to emphasize this point in his account. To identify the spirit merely with civilization is limited, because Demant also sees civilization as a contingent phenomenon happening only in some parts of the world. To identify the civilizing impulse with history gives a much broader meaning to the civilizing impulse, because the relatively uncivilized parts of the world still have a history. For Stanley, see *Church and the World*, 219.

74. Demant "Man and the Social Order," in *Christian Belief To-Day*, 119.

fore transcendent, in that it is essentially dependent upon God although He is wholly distinct from it; it is noumenal, in that its pattern is never a phenomenon to be observed, but its true meaning can be apprehended only by human intelligence; it is eschatological, in that it reaches its fulfilment only in God's final perfecting of creation. The natural order affects the phenomena of human cultures but is never embodied totally in any of them."[75] By rational, and preferably, redeemed reflection, the human mind can discover the truth about the natural order intended for society. Such an order is dependent upon God and, ultimately, will not be perfected until the last day. However, it is the task of the church, Demant argues, to foster a "social order which takes account of the frailty of man and at the same time seeks to buttress him from the worst effects of it."[76] Demant details what this means in practice, and the sense in which modern society is violating the natural order. For example, he writes that the "cultural side of life, its arts, knowledge and ceremonies — all that qualifies life and does not merely preserve it — has a precedence over politics and economic activity."[77] To the obvious criticism that such things need paying for and therefore cannot be more important than economic activity, Demant writes,

> It is a metaphysical and not a physical or moral precedence. Life must be sustained by economic activity, it must be protected and coordinated by politics, before it can be enriched and adorned. They have a physical priority over the cultural stratum . . . Cultural activities have a metaphysical priority in that in them the spirit of man operates most centrally from within outwards, less conditioned by the determinism which of necessity belong to political and economic activities . . . Therefore, a society in which the cultural life has not a certain priority in this sense violates the natural order of man's inner structure. It can be violated in several ways: if provision is not made for people to teach and carry on the religious, educational, aesthetic, and scientific arts; if any class is so exhausted in one of the more practical tasks that it has no opportunity, energy, or guidance for cultural pursuits; if the cultural domain is treated as an adjunct for political consolidation, as this sphere is in totalitarian societies; or if it is prostituted to keep the economic process going, as it largely is in the democracies.[78]

75. Demant, *Theology of Society*, 83.
76. Demant, "Man and the Social Order," in *Christian Belief To-Day*, 125.
77. Demant, *Theology of Society*, 86.
78. Ibid., 86ff.

The model Demant is developing is one which is very general. The natural order of society demands that the telos of society is, ultimately, the spiritual, but then, closely related to it, the cultural and aesthetic. A society which allows men and women no opportunity for these things is unnatural. To make work an end in itself is unnatural.

One possible confusion must be eliminated at this stage. For a society to recognize its dependence upon God does not mean that everyone in the society is Christian. Rather, it is a society in which Christian values and virtues are able to flourish. Demant often quoted with approval Eliot's concept of a "society acceptable to the Christian judgement as 'a society in which the natural end of man—virtue and wellbeing in community—is acknowledged for all, and the supernatural end—beatitude—for those who have eyes to see it.'"[79] It is a society where spiritual virtues can prosper and, therefore, anything cultural and aesthetic must be given a priority.

Demant has been criticized, at this point, on two grounds. On the one hand, by Peter Mayhew for failing to be more specific in his political policies. He is including Demant in the Christendom group, when he writes, "The Group was composed of educated persons who delighted in discussion of principles. The people of the Church (and of the nation) were concerned more with the doing (or not doing) of what was right than with the reasons for declaring its rightness. Christendom thought hard concerning the good which ought to be, not hard enough concerning how the good should be brought about."[80] On the other hand, by Michael Taylor who believes that Demant's outline of the natural order of society is too rigid. He cites Reinhold Niebuhr with approval, "Dr. Niebuhr goes as far as to say that 'historical development which has increased man's mastery over nature and his corresponding capacity for both good and evil, has rendered most of the norms of natural law irrelevant.'"[81] And Ronald Preston makes the same criticism when he writes of Demant: "This is the whole weakness of his position: a too detailed and specific deduction of the content of natural law and of the desirable social system to be based on it, so that the whole concept becomes insufficiently transcendental."[82]

---

79. Demant, "Man and the Social Order" in *Christian Belief To-Day*, 125.

80. Mayhew, *Christendom Group*, 52ff.

81. Taylor, *Christian Social Thinking of V. A. Demant*, 86. Quoting Niebuhr, "The Problem of a Protestant Social Ethics," in the *Union Seminary Quarterly Review* XV, no.1, 1959, p. 7ff.

82. Preston, "The Theology of the Malvern Conference," in *Christianity and Society*. Ronald Preston admits to a difficulty in interpreting Demant. Preston writes "The remark 'mankind is always seeking it' might be considered an indication that Dr. Demant thinks of it as a norm which will always stand over against the partial achievements of

It is very difficult for Demant to satisfy both critics. However, the following must be said. First, Demant is deliberately general, because he does want to make certain very limited universal claims. He writes, "In every situation there are elements that belong to human nature at all times, but the relationship of these factors to one another and their results in the objective world are affected by the unique, unprecedented and unrepeatable constellation of historical facts at the time."[83] There are certain very general norms, such as, that the economic and political are secondary to the cultural and aesthetic, which are true of all human society everywhere. The question is: can this be held despite the enormous cultural and anthropological variety in the world and in history?

The attempt to answer this question provokes the prior question, whether any comparisons between cultures are possible. Comparisons between cultures are very complicated because the same activity might have a different significance in different cultures. Polygamy is not the same in Africa as it is in Cambridge. Polygamy functions within the African culture as a welfare state, an extended family, and as the context for procreation. The equivalent in our culture would have to be a combination of welfare support and monogamous marriage. Providing Demant is not too rigid regarding precisely what activities are cultural and what are economic, the general judgement can be sustained. If an activity has an economic (in the sense of directly related to production) significance, claims Demant, then it should have a lower status than those activities which have a religious significance. Precisely what is the African cultural equivalent of the obsessed business person living solely for profit is a matter of comparing the significance and function of activities. Such judgements are very difficult but not impossible. But provided they can properly be made, Demant's position is sustainable.[84]

a particular era ... but the last sentence implies something realizable after the war." The overall tenor of Demant's thought is better reflected by Preston's first interpretation. Certainly in *Religion and the Decline of Capitalism*, Demant is unequivocal. "Society is always sick" (p. 157). But he does believe that some societies are more sick than others; and it is the task of Christian Sociology to try and redeem society. This particular passage, on which Preston is commenting in the Malvern Conference volume, is puzzling. It appears to reflect a sense that after Hitler there cannot be yet another reaction. Demant does write, "so far as I can see" which is an appropriate qualification. On Preston it is worth noting that his criticism here of a too strict definition of natural law must be contrasted with his assertion in *Church and Society in the late Twentieth Century: The Economic and Political Task*. Here he writes that the Christendom group were "vague as to the 'natural' order to which we should return" (p. 23).

83. Demant, *Theology of Society*, 115.

84. For a general discussion of the problems related to judging cultures see Wilson, *Rationality*. The solution that I am proposing is heavily dependent upon the work of Hughes, *Authority in Morals*.

Certain policy requirements flow from the observation that cultural activity is more important than economic activity. It must imply that a nation which merely invests in industry, in defense, and in administration, has become an "unnatural" society. This is because the purpose of work, defense and administration, is education and art. The policy implication is that the priorities should be adjusted by financing education and art instead of administration and defense. What emerges is that Demant's idea of a natural order of society invites only limited and rather general claims.

A final social parallel with the human spirit relates to the proposal that society, like the human, can have an inner and outer life. The distinction between the inner and outer life of a culture is very important for Demant. He believed that many of the conflicts in our culture are a result of a conflict between the conscious aims and the unconscious assumptions. The terms to describe this duality of culture posed a real problem for Demant. In *The Religious Prospect*, where the distinction is most strongly developed, he uses the terms "doctrine" and "dogma." He attributes this distinction to T. E. Hulme, quoting a passage from Hulme's *Speculations*. So an examination of *Speculations* will clarify Demant's meaning. Hulme is contrasting two periods. First, the Middle Ages in Europe, from Augustine to the Renaissance. Second, the period from the Renaissance to the present. The first period was dominated by religious assumptions and the second by humanistic assumptions. The main difference between the two periods lies in their conception of humanity. This is not an incidental difference, it permeates all human activity. For in the Middle Ages it was assumed that there are absolute values and that humanity is, though created perfect, now flawed; whilst in the second period, these assumptions are reversed, so there are no absolute values and humanity is essentially good. These assumptions which characterize each age are unquestioned; they are taken as facts; they are fundamental categories; they are the framework through which all human activity is interpreted. Although Hulme does not actually describe these assumptions as dogma, he does make the connection when he writes "The more intimate connection with dogmas I referred to depends on the fact that dogma is often a fairly intellectual way of expressing these fundamental categories—the dogma of original sin, for example."[85]

Demant takes Hulme's insight that an age has these unquestioned assumptions which are distinct from conscious beliefs, and calls the former "dogma" and the latter "doctrine." F. L. Cross was the first to criticize Demant's use of the word "dogma" to describe these assumptions.[86] The fact

85. Hulme, *Speculations*, 68.
86. Cross, "New Orthodoxy."

is that dogma does not mean the set of assumptions which make up the interpretative framework for an age. *The Oxford English Dictionary* suggests two meanings for "dogma": 1. that which is held as an opinion, a belief, principle, tenet [this clearly overlaps with "doctrine"]; 2. the body of opinion formulated or authoritatively stated, systematized belief. Neither sense corresponds to Demant's meaning.

Clearly Demant was sensitive to this criticism, so elsewhere he developed the concept using different terminology. In *Our Culture*, Demant's chapter is called "The Aims and Assumptions of our Culture," and it is here, that he makes the analogy with the individual explicit. He does this in two ways. The first is a human analogy between the head and the masses. "The head is that part which is clear and precise, which knows what it wants. The masses represent the impulse, feelings, memories, dogmas and habits."[87] He is quoting the ideas of M. Denis Saurat, in *Regeneration*. The second has already been referred to, namely the conflict described by St. Paul between the law of God which he would like to obey; and the law of his own members which gives rise to sin. In the same series of lectures, Demant uses the terms ethos and logos. Demant writes, "That our cultural crisis is due to the ethos derived from Christianity having become separated from and deprived of its specific logos. In other words, certain dispositions in respect to action, will, behaviour, have been formed by Christian dogma and cultus; these dispositions remain operative after the word, the doctrine, the shape of things, out of which the dispositions were born, have disappeared."[88] The origins of many of our ideas, argues Demant, are found in Christianity. However, we have undermined the roots of these ideas, even though we retain many of them. There is a conflict between the inner and outer life of our culture. In *Religion and the Decline of Capitalism* Demant calls the chapter devoted to this theme "Aims and Axioms." These terms are legitimate. The *OED* defines axiom as "a proposition that commends itself to general acceptance, self-evident, well-established or universally conceded principle." Demant believes that these hidden assumptions are treated as if they are self-evident.

The basic idea can be summarized as follows: just as each person has an inner and outer life which need to be in harmony, if there is to be any possibility of his aims being realized, so a culture has an inner and outer life which need to be in harmony. Without this harmony men will be bewildered why their efforts to succeed fail so frequently. This Demant believes is our modern-day problem. However, this is to push beyond my present

---

87. Demant, *Our Culture*, 3.
88. Ibid., 99.

argument; here, we must explore the other respects in which the analogy between the individual and society is developed.

SOCIAL EQUIVALENT OF HUMAN SIN

With the individual, sin is the act of denying one's transcendent roots. In so doing the human spirit ejects itself into one of the peripheral layers which are around the center. This layer assumes a disproportionate importance; it becomes the interpretative key in terms of which all else is explained. The social equivalent can be described in almost exactly the same terms. It is the act of denying the corporate dependence on God. And in the process one of the peripheral layers of human society is elevated to a status of undeserved importance.

There are three related aspects to sin at the level of a culture. First, such sin involves secularism. Demant defines secularism in the following way: "Secularism means the erection of a subsidiary secular goal into the place of the supreme purpose of human existence."[89] Secularism is the assertion of human pride; it is a denial of the transcendent basis of human life and elevating an aspect of the temporal. In *Religious Prospect* he talks of this as the denial of Being and belief that all is Becoming. Although there are several different forms of secularism, they all have this in common: for them, the meaning of the world lies within itself. Or as Demant puts it, "It is the 'monistic' one-story universe of all forms of secularism which constitutes their common lineage."[90] The second element which is involved in a cultural sin, arises when the State claims what God alone can claim. This was the error of the totalitarian regimes of the 1930s. Demant declares emphatically that "no aspect of the temporal process, state, race, tribe, or economic activity, has an absolute claim to the total life and loyalty of man, for that claim would be putting an element of the created order in the place of God."[91] And "when the State claims what only God may claim, the proper place not only of politics, but of the arts and industries, is denied. The natural order is violated."[92] This leads to the third element, that the action displacing God is a violation of the natural order. This means that the spirit of society has been ejected making it unnatural and unbalanced. The displacement of God is not an incidental feature which may or may not occur in a society, on a par with other features; its effect is to distort every human activity in that

---

89. Demant, *Theology of Society*, 62.
90. Demant, *Religion and the Decline of Capitalism*, 113.
91. Demant, *Theology of Society*, 79.
92. Demant, *Religious Prospect*, 116.

society. Society becomes frustrated and problematic. To illustrate this claim, he details the manner in which our society has become unnatural and unbalanced. He writes, "In the nominally liberal state politics are subservient to economics as a means to a sum of money. The natural order of economic activities is completely inverted. Agriculture has been the despised lackey of commerce, commerce the harassed agent of loan-finance. Consumption, or the use and enjoyment of things, is regarded as necessary to stimulate production, production as necessary for making work and activity."[93]

So the social equivalent of sin is seen in the process of secularism. Secularism is the denial of social dependence upon God, and the result is the elevation of an element of that society into the status which belongs to God alone. It is a violation of the natural order.

THE SOCIAL EQUIVALENT OF REDEMPTION

This is where the analogy reaches its limits. Although there is a sense in which society can be restored, it is not the same as it is for the individual. The individual has to respond to God's grace, and he effects the restoration. Society is not redeemed in this way, save perhaps in the Last Day when the Kingdom of God is ushered in. An acceptable order can be achieved by human strivings. Such an order will acknowledge the central importance of religion and will see the spiritual as the appropriate end of every other aspect of human life. This depends upon individuals realizing the need for it. Demant writes, "It is only when men are ready for the continued task of remaking their order of life in the light of their loyalty to the divine reality which transcends, while it provides the pivot of, the immanent order itself, that the true autonomy of each function is assured."[94] Society is restored through human strivings. This, of course, is the idea behind Christian Sociology.

Therefore, for Demant society is technically "always sick. It is always sick because it is never free from destructive forces, such as division in human aims or discrepancies between central policies and personal goals; there are anglings for power and plain human sin. But society has at the same time its own recuperative impulses and powers; there is a self-healing principle which tends to bend policies, theories, conflicts and behaviour, so as to serve the needs of human existence."[95] Judgments about the goodness

---

93. Ibid., 240.
94. Demant, *Theology of Society*, 90.
95. Demant, *Religion and the Decline of Capitalism*, 157.

or badness of a society are judgments about the progress of the respective human impulses for goodness and badness.

Finally, Demant draws a further analogy: "In the personal life the true centrality cannot be recovered by the individual man through his own willing; he must lose his self in the Divine Action operating upon and through him, a process begun and carried through by the spiritual culture we call the practice of religion. So also, the centrality of the spirit in its sociological force cannot be recovered by moral desire alone, but requires that this desire be sustained and that real will be formed out of it, by a social order that provides a habitat for the soul."[96] As has been already noted, Demant did not suggest that the restoration of society is simply a matter of God's grace. So here, Demant is emphasizing the need for both the inner and outer life of a culture to be in harmony. Simple decision and willing in the outer life of a culture is never enough. The subconscious assumptions of a culture must be in harmony with these aims. The inner life is not just a question of mental ideas. In *Our Culture* Demant identifies three influences which mold a culture. First, the ideological influence which includes both the doctrines and dogmas as outlined above. This is the realm of ideas. Secondly, the ritual, the conventions which underlie human actions. So, to use his example, are holidays marked by the closure of banks as on bank holidays, or by the decent observance of holy days of the church? Elsewhere it was a concern about the rituals of society which made him defend the convention of wearing Sunday best, even if you do not go to church.[97] Third, the structure and organization of society; "this includes the order of rank, importance and status, accorded to different kinds of person, the occupations deemed more or less essential, central or normal."[98] This includes the economic factor in human life. This will prove important when we come to the Gifford Lectures, for there Demant defines the penumbra of a culture as including, "axioms about existence, world views, routines taken as norms, rituals and emotional bents, images and archetypes."[99] This penumbra is part of the inner life of a culture at conflict with the outer life.

The final parallel between the individual and the social is an extension of his discussion. He sees a social equivalent of the individual "link-in-contradiction." It is to this that we now turn.

---

96. Demant, *Theology of Society*, 79
97. Ibid., 246ff.
98. Demant, *Our Culture*, 5
99. V. A. Demant Unpublished Papers. Gifford Lectures. Series 1, Lecture 1. University Summaries.

SOCIAL EQUIVALENT OF THE LINK-IN-CONTRADICTION[100]

It has already been noted that the idea of the inner and outer life of a culture is central in Demant's system. The reason why this is so important to Demant is that this is the essential problem facing our culture. Logically, there are three possible relations for the inner and outer life to bear to one another. First, they can be harmonised with each other, recognizing their total dependence on God, thereby maintaining the natural social order. Secondly, they can be harmonized in rebellion against God, swinging destructively from their natural order in an act of pride and independence. Although the link between God and humanity cannot be broken, this would represent a united attack against that link. Thirdly, they can be in conflict with each other, with the inner and outer life out of harmony, thereby generating frustration. If either of the first two prevails, then there is very little that needs or can be done. In the first case, there is no problem. The culture is on the way to restoration. In the second case, the culture is locked into rebellion, with no internal pressures which might trigger a change of direction. However, our culture is an example of the third case. We are a result of a Christian ethos, which has tried to maintain the appropriate aims in our outer life, but has denied this ethos in our inner life. From this, Demant believes, flows our current crisis, namely, our inability to do anything to ameliorate our position.

Our society, within its inner life, is denying our eternal dependence. In so doing we are giving some aspect of the temporal world an undeserved significance. To maintain the analogy with the individual, the spirit of our society has ejected itself into one of the layers of our society. However, the link between God and the world cannot be broken; so our culture swings in frustration, refusing to settle where it should. This explains the dialectic which Demant believes is an appropriate way of interpreting history. As a model, it is considerably better than the "liberal progressive" conception, which just sees a movement from worse to better in history. Rather, history is made up of conflict, and this is best explained, by the "pull of something independent of the time process and yet which actuates it, (which) provides a more ultimate explanation of the revolutions of cosmic and human history, than a dialectic whose terms are within the process itself."[101] Demant feels that talk of a dialectic is wholly appropriate for the theist and more so than for the Marxist. The dialectic arises because humanity having rejected

---

100. Demant, *Religious Prospect*, 195.
101. Demant, *God, Man and Society*, 154.

the transcendent center, gives priority to first one element in the culture, then another. Demant thinks that if we look "at these revolutions of post-Renaissance Europe in a dialectical way, we get a forceful impression of a series of struggles to embody a wholeness of life, each answering the last, but missing the wholeness by giving absolute, divine value to the previously neglected elements of it."[102]

The central problem which Demant is grappling with here is this. Virtually all people consciously seek a better life, and exhortations abound, hoping to persuade everyone to be good; yet human society is not improving. Demant believes that his analysis explains why this is so. There are two related problems. First, the problem that the conscious aims of the culture are incompatible with its assumptions. The inner and outer life are not in harmony. Secondly, whilst the culture stubbornly refuses to acknowledge its transcendent basis, it finds itself swinging from one layer to another. Demant gives two examples of these frustrating dialectical swings which he identifies in western Europe in his day. The first is the political swing from the liberal state to the totalitarian one. The second is from the capitalist, individualistic market principle to the socialist, collectivist state principle. Both are reactions to the same underlying crisis, namely, the fact that in the inner life of the culture there is a refusal to recognize the appropriate transcendent ground of all human life.

The text of the Giffords that follows seeks to be readable. We have used a variety of devices to achieve this end. Where Demant lapses into notes, which need some significant editorial clarification, we have used square brackets, often with an explanation. Where Demant's note needs less editorial clarification, we have used italics. Sometimes Demant's note is very brief, but we have used italics when we are confident as to the meaning because it is a classic Demantian theme. In both cases, we describe precisely what Demant had written in the footnotes. As some points, we use bold - this marks occasions when Demant had crossed out what follows. But we include it here because even his crossed out text illuminates his argument. With these preliminaries established, we now turn to the Giffords.

102. Demant, *Theology of Society*, 134.

SECTION TWO

The Giffords

Introduction

I

A Gifford lecturer may fittingly ask himself whether his chosen subject could be properly considered as a contribution to "natural theology." It is a necessary question because Lord Gifford intended the endowment of this lectureship to be used not merely for an academic exposition of what he called natural theology, but preeminently the presentation of it as a desirable discipline. The Gifford Lectures were meant to commend the subject and not only to describe it. His reasons must have been clearer to his contemporaries than they are to us nearly a century later. The terms of his will take for granted that he regarded natural theology as a unifying force among religious believers, in contrast to the divisive effects of the historical religions and churches, with their warrants in some kind of revealed truth. He also assumed that natural theology was a straightforward alternative to revealed theology, and that its avoidance of supernatural and miraculous elements would thereby give it more cogency in the minds of all sensible men.

For two reasons it is of significance for me to identify, as far as possible, in what sense Lord Gifford understood natural theology. One is that I find any coherent body of thought which has commanded attention, to be an exciting thing. It cannot be taken for granted as a necessary phase in the mental development of mankind or as a stage in social evolution, or as an occasional concentration of a diffused essence in universal human knowledge. It has a significance and morphology of its own which cannot be discerned in terms of what it came out of or what it leads into in a process of continuity. The second reason I have for seeking the affinities of natural theology in Lord Gifford's understanding of it, is that it enables me to interpret my own account of religion and ethics in Christendom with some fidelity to the terms the founder laid down.

His affinities are undoubtedly with that system of religious thought which ranges roughly over the seventeenth and eighteenth centuries and can conveniently be denoted as the natural theology of the Enlightenment, with close connection with Deism. As Lord Gifford used a terminology which has close resemblances to that of this Enlightenment theology, he must be regarded like St. Paul "as one born out of due time," for nearly a century elapsed between the foundation of his lectureships and the close of that vigorous but comparatively short-lived Enlightenment tradition. The nineteenth century saw that tradition displaced by a number of new approaches to religious phenomena.

In his *Trust Disposition and Settlement of 1885* establishing this lectureship, Lord Gifford defined the subject in these terms: "The knowledge of God, the Infinite, the All, the First and only Cause, the one and sole Substance, the Sole being, the Sole Reality, and the Sole Existence, the knowledge of His Nature and Attributes, the knowledge of the Relations which men and the whole universe bear to Him, the knowledge of the Nature and Foundation of Ethics or Morals, and of all Obligations and Duties thence arising." This language might suggest that Lord Gifford had been influenced by Spinoza two centuries earlier rather than by the intervening exponents of the Enlightenment. The Foundation document requires that "natural theology" shall be exercised "without reference to, or reliance upon, any supposed special, exceptional or so-called miraculous revelation." There have not been wanting holders of this lectureship who have questioned the distinction between natural and revealed theology and have insisted that all knowledge of God or divine things are in some sense revealed. But Lord Gifford has left us no doubt that what he intended to exclude was any religious affirmation which derived its authority from a specific revelation or sacred scriptures or a historical record of divine acts or such images as Christ the Paschal Lamb.

A precursor of Enlightenment natural theology was Francis Bacon (1561–1626) who put it this way. "Natural theology is rightly called also divine philosophy. It is defined as that spark of the knowledge of God which may be had of the light of nature and the consideration of created things; and thus can fairly be held to be *divine* in respect of its object, and *natural* in respect of its source of information."[1]

An even earlier forerunner was Raymond Sebonde whose treatise *Natural Theology or Book of Creatures* became influential through being translated by Montaigne. In his prologue to this work he wrote, "This science alleges no authorities, neither Holy Scripture nor any doctors, nay rather

---

1. Bacon, *The Two Bookes of Sr. Francis Bacon*, III.2.

it confirms Holy Scripture, and by means of it a man believes firmly in the Holy Scriptures. And so in the order of our procedure it comes before Holy Scripture; and so there are two books given to sue of God, to wit the book of the world of creatures or book of nature, and another which is the book of Holy Scripture."[2] In brief, Sebonde held the written word to be superfluous, but it could be confirmed by the book of nature.

Early in the seventeenth century Edward, Lord Herbert of Cherbury enunciated in a slightly different form the priority of natural religion. In his major work: *De Veritate print distinguitur a Revelatione, Verissimil, Pissibili, et a Falso* (Paris 1624) he presents natural religion as a common feature in the various historical religions, but he regards it as able to stand alone by the side of them. These "common notions" as he calls them, are given universally by a kind of inner light to all men. Although an individual person may receive special revelations and gifts of grace from a particular providence, these are not necessary for man's knowledge of God. The essentials of religion are within the hearts of man, apprehended by the natural reason, and are proven by moral virtue and the right use of our faculties. Lord Herbert's position represents a step further away from that of both Francis Bacon and Raymond Sebonde, both of whom held to a recognizable identity between the divine object of natural and revealed religion.

Perhaps the most typical representatives of this school of natural theology in England, though hardly its greatest figures were John Toland and Mathew Tindal. The sub-titles of their famous works are indications of their position. In 1696 Toland published his *Christianity not mysterious, showing that though there is nothing in the Gospel contrary to reason nor above it, and that no Christian Doctrine can properly be called a Mystery*. And in 1730 Tindal issued *Christianity as old as the Creation or the Gospel a Republication of the Religious Nature*. Both these men upheld an original endowment given to the human reason coeval with creation. They attached no importance to the person of Christ; they underestimated the force of evil; they believed they were removing all obstacles to a new heaven and a new earth. What was specific in the New Testament they regarded as the product of superstition and credulity. For them, in line with others of this school, revelation can add nothing to the religion of nature apprehended by reason. We might say that they mentally projected the omnipotence of reason as understood in their own period upon the creation of the world. This looks like a touching remnant of desire for a theological warrant.

Toland and Tindal figure in the literature as among the Deists, and Toland proclaimed himself as avowed pantheist, and this is not incompatible.

---

2. Raymond, *La theologie naturelle de dom Raymon Sebon* . . .

Tindal's *Christianity as old as Creation* has been considered the Bible of Deism. A more complex form of deism is found in the work of William Paley who wrote *Evidences of Christianity* (1744) and *Natural Theology* (1803) at a time when nature was looked upon as a mechanism. His evidences for God's existence constituted a form of argument from design, as in the famous "watch" model where the divine designer set the works in motion and dictated the laws of their behavior. In the same vein Paley accepted miracles as witness to a supernatural and arbitrary intervention into the world's clockwork. Moreover, he found proof of God's initiative from beyond the cosmic whole, in the originality of Christ's character which could not be accounted for in terms of its antecedents or environment.

This turn of attitude presaged the demise of the whole movement. The appeal of Enlightenment natural theology was soon blunted by several influences. First came the attack upon it by its own followers, such as the skepticism of Hume and Voltaire. Hume rejected entirely the fundamental axiom of natural theology which he describes as belief that "the cause or causes of order in the universe probably bear some remote analogy to human intelligence." He averred that a well-disposed mind would feel an intense longing that "Heaven would be pleased to dissipate, at least, relieve, this profound ignorance by affording some more particular revelation to Mankind and making discoveries of the nature, attributes and operations of the divine object of our faith."[3]

In brief, that human reason is as mysterious and unreliable as any revealed doctrine. And Voltaire poured scorn upon the rational optimism which marked the faith of his predecessors in the field of natural theology, especially God's providence and goodness. But perhaps the climax of revolt came not in the field of thought, but in abhorrence at the sanguinary results of the French Revolution, when Robespierre, deserting the tolerance of the older deists, celebrated the Festival of the Supreme Being in the age of terror to the orchestration of the guillotine.

II

There had naturally been some minds who realized the strength of the philosophical "natural theology" of the Enlightenment before its demise, who appreciated its attractiveness and learned its language, but who rejected its postulates. Such a one was the poet John Dryden who penned some sonorous and poorish verse to express the relation between the light of nature

---

3. Hume, *Dialogues Concerning Natural Religion*, Part VII and XII.

and the light of faith as he saw it. Here are the opening lines of his *Religio Laici* or *A Layman's Faith*,

> Dim, as the borrow'd beams of moon and stars
> To lonely, weary, wand'ring travellers,
> Is reason to the soul; and as on high,
> Those rolling fires discover but the sky
> Not light us here; so reason's glimmering ray
> Was lent not to assure our doubtful way,
> But guide us upward to a better day.
> And as those nightly tapers disappear
> When day's bright lord ascends our hemisphere
> So pale grows reason at religion's sight:
> So dies, and so dissolves in supernatural light.

In the preface Dryden explains: "Revelation, being thus eclipsed to almost all Mankind, the light of Nature as the next in Dignity, was substituted, and that is it which St. Paul concludes to be the rule of the Heathens; and by which they are hereafter to be judged. If my supposition be true, then the consequences which I have assumed in my poem, may be also true; namely that Deism, or the principles of Natural worship, are only the faint remnants or dying flames of revealed Religion in the Posterity of Noah."[4]

There are two ideas in these pages. On the one hand, Dryden refers to the older Christian tradition of a natural light vouchsafed to the heathen, by which all men are judged, but from the inadequacy of which the Christian believer is rescued by the light of Christ, according to St. Paul in the Epistle to the Romans. In a similar way Dryden regards the philosophical natural theology of his own time as a guide toward the "better day" of Christian faith. But then he changes the image to one where this natural theology is but an afterglow in the twilight of revealed religion. We shall see that this second image is the better one for understanding what happened to Enlightenment natural theology.

There are greater names of those who served to displace the philosophical theology of the Enlightenment. The most influential was Rousseau, one of its own children, who preached a natural religion which had no need of a revelation and a faith based on some aspect of human nature. Not reason or evidences of design, but the emotion of awe, the sense of mystery, the feeling of aspiration, an innate sense of right and wrong, provided mankind with infallible guides. What God says to the human heart is that all men need to listen to, and if men had done so there would be only one religion. Rousseau was one of the most powerful influences in the history of the

---

4. Dryden, *Religio Laici or A Laymans Faith*.

western world; he is at the root of the great wave of humanitarian liberalism which had its heyday in the nineteenth century. The philosopher Kant said he had learned from Rousseau to rely upon the intuition of the common man, for Rousseau placed the evidence of sentiment and emotion above the metaphysical proofs of the natural theologians.

Nearly a century earlier Pascal delivered his attack upon "le Dieu des philosophes." This scientist and mathematician sent the readers of his "Pensées" to the revealed facts of Christianity. "The God of the Christians is not a God who is merely the creator of geometrical truths and the order of elements, like the God of the pagans and the Epicureans . . . But the God of Abraham, the God of Isaac, the God of Jacob, the God of the Christians is a god of love and consolation, a God who fills both the souls and hearts of His own."[5]

For Pascal, the root convictions of religion are not reached by observation of nature or by philosophical deduction, but by the promptings of "the heart." In his well known dictum "the heart has its reason which the reason does not know" the heart must be understood, not as mere feeling or imagination, but as the metaphor for immediate certainties, physical as well as religious. From these immediate data of consciousness the reason operates. "The principles are felt, the propositions conclude; and the whole with certainty, though by different routes."[6] None has given a higher place than Pascal to the power and dignity of human thought. "By virtue of space I am comprehended and engulfed in the universe as a mere point; but by virtue of thought I comprehend it."[7] The infinity of the universe is known as one of the immediate data, but its nature is an unfathomable mystery. Pascal reiterates that the range of human thought exalts the mind, but that its limits duly humble him. Hence "the greatness and littleness of man." But there is no anti-intellectual fideism in Pascal. "If one submits everything to reason, our religion would have nothing of the mysterious and of the supernatural. If one violates the principles of reason, our religion will be absurd and ridiculous."[8] Pascal quarreled with the natural theologians of the Enlightenment because of their refusal to face the baffling character of the infinitely great and infinitely small and he argues that when one has been immersed in and overwhelmed by the riddles and inconceivability of the natural world one can expect to find mysteries also in religion.

---

5. Pascal, *Pensées, D'après L'éd. de M. Brunschvigg*, 556.
6. Ibid., 282.
7. Ibid., 348.
8. Ibid., 214.

Less philosophically and more stridently the poet William Blake attacked the modern natural theology. In tumultuous outpourings of esoteric genius, he derided that form of it called Deism. His appeal was, however, not obviously to revelation, but rather to the inspiration of poetic genius. This mystic and visionary directly addresses the Deists in prose paragraphs of "Jerusalem": "He never can be a friend to the Human Race who is the preacher of Natural morality, or Natural Religion ... You O Deists! profess yourselves the enemies of Christianity, and you are so. You are also the enemies of the Human Race and of Universal Nature ... Deism is the worship of the God of this World by the means of what you call Natural Religion and Natural Philosophy." And in an Appendix to the Prophetic Books, one finds Part the First entitled "There is no Natural Religion." There Blake declares "Man by his Reasoning Power, can only compare and judge of what he has already perceived." Also "if it were not for the Poetic or Prophetic character, the Philosophic and Experimental would soon be at the Ratio of all things; and still, unable to do other than repeat the same dull round over again." In aphorisms headed paradoxically enough, "All Religions are One," we find "As the true method of knowledge is Experiment, the true faculty of knowing must be the faculty which experiences." Further, "The Religions of all Nations are derived from each Nation's distinctive reception of the Poetic Genius" which is everywhere called the Spirit of Prophecy. "The Jewish and Christian Testaments are an original derivation from the Poetic Genius." In his wild apocalyptic way Blake represents two distinct reactions against the natural theology of the seventeenth and eighteenth centuries. He finds the data in religious experience rather than in the conclusion of deductive argument, and he sees the faiths of mankind as disjunctively varied growths from an original root.

A century before Blake Europe had been subject to other religious insights which had not been quite overwhelmed by the rationalistic optimism of the natural theologians. The dark hidden and paradoxical nature of the divine existence, expounded in the medieval spiritual teachers, was discovered again through the powerful influence of Jacob Boehme whose theosophical mysticism greatly influenced the German idealist philosophers and attracted the enthusiastic attention of William Law, Isaac Newton and John Wesley in England, for a time at least. These men found in the neo-gnosticism of Boehme a vital insistence upon the dark side of the divine nature, along with the scandalous fact of evil and its consequence in a tragic sense of life. In this they were overcoming the shallow optimism and defenses of God's providence which had misled the natural theologians into accepting plausible arguments for the harmonies of nature.

Another signpost later in the same direction can be detected in the young Goethe who at the end of his *Dichtung und Wahrheit* announced his discovery of the daemonic element in existence. In spite of his early admiration for the Encyclopedists, on whom he made some caustic remarks, Goethe describes how from childhood he sought "various ways to approach the supernatural, first looking with strong inclination to a religion of nature; then clinging with love to a positive one; and, finally, concentrating himself in the trial of his own powers and joyfully giving himself up to a general faith." In this search,

> He thought he could detect in nature—both animate and inanimate, with soul and without soul—something which manifested itself only in contradictions, and which, therefore, could not be comprehended under any idea, still less under one word. To this principle, which seemed to come in between all other principles and separate them, and yet link them together, I gave the name of Daemonic, after the example of the ancients and others with similar experiences . . . Although this Daemonic element manifests itself in all corporeal and incorporeal things, and even expresses itself most distinctly in animals, yet it is primarily in its relation to man we observe its mysterious workings, which represent a force, if not antagonistic to the moral order, yet running counter to it, so that the one may be regarded as the warp, and the other as the woof."[9]

Goethe had early declared himself a partisan of the Enlightenment, but he ventured to predict that on its principles the poetic value of the scriptural writings would eventually be lost together with their prophetic significance.[10] He put a query to the assumption that a particular religion arises on top of natural religion, and he remarks that when some of the natural theologians assigned equal right to all positive religions, these all become equally unimportant and uncertain. Goethe repeatedly announced the need for some revealed religion such as fascinated him in the Bible, holding as he did that natural religion required no faith. It is interesting to note that he uses variously the terms "positive" or "particular" for what others called "revealed" religions. How striking it would have been if at the end of his memories Goethe had associated his discovery of *The Daemonic Element* with his commitment to some kind of positive religion. "The Positive Religions" became a common phrase in later discussions where, it would be contended that "natural theology" was an eviscerated derivative from some

---

9. Goethe, *Poetry & Truth*, Book XX.
10. Ibid., Book VII.

INTRODUCTION 83

positive religion, and not a neutral basis upon which it could or could not arise.

A powerful and somewhat baffling figure in this intellectual gallery was Golthold Ephraim Lessing (1729–1781), a near contemporary of Goethe. His acute and restless mind was displayed with outstanding artistic and literary gifts. Though inclined to be scornful of the deists he shared their reverence for "the necessary truths of reason" and their rejection of "the accidental truths of history." He gave little weight to the sacred traditions of actual religions and contributed controversially to the contemporary work of the biblical critics. Lessing wrote a short note on *The Origin of Revealed Religion*. After laying down that every man is committed and bound to the natural religion which acknowledges one God, he argues that each man's natural religion differs from another's, because of their varying capacities; therefore, for the sake of community conventional bonds are needed. "Out of the religion of nature, which was not capable of being universally practiced by all men alike, positive religion had to be constructed, just as out of the law of nature, for the same cause, a positive law has been constructed ... This positive religion received its sanction through the distinction of its founder."[11] The conclusion of the matter is stated in Lessing's dictum that all positive and revealed religions are equally true and equally false, true for each believer, false for others.

Here, in Lessing, we find revealed religion and the positive religions closely affiliated, as against the only absolutely necessary natural religion. But he did not wholly attribute them to the corrupt effect of superstitious priesthoods, as other natural theologians of the Enlightenment did. He gave the positive religions a relative value, as stages in the passage of humanity from primitiveness to maturity. There is considerable incongruity in Lessing's varying attitudes to the natural theologians of his time. He magnificently exemplifies the quality which Emerson admired when he wrote, "with a foolish consistency a great mind has simply nothing to do." But of two convictions Lessing seems to have been unswervingly tenacious; his rejection of the transcendence of God and his refusal of allegiance to any of the positive religions.[12]

III

I have now reviewed, imperfectly and too selectively, the natural theology of the seventeenth and eighteenth centuries, and then some influences at work

11. Lessing, *Lessing's Theological Writings*, 105.
12. Ibid., 45.

in the same period which recovered or stimulated counteracting tendencies. Before describing these tendencies more fully, two summary observations on the distinctive character of the natural theology I have reviewed, can be made.

First, we have noted two contending attitudes to its status. One of them, taken by most of its exponents, regarded natural theology and religion as a given datum of the human mind. It was exemplified by Rousseau and Voltaire for whom "la religion naturalle ne peut contenir que les principles de morale communs au genre humain,"[13] with the implication that revealed or positive religions are unnecessary and pernicious over-beliefs. The opposing attitude held that the natural religion or theology of the philosophers was a twilight or ghost of the living religion. John Dryden spoke of the dying flames of natural theology. In the nineteenth century S. T. Coleridge referred to "our Alogi who feed on the husks of Christianity" and could hold "their own Remnants of a Creed."[14] A century later Ernst Troeltsch, in the same vein, for all his emphasis upon the relativity of religious phenomena, insisted that "the rational religions are in every instance only offshoots of the positive historical religions, and for all their speculative subtlety, in no case do they possess a strong, independent religious impulse."[15]

In the second place, for the sake of comparison with the interests that replaced it, the natural theology we have been sketching was, in its genuine intention a theology, and not merely a description of religious phenomena. Its upholders inherited an idea of God derived from the biblical monotheism which had been carried through the Christian centuries by the church. Their problems became acute when they sought to use this idea of God as the basis for the new science and philosophy. It became assumed that this monotheistic dogma could survive the disappearance of its historical expressions, its revelatory deliverances, its sacred scriptures, its ritual communications, and its devotional canalizing of the powers of the soul. The fundamental instability was due to the shift from God as an object of cognition and worship, to God as the principle of intelligibility. The transition is obvious in the early stages of the period. We have already recorded that Francis Bacon wrote: "Natural theology is rightly called also divine philosophy. It is defined as that spark of knowledge of God which may be had by the light of nature and the consideration of created things; and thus can fairly be

---

13. In English, the translation is "natural religion can only contain the moral principles common to the human race."

14. Coleridge, "On Spiritual Religion" in *Aids to Reflection in the Formation of a Manly Character.*

15. Troeltsch, *Absoluteness of Christianity and the History of Religions*, 93.

held to the *divine* in respect of its object, and *natural* in respect of its source of information."[16]

And very soon afterwards René Descartes was saying: "the certitude and truth of all science depend on knowledge of God and on that alone." The reason for this is: "the certitude of all other truth is so dependent on this one that without the knowledge of God it would be impossible to know anything else."[17] For Bacon, God is still the divine object, but the principle of knowledge is natural. For Descartes, God constitutes the power of man's knowledge of the world; and he relegates man's knowledge of God to the sphere of faith, separate from intellectual knowledge or rational demonstration. So, religion began to lose any theological warrant, and a process was started which encouraged the view of religion as mass delusion or merely a subject for historical curiosity.

I have hinted that before the end of the eighteenth century the specifically theological concerns of natural theology gave place to new religious interests. The transition has been described by Arthur O. Lovejoy in his magisterial work, *The Great Chain of Being*:

> It is one of the instructive ironies of history of ideas that a principle introduced by one generation in the service of a tendency or philosophic mood congenial to it often proves to contain, unsuspected, the germ of a contrary tendency—to be, by virtue of its hidden implications, the destroyer of that *Zeitgeist* to which it was meant to minister. There are few more striking examples of this irony than that which may be found in the principles of plenitude and continuity. As we have seen, they were invoked in the seventeenth and early eighteenth century primarily as a support for the doctrine of the essential logicality of the world. They were designed to justify the belief in the rationality, the perfection, the static completeness, the orderliness and coherence of reality...the ultimate effect of their vogue was to introduce subtly and gradually into the European mind several of those tastes and those philosophical presuppositions which at the end of the century took form in a conscious and aggressive revolutionary movement in thought, that to which the name of Romanticism is commonly applied.[18]

The rise of Romanticism may not be the most enlightening of terms by which to identify the transition we are concerned with. But one

---

16. Bacon, *Proficience and Advancement of Learning*, III.2.
17. Descartes, *Method, Meditations and Philosophy*, 262.
18. Lovejoy, *Great Chain of Being*, 288.

characteristic of thought about religion, which was becoming prominent, had this in common with Romantic thinkers, litterateurs, and artists, that interested attention was now directed to the variety, individuality, and sometimes the incongruity of human phenomena. Lovejoy points out that "The Enlightenment was, in short, an age devoted at least in its dominant tendency, to the simplification and the standardization of thought and life—to their standardization by means of their simplification . . . When the contrary principle began widely to prevail . . . it came to be believed not only that in many, or in all phases of human life there are diverse excellences, but that diversity itself is of the essence of excellence."[19] It stimulated "the endeavor to reconstruct in imagination the distinctive inner life of peoples remote in time or space or in cultural condition."[20] This endeavor is just what we find promoting a new attitude to religion. Instead of seeking the theological common structure of religious beliefs by philosophical articulation, the mind of the age was in the nineteenth century turning to survey the actual religions by which men live.

For some centuries Europeans had been interested in reports of religious belief and practices in distant lands. As early as the fourteenth century they had become aware of a widening geographical horizon, reaching from Iceland to remotest Asia. The Portuguese reached India, Spaniards and Italians got to Poland and Russia. Jesuits told about the Chinese and the Indian cultures. Explorers, missionaries, administrators, and scholars, had before the modern world, taken notice of other people's religion, not altogether in the interests of the conquest, conversion, economic gain, and political control. But not much before the nineteenth century can we trace a number of confluent approaches to what may be called "the history of religions." The emergence of social anthropology as a human science as well as a guide to colonial authorities, disclosed the large place held by religion in the human enterprise. At first the origin of religion was a dominant enquiry and its secret was sought for in its primitive forms. The influence of E. B. Tylor's *Primitive Culture* and J. G. Frazer's *The Golden Bough* fostered accounts of religion in terms of its origins. Under the spur of Darwinism theories of biological evolution were early misapplied to the religious career of mankind as well as to history in general and to the movements of thought. Books appeared with titles like *The Evolution of Religion*, *The Evolution of Morals*, and *The Evolution of the Idea of God*. This developmental hypothesis began to lose its cogency by the end of the nineteenth century, and religions became

---

19. Ibid., 292.
20. Ibid., 293.

more the subject of enquiry into the various ways men coped with their cognitive problems and the social setting of their personal goals.[21]

Besides the contribution of the anthropologists a greater stimulus to the ranging of religion among the subjects of humane studies came from those who had discovered its place in the cultures outside Europe, in India, China, the Arab world, and in the ancient civilizations. The Hindu *Laws of Manu* had been translated by Sir William Jones in 1794; Max Muller began to edit and translate *The Sacred Book of the East* in 1875, and a *World Parliament of Religions* met in Chicago in 1893. The comparative study of religions was becoming a serious and fascinating occupation.

The spreading interest in the actual religions of mankind was reinforced in the twentieth century by recognition of religious certainties in the obscure hidden life of men, below the level of conscious and intellectual doctrine. A key document representing this trend was William James's *Varieties of Religious Experience*, Gifford Lectures delivered at Edinburgh in 1901–1902. That great work gave an account of religious experiences of men and women, mainly in the western world but also with a sympathetic glance at the Far East. It covers facts like the processes of conversion, the nature of saintliness, mystical insights; and also, such unusual tormented phenomena as the sick soul or the divided self. Moreover, it called attention to the positive significance of mythology, symbols, visions and images of the divine in the hidden depths of the self. All this James placed in the category he called "The Reality of the Unseen." He found a framework for classifying these phenomena in the idea of the *sub-conscious* which was then "a well accredited psychological entity."[22] These lectures of William James became a powerful launching pad for a new kind of study of religions, though it has been subjected to a number of criticisms for its method. It stressed the importance of feeling as a realm of certainty, and then wrote about it as if feeling were entirely a subconscious experience. The book was judged to be one-sided, drawing its raw material too much from morbid and irrational levels. It was misleadingly individualist in that it placed the subconscious forces in the private sphere. The validity of both clear and subliminal experiences was tested too narrowly by their moral results, in accordance with the author's pragmatic assumptions.

In particular, these magnificent lectures never made quite clear whether the intimations given in religious experience warranted belief in the reality of God. James was aware of this criticism and made some effort to meet it. In one place he calls "the subconscious" self "an intermediary between the

---

21. Cf. Evans-Pritchard, *Theories of Primitive Religion*.
22. James, *The Varieties of Religious Experience*, 511.

self and God," and in order to prevent a possible subjectivist interpretation, he adds, "God is a causal agent as well as a medium of communion." In the concluding chapter he admitted that he believed feeling to be the deepest source of religion, and that intellectual formulae are secondary products "like translations of a text into another tongue." He classed the doctrines of theology and the conclusions of philosophy as "over beliefs," necessary to redeem religion from an unwholesome privacy and to give it public status. That is the task of reason. The main theme of William James's *Varieties of Religious Experience* is that religions have their origin in the depths of the soul, and that formulated beliefs are possible superstructures, which may certainly be required but do not penetrate to the source of religion. Much has come about since he wrote in fulfillment of his plea that theology should abandon metaphysics and transform itself into a science of religion. Encouragement to pursue such a science of religion was mightily reinforced by the work of clinical psychologists like C. G. Jung. Following the discovery by Freud and others that the human personality has a powerful set of forces in a realm normally hidden from its conscious awareness, Jung approached religious phenomena with the key of "the unknown self." In an early work, he wrote "within our own unconscious psyche there are active those powers which men have always projected into space as gods and then worshipped them with sacrifices" and "God is a psychic fact of direct experience."[23] This does not mean, he makes repeated efforts to convince his readers, that God does not exist or does exist. As an empirical scientist, he disclaims any title to draw philosophical or theological conclusions. But he insists that it would be dishonest for a psychologist to assert that the psychic image of God does not have the most powerful influence in the soul. In his commentary upon the Chinese classic, *The Secret of the Golden Flower* he rebuts the charge of "psychologism," namely the view that what man knows is only his subjective state. "That charge," he writes, "applies only to a fool who thinks he has his soul in his pocket."[24]

It would be hard to exaggerate the influence of Jung and his followers upon the rise of the now popular study of the religions. He held that the multiplicity of unconscious religious forces explain the manifold religions of mankind. There is therefore a ground common to them all and people can learn of it by looking, with psychological help, in the hidden abysses of the self, individual or collective. There they would find, not indeed Christ or God, but all the turbulent forces with which salvation and scriptures and churches have to do. Because Jung finds in these unconscious strata symbols

23. Daking, *Jungian Psychology and Modern Spiritual Thought*, 107.
24. Jung, *Secret of the Golden Flower*, 129.

of uncreated and undifferentiated deity, he interprets the various religions as different ways of coping with the disharmonies between conscious and the unconscious elements. He repeats that while philosophical and dogmatic formulations divide, the problems they attempt to systematize are the basic stuff of man's inner life. So he can say, "If I accept the fact that a God is absolute and beyond all human experience, he leaves me cold. I do not affect him, nor does he affect me. But if I know, on the other hand, that God is a mighty activity in my soul, at once I must concern myself with him; he can then become even unpleasantly important, and in practical ways too, which sounds horribly banal like everything appearing in the sphere of reality."[25]

Jung knew that all religions are therapies for the sorrows and disorders of mankind, and interprets insanity as the consequence of failure to assimilate the unconscious content of the psyche to the luminosity of consciousness. Such failure he regards as pre-eminently a characteristic of the modern western mind. So he draws heavily upon Eastern wisdoms, Hindu, Chinese, and others, as well as upon pre-Renaissance western religious traditions, for therapeutic counterweights to modern western distortions. The enormous vogue of salvation techniques from the east in this late twentieth century western world on the part of masses of people who have never heard of Jung, testifies to the strength of this appeal. And Jung himself has uttered a warning that there is no salvation for a westerner to be found from artificial imitation of the East. "Of what use" he writes "is the wisdom of the Upanishads or the insight of the Chinese Yoga, if we desert the foundations of our own culture as though they were outlived errors, and like homeless pirates, settle with thievish intent on foreign shores?"[26] This warning springs from Jung's condition that the apparent disappearance of religious feeling in modern man is in reality its banishment to the deep levels of the psyche. The result is not merely a loss but also a menace, for gods and demons, heaven and hells, are ineradicable from the nooks and crannies of the human mind. If the mind is deprived of heaven above and hell beneath, it makes heaven and hell on earth. Much of Jung's teachings suggest a picture of the fearful vengeance wrought on earth when the human spirit cleanses the sky of its gods and the underworld of its demons. Removed from consciousness these realities tear holes in the hidden psyche, making for conflicts inside man and for wars on earth between terrestrial heavens and hells."[27]

25. Ibid.
26. Ibid., 146.
27. See also one of Jung's interpreters: Victor White, *God and the Unconscious* (1952); *Soul and Psyche* (1960); and kindred themes in Miricea Eliade, *The Two and the One* (1962), *Le Sacré et le Profane* (1965).

Religious studies pursued independently of concern with the theological validity of any actual religion seem to have claimed the interest of a number of people, even of those who needed no faith and sought no conviction. Religion became a subject of investigation and occupied the attention of at least six kinds of mind. First, there were those who knew the power of religion and wanted that power to be destroyed. In the nineteenth century the outstanding investigators who studied religion in order to attack its influence were Feuerbach and Comte, Marx and Nietzsche.[28] Secondly, there were those for whom religion was a fascinating field of enquiry, especially in its influence on social cohesion, like De Maistre and Max Muller. Thirdly, there were the hopeful searchers after a common ground in the religions which could serve for the unification of mankind. Fourthly, there were those who looked around for new fields of enquiry which could attract financial resources under the heading of academic research, or which could provide teachers with school substitutes for the older Christian religious education. Fifthly, there were many who craved for religious enlightenment which the Christian churches were no longer able to offer, and who consequently turned to non-Christian faiths, mystical movements and therapeutic techniques. Sixthly, multitudes in the west found, to their immense relief, a vicarious piety by becoming "interested in religion" without obligation to commit themselves to any particular belief or cult.

The shift from theological concern to interest in religions did not only mark a widespread diversion of sensibility. In response to such diversion and reciprocally fortifying it, appropriate academic and popular scholastic habits were cultivated. Faculties of Theology in European universities were in many cases replaced by departments of "religious studies"; and even where teaching positions in Christian theology were retained, its biblical and doctrinal foundations were attenuated in order to make room for second-order subjects such as the comparative study of religions, the sociology of religion, the psychology of religion, and the art of pastoral counseling. In Britain, the compromise over religious education in schools has lately allowed sketchy surveys of the world faiths to be given to children, which relieved teachers from the appearance of dogmatism and from which, it was hoped, the young would find something on their own to enlist their allegiance.

---

28. For the present writer's estimate of these critics, see Demant, in *Religion and the Decline of Capitalism*, chapter V, "The Criticism of Religion" (1952), cf. E. E. Evans-Pritchard, *Theories of Primitive Religion* (1965), chapter III, "Sociological Theories."

IV

It was during an earlier phase of interest in the studies of religion that many former Gifford lecturers made their special contribution. The learned world is inestimably indebted to the establishment of the Gifford Lectureships at the end of the eighteenth century, for so many profound and extensive studies in the history of religions. This has of course not been exclusive concern of the distinguished lecturers; nor was it indeed the primary design of Lord Gifford himself. So, appropriately, many Gifford Lectures were devoted to the theology and philosophy of theism, to the moral and psychological questions of human nature, to the history of human cultures, and to the relation of Christianity to the physical sciences. As I have myself embarked upon an enquiry into the status of ethics in the historical religion of Christendom, I am involved in the contributions made by predecessors in the field of religious studies. I note with interest, therefore, that one of the very earliest Gifford Lectures was the Dutch scholar, Cornelis Petrus Tiele, who between 1896 and 1898 took as his subject at Edinburgh, *The Elements of the Science of Religion*.

I also note that the first Gifford lecturer at St. Andrews was Andrew Lang who discoursed on *The Making of Religion*, 1888–1890. I take this opportunity of saluting his memory, for his writings were part of my own background when I was studying social anthropology with Dr. R. R. Marett at Oxford. Marett, also a Gifford Lecturer later on at St. Andrews, described Lang's contribution as contending for "The High Gods of Low Races." An attendant at Lang's Gifford Lectures describes their purpose and reception somewhat ironically as follows:

> Lord Gifford, a Scotch Judge, suffered much from skeptical doubts and wished to deliver others from them... The judge desired that a number of able men should apply their minds to the contemplation of this universe, in the hope that light might be brought to darkened souls, and assurance to perplexed. I cannot but say that these lectures, in several cases, appear to me to have been eminently successful in bringing their bearers to the state of mind from which Lord Gifford designed to deliver them. The resultant conclusion, in more than one case, has been briefly this: *Nobody knows anything at all about the matter*. Mr. Lang gave his Introductory Lecture in St. Salvator's Hall on Thursday, January 17, at 5 p.m.... The lecture was a very remarkable one. There was an extraordinary brightness of treatment... Yet, it

must be said, that the occasional bit of serious counsel and deep feeling came home in a singular way.[29]

While I am acknowledging my indebtedness to previous Gifford lecturers, I wish specially to recall two of them who have specifically brought up the question of the relation between revealed and natural religion. One was Professor A. E. Taylor who delivered his series at St. Andrews in 1926–1928 under the title *The Faith of a Moralist*. There he elaborated considerations which forbid us to hold the two to be independent and alternative fields of study. In Taylor's magisterial volumes he works out a critique of three possible views of the relation. One of them he dismisses at once, the view that a genuine natural theology and an equally genuine revelational theology might be in real contradiction. The second view he rejects is that a revelation, if there is such a thing, would leave the results won by the aid of "natural human reason" standing without modification, merely supplementing them by revealed disclosures. A third position is Taylor's own, namely that revealed religion does not merely supplement natural religion but transforms it in such a way that all truths of natural theology would acquire richer and deeper meaning when seen in the light of a true revelation. And he adds specifically: "In Christian societies natural theology has only been pursued with steady devotion by men who, in point of fact, were earnest believers in an historical self-disclosure of the divine, and active adherents of a positive institutional religion."[30]

Taylor's exposition was that of a moral philosopher. I have next to record the enlightenment received from Christopher Dawson who I have come to regard as the wisest historian of human cultures. In his Gifford Lectures at Edinburgh in 1947 he delineated the natural theology of the Enlightenment as a unique variant of such other manifestations as the natural religion of the pre-Socratic Greeks, and the natural theology of the medieval scholastics held in a dialectical relation with revelation. Dawson's first series, entitled *Religion and Culture* gave an historical account of the rise and demise of the pattern of religious thought known as natural theology in the seventeenth and eighteenth centuries. In his interpretation, this school of natural theology turns out to be a highly specialized product of western religious culture, distinct from ancient religious philosophies like those of Greece and India, and distinct from self-sufficient religious traditions like those of Egypt or China. Every school of natural theology is shown to have been preceded by a revealed theology in most cases derived from it.

---

29. Boyd, *Twenty-Five Years of St. Andrews*, 324–25.
30. Taylor, *The Faith of a Moralist*, 20.

The widespread interest in religious studies during this latter part of the twentieth century raises three considerations which may fittingly conclude this treatment of the natural theology of the Enlightenment and its sequels. They are, firstly, the ambiguity of the term "religion"; secondly, the search for a common essence in the world of faiths, and the contrary instance upon the variety, conflicts, and historical individuality of each religious culture; and thirdly, the tremendous upsurge of popular religious fervor in the western world in the nineteen seventies.

The first of these issues is brought out by the realization of how very modern and predominantly occidental is the use of the term "religion." And the significant historical fact is that this use originated with the debates over natural and revealed theology in the seventeenth and eighteenth centuries. The general noun "religion" came into vogue as meaning beliefs in the sense of the things believed in, and not as the act of believing or the proper attitudes towards them. Immanuel Kant's famous distinction is typical. "That type of religion in which I must know beforehand that something is a Divine Command in order to be able to recognize it as my duty, is revealed religion . . . On the other hand, that kind of religion in which I must first know that something is a duty, before I can admit it to be a Divine Command, is natural religion, that is, religion within the limits of mere reason."[31] And Bishop Butler expounds Christianity "first, as a republication and external institution of natural or essential religion, and secondly, as containing an account of a dispensation of things not discoverable by reason."[32] Both Kant and Butler were defending the two kinds of knowledge necessary for the moral life, and did so in terms of beliefs understood as certainties to be counted upon.

Before the expositions of natural theology and religion in the seventeenth and eighteenth centuries no one ever used "religion" as something revealed or disclosed by reason and observation. This has been demonstrated with great thoroughness by the American scholar Wilfred Cantwell Smith. The English translations of the New Testament, from the Authorized to the Standard Revised text, have very few mentions of the words "religion" and "religious," and in these cases, renders the Greek *thrēskeia and thrēskos* with the force of reverence, worship, piety, and devout, pious, or holy, denoting the quality of ritual acts.

Augustine in the fifth century wrote a short treatise, *De Vera Religione* where the term stands for worship of the one true God, which unites the devotee to him. He also uses the Greek term *latria* for the service due to a

---

31. Kant, *Religion within the Limits of Reason Alone*, 153.26–29; 154.01–5.
32. Butler, *Bishop Butler's Analogy of Religion, Natural and Revealed*, 199.

master. In the thirteenth century St. Thomas Aquinas made frequent use of *religio* for the bond which unites the soul with God. *Religio*, he declares, is not faith, but a witnessing to faith by outward signs. The term applies not to beliefs but to states of life like those of monastic orders, or as an activity of the soul prompting it to the due worship of God. Aquinas recognized two kinds of knowledge. He maintained, of course, that there is a natural knowledge which he attributed entirely to the work of reason. He held it in high esteem and gave it credit for man's apprehension of the existence of God, and of good and evil. But he insisted that for other objects of knowledge like unity in Trinity of Godhead, or the redemptive work of Christ, or the major specifically creedal statements in the form "I believe . . ."; for these faith is the faculty by which the divine realities are known. Further, the two leading figures of the Protestant Reformation are in line with their predecessors in this terminological respect. For Luther *credere* is something a Christian does; it is the act of believing, not what he puts his faith in. And Calvin affirmed that the purpose of his treatise *The Institutes of the Christian Religion* was to do good to the church by maintaining "the pure doctrine of Godliness."[33] It appears therefore that only after the early reformers did the habit arise of employing the term "religion" for the substance of the things believed. In the medieval context religion referred not to the objects of a person's allegiance, but to a grounding in Christian piety.

A second set of questions has arisen out of the wide spreading study of religions. It concerns curiosity whether there is a common essence in the world faiths or whether every one of them is a specific historical development with its own individual character and no shared underlying basis. Are the religions of the world various manifestations of a universal religion, or can such a universal essence only be posited by the abstract intellect which ignores the particularist forms in which the historical faiths have appeared? A vast literature has grown up around these questions. One body of conviction maintains that all the religions say fundamentally the same thing, a kind of kernel in them all to be discerned by penetrating through the dispensable and divisive husks of doctrinal and traditional affirmations. Such a postulate of a common essence has impressed some students of comparative religion, prompted by expanding acquaintance with the world religions; and for many enquirers, by the surmise that the faiths of the Far East have some sources of insight which are missed in western religious systems. Arnold Toynbee has voiced the hope that diffusion of the common essence of all religions would be a force for the unification of mankind. Aldous Huxley looked for the most conspicuously comprehensive layer of the religions in

---

33. Calvin, *Institutes of the Christian Religion*.

their mystical and contemplative elements.³⁴ In a tantalizing esoteric treatise, *The Transcendent Unity of Religions*, Frithjof Schuon promulgates a unity in the religions which is metaphysical and one, to be contracted with the phenomenal religions which are many and divisive.³⁵ The keynote of this work is the term "transcendent" which has the force given it by Meister Eckhart's dictum: "the more God is in all things, the more he is outside them" which carries the corollary that phenomenal religions represent a fall from the *noumena* of metaphysical reality. My own conclusion is that the most cogent version of the common feature of all religions is to be sought not in the field of beliefs, doctrines, or ethics, but in the conviction of a sacred realm behind the mundane world which is in continual need of renewal from its sacred counterpart, the process known most generally as salvation. This conviction of a sacred transforming power is common to all religions, whether they are theistic, pantheist, Catholic or Protestant, Hindu, Buddhist, or Islamic. But it is necessary to add that in many of its forms belief in a sacred transforming power sees it as destructive and demonic, as well as therapeutic and beatific.³⁶

A contrasting position which turns its back upon the search for a common element in religions is found in the work of two eminent German thinkers of the early twentieth century. Ernst Troelstch maintained that all conceptions of a common spirit are a fantastic delusion. Troelstch will have nothing to do with a common essence of all religions, or with a syncretistic amalgam or a monistic evolutionism. What history confronts us with is a small number of great religious orientations, each with its own concrete individuality and inner principle which informs its worldview and its norms. "The great revelations of the various civilizations will remain distinct" he writes, and "each racial group and religious culture will strive to develop its own highest potentiality." He also contends that the great rational systems, neo-platonic, Catholic, and Protestant, are only offshoots from the positive historical religions. He sees the creative power pulsating only in the historical religions, and he is suspicious of every philosophical attempt to sever connections with history in order to reach a rationally apprehended universality.³⁷

34. Huxley, *The Perennial Philosophy*.
35. Schuon, *The Transcendent Unity of Religions*.
36. Modern recognition of the sacred realm owes much to Rudolf Otto's famous study, *The Holy*, and finds its more precise formulation in works of Mircea Eliade, specifically *Le Sacré et le Profane* (1965).
37. These affirmations of Troeltsch are to be found in translations of his works: *The Absoluteness of Christianity* (1972) and *Christian Thought* (1923), especially Section II, Lecture 3, "The Common Spirit."

A similar emphasis, with slightly different presuppositions, is expressed by Max Weber in his essay "The Social Psychology of the World Religions," where he writes: "In no respect can one simply integrate various world religions in a chain of types, each of them signifying a new 'stage.' All the great religions are historical individualities of a highly complex nature; taken together, they exhaust only a few of the possible combinations that could conceivably be formed from the very numerous individual factors to be considered in each historical combination."[38] A century earlier Friedrich Schleiermacher in the first of his renowned writings, *On Religion, Speeches to its cultured Despisers*, had ingeniously interwoven the two strands just delineated, namely the presupposition of a common spirit underlying all religious phenomena and the apparently contrary assumption of historically developed independencies. The common spirit he identified as a feeling of utter dependency, first as a mood, and in this later works as the exclusive definition of religion. But even so, in the Fifth Speech of this early work, the one entitled "The Religions," Schleiermacher defends a doctrine of the plurality of religions, a plurality which is not accidental but of their essential characters. He addresses those who hold on to a philosophical natural religion in terms like the following: "I would, as it were, conduct you to the God that has become flesh; I would show you the religion when it has resigned its infinity and appeared, often in sorry forms, among men; I would have you discover religion in the religions.... This multiplicity is necessary for the complete manifestation of religion. It must seek for a definite character, not only in the individual, but also in the society ... You will then find that the positive religions are just the definite forms in which religion must exhibit itself—a thing to which your so-called natural religions have no claim."[39]

V

Any account of the tendencies which followed the demise of the natural theology of the Enlightenment and the subsequent interest in the study of religions, must refer to the upsurge of popular religion in the last three decades. It is impossible to delineate this phenomenon briefly or concisely. It consists of a random confluence of energies made up of at least three main impulses, namely, social revolt against the political structures and industrialist economics; search for direct experience which reaches below the level of intellectual and scientific deduction; and thirdly, borrowings from the religious tradition of the Far East and from the mystical insights of western

---

38. Weber, *From Max Weber*, 292.
39. Schleiermacher, *On Religion*, 211–17.

Christianity. While intellectual investigation of these three impulses can separate them, their occurrence in this period in some connection with one another is of peculiar significance. While the main provenance of this triple impulse seems to be the western region of the United States, it is spreading to South America and eastward into Europe. It has already elicited a growing volume of descriptive literature.

The social component is chiefly a movement for liberation from the momentum of political, economic, and technological trends in modern occidental societies. It goes with protest against injustice endured by oppressed peoples, and against systematic schools of thought in morals, law, and discipline built up in western Europe from the ninth century onwards. So, it tends to foster anarchy and violence, and inclines to permissiveness in personal behavior. In many respects, its ethos is radical and revolutionary, although it contains also a strand of non-violence, along with disgust at the corruption produced by the mass media in the service of the multiplication of wants for commercial exploitation. For these reasons adherents of this tendency are often called "drop outs" and the trend itself has been labelled "The Counter Culture." Among other elements in this uncoordinated set of impulses are to be found programs for the conservation of the earth's resources and for remaking of more spontaneous growth communities. They represent a disposition to counteract the determinism of modern occidental societies in which technological mastery of the terrestrial environment has become paramount. This disposition is in sharp contrast to the ethos which was shared by both the free-enterprise of the capitalist era and Marxist Communism, its critical opponent. Both these powerful systems stood for an estimate of man which regarded him as primarily *homo faber* whose essential humanity is expressed in purpose and utility. This doctrine of man is often referred to as Promethean or Faustian, and the struggle against its results aims at a more accepting and less destructive attitude. One result of this revolt is a growing number of attempts to create communities of economic self-sufficiency by acquiring a piece of land and living on it as far as possible, independently of the industrial system in both its capitalist and community forms.

Sometimes these movements for liberation have millennial overtones, but these are not universal. Mostly they encourage an attitude of taking life as it comes, riding with the flow without strain or effort. Certainly, this social aspect of the newest religion has not produced a systematic social doctrine as an alternative to the assumptions of the recent "work and effort" culture of the western world. It has turned its back upon all such doctrines as were embodied in for example, Plato's *Republic*, Carolingian Europe, medieval hierarchies, Calvin's theocratic republic, More's *Utopia*, Rousseau's *Social Contract*, Hitler's Third Reich, and Mussolini's Corporate State.

The second component in this confluence of impulses is the search for modes of consciousness which have the character of direct experience. It is a movement for liberation from the allegedly constricting impact of scientific inference, of political doctrines, intellectual deduction, moral codes, and theological formulations. It could be called "the psychic" dimension. If that term had not been improperly appropriated by the spiritualists and occultists, we might name it a demand for enlightenment through psychic immediacy.

It has its high priest among the intellectual exponents of the untutored forces within the human being. In England R. D. Laing campaigns for a re-discovery of our own inner world were *The Divided Self* is healed and repression is abolished, for society, family, and schooling induce an inauthentic self which suffers an "ontological insecurity." In the United States Norman O. Brown, author of *Life Against Death* and *Love's Body*, maintains that all culture is repressive, and, along with Laing, finds the rationalizing formulations of civilization so deleterious to psychic unity that only in madness can health be fully realized, though he allows that it must be a "holy" madness.

These and many other psychiatric healers offer a therapy for becoming one with the stream of life, of being rocked in the cradle of the deep, of returning to the mother's womb, of re-finding man's original innocence. What a bliss that would be! It is an age-long quest, and now in the modern world it seems to require a discarding of all the conscious systems of the mind which have fathered the march of civilization. The same kind of recovery from disintegration of our unitary consciousness is offered by recent therapists by means of psychedelic drugs. Its most notable practitioner is Timothy Leary, author of *The Politics of Ecstasy*. The human race has always found ways of getting behind the distorting effects of extroverted intellectual exploration, and today in the acutely disturbed state of mankind these psychedelic aids to recovery are in great demand. Some are cures for depression; they prevent fatigue and are known as "pep pills"; their effect is to make people "high." Others, like LSD (Lysergic Acid Diethylamide) induce hallucinations, a change in perception and a sense of euphoria. Its use is called "tripping." Resort to these two kinds of psychotropic agents is on the whole a private experience. In contrast, cannabis, or "pot" is smoked communally, with others, and is probably the least risky of them all, but similarly, addictive. From all accounts, these psychedelic practitioners often display a missionary impulse; they are adepts with an exalted status, who would spread the blessings they enjoy.

There is now a vast literature commending impulse, passion, feeling, play, and enjoyment as gateways to the deepest human wisdom. These ways go with emphasis upon wordless communication, by touch and ritual action. They affect sexual behavior, either by loosening all restraints or by unisex habits, gestures, and physical contracts between men and women. Other ways encourage mental techniques of a Yoga character for psychic poise and for forging a link between personal existence and the cosmos, as we get in resort to horoscopes and astrology.

The religious component in this late twentieth century religiousness owes much to the spreading knowledge of the world religions. This knowledge has a purpose of its own. "Religious Studies" can be pursued in the frame of mind which compares species of, say, insects or archaeological remains, a study that does not commit enquirers to compelling convictions. For many students of religion their interest is kindled just because it serves to eliminate the need for any commitment. But the recent impulse to learn about other faiths is followed by men and women who are seeking to be disciples, not just students. They are ready to put themselves to school with initiates and guides who can give them certainties of a vital, direct experience, and to learn from other believers. The outstanding manifestation of this search is the welcome given by many western minds to the religious traditions of the Far East, especially those of Buddhism, Hinduism, and Taoism. The popularity of Zen doctrines and exercise is a striking symptom of a need for some sort of timeless bliss. It is part of a religious revival which in mystical religion provides an antidote to the conventional "scientific" account of man and its technocratic idolatry, as well as to the western theological support for an undated millennium in the future. This aspect of the new religiousness fastens upon the oneness of the human self with the cosmic whole; it leads to enlightenment in serene or ecstatic union with the Great Self—what the older western books called "In Tune with the Infinite" or "The Light of Asia." It is the quest for a vision in which the divine, the human and the natural realms are known as one on their inner side, and no longer as objects to be grasped by the discursive intellect or empirical testing or inferred from revelations of a hidden god. The wisdom of the East tends to look for the secret of being through contemplation and to regard consciousness as the total reality, but not at all to be found in terms of problems and their solution in our western fashion.

The wisdom of the East, in its westernized "eclectic" context, acquires a number of phenomena which are not of its essence though interwoven with it. So, we find it hitched on to such groups as the Jesus People and to "speaking with tongues," along with various aspects of Pentecostalism and pop music. Sexual abandon and drug addiction contribute to the modern western search for ecstatic fulfillment; so do dance and rhythmic beat music. Devotees are also being led to discover the great mythologies of the past, to learn esoteric texts like the Jewish Kabbalah, the Taoist *Tao Te Ching*, as well as the rituals of Shamanism, magics and counter-magics, demonology and exorcism. More fundamentally, there is a return to appreciation of a sacred realm behind the world of phenomena, which is known as a source of healing and re-creation. All these manifestations of religious eclecticism seem to signify two things. First, a disillusion with a thoroughly scientifically directed utilitarian and technocratic culture; secondly, a faith that these esoteric levels of awareness display a common factor in the religious traditions of the world. This faith is mostly grounded in the fact that the mystical strand in both eastern and western religion looks more alike than the theologies and the cults. But the learned exponents do point out that divergence of the various mystical schools is as great as that of the doctrines and philosophies.

The three components I have epitomized, the social, the psychedelic, and the religious, make up an energetic and unstable mélange. Their appearance at this time in combination is a new phenomenon, though their components are all of age long parentage. Their confluence as a whole has no comparable predecessors. It is not marked by the genuine syncretism of the various strong religious forces of the early church; nor does it display the robust and violent character of the doctrinal conflicts between orthodoxy and heresy in the later middle ages. The nearest similarity might be detected in the fourteenth century, with its quivering proclamation of an "Inner Kingdom," the precursor of all modern idealisms.

To assess the historical significance of this twentieth century religiousness we can note the extent to which it represents a reversal of the mental forces which have created the modern world. In Max Weber's terminology, these forces made for what he called "disenchantment." As late as 1919 he had written: "The fate of our times is characterized by rationalization and intellectualization, above all by the disenchantment of the world. Precisely the ultimate and most sublime values have retreated from public life either into the transcendental realm of mystical life or into the brotherliness of direct and personal human relations."[40] Further he notes: "In principle, the empirical as well as the ethically orientated view of the world develops refutations of every intellectual approach which in any way asks for a 'meaning' of inner worldly occurrences. Every increase of rationalism in empirical science increasingly pushes religion from the rational into the irrational

---

40. Weber, *From Max Weber*, 155.

realm; but only today does religion become *the* irrational or anti-rational supra-human power."[41]

In these terms, what we are witnessing today is the re-enchantment of the world, whether it comes from hopes of a social apocalypse, from toxic stimulants and narcotics, or from religious thumb sucking. It could be called a vast movement for universalizing the contemplative and play elements in life. Philosophically it comes to rejecting the objective consciousness which has been the dominant criterion of the occidental mind; and replacing it by immersion in the inner stream where mental and historical happenings are but surface ripples on the ocean of universal selfhood. The more dithyrambic manifestations of this tendency are evidence of the fact that in the midst of an advanced civilization we are reaching a stage which reinstates group attitudes that formerly belonged to primitive ecstatic religions. "New lamps for old" might well be the motto for the diverse ways in which very modern men and women are ready to exchange the recent conceptions of scientific enlightenment for more ancient ways, provided these have the magical qualities symbolized by Aladdin's lamp. To put it in another way, we in the West are exhorted to renounce our culture's entrenched prejudice against myth, ritual, religion, and belief in salvation from a transcendent realm. In place of hope in a technological utopia, or a perfect government, or some unshakeable theory, or luck in the rat race, or endless research enquiries, the new religiousness represents a recall to age long modes of consciousness. This recall contains a lot of counterfeit sanctity, magical rubbish, drug experimentation, and light from Oriental brands of mediation and contemplation; however, it does testify to the recurring fact that if the "supernatural" is ejected through the front door it invades the human consciousness through the back door, often with a lot of demons in its train. The supernatural or preternatural will not be indefinitely excluded.

What a change from the attitude represented by Sir James Frazer's lament over the contents of mankind's religious museum which he did so much to catalogue. In his *Aftermath, A Supplement to the Golden Bough*, he referred to his work as witness to "the tragic chronicles of the errors of man, foolish, vain efforts, wasted time, frustrated hopes." Now, forty years later, we see these "superstitious" realms explored for their rescuing value. To relate these conclusions to the starting point of this addendum, the new religiousness stands for all that was rejected by the natural theology of the Enlightenment which attempted to catch the Universe in a web of theoretical observation and unrevelatory rationality. By contrast, the religious trend we have been considering appears to be a fideistic form of surrealism which,

---

41. Ibid., 351.

in art and literature, expresses the unconscious mind in images and intimations of the inner world in much the same way as dreams do. The final curiosity about this latest phase of modern religious history is its occurring after two centuries of resolute secularization of public life and private unbelief.

Series I

The Religious Climate

Series I, Lecture I
Ethos and Logos[1]

The relation of ethics and religion has today become one of peculiar insistence and complexity. It is not primarily a problem for philosophers, theologians, teachers, or students of human culture, but a practical and urgent question for millions who are considering how to live at all with any purpose or guidance in the modern world. It has become insistent because of a suspicion that western society in the twentieth century has come to the end of a period in which ethics, along with other disciplines, could operate with a certain independence or autonomy, with principles of its own not owing their warrant to any total pattern of life such as the higher religions provided in earlier cultures. And this part of our western world has so far resisted the totalitarian social dictatorships which so successfully cope with the problem by canceling that independence in ethics, religion, art, and science which has marked the character of recent European civilization.

There is said to be a serious moral degeneration in our time or a failure of moral development adequate to cope with situations brought about by scientific achievement. There is also said to be a poverty of ethical doctrines sufficiently convincing to form the basis of a public moral sentiment. And these failures are then widely attributed to the collapse of the humanist attempt to separate morals from their roots in religious belief and practice. At the same time secular ethical humanists are alarmed about the moral deterioration. They take the opposite view and say that it is due to official powers in the church, press and broadcasting, maintaining a sustained propaganda that Christian faith is the only firm foundation for morals. That faith, they contend, is untenable, and the propaganda ought to present the building up

---

1. Demant's notes include two separate drafts of this lecture. The second draft, although more complete, is unfinished. This text contains the second draft in its entirety and then picks up with the corresponding place in the argument of the first draft.

of a public conscience on some secular basis such as the requirements of good citizenship.

The alleged decline of morals cannot be taken at its face value. However much traditional morality has lost its hold, there is no lack of moral concern. We can detect no absence of moral persuasion or exhortation, although this is offered more for socially desirable behavior than for personal integrity (or holiness). Where personal integrity is proclaimed as the one real moral achievement—as it is among many of the younger generation—it is sincerity that is in mind; oblivious of the fact that sincerity informs many of the most destructive movements of our time. On the other hand, there appeared a curious recent phenomena in Britain, which suggests among the less sophisticated population that morals on their own may not arrest the alleged moral decline. Mrs. Margaret Knight delivered her broadcasts a few years ago on *Morals without Religion*, in which she said; "Because we are naturally social beings, we live in communities; and life in any community, from the family outward, is made much happier and fuller and richer, if the members are friendly and cooperative than if they are hostile and resentful.... Most people are prepared to accept as a completely self-evident moral axiom that we must not be completely selfish, and if we have our moral teaching on that we shall ....be building on firm enough foundations."[2]

There are many questions one might ask about that kind of statement, such as: what kind of life does unselfishness want for the neighbor? (For cooperation can exist for base ends.) Is there no ethical place for the rebel? Does not this cozy morality assume the speaker to be living in a relatively settled community? Does it not ignore the terrible strength of egoism and self-deception? And does it not skate over the perennial genuine conflicts between personal goals and social solidarity? But what was really significant about these broadcasts was the outcry they produced. No one could say they embodied a revolutionary or subversive doctrine. They contained an admirable, sincere, and capable expression of a philosophy which thousands of people, intellectuals and ordinary folk, had been living by for over a century. Here was a humanist faith of serious respectability. Yet, a kind of panic seized, not so much upon the religious world, but a good position of the educational interest; and public nervousness was exploited by that section of the press which one would regard as the most morally irresponsible. The frightened reaction could by no means be regarded as a measure of religious conviction. It was, I think, the expression of a deep though inchoate suspicion that religious backing for morals may be the only one which will be effective in a period of confusion, doubt and dissatisfaction. The growth

---

2. Knight, *Morals without Religion and other essays*.

of anti-social behavior, calculated delinquency, of swaggering violence and cruelty, have no doubt impressed upon a public without religious allegiance that something more powerful than injunctions to be good neighbors is needed in order to make children "considerate to those who work for them, and courteous to all, honest and truthful, and mentally and physically courageous."[3] It is of course, true that these qualities mark the lives of many who have no religious faith, but the alarm is the symptom of the malaise. A contribution of people under thirty to an essay competition on "Faith and Reason" in the *New Statesman* revealed that the majority of the entrants could not accept either faith or reason as a foundation for conduct. It did not reveal with what this void was to be filled, but it did provide a hint that ethics must take hold of a people at a deeper level that that of the reasonableness of humanist morality, whether this takes the form of realizing men's common citizenship or some more personal kind of self-fulfillment. In brief, it seems that this faith of ethical humanism is as shaken by the contemporary situation as is the Christian moral tradition, if not more.

An interesting contribution to this question of whether the modern western world is suffering from moral deterioration has been made by Professor Michael Polanyi.[4] In his Eddington Memorial Lecture *Beyond Nihilism*, he contends that "the past two centuries have not been an age of moral weakness; but have on the contrary, seen the out break of a moral fervor" and he believes that "this fervor which, in our own life time, has outreached itself by its inordinate aspirations and thus heaped on mankind the disasters that have befallen us . . . We have yet to discover the proper terms for describing this event. Ethics must catch up with the pathological forms of morals due to the modern intensification of morality. We must learn to recognize moral excesses. I shall suggest that modern nihilism is a moral excess from which we are suffering today."[5] The thesis is that nihilism, or the negation of all traditional moral teaching, is itself a form of moral inversion which stems from earlier millenarianism movements and owes a tremendous impetus to Rousseau. Its romantic disposition, which informs modern totalitarian democracy, has undone the influence of the ethical rationality of the Enlightenment. But Polanyi can, out of his intimate knowledge of continental political movement today, detect a reaction at the present time recoiling from the negation in the direction of a recovered civility.

I cite this important and apparently paradoxical argument in support of my own contention that there is no lack of moral impulse in the twentieth

---

3. Source of quotation unknown.
4. Polanyi, *Beyond Nihilism*.
5. Ibid., 1–2.

century West, though I would demur to Polanyi's ascription of these pathological form of morals to "the modern intensification of morality." The term "moral inversion" is less misleading, suggesting as it does that "immoralism" as an ethic is by a kind of Heractean enantiomorph dependent on what it negates.

The two powerful movements of Communism and National Socialism exemplify the moral dynamism of our time, detached from and opposed to the Classical—Christian—Humanist body of ethical teaching. They did in their own way do for their adherents what ethics geared to a religious faith had done in the past. It is not only that they provide a kind of unity between personal and social conduct, between the goals of their program and dogmas about the nature of existence, and between the dominant faith and the community's art, science, education, industrial effort, and political structure, by placing them all under the control of the rulers. More important, their moral and social aims are presented convincingly as the operative point at which a universal purpose in the scheme of things is in action. The worthwhile life is not only a good to be striven for; it is inherent in the march of destiny. These movements had in this respect something of the force of religion. That is why disillusionment with them has left former believers and external admirers with a void more abysmal that that between the Christian churches and the populace in the democracies.

Another aspect of the strength of moral sentiment in public life is the transfer of moral allegiance from churches and personal claims to society itself and the state as its supreme organ. The separation of the sacred and the civic realms, which has marked the growth of liberal society since the seventeenth century is now being obliterated. Twentieth century political debate is no longer in terms of the best way of ordering the natural community. In internal affairs, and still more in international propaganda, political regimes are defended as representing the righteous or holy cause in an otherwise immoral world. The liberal state of the west has largely become the moral state to the alarm of many liberal observers. The Russian state has always been regarded as the holy community.[6]

No wonder there is indifference toward and even boredom with ethics, to which Professor H. D. Lewis has called attention.[7] "It is not a case of simple ethical skepticism, although, heaven knows, there is plenty of that. Skeptics are as a rule quite ready for debate. But the phenomenon with which we are confronted today is that of a large and influential body of philoso-

---

6. Here ends the second draft of lecture one, which was not completed. Demant's notes continue at the corresponding point in the first draft.

7. Lewis, *Morals and Revelation*.

phers who find any sort of examination of ethical questions along the lines we traditionally know as moral philosophy tedious and little worthy of the attention of those who truly know what philosophers ought to be doing."[8] Yet as he points out there has been a solid body of thinking on ethics in this half century on the part of British philosophers, turning on such questions as how to define "the right" and "the good" and what is meant by a moral judgement. What is lacking is any body of ethical doctrine with formative power on the public mind comparable, shall we say, to Aristotle's *Ethics*; the works of Aquinas; Calvin's *Institutes*; Hooker's *Ecclesiastical Polity*; Hegel's *Philosophy of the Right*, *The Communist Manifesto*, Marx's *Das Capital*; Mill's *Utilitarianism*; or Nietzsche's doctrine of the Superman.

I am inclined to think that the present indifference to ethics and alleged boredom with it, spring less from lack of concern with the theory and practice of conduct, than from bewilderment and frustration. Much more is expected of the unaided moral judgement in our atomized and collectivized society, than it had to bear when the individual's "conscience" was supported by strong church life or by the community sense of naturally grown group loyalties. I am told that in a village where everybody is known to one another a young man will not drive his motor bicycle to the public danger. He is more deterred by the prospect of a slanging from the old women next door than by moral precepts of the State or the threat of police action. As Professor A. D. Ritchie pointed out, "Stable, nearly self-contained communities based on small scale agriculture and industry require only very little government or organization of any sort. (There was a time when the laws of Rome were comprised in Twelve Tables and every citizen could see and understand them.) But large scale industry and dense urban aggregation depending on world wide exchange of commodities require a great deal, and a mass of rules which are technical and not moral in any obvious way."[9]

The matter has been considered more concretely by Gustave Thibon, one of the most sage-like of the French moralists: "The peasant, in order to accomplish his social duty, has only need of a minimum of moral grandeur. An anonymous employee, however in order to give himself to his task with as much energy and application as the humblest of laborers would almost have to be a saint."[10] Thibon adds that he has no idyllic illusions about peasants. From the point of view of pure morals they are no better than their uprooted brethren: "selfishness, envy, hardness afflict them often more

---

8. Ibid., 78.
9. Ritchie, "Christian Religion and Contemporary Thought," 203.
10. Thibon, *Retour au Reel*, 30.

violently and lastingly but their faults are less opposed to the equilibrium of the individual and the collective life."[11]

This is of course, only one aspect of the complexities introduced for the moral conscience by the weakening of all social bonds except the one between the naked individual and the naked state, and the impersonal bonds of the buying and selling relationships. What I am seeking to emphasize is that our age in this part of the world is laying upon individual discovery and action in ethics much of what previously was looked after by indeliberate community consciousness. And this takes place at a time when ethical thinking and pronouncements in the world—I am not now considering the academic sphere—tend to be concerned more with the influence of behavior upon social solidarity and harmony than with interpersonal values. We are familiar with the exhortation from pulpit, political platforms, and publications, to populations to become more responsible in vast world affairs and in economic activity on a national scale just when the exercise of moral responsibility in the smaller areas of life such as the family, neighborhood, work associations, is being weakened by the deprivation in these spheres of their natural function. Further, there is the call for greater moral stature in view of the immense powers of destruction given by applied science—not only by nuclear instruments of war and genocide,[12] but also by colossal mistakes possible in destroying the sources of life. These dangers spring from the assumption that to do things technically is always the best way of doing them. Moralists are often addressed by distinguished members of the scientific world with a complaint that morals and religion have not made human nature good enough to play about with the resource of power now at our disposal. "Society be good, or the bombs will get you," is a favorite theme in lay sermonizing as well as in the pulpit, where preachers often seem more at home with this kind of secular moral terrorism than with older threats of hell fire. Our great octogenarian Bertrand Russell was among the moralists. In some recent broadcasts in *Living in the Atomic Age*, he prescribes a first estimate of self-interest combined with the old virtues of love, joy, peace, mutual help, and courage for an age whose technical power and closely knit interdependence makes the faces of egoism more calamitous than in earlier periods. In brief, he prescribes a complete change of human nature—a much more moralistic and utopian solution than what his contemporary, John Maynard Keynes, recognized as "traditional wisdom or the restraints of customs. . . . .the extraordinary accomplishments of our predecessors in

---

11. Ibid.

12. Here Demant included a note which reads: "interdependence and centralization."

the ordering of life (as it now seems to me) or the elaborate frame work which they had devised to protect this order."[13] I am still laboring the point that indifference to ethics is not due to want of calls upon the moral sense of men. To take one more example of extra weight added to the moral burden of individuals. The relation of men and women in wedlock is less than it used to be a combination of mutual attitudes and respect for an institution which carries the parties over many a bad patch. Loss of supporting framework of the institution puts the relationship entirely upon the personal, moral attitudes of the two human beings concerned. (In America, where the institution is still more disregarded than with us, the personal fear of failure gives women neurosis anxieties about growing older, and men get stomach ulcers in worry, endeavoring not to put a foot wrong.)

In countless ways our age has enlarged the area of life where deliberate and conscious moral behavior becomes a necessity not only for the good life but for existence itself. I can hear the moralist "fanatic" calling out, "And a very good thing too!" for he believes, or pretends to, that men's moral capacities increase *pari passu* with the size of the problems they have to cope with. I shall have a bone to pick with this moralist in a later lecture, so I will not call him bad names yet. What I am anxious to establish is that indifference to ethics today and a sense of tediousness at the mention of ethics, derives as much from a situation where fantastic demands are made upon human moral powers, as from a decline in religious warrants for moral behavior or from an alleged moral degeneration. In this judgment I find myself supported by the words with which Dietrich Bonhoeffer opens his posthumous book *Ethics*. Bonhoeffer was put to death in Nazi Germany where he was confronted with, as he phrases it, "not something men did but what they had become."[14] He writes: "Rarely has any generation shown so little interest as ours in any kind of theoretical or systematic ethics. The academic questions of a system of ethics seems to be of all questions the most superfluous. The reason for this is not to be sought in any supposed ethical indifference on the part of our period. On the contrary, it arises from the fact that our period, more than any earlier period in the history of the West, is oppressed by a super abounding reality of concrete ethical problems ...the man with a conscience fights a lonely battle against the overwhelming forces of inescapable situations which demand decisions."[15]

[Here Demant has a reference to an article by Michael Polanyi. In the article, Polanyi concurs as he writes of how the abundance of ethical

---

13. Keynes, *Two Memoirs*.
14. Bonhoeffer, *Ethics*, 3.
15. Bonhoeffer, 5.

problems leads to this contemporary dilemma: "The idea that morality consists in imposing on ourselves the curb of moral commands is so ingrained in us that we simply cannot see that the moral need of our time is, on the contrary, to curb our inordinate moral demands, which precipitate us into moral degradation and threaten us with bodily destruction."[16]]

It is distressing to find that this situation of greater moral demands with fewer moral resources, is almost completely bypassed by the characteristic religious messages of our time. On the one hand, we have the pulpit platitudes nagging men to be more cooperative, usually in relationships they have never experienced, like a sermon I have heard a hundred times. It often begins with the atom bomb and ends up with the World Council of Churches. You know that sermon and can fill in the headings. "The world is in a terrible state, the cure is Christianity: we are weak because we are divided, therefore let us act together!" (with the assumption that if weaknesses are joined up somehow a great strength will ensue). It all amounts to a hypothetical commonplace in place of a gospel. "If only the world were better than it is, it would be better." On the other hand there is the serious recovery of the gospel and its theology, often with the cogent message: "let the church be the Church," and a reliance on revelation as the only avenue by which the word of God reaches mankind. This theological message rightly repudiates the ethical fatuity described above, but on the whole it has no word of moral guidance for the world in which the church is set. Differing as they do almost as opposites, these two kinds of Christian utterance agree in one thing, namely that the intractability of the modern situations to moral guidance is due to human sinfulness. This so general a generalization only acquires a useful meaning if it is regarded as a negative, a direct contradiction of any view which assumes that all evil in the world can be overcome by a change for the better in the structure of social living, and as a challenging statement that its roots are in the human heart. But as a serious theological contribution to the understanding of our society or any other age it is useless. Sinfulness, as Christians understand it, is with man in every time and place. However, sinfulness takes particular forms and structures at particular times. Thus the alleged Christian message has a gap in its argument, if it ascribes the special social troubles and moral dilemmas of today to the same general fact which is shared by us with men in the days of the flood, or the fall of Rome, or the wars of religion, or the hungry Forties. True as it is in Christianity, when rightly understood that "before God man is always in

---

16. Polanyi, "Beyond Nihilism," 34–43.

the wrong," it cannot as a bare assertion be the basis of any moral guidance in the human situation at a particular time.[17]

In what follows, I shall not attempt a theological interpretation of our time and its ethical situation, partly because I have given what limits I can elsewhere but more seriously because if I had anything cogent to say I should be too busy prophesying with no time for academic lectures. But I am embarking on an examination of the relation of ethics and religion in Christendom, which I think will throw some light on our contemporary situation. Two preliminary explanations are necessary. The first is to say that I am using the term Christendom not as a designation of a Christian society, or the redeemed community or of the church or a realm under the tutelage of theology. I am using it for the society and culture of the western world where Christianity, along with a number of factors of different origin and some rival ones, has been the dominant religion. The second is an admission that I am a believer in the autonomy of ethics, that is in the possibility of ethical systems or attitudes which do not derive their warrant from religious belief; and I do not think that Christian believers do their religious cause any good by contending for the unreality or unreliability of ethics unless it is religiously founded. I shall contend, however, for the view that ethics, when it is a body of doctrine about the aims and conduct of life, never stands alone unrelated to assumptions about existence, about what "is"; unrelated to the culture of an epoch, or society; or to the drive given to aims by a religious faith and its embodiment in a religious community.

The problem of religion and ethics as it currently exists is the product of a history. In primitive societies, ethics, religion, and daily life were all bound up together. As Christianity developed, Platonic thought was interwoven with Christian ideas and therefore one could not consider religion without philosophy and ethics. Now ethics and religion are disciplines and categories unto themselves. There is a division in the narrative. Today the ethical has been separated from the religious in contemporary thinking and there are many ethical aims in our world that are independent of religious claims. This treatment of ethics as an independent discipline developed with the Scholastics in the thirteenth century.[18]

---

17. Here Demant included the note: "cf. Catholic approach in *Moralle Chrictenne et Requetes Contemporaries*. (Casterian Paris 1954, 19ff.) and Protestant Ste: Christ."

18. This paragraph is an expansion by the editors of notes that read: "Penumbra. And on opposite side; also: the problem of religion and ethics as we have it. Is the product of a history. Early religions primitive and essential. Plato with Christianity closely interwoven—Theodicy. Now separate in that many ethical aims are independent. Not separated in thought until 13th Century."

Part of the alleged crisis in morals, to which I have referred, is that we live with ethics for man and society inherited from a culture which is no longer there to back up the intentions and wills of men. The culture was by no means entirely religious. In fact one part of a culture, namely powerful axioms concerning the nature of human existence, took secular and often anti-religious forms. But in so far as such axioms formed a mental climate so ingrained that it was not very deliberately attended to, it supplied the same kind of support to the ethics as a religious tradition does to its ethics. The most influential of these mental climates in the past two centuries—perhaps the only one which swayed public life before the advent of Marxism—was the powerful alliance of Utilitarianism with evolutionary naturalism. The rationalized hedonism of the eighteenth century became alive in the Utilitarians of the nineteenth because the latter could put behind their ethical theory and aims a doctrine that self-interest was making for personal and social fulfillment by a law of development which was wider and deeper than the wills and minds of men. This was possible by the application—or I would say the misappropriation—of the biological theory of evolution to human society. Into this blend of rationalism and naturalism was injected the ethical and social aims of western Europe which were then regarded as what the social evolutionary process was carrying to greater heights. Already in the eighteenth century Hume had based ethics on Nature rather than reason. He accepted the conventional moral and social standards of a relatively settled Britain and found all the backing he needed in human nature itself. James Mill in 1805 wrote that "those circumstances in the constitution of the world, which seemed opposed to the establishment of perfect happiness or virtue on the earth, prove nothing" and he held that the causes which check the "natural and fixed" tendency of human nature to perfection can only be temporary and accidental."[19] Herbert Spencer took as his criterion of the good or bad conduct the test whether it was more or less evolved. War, for example was bad because it represented a retrograde obstacle to the more highly evolved industrialism.[20]

Leslie Stephen wrote *The Science of Ethics* on the theme that the more advanced a society is, the more the individual is bounded by far reaching sympathies with his fellows and devises more comprehensive codes of conduct accordingly.[21] This belief in the emergence of rational moral and social incentives as the result of the passage of time and history has been pretty well demolished in theory and by the tremendous uprising of collective wick-

19. James Mill quoted in Halevy, *The Growth of Philosophic Radicalism*, 276.
20. Herbert, *Various Fragments*.
21. Stephen, *The Science of Ethics*.

edness in the twentieth century, but it retains a strong hold on the ethical sentiments and language of ordinary people. People will say "progressive" when they mean "good," and "reactionary" when they mean "bad." Its vitality, which is what I am concerned with, springs not from its ethical doctrine but from the faith induced by the dogma, that this ethic was in the line of a universal, natural and inevitable process. It has survived in the mentality of multitudes in Britain and America, and some natives of other continents, in spite of the demolition made of it by writers in England like T. H. Huxley, Coleridge, and Carlyle, or of Nietzsche and Marx on the Continent. And I would say that there has been no big wave of ethical doctrine of comparative force in the western democracies able to form a public philosophy. Not all the intellectual and social revolts against it has shaken the naive fideism of its adherents in the popular and educational worlds of this country.

In my terminology, which I am now about to explain, the axiom of "evolutionary naturalism" was part (or became part) of the penumbra of the ethics of Utilitarianism. It was a view of the nature of things surrounding the clear moral and social aims of the nineteenth century humanists and their successors. And it was this part of the penumbra that gave the ethics its vitality.

AN ACCOUNT OF MY TITLE AND ARGUMENT

Ethics deals with one part of man's purposive life, his aims, goals, and strivings. Therefore, the field of ethics is a moral field in this world of purposes. All of ethics presupposes that there is a gulf between what "is" and what is desired. This gulf is apparent as man conceives the world as it ought to be and yet finds the world to be otherwise. This desire for the world as it ought to be can be seen in a time period, a community or an individual.[22]

Ethics is concerned with things men want to be and do; possessions they want to obtain; the kind of life want to live; systems they want to live under. In short, a describable state of things to be worked for. What makes certain aims or goals of men ethical—for there are other purposes—it has been the task of moral philosophers to define.

Now I am calling attention to the commonest of human experiences in ethics, but also in other purposive endeavors. It is that the aims and

22. This paragraph is an expansion by the editors of notes which read: "Ethics deals with one part of man's purposive life, aims, goals, strivings;
Field of Ethics: is moral field in this world of purposes.
Presupposes: a gulf between—what 'is' and what want—in ethics. What they want because they conceive it as what ought to be. This can be seen in a period, a community, or in an individual."

intentions often do not bring about the results willed. What men want for moral or other reasons is not what they actually achieve. This is part of the mystery of the will, and forms part of the material for the problem of freedom and determinism; for the discrepancy between what is achieved and what is willed. Not always due to insuperable obstacles in the environment, but to obstacles in the same man or group of men. Where this is so, the grim voluntarist will say they have not willed hard enough; or that their ideals are not sufficiently compelling; he will exhort people to pull up their moral socks.[23]

Others will be so impressed with the way human intentions are defeated that they will adopt some form of determinism or pessimism like Arthur Schopenhauer. Mr. Isaiah Berlin has written about such exponents of Historical Inevitability, who regard human purposes as negated by the march of events, a position which he seeks to demolish. He has also made a study of Leo Tolstoy, to show that Tolstoy regards it as the great illusion to suppose that individuals can by their resources, understand or control the course of events.[24] It is the theme of Sophoclean tragedy, namely that Oedipus and other strong characters bring about results the opposite of what they intend, and other things they never thought of.

Christians will often use this discrepancy between what men will and the things that ensue, as a support for the doctrine of providence—the Might of God overruling and deflecting the intentions of human beings. The Lord becomes the God of the gaps. "Man proposes, but God disposes." No wonder, that the critics of religion fasten on this kind of language and describe the religious attitude as a compensation for or reflection of man's impotence in making history. The Marxists hold that as human mastery over nature and history increases, the religious impulse will diminish. Friedrich Engels jibes at Eugen Duhring for wanting to stamp out religion, for says Engels when the human race has controlled its material and social environment, religion dies a natural death. He writes, "When therefore man no longer merely proposes, but also disposes—only then will the last extraneous force which is still reflected in religion vanish; and with it will also vanish the religious reflection itself, for the simple reason that there will be nothing left to reflect."[25]

There is no need to enumerate further the many ways in which the human mind has reacted to this commonplace fact—that achievements

---

23. Here Demant includes the note: "cf. VAD Mischief of Ideals." This is a reference to chapter 7 in *Theology of Society*.

24. Berlin, *Hedgehog and the Fox*, 67.

25. Engels, *Herr Eugen Duhrings Revolution in Science*, 348.

and aims so often appear unrelated or contradictory. We have, however, to consider one special way in which the discrepancy arises. Human aims, moral as well as political, intellectual, artistic, or emotional, are only the most clarified part of men's purposive existence; behind and surrounding these sharply conscious purposes are forces in the same people which give a certain undirected direction to their lives—as when we pick up the newspaper without definitely resolving to do so. These are also forces at work in the hidden parts of the inner life which may or may not be working in the same direction as the will and the mind.

It is part of the human experience to become aware of these forces, or at least the effect of these forces, which are within one's self and yet also sometimes contradictory to one's goals. One need look no further than the apostle Paul's famous struggle between his own aims and his actions. As Paul writes in Romans: "For I know that in me (that is, in my flesh,) dwelleth no good thing: for to will is present with me; but how to perform that which is good I find not. For the good that I would I do not: but the evil which I would not, that I do. Now if I do that I would not, it is no more I that do it, but sin that dwelleth in me."[26] The human dilemma is that man constantly aspires to be better or at least different than he is and yet is often unable to change. This can be seen not only in Paul's writing, but also in Augustine's thoughts on the divided will in his Confessions.[27]

Denis Saurat in his work *Regeneration* uses social analogy to describe the parts of the inner life of man, which he calls the head and the masses. (Religiously, the will and the soul). The head is that part which is clear and precise, which mines what it wants. The masses represent the impulses, feelings, memories, dogmas, and habits. The head itself has two parts: the power which makes decisions, and a number of talents which carry them out: "The relation between the main parts, the head and the masses is complicated and not clear... Ultimately the head is only the clarified concentration of the masses. It can only act on them because it represents them truly, because it is that part of themselves that they have clarified and of which they have become fully conscious. But this is not always clear, and many a man in a crisis finds himself deciding and doing things of which he had never thought and which he would have believed himself incapable of doing. A new head has been thrown up by the masses in an emergency."[28]

26. Romans 7:18–20.

27. This paragraph is an expansion of Demant's notes that read: "Change habits, want to commit.

St Paul Romans 7 and 8; Augustine: confessions 7, 10 and 11 'Divided will self against self.'"

28. Saurat, *Regeneration*, 8.

If our action is to be congruous with our intention, there must be a certain harmony and mutual reinforcement between these two elements. They must also have their distinction: if all is masses there is no freedom; if all is head there is no power.

When these two elements are not in harmony, we find ourselves incapable of achieving our aims or resolves. Think of the man who sets out to conquer his addiction to alcohol. Though he may with his head fully intend to quit drink, his impulses, habits, and feelings work against this end. Or similarly, the writer who fully intends to write, but finds himself unable to do so.[29]

Effectiveness of aims depends on whether they are the concentrated business end of forces in the soul; or merely desires induced by superficial disparate factions, by accepted codes or external loyalties, by adverse judgments of others—in which case aims not reinforced by forces or structure of whole inner life.

Also, a man may only be free to pursue his aims if he is settled and established in other parts of his life.[30]

This same problem is found in the history of thought and social systems. Rationality has been the great aim of several periods. The two well known periods of rationalism are examples. In Greece, the period from the foundation of the Lyceum in the middle of the fourth century BC to the end of the third century BC was marked by the attempt to handle life and attain moral perfection by reason and knowledge. It was a short-lived experiment and Professor Dodds, in *The Greeks and the Irrational*, wonders why.[31] He himself gives hints as to the cause, when he refers to the extent to which Plato earlier and Aristotle had recognized the part played by the less rational turbulent hidden forces in life. Aristotle had allowed that men cannot live on the plane of pure reason for more than very brief periods.[32] I would deduce from this piece of history in thought that men are free to pursue the aims of a pure rationalism when their emotional life is looked after by some other influence, such as was recognized by Plato and Aristotle in the coryliantic dances, the religious view of dreams, the cathartic effect of music, and other manifestations of the mystery cults. These dealt with the

---

29. This paragraph is an expansion of Demant's notes that read: "Pastoral Problems aims, resolves—incapacity.
Drink/habit."

30. This paragraph is a summary of notes that read: "Another aspect is the situation where a man is only free to pursue aims; if he is settled and established in other parts of his life (pastoral examples)
Society—work—Love."

31. Dodds, *The Greeks and the Irrational*.

32. Aristotle, *Metaphysics*, 12 1072B.

phobias and anxiety states (*deimata*) and the rest of the demonic elements in the human psyche.

The modern cause of the eighteenth century tells the same story, that when the rational intellect is sufficiently powerful to suppose it can dispense with other ways of managing the sub-rational elements, and considers that reasons contain them, then its influence begins to waver. In France and Britain what strikes one about the literature of the "age of reason" is that the life of men was more under the sway of passion and erotic passion than of deliberate ethical reason. The rationality of a period can thrive if the culture of the epoch has underneath it the harmonizing of the instincts and other vital forces by religion, art, and traditional institutions such as the eighteenth century inherited from the past. When this foundation is ignored, the sub-rational face becomes uncontrolled and dehumanized and the top story of rationality cannot cope with the situation. So we had to have the Romantic reaction and other movements to compel a recognition of the needs of the soul.[33]

I have myself attempted in an earlier work to show that the aims of what was called the free-market economy were successful so long as it could count on a social tissue underneath that was inherited; when the superstructure weakened this underlying pattern, the period of free-enterprise was doomed and gave place to various forms of economic collectivism.[34] In another book I traced the aim of the Liberal age—namely the aims of embodying in social institution the significance and status of the person—traced these aims to a long tradition in which they were active though not explicit in the thought of Christendom where they were based in certain axioms of the relation of man to the cosmos—and the religious axiom of the human substance in some direct relation to the divine substance; and argued that when this axiom was displaced by another which regarded man as only part of the cosmic process—the aims of giving status to persons were defeated by totalitarian tendencies.[35] These underlying culture patterns,

---

33. Demant wrote notes opposite the previous two paragraphs, some of which are expanded in his full text and some of which are not. The notes read: "Philosophers theories and problems derived from their sometimes accepting its influence, sometimes in correcting its bent.

Aristotle—city state.

Kant's Pietism and period when patterns of life broken up; therefore could only contribute a gearinuips ethicle, instead of a vorant wrtingl..(cf. Mannheim p16, 112).

Bertrand Russell's History of Western Philosophy.

H. Lewis History of Philosophy.

St. Paul faith only is became protected Reason?"

34. cf. Demant, *Religion and the Decline of Capitalism*.

35. cf. Demant, *Religious Prospect*.

along with the axioms and outlooks on the nature of existence—the hidden forces in the soul—are rarely in the consciousness of the period, they are not talked about. It is the aim that we talk about. Therefore we should not judge the character of a man or a period by their "interests" only; we should ask not only what they stand for, but also what they stand on.

All these secular examples of the relation between the clear part of man's purposive life and the "penumbra" which surrounds it have been mentioned in order to give an idea that it is a perennial human problem—seldom attended to by moralists, political and social reformers, and preachers. It is of course known to the educators who are aware of the need to form character, to give a certain bent to the soul, to wise psychological therapists, as well as to competent pastoral guides.

This introduction is meant to head up to a realization that in the religious tradition of the race, ethics are never a body of doctrine about conduct standing alone, or even the main conscious element in the teaching to which all the rest of religious life is meant to minister. Moral insight and endeavor are induced as a kind of by-product of a number of other influences which are not specifically ethical.[36] The forces of religion are mostly brought to bear in the "indicative" forms of expression, rather than in "imperative" commands. "Commands" are effective as a narrow point of a triangle or pyramid comprised mainly of other ingredients. These ingredients comprise: axioms about existence couched in terms of bits of history, chronological, or mythological, parables, and dogmas about the nature of things or the constitutions of the universe in which man's life is set.

All of these things form a climate, which I am calling the penumbra of ethics.[37]

Penumbra. Dictionary definition; partly shaded region around the shadow of an opaque body, especially around the total shadow of the moon or earth in eclipse. In its use as a metaphor for what we are considering it is a sharp, distinctiveness of the central disk, which I am using analogically for the ethical aims; although in astronomy that central disk is not bright but dark, and the shaded surround represents all those elements of religion which are less sharp and distinct ethically, but which in various ways create, feed or weaken the ethical impulse. *It is the border land between conscious intentions and aims on the one hand, and the unconscious forces which affect these conscious intentions on the other.*

---

36. Here Demant included the note: "like the influence of literature, Dickens's descriptions of the [unreadable] are its condemnation—without moral imperative attending."

37. This text was added to address a gap in the notes.

This chapter is called "The Ethos and Logos." This is the terminology I prefer.[38] It has a certain direction, this combination of human forces, not given by the ethical aim itself. It provides an "ethos" as we usually use that term, a disposition or spirit, or what I call "a bent of the soul." The ethos lies behind the aims of men, enforcing them or pulling against them. When the aims are backed up by the "ethos," the will is free and successful—as free at any rate as the external limits of human life allows. When the forces in the soul are not in line with the aims and intentions, there is frustration, a sense of being completely determined. This situation is known popularly and misleadingly as a gap between achievement and ideals; or psychologically, as schizophrenia; or theologically, as the divided will of St. Paul and Augustine. One of the most powerful elements of the "ethos" in men is their world view—or as the Germans call it, *Weltanschauung*. Collingwood's term is "ultimate presuppositions"—I have dubbed it "axioms."[39] In the context of these lectures I refer to it as "the Logos," using the term with a force more like that of the Jewish Alexandrine logos—something active and in man of which he is to some extent a passive recipient; and in the modern usage of "word," as merely what is uttered in speech—*sermo*, as Erasmus unfortunately translated Logos in his Latin translation of the New Testament.

---

38. This text was added to address a gap in the notes.
39. Collingwood, *Essay on Metaphysics*.

Series I, Lecture II
God, Man, and the World

THE FORMULATED DOCTRINE ABOUT the relation of God and the world, and about the place of human existence in this relation, as well as the moral teaching implied in man's place and destiny, these doctrines depend for their force upon outlooks not clearly delineated. These outlooks grow up as standpoints or attitudes from forces that impinge on the mind at a deeper level than its thought. Thought seeks to clarify an experience which is derived from history, culture, religious, or aesthetic happenings. And these outlooks lie behind ethical systems, as they lie behind formulated doctrine—they are part of the climate of ethics.

In intellectual discourse we have to use the language of discursive thinking and do our best when this has to convey something of the underlying outlook. We shall now endeavor to grasp the main world pictures or outlooks about what in our western terminology we call the relation of God and the world; or to put it more generally, the relation between the phenomenal world in which men live and act and observe and question—and the source of meaning for the world in which they do these things.

[Here Demant references H. A. Hodges's discussion of standpoints and attitudes. In his Riddell Memorial Lectures, Hodges considers different possible outlooks. First, though, he reminds his audience that there are irreconcilable differences between the ways in which different cultures understand the relationship between these two spheres of God (or the source of meaning) and the world. "There are real and fundamental conflicts, conflicts which no amount of dialectical or analytical manipulation can resolve."[1] In addition, Hodges notes the importance of how an individual's culture or worldview will substantively shape his thinking. "These fundamental needs or desires are the basis on which his whole life-structure rests. . . these basic

---

1. Hodges, "Languages, Standpoints and Attitudes," 44.

attitudes of which I speak have the power of opening up or closing whole worlds of experience."²]

There are three main outlooks, each with their doctrinal expression. The first regards the eternal world, beyond time and change and multiplicity and determinate beings, as the only reality of significance. All that we mean by the world, nature, human history, discrete objects and events, are, if not illusory, at least devoid of significance in their own right.

This is the characteristic outlook of the religions of the far East—Hinduism and Buddhism. But it has to be said that in them the problem is not set out in this peculiarly western way as a question of eternal and temporal worlds; it has also to be said that it is only the advanced speculative, metaphysical ways of thought in India that come into this picture. Brahman in the Vedanta of Shankara (c. AD 800) is not the eternal God as we understand it: Brahman is universal consciousness and therefore indeterminate or infinite. Nothing determinate is real; the existence of separate and definable beings is illusory; there is no objective world in our sense; things do not exist even in Brahman, they are Brahman and any idea that they are real is part of the dream state from which the adepts seek awakening. Above all this is no human self confronting a not-self. Things are in no sense a way to or a pointer to Brahman, they are when given significance a blind alley in the search for the knowledge of the One, which is beyond our awareness of objects.

Buddhism in its purest form is found in Tibet, a version of Mahayana Buddhism. There the purpose of ritual is to prepare the mind for metaphysical realization, to put it on to pierce the veil of the finite and to seek deliverances in knowledge, that is in identification with the Supreme and infinite Reality. The latter is devoid of every determination whatsoever, even unity or goodness.

Another form is found in Plato, where the eternal, only really real world transcends the temporal and historical. See *The Republic* (500 BC) "For surely, Adeimantus, he who has his thoughts truly set on the things that really exist, cannot even spare the time to look down upon the occupations of men . . . On the contrary he devotes all his time to the contemplation of certain well adjusted and changeless objects."³ Or in *The Phaedrus*: "The region above the heaven was never worthily sung by any earthly poet, nor will it ever be . . . For the colourless, formless, and intangible truly existing

2. Ibid., 50–51.
3. Plato, *The Republic*.

essence, with which all knowledge is concerned, holds this region and is visible only to the mind, the pilot of the soul."[4]

[Here Demant references John Scotus Eriugena who describes a similar understanding of creation in his 9th century work, *De Divisione Naturae*, saying, "Creation is, therefore, a process of unfolding of the Divine Nature, and if we retain the word, Creator, in the sense of 'one who makes things out of nothing,' we must understand that God 'makes' the world out of His own Essence, which, because of its incomprehensibility, may be said to be 'nothing.'"[5]]

RELATIVE UNREALITY OF PHENOMENAL WORLD

There is a second form of this outlook, often combined with the first, namely, that the world of nature, man and history is the very root of evil. What we call the creation is the first act by which falsity comes into being. In the archaic cultures we have numerous teaching and rituals which imply that only by recurrent contact with divine archetypes can men overcome their ties with the evil principle of this world—the evil principle is the existence of a cosmos distinct from the creative reality.[6]

Aldous Huxley rejects the biblical and Christian scheme for refusing to regard "the passage from the unity of spiritual to the manifoldness of temporal being as an essential part of the Fall." He writes, on the contrary "the incomprehensible passage from the unmanifested One into the manifest multiplicity of nature from eternity into time, is not merely the prelude and necessary condition of the Fall; to some extent it is the Fall."[7]

In complete contrast to this first outlook, that only the infinite world is truly real, stand all the dominant outlooks of the modern world. These hold that only the sub-limar flux of existence is real and the abstractions which the human mind can distill out of the flux. It is the outlook shared by the older liberals for whom all the forces in existence were immanent in the world process—where there were only two possibilities; moving along with the world process or hanging back. There is no dimension other than the temporal. There is nothing absolute which is not in the moving process of

---

4. Plato, *Phaedrus*, 78 (247c).

5. Eriugena, *De Divisione Naturae*. Quoted in *The Catholic Encyclopedia*, vol. 5 (Encyclopedia Press, 1913) p 521. The exact reference reads: "Degrees of Being," cf Duns Scotus Eugenia Guenon 84–85."

6. Demant included a note at the end of this paragraph that read: "VAD more wanted."

7. Huxley, *The Perennial Philosophy*, 209.

history. Then a teleological element was combined with this purely immanentist outlook. The process was moving to a fulfillment along its own time. This was the conception of progress which, as Professor Bury wrote, implied that "as the issue of the earth's business, a condition of general happiness will be ultimately enjoyed, which will justify the whole process of civilization."[8]

The dogmas of Marxism and National Socialism did not counter the doctrine of progress only, which informed the Liberal doctrine they displaced. They shifted the emphasis from the single person to the collectivity, still within the one world plane.[9] We must not refer in particular to the assumptions of a one-world, this world view which underlies all our modern western education, philosophy, social science, and doctrines of social reforms. In its many transformations idealistic, rationalist, vitalist, evolutionary, revolutionary, the dogma of cosmic existence as the only real existence is the working dogma of the nineteenth and twentieth century. And where it takes on a religious dress God is regarded as the cosmic machine or the invigorator of human purposes conceived as furthering the cosmic process.

ETHICAL TEMPER

Each of these two main outlooks produces its own ethical temper. Let us consider each in its most extreme form. In the Eastern outlook where no thing or act which can be defined is wholly real, and where consciousness in itself—not of an object, thing, or act—is the only true reality, there the subject and agent of freedom is not will but consciousness. Ethical values are not an end for which freedom and consciousness are the instruments. That is the ethereal which leads to pure consciousness—it does not flower into action—in fact action is part of the illusory world. I recall a Taoist proverb which has sometimes soothed me, it says, "Whatever you do makes things worse." Because determinate things are transitory, the Oriental will have no moral precepts which are valid under all circumstances.

Two of the Buddhist Padmasambhava's six prescriptions for the perfect life run thus:

> To be indifferent to all, Behaving like the dog or the pig that eat what chance brings them. Not making any choice among the things which one meets. Abstaining from any effort to acquire or avoid anything. Accepting with an equal indifference whatever comes: riches or poverty, praise or contempt, giving up the distinction between virtue and vice; honorable and shameful,

8. Bury, *The Idea of Progress*, 5.
9. See Demant, *Religious Prospect*, 86ff.

good and evil. Being neither afflicted, nor repenting whatever one may have done and, on the other hand, never being elated nor proud on account of what one has accomplished.

Moreover, "To consider with perfect equanimity and detachment the conflicting opinions and various manifestations of the activity of beings. To understand that such is the nature of things, the inevitable mode of action of each entity and to remain always serene."[10]

These Oriental forms of denying significance to what happens in the world, regarding it not as making for or against a purpose, but all happenings—the good or the evil, as ripple after ripple which moves on the surface of the ocean and subsiding in it again—this religious and moral climate looks to us westerners as often unprincipled. It has however its own principle—a felt sympathy for all persons and things. It does not lead anyone to lay down their life for any specific determinate form of behavior, or suffer loss for a point of honor or truth, like a medieval knight, or a Scottish Covenanter. Still less will it inflict suffering for an ultimate good; for that too is a determinate unreality. There is compassion for the neighbor, human, animal, and inanimate things. To cause anyone, self or others, any suffering in the name of loyalty to a predetermined aim or goal, or for a cause is against good sense. A true Oriental would not understand such attitudes so familiar to us as fidelity to a promise, deprivation today for the sake of an undated millennium in the future, destruction of a house or a cricket pitch here because of a plan for the region as a whole, or the kind of principle which would wish the loss of people in order that justice might be done to one man. The Oriental is afraid of 'loss of face', so he will not commit himself. "Wock jeh," perhaps is the Cantonese rich show boy's reply when asked if he will get you to the train at a certain time; infuriating to a westerner who wants to hear "Yes, Sir, whatever happens you shall get there." It is an open, tolerant, expedient, and strategical attitude to life in the world.

Ethics within the Greek worldview is both similar and dissimilar to the East. Plato commends a sort of self-abnegation and detachment from bodily pleasures that is at home in this Buddhist perspective. On the other hand, his exploration of the best form of government reveals a different sort of answer to what is good for the soul, contrasted with the Eastern emphasis on individual acceptance of what comes.[11]

How different from the ethical temper of the opposite western world view represented by the seriousness accorded to the one temporal and

---

10. David-Neel, *Magic and Mystery in Tibet*, 268–9.

11. This paragraph is an expansion by the editors of the notes that read: "left out Greek. Ethical temper similar and yet dissimilar."

historical world of the modern West, where the permanent self of man sets itself aims which override all considerations of mere living and making the best of one's immediate experiences and contacts. Ours is a world of "ideals"—for which men will endure hardships and conflict—causes with an imperative note in them. And the more these causes are purely this-worldly, the more immediate satisfactions are sacrificed for them.

The spirit of adventure that sent man across oceans—though mixed with commercial and political motives, is a western affair—the South American Indians were astounded at both the devotion and unscrupulousness of the Spanish invaders. The mentality of Industrialism found a response in the masses when it called on them to endure deprivations for the sake of wealth in the future; today countries are seeking to generate towns, in order that in the future they may enjoy the alleged benefits of a technical civilization. More victims have perhaps been sacrificed on the altar of "progress" than on those of heathen cults. When the "absolute good" is insinuated somewhere into a pure, this-worldly scheme (as it is in the various nationalisms, or in the classless society of the Communists, or the savior race of the Nazis), we see as true the self-deceiving ethical temper at work with much expediency. At any rate, it puts on the moral disguise of making life serve a cause.

Now this characteristic western attitude is a secularized version of a disposition largely formed by the religious climate of Christendom, wherein the source of existence and of values is not immanent in the world process, nor is it quite outside it in the eternal ideas or the undifferentiated cosmic consciousness. Christianity with its roots in the Bible and affected by its contact with Greek rationalism and some later influences, has in the main traditions accorded reality and significance to both the eternal and temporal orders. Therefore, it has seemed dangerously other-worldly to the humanist, Marxist, and social scientist, or to the experts who handle the psyche troubles, as if when they go deep enough into the unconscious, they still do not come to a borderline across which lies something extra human. Historical Christianity has appeared to be closely connected with history, social reform, the bodily life of men—to those who look at it with the mind of an Oriental, or with a certain kind of Greek idealism, or with some forms of mystical detachment.

We have now to see how this two-world view of Christianity appears in its doctrine, remembering that the doctrine of creation which attempts to express it and the Christological formulations which seek to safeguard one unique event in the relation of the two worlds, are conceptual expressions of an outlook formed by religious history. We can get an idea of what is involved by a conspectus of the task which the Christian church had to shoulder in coping with heathen thought in the first five centuries of its history and compassing this with the situation confronting Christian thought in the modern world of immanentist secularism.

[Demant here references an article he published in 1947 and the work of Vladimir Solovyev. Demant writes how an early "heathen thought" that Christianity contended with was the heresy of Arianism. "The struggle with Arianism... was a struggle to safeguard the biblical God who is really personal."[12] Whereas some early Christians sought to abandon this personal God in favor of pure transcendence, today the church must deal with a similar though opposite impulse. Demant writes that the church must work at "the task of overcoming the basic heresy of Modernism—denial of the transcendent."[13] Solovyev also sees this dynamic in the development of religious thought, as is evident in the following quotation from his *Lectures on Godmanhood*.] "The pagan world which blossomed out in Hellenism established divinity as primarily the all. Of the two necessary *momenti* of the divine actuality: the personal or subjective and the ideal or objective—that world perceived and expressed in definite way only the second. Judaism, on the contrary, comprising in this respect the direct opposite of Hellenism, perceived and in a definite manner realized the first momentum, that of the personal and subjective actuality; it cognated Divinity as the extant One or pure Ego."[14] What this story tells is the working out in Christian thought and history of the consequences of an outlook on the relation of God and the world referred to in shorthand as the doctrine of Creation and of the Incarnation and Atonement as in some sense a new creation.[15]

The background is the Old Testament picture of the World's relation to the Creator. It is however quite clear that Hebrew religion does not begin with the axiom of God as Creator. It begins with Jehovah as the tribal God; the Lord of man's life: first of the nation and its history, then of other nations. Genesis 2:7, Life and man are formed by him and thereby an ethical obligation of life to its lord is incurred. Genesis 1 represents the creation of the world out of chaos; but not as a work (*ergon*) or the product of craftsmanship or by generation. Bultmann points out that the characteristic note is that God transcends the world. "The Lord hath prepared his throne in the Heavens; and His kingdom ruleth over all."[16] The transcendence of God receives its classical expression in the doctrine of the *creatio ex nihilo*, a no-

12. Demant, "Ancient Heresy and Modern Unbelief," 83.

13. Ibid., 85.

14. Solovyev, *Lectures on Godmanhood*, 54.

15. Not having access to his lecture note book, the editors removed Demant's note which reads: "The following New Testament passages are selected examples. Lecture Note Book."

16. Psalm 103:19.

tion utterly inconceivable to the Greek mind, though a logical development from the premises of biblical thought.[17] God's revelation in nature is not seen in the ordered course of Natural history, but in unusual and terrifying occurrences like storm and earthquake.

> In the last analysis, the Old Testament doctrine of creation expresses a sense of the present situation of man. He is hedged in by the incomprehensible power of Almighty God. If Jehovah withdraws his breath, man returns to the dust from which he sprung . . . hence the doctrine expresses man's sense of utter dependence on God. This sense of God as our Creator implies an awareness of our own status as creatures. But God has given man a certain dignity in the world. Genesis 1:26 says that man was made in the Image of God. Man then, though a creature, is not just part of nature or its processes. He is not a part of the objective world, but stands over against it. Man is not interpreted in the light of the world, but the world in the light from him . . . In its earlier stages Hebrew thought did not think of Jehovah as the God of this world. But the cause to be conceived as such in the teaching of the prophets. He was essentially righteous will, demanding righteousness from men. The center of interest. . . is the purpose of God and his moral demands.[18]

This quotation from the first chapter of Bultmann's *Primitive Christianity* gives, in epitome, an outlook in which man's relation to the world is something different from and subordinate to his relation to God. Thereby there is set up a certain duality in his life and the task of adjusting the two responsibilities in the same human breast.

[Opposite the previous paragraph Demant included a note considering possible comparisons with Zoroastrian dualism.[19] He mentions W. S. Haas's work exploring the fundamental differences in how the East and the West think about the world. Haas sees reason as the key concept in the West while consciousness is central in the East. He writes of how reason became

---

17. Here Demant references Jubilees 12:4 and 2 Maccabees 7:28, both of which speak of God's creation of the world.

18. Bultmann, *Primitive Christianity*, 22.

19. Apart from the Haas quote, which has been reproduced, Demant's notes read: "Comparisons with Zoroastrian dualism: Zurivan R. C. Zachner general note book.
Greece: W. S. Haas, Destiny of the Mind, 138.
cf. E. R. Dodds. *The Greeks and the Irrational* (California) shows how Zeus was moralised from the Odyssey onwards—until justice is accepted as a principle bonds or over the Gods. pp32–55."

so pervasive in western thought. Demant's notes include this quote from Haas:

> In Greece there can be traced an evolution in the course of which a distinctly monotheistic trend arose which separated itself from popular religion and was given expression by poets like Hesiod. In it Zeus, losing his mythological character and overshadowing if not extinguishing all other deities, became the Godhead, the creator and ruler of the universe. In the *decis* we hear this idea was supplanted by the conception of the *arche*—a conception of quite another order, that of a powerful beginning—not an end. In conceiving the idea of *arche* the Greek mind secularized the Godhead. Taking over all the power and potentialities contained in the notion of the Godhead, the idea of *arche* started the West on its way to rule the universe in thought and to a more modest degree in action.[20]

Along similar lines, E. R. Dodd's work has shown how Zeus came to be moralized from the Odyssey onwards, until he became "the embodiment of cosmic justice."[21]]

The point is two-fold: first, the Christian conviction of the reality of two worlds is a combination of these Greek and Hebrew elements; second, the Hebrew element also points to a further duality. Man has a relationship with both God and the world. This is derived from the doctrine of creation.[22] Doctrine of Creation is expression of outlook which gives significance not only to the created order as a whole, but to each part of it.

[Here Demant references specific pages in his work, *The Religious Prospect*, in which he writes how the Christian doctrine of creation necessarily values the individual and the particular.

> The doctrine of the creation of the world by God implies that the world has the source of its meaning outside itself. Creation is the denial that the world is God. Because the source of the world's meaning is not in the world itself, each part has its meaning from the source and not ultimately from its relation to the whole. Where the cosmos is held to carry its own meaning, or when God is conceived as the whole world process, then no single thing or event exists in its own right but only as an element in the process . . . And when Newman said, "Religion has to do with the real, and the real is always particular," he

---

20. Haas, *Destiny of the Mind*, 138.
21. Dodds, *The Greeks and the Irrational*, 35.
22. This text was added to address a gap in the notes.

was underlining the Christian sense that particulars, individuals, and communities have final causes of their own. This sense comes from conviction of creation in which universals and particulars can neither be resolved into each other.]²³

The doctrine of creation also implies a "double relationship of kinship and contradiction between the world and God."²⁴ There is a distinction between the two although creation was not originally hostile to the divine. It is only as a result of the Fall that this contradiction exists, such that there is both affinity between God and the world, but also enmity because of human sin.²⁵

With this duality in mind, the dual relationship of man to the world and man to God—which in the Bible is a one-sided duality in that man's responsibilities in the world are part of his responsibilities to God—we can perhaps make something of Albert Schweitzer's interesting but somewhat puzzling book, *Christianity and Ethics*.

Having put aside the ethics of the New Testament as entirely conditioned by its eschatological perspective—valid only for the short interval before the end of the world, and therefore quite irrelevant for the human race in history, he later searched in European philosophy and the religions of the world for an enduring ethical system. In these Dale Lectures of 1922, he maintains sufficient of the biblical outlook to assert that the basis of ethics is what he calls a life-view, which has its own independent source, and is not derived from a world-view. And he reviews with considerable insight—though with some confusing jargon—the work of the moral philosophers from the pre-Christian religions to the machine age.

He divides religions rather crudely into monistic or dualistic categories, putting the Jewish prophets and Christ among the teachers of the second kind. "These religious thinkers" he writes, "do not start from an investigation of the existence which manifests itself in the universe, but from a view of the ethical which is quite independent. . . . Accordingly they assume the existence of two world-principles, the natural and the ethical."²⁶ Note, ethics is not the dualism of two divinities as in early Mazdeanism. He goes on,

> The first [the natural principle] is in the world, and has to be overcome; the other is incorporated in an ethical personality

23. Demant, *Religious Prospect*, 47–49.

24. Ibid., 168

25. This paragraph is an expansion by the editors of Demant's note that reads: "Also implies a double relation: near and far between God and world. when creation is complicated by rebellion of creature, which is sin. cf. Demant, *Religious Prospect*, 168, 169.

26. Schweitzer, *The Philosophy of Civilization*, 110.

which is outside the world and endowed with final authority. . . . The weakness of dualistic religions is that their world-view, because it rejects every kind of nature-philosophy, is always naive. Their strength lies in the fact that they have the ethical within themselves, directly present and with undiminished force. They have no need to strain it and explain it, as must the monists, in order to be able to conceive it as an effluence from the world-will which reveals itself in nature.[27]

Then Schweitzer produces an apparently paradoxical thesis to account for the fact that Christendom has inaugurated a reforming and actively ethical disposition. "The world-view of Jesus is thoroughly pessimistic so far as concerns the future of the natural world. His religion is not a religion of world-transforming effort, but the religion of awaiting the end of the world. His ethic is characterized by activity only so far as it commands men to practice unbounded devotion to their fellow-men, if they would attain to that inner perfection which is needed for entrance into the supernatural kingdom of God."[28]

Yet Christians throughout history have acted quite differently.[29] "Christianity now treats world—and life—affirmation as valid. But how could this volte-face of Christianity be bought about? Because of the fact that in spite of its pessimistic world-view it upholds an ethic which, so far as it touches the relation of man to man, is activist."[30] Schweitzer seems to be saying that the optimistic ethics of Christianity, capable of making men ready for the kingdom, rightly got detached from its original pessimistic world view, and became the inner spring of world transformation, and active devotion to man and his future on earth. You must read this neglected work to see the full force of his thesis.

Its connection with my theme in this lecture is that it does provide a historical religious account of the peculiar world-changing and social-reforming spirit of Christianity as it spread westwards—a phenomenon the uniqueness of which we are bound to miss if we have never looked over the borders of our own culture and taken our ideas of normal mankind from it alone. And it is an account which rests firmly on the two world view giving significance to both the eternal and temporal orders, which I have tried to delineate. Modern secular critics of Christianity who charge it with neglecting human life and civilization on earth, do become such critics because

27. Ibid.
28. Ibid., 146.
29. This text was added to address a gap in the notes.
30. Ibid., 145.

they share a disposition which only a culture imbibed with the Christian spirit could engender.

Series I, Lecture III
Moral Goodness and Blessedness

IT WAS IMPLIED IN Lecture One, that everything that has happened within the human field where Christianity has been the dominant religion, even the revolts against it, is conditioned by that religion. That is an over statement, but sufficiently accurate when by "everything" we understand the chief movements of the human spirit and the intelligence which seeks to catch, identify, understand, and direct those movements.

We are now to attend to a pair of outlooks, moods, philosophies, and tempers which has its counterpart in the culture of Christendom outside the religious sphere, operating in realms where its problems are discerned in purely secular terms. It is the tension between intense awareness of the moral struggle as the central specifically human fact, the destruction of good and evil, and the choices with which it confronts man as man on the one hand; and an awareness that this struggle, however deep, though it seems to invade all human existence, is, yet cannot be, the characteristic of the deepest layer of man's meaning and purpose. It must be given its due value respect, but it must certainly be something secondary and derived, an alienation of some sort from the source and end of life.

The one sees the good life entirely in terms of moral effort; the other a condition where moral effort is transcended or even not undertaken. For the one, the moral good is the sense of striving for the supreme excellence; for the other the supreme excellence is beyond good and evil as commonly understood. For these two conceptions or outlooks I have chosen as the title of this lecture "The Moral Good and Blessedness" with full awareness that it is possible so to extend the sway of the adjective "moral" so that it can be made to cover all types of excellence which men may aim at, to let it mean all that is covered by the term "values" in certain recent ethical religious movements of thought.

Orientals often regard our western desire to be always doing good or reforming something as a sign of crudity and unwisdom. That is because with us, ethics have acquired a certain autonomy—moral values can be thought about as a distinct set of categories—distinct from biological, social or aesthetic. "Western ethics relies on either a set of commandments such as the Decalogue emanating from God, the natural law and the like, or it is founded on something rationally demonstrable, be it love, altruism, the common good, the well pondered on right of the individual and the like, up to such formal definitions as Kant's categorical imperative. The applications of these moral principles to the basics of emerging situations forms an essential part of ethics."[1] In the East, by comparison ethical values constitute no more than stepping stones leading to the entrance to the state of pure consciousness. Contrary to western ethics, which aims essentially at action, the realization and verification of the state of freedom does not point beyond itself and activity is incompatible with the blessedness of consciousness. Our classical Christian and humanist ethics appear therefore to the Oriental mind to run far too deep in our religious and consciousness.

To those in our western culture whose paragon of man is the noble Greek ideal enjoined with the caring consciousness of a *Kalos kagathos*—in whom there is no tension between duty and desires—to such a one the Judaic-Christian moral seriousness that makes moral will and the conquest of evil the very nerve of true humanity ruins man's proper excellence.

So it has come about that by a quite misleading shorthand those who cannot bear morals to be the whole of the good life have been named "Hellenists" and those for whom man's striving for fulfillment never gets outside the field of moral striving have been called "Judaic." This pair of labels, which introduce an element of caricature in impressions of Greek attitudes to life and of the Biblical picture, were described by Matthew Arnold, who laid himself open to being called a Hellenist. Wallis Pater was another who was called a Hellenist, and here the label applies more accurately. Both represent, in their conscious preferences, the type of mind which makes morals subservient to an ulterior condition of abiding satisfaction of an aesthetic kind. Nietzsche, as we shall see, was the outstanding example of this attitude in the end of the nineteenth century.

The opposite outlook is that of moralistically minded people for whom any hope of getting beyond the moral struggle is derogatory to human nature. It is well put with some asperity in C. S. Lewis's description of the coherent modernist ecclesiastic who is allowed to pay a trip to Heaven to see if he wants to stay there. Like most of the visitors he has his doubts, because

---

1. The editors could not find Demant's source for this quotation.

the idea of an abiding satisfaction in conduct or in thought seems to him unworthy.

"Will you come with me to the mountains?" asks the spirit of young man who is sent to show him round. "It will hurt at first, until your feet are hardened. Reality is harsh to the fact of shadows, but will you come?"

"Well, that is a plan. I am perfectly ready to consider it. Of course, I should require some assurances. . .and should want a guarantee that you are taking me to a place where I shall find a wider sphere of usefulness . . . and scope for the talents that God has given me. . .and an atmosphere of free inquiry. . .in short, all that one means by civilization and. . .er. . .the spiritual life."

"No," said the other. "I can promise you none of these things. No sphere of usefulness: you are not needed there at all. No scope for your talents: only forgiveness for having perverted them. No atmosphere of inquiry, for I will bring you to the land not of questions but of answers, and you shall see the face of God."

"Ah, but we must all interpret those beautiful words in our own way! For me there is no such thing as a final answer. The free wind of inquiry must always continue to blow through the mind, must it not? 'Prove all things' . . . to travel hopefully is better than to arrive."

"If that were true, and known to be true, how could anyone travel hopefully? There would be nothing to hope for."

"But you must feel yourself that there is something stifling about the idea of finality? Stagnation, my dear boy, what is more soul-destroying than stagnation?"

"You think that, because hitherto you have experienced truth only with the abstract intellect. I will bring you where you can taste it like honey and be embraced by it as by a bridegroom. Your thirst shall be quenched."

"Well, really, you know, I am not aware of a thirst for some ready-made truth which puts an end to intellectual activity in the way you seem to be describing. Will it leave me the free play of Mind, Dick? I must insist on that, you know."

"Free, as a man is free to drink while he is drinking. He is not free still to be dry." The Ghost seemed to think for a moment. "I can make nothing of that idea," it said.

"Listen!" said the White Spirit. "Once you were a child. Once you knew what inquiry was for. There was a time when you asked questions because you wanted answers, and were glad when you found them. Become that child again: even now."

"Ah, but when I became a man I put away childish things."
"You have gone far away. Thirst was made for water; inquiry for truth."[2]

What the episcopal ghost in this passage stands for is attachment of supreme significance to keeping on in a striving for which there is no goal. It is the attitude towards intellectual pursuit parallel to the one I am trying to identify in the moralistically minded person for whom the moral struggle has no term and should not have any. You find this temper in Gotthold Ephraim Lessing in eighteenth-century Germany. In *Eine Duplik* (1778) he writes the well-known words:

> It is not the truth which a man possesses or supposes himself to possess, but the honest pains which he has taken to come at that truth that constitutes his significance. For it is not by the possession, but by the search for truth that he develops the powers wherein his ever-growing perfection consists. Possession brings quiet, indolence, pride.
>
> If God held all truth in his right hand, and in his left hand nothing but the ever-active impulse towards truth, though coupled with the condition that I must forever wander in error, and were to say to me, "Choose," I should throw myself humbly upon his left and should say: "Father give! the pure truth is for thee alone."[3]

We understand this attitude, but must put the question whether there is not some hidden insincerity in this attitude which prefers ignorance to knowledge and out of choice renounces the arrival of knowledge.

The moralistic attitude as I call it, is sometimes hidden in the religious scheme of a writer. I think this is true of Milton. When people say, "Of course: Satan is the hero of *Paradise Lost*" they are right without knowing quite why. The fact is that John Milton hails Satan so because he fundamentally loves him, for having started this wonderful fray of the forces of good and evil and that is also why *Paradise Regained* is such a failure. He really revels in the dualism which evil has set up, for it supports the concept of life as a battle. With the publication of Milton's *Christian Doctrine* in English in 1825, it became clear that *Paradise Lost* was not a poetic version of orthodox puritan salvation orthodoxy, but a disguised undermining of it.

---

2. C. S. Lewis, *The Great Divorce*, 40ff.
3. G. E. Lessing quoted in Wicksteed, *The Religion of Time and the Religion of Eternity*, 103.

It is not only that he makes Satan and evil both trivial and comic, not so much a fiendish awareness as the permitted challenger, power, and opponent in the same life and one who compels us to play the game well, to establish the good living; for good is nothing but the battle for it. Evil here is not the original sin in man's heart, to be overcome by Christ's victorious atonements. Milton's evil is objective, a legitimate and eminent force in the universal scheme of things. The same attitude is to be found in the "Areopagitica" and "Samson Agonistes."[4] It was for this absolutizing of the conflict of good and evil that Blake disliked Milton; Blake who believed in the Marriage of Heaven and Hell, and who knew the truth of his own combative personality, who wrote "Damn braces, bless relaxes."

For the pure, moralistically-minded man, there is a need to find and confront temptation. It is almost as if,[5] "Lead us not into temptation" is the prayer of pure moralistically-minded man.[6] The moralistic attitude regards the conflict of good and evil as absolute and sees no other fulfillment of human existence than its pursuit, "there's no discharge in that war," no Sabbath next.[7] This attitude is seen at its best in the Pharisees of the Gospel. Bonhoeffer writes, "The Pharisee is that extremely admirable man who subordinates his entire life to the knowledge of good and evil and is as severe a judge of himself as of his neighbor to the honor of God, whom he humbly thanks for his knowledge. For the Pharisee every moment of life becomes a situation of conflict in which he has to choose between good and evil."[8]

It is felt that the only legitimate form of moral good, is that which strives with evil.[9]

ETHICAL WEIGHT OF THE HOLY

The Bible has its own versions of the place of the moral conflict, it is the warp of the pattern; the woof, however, is made up of the intimations that the moral conflict is not original or final; that it is a sort of grimace of the face of human reality. There is surely no need to stress what Tillich calls the

---

4. Following this paragraph, Demant includes the reference: "Elizabeth Mideols: Milton in the Yewtree Temperament: in Faith and Freedom vxvii Part 3. 1954. Number 21."

5. This text was added to address a gap in the notes.

6. Following this sentence, Demant includes the note: "Pharisee: cf. Bonhoffer," which Demant expands upon in the following paragraphs.

7. Ecclesiastes 8:8, KJV.

8. Bonhoeffer, *Ethics*, 151.

9. This text was added to address a gap in the notes.

"weight of ethical material" in the Bible. There is at the start the enigma of a commandment and a prohibition in Eden; though as we shall consider in a moment this cannot be considered as a moral commandment and prohibition. Anyhow, man defies them and loses his innocence. Then the knowledge of good and evil arises; there is envy, murder and deceit and a sense of guilt. The judgement of the flood, and in place of primal innocence mankind has to put up with a covenant of which its part is obey the Law given through Moses. The prophets thunder against injustice, and the second exile is imposed to drive home the truth that being the Lord's chosen was not to be taken as a moral "most favored nation clause" in the covenant between God and man. Bultmann notes how in the Old Testament heritage "The judgements passed on man and his activity are not derived from an ideal conception of man or the Good. The ethical vocabulary of the Old Testament is not derived, as with the Greeks, from the plastic arts or craftsmanship. It comes partly from the law court and commerce, partly from the *cultus*. Hence there are no such laudatory epithets as 'becoming,' 'decent,' 'harmonious,' 'well-proportioned,' 'graceful' and the like. Instead, we get such terms as 'true,' 'faithful,' or (from the *cultus*) 'whole,' 'without blemish,' 'unspotted.'"[10]

And the New Testament though primarily a gospel of the new life, offers it as a new righteousness. The atoning work of Christ is delineated as an act of the divine initiative by which believers can fulfill the inexorable demand of righteousness, though it be no longer their own righteousness.

Readers of Rudolf Otto's book, now over a quarter of a century old, *The Idea of the Holy*, will remember his account of the way the Bible combines with moral demands, the idea of the holy in him who makes the demands; and holiness is a category quite different from morality in origin. The Bible says "*Tu solis sanctus*," but once it has been grasped, writes Otto, that "*qadosh* or *sanctus* is not originally a moral category at all, the most obvious rendering of the words is 'transcendent' (*supramundane, überweltlich*)."[11] In the light of this holiness of god, "Mere 'unlawfulness' only becomes 'sin,' 'impiety,' 'sacrilege' when the character of *numinous unworthiness* or *disvalue* goes on to be transferred to and centered in *moral* delinquency. And only when the mind feels it as 'sin' does the transgression of law become a matter of such dreadful gravity for the conscience, a catastrophe that leads it to despair of its own power."[12]

---

10. Bultmann, *Primitive Christianity*, 48.
11. Otto, *The Idea of the Holy*, 54.
12. Ibid., 54–55.

[Demant here references St. Paul's writing on the relationship between the Law and the Gospel. Although Paul makes many moral demands on those to whom he writes, he ultimately sees the Law as insufficient. Paul is always pointing back to faith in Christ or the righteousness of Christ, as he does in the oft-cited verses from Galatians 3: "Wherefore the law was our schoolmaster to bring us unto Christ, that we might be justified by faith. But after that faith is come, we are no longer under a schoolmaster."[13]] Having appreciated the depth to which the moral element in biblical religion goes, let us now see that it does not run all the way.

[Here Demant references a chapter from his book, *Christian Polity*, where he writes of how human identity as creatures made in the image of God completely changes the Christian view of morality (which he refers to as contract-based thinking); e.g., "to such a world He comes as an enigma, 'the Riddle of the New Testament,' speaking words which say, not 'I do this for you, do this for me,' but 'I am' and 'Ye are,' 'Ye shall become.' And he enters into this contractual world, pays a price, meets a cost, earns a salvation, so that once and for all the whole sorry business of contract can begin to be superseded through the leaven of a new history beside the old."[14]]

This two strand religion can be seen as having the characteristics imaged in the main picture of the historic world as set between the two noumenal realities of Eden and the Kingdom of God. The paradox of ethics: "if morality is the struggle against evil it leads to its own overthrow,"[15] then receives the answer "why yes," but this is not an achievement in the terrestrial existence, and if the distinction of good and evil is thought to be overcome in history and the conflict stilled, then hell is created on earth. Still there are intimations in the Christian's consciousness that behind the involvement of man in history is fall and moral struggle. Then a good beyond moral good and evil is derived: "O that my ways were made so direct that I might keep thy statutes."[16]

This world is set between Eden and the Kingdom of God. The Christian longs for the Kingdom, when moral striving shall cease. And yet, there is in this world a very real sense that good and evil have a corresponding relationship.[17]

---

13. Galatians 3:24–25.
14. Demant, *Theology of Society*, 33–34.
15. The editors could not find the source for this quotation.
16. Psalm 119:5, Coverdale translation.
17. This paragraph is an expansion by the editors of Demant's notes, which read: "Therefore Eden—Fuller (Distinct Good and Evil)—Kingdom of God
   Eden—and Kingdom. Original harmony—good (1)
   History—correlative good and evil—good (2)."

[Here Demant references Charles Williams's book, *He Came Down from Heaven*. In his text, Williams discusses this paradox of ethics and how it develops. He begins with Eden, "The Adam had been created and were existing in a state of knowledge of good and nothing but good."[18] Williams goes on to describe the Fall.

> Man desired to know schism in the universe. It was a knowledge reserved to God; man had been warned that he could not bear it—"in the day that thou eatest thereof thou shalt surely die." A serpentine subtlety overwhelmed that statement with a grander promise—"Ye shall be as gods, knowing good and evil." Unfortunately to be as gods meant, for the Adam, to die, for to know evil, for them, was to know it not by pure intelligence but by experience. It was, precisely, to experience the opposite of good, that is the deprivation of the good, the slow destruction of the good, and of themselves with the good.

Thus in history, human beings know both the good and its opposite, and these forces are correlative. Humans cannot achieve the good, by morality or any other means. And yet, there is still a possibility for good to exist that is beyond moral good and evil.

> It is a recurrent effort, since it is a recurrent temptation: if this or that could be done, surely the great tower would arise, and we should walk in heaven among gods—as when the orthodox of any creed think that all will be well when their creed is universal. Yet the recurrent opposite is no more true, for unless something is done, nothing happens. Unless devotion is given to a thing which must prove false in the end, the thing that is true in the end cannot enter.[19]]

---

18. Williams, *He Came Down from Heaven*, 19.
19 Ibid., 20.

Series I, Lecture IV
The Mystery of the Will

SEVERAL MODERN PHILOSOPHERS HAVE remarked, with some air of complaint that early philosophy has no doctrine of the will. But why on earth should anyone have a doctrine of the will anymore than a doctrine of digestion if you only need it when something goes wrong.[1]

In our western religious and moral culture the question of the will has been acute because, more than in any other culture, men in this one have imposed their wills on their environment, made artifacts out of what is given by nature, made political systems on top of tribal togetherness, economic processes of buying and selling on top of naive exchange of goods and energy. Our moral theories have been as largely concerned with the facts of the moral consciousness as with the good kinds of life men have striven for. And the will seems to have become the central mystery of the moral life, at any rate since Kant proclaimed that there is nothing good but the "good will." In this classical-Christian-humanist culture though, when it reaches philosophical levels, it has been pre-occupied with the crises of free will and determinism, and with the relations of freedom and knowledge the will and the mind.

I am about to suggest that this kind of debate is one which could only arise in a universe of discourse formed by a specific intellectual and religious history. Because that is so, philosophic students who live and work within the universe of discourse are surprised when they discover that men act and talk on the assumption that they have a certain freedom. They do so without our doctrines and counter doctrines about whether the human will

---

1. Immediately following this paragraph, Demant includes the following text, which seems to the editors to be a draft of ideas he develops in subsequent paragraphs: "Our Western culture marked tremendous impact of the human Will upon its environment. Will not intelligence. No wonder, therefore, that it has also been marked by endless arguments about the will, which still remains a mystery."

is quite self-determined or controlled by external forces, or about whether the knowing act preceded the choosing act or vice versa. One might as well be surprised that the birds of the air do not write PhD theses on "Ornithology," or that mankind seems to have taken enough relaxation from the arduousness of its career without knowing anything about the physiology of sleep or the value of prophylacting against "weight starvation."

The fact is that the human will, which has been the subject of so much discussion in Christendom, awaits secular cultural heirs and this discussion has helped to provide philosophers with jobs and stipends—yet the human will is the discovery of a particular phase of human consciousness; in other places and times men get on quite well without that discovery. Nicolai Hartmann writes, "The older ethics was astonishingly superficial in treating the question of freedom. Ancient thinkers took freedom for granted as something self-evident, which clearly shows how little they knew of the metaphysical difficulties which they passed over in so doing. . . . Such is the freedom of choice which Plato proclaimed in mythological form; such also is Aristotle's statement that man is free to know what is good and to be virtuous."[2] Poor ancients! not to have the blessing of coping with difficulties introduced by subsequent developments!

Hartmann does hint at some of these developments—which introduced difficulties! "The Church Fathers and the Scholastics had a firmer grasp of the problem; but it was not so much moral as religious freedom that they had in mind, not freedom in relation to the course of the world, nor in relation to moral requirements as such, but freedom as over against God . . . moral freedom exacts far less than religious freedom, that is to say, because over against an all-powerful and all-knowing Being the question of scope for choice on the part of a finite entity is much more unfavorably placed, than merely over against commandments and values which as such exercise no foresight whatever."[3]

Spinoza takes up the question of the ethical and finds human freedom lacking. Hartmann says of Spinoza, "According to him everything (the series of the modi) issues from the necessity of absolute substance; nothing therefore can be otherwise than it is."[4] Later, Kant detached human freedom from the pantheism of Spinoza.[5] This generated the Enlightenment's virtue of autonomy. Thus Autonomy: moral consciousness is no longer protection against all

2. Hartmann, *Ethics*, 30.
3. Ibid., 31.
4. Ibid., 31.
5. This paragraph is an expansion by the editors of Demant's notes which read: "Spinoza substitute 'The necessity of absolute substance is for decisive overruling; then Kant detached human freedom from the pantheism of Spinoza."

powerful providence, for, if recognized at all, providence is the moral consciousness itself.[6]

But it was the religious debates about freedom that had sharpened the problem to the point at which Kant took it up. For it is only in the religious universal discourse that man has to cope with the two freedoms; over against the world and over against God. The first presented few puzzles, precisely because freedom over against the world was what western man within the Greek and Christian world thought he was good at—he was arranging life and not just going through it—(intellectual problems are born of failure or at least frustration); and the European man was characteristically the man who was making his own world. It was the second kind of freedom which discussed throughout the early church and Middle Ages and Reformation disputes, sharpened the idea of the will. The mystery of the will was not solved by Christianity; the problem was created by it.

For "if man is free only as against the course of nature, but not against the commandments of God, then it is altogether beyond man's power to transgress the commandments, hence also to decide in accordance with them."[7] But the mind of Christendom has firmly insisted on this freedom against God—how otherwise can one account for the Christian attitude to human accountability, responsibility, and sin. At the same time God's sovereign will is over all creaturely things.[8] Here is a nice kettle of perplexities, which I contend would not have occurred without the religious debates about it; for as I hope it is now clear these debates were not about man's freedom and determinism imposed by his involvement in the world.

Let us now try to trace back some of these stages leading to these debates. Not every religion or religious philosophy is bothered by the mystery of the will. In Far Eastern religious thought, though it has an elemental idea of freedom, there is no conception of the will, in our sense; for the human will as we westerners understand it is part, a very central part, of the self as subject comporting objects, this contrast is a western device; the human will with us, too, is a kind of cause, a self-moving cause; and causality is a Greek concept.

In Iudian and Chinese religion there is no problem of a conflict between the divine and human purpose, for there is not any purpose: from the *Bhagavad Gita* we read "It is I (Brahmas) devoid of every sensible form, who have developed all this universe . . . immutable in my productive power

---

6. Following this sentence Demant included the note: "Fundamentals from Religion."

7. Hartmann, *Ethics*, 109.

8. The editors removed the second half of this sentence which reads: "is the human will away these creaturely things that cannot be or act outside God's will."

(Shakti, Prakiti) I produce and reproduce the multitude of beings, without a determinate aim, and by the sole virtue of that productive power."[9]

In the rest of the Vedanta you can read all about what are called the "envelopes of the self"—but these are all in terms of intellect, consciousness, essence, knowledge—reflections—nothing corresponding to the will, which in our mental universe is the most central envelope of the self, nearest to that ultimate mystery of the subject which we call by the same name "I."

The fact is that eastern consciousness is content that existence is ineffable: so there is not the concept of free will as opposed to determination to which we are accustomed. And it is also, I think, true that free will and determinism are two concepts which arose together, like Jacob and Esau, struggling in the same womb. This development is largely the work of the Greeks and I shall show how when it was met by the Judaic Christian axiom of the will of God, these two influences molded the mentality of the western world—with its intense consciousness of the power of the will and equally of the limits to which it is subjected.

It is important always, when confronted with a recurring debate, like that of free will and determinism, to realize that most oppositions of that kind are twins of the same mental parentage—and that other families have no twins at all. So, it seems to me, this problem arose when Greek thought first made a distinct object of the external world and could "stand off from established custom and ask the reason why"—thereby dividing existence into two, the inner and outer life, or subject and object; and then objectified the mental concepts, general ideas, which are much tidier than the irrational [unreadable] of particular things, wants, feelings, and energies.[10]

There was a further step they took, that of turning man inside out and trying to see his inner life which looks out from a center—as part of the objective world—so you began to have studies of the soul and its constitution. (I am not going into all the consequences of that attempt to treat that ultimate subject as an object, and its impossibility beyond a certain point—a story which leads up to the protest against the attempt as the part of certain modern existentialists). But I am concerned to point out that what we call the will part of the inner life, when experienced from inside—is known as free; when looked at as an object, part of the objective world—then the mind cannot accept its freedom but is bound to see it as determined by extraneous causes.[11]

9. *Bhagavad Gita*, ix.4 to 8.

10. Citation for quotation: Edwyn Bevan, *Christianity and Hellenism* (London: Allen and Unwin, 1921), 14.

11. Here Demant includes the reference: "Bergerac: Dormics Immediateo de la Conscience, Tuce and Free will."

[Demant here references Scottish philosopher David Hume's ideas on free will in the text, *Enquiry Concerning Human Understanding*.] Hume explores the challenge of human beings understanding that outside causes influence human behavior, while at the same time being aware of the individual's freedom of choice in a given moment.

> For what is meant by "liberty" when the term is applied to voluntary actions? Surely we can't mean that actions have so little connection with motives, inclinations, and circumstances that the former don't follow with a certain degree of uniformity from the latter, and that motives etc. support no inference by which we can infer actions. For these are plain and acknowledged matters of fact. By "liberty," then, we can only mean a power of acting or not acting according to the determinations of the will; i.e., if we choose to stay still we may do so, and if we choose to move we may do that. This hypothetical liberty is universally agreed to belong to everyone who isn't a prisoner and in chains.[12]

It is not that mankind has always to choose between belief in free will or an endless chain of causality which makes freedom an illusion. It is that the rise of the idea of cause and effect—which governed the external world in the mentality of the western world from the time of the Greeks and idea of free will emerged side by side as counter positions in the same universe of discourse. The Greek idea of causality in the objective world is the secular counterpart of the religious belief in Moira, the inexorable fate which rules over gods and men, and yet human responsibility was not denied in either case. Though intellectually incompatible with both fate as the power behind the gods and with causality as the law of the cosmos, *human responsibility* was an important mental concept. In the religious field the tension between fate and freedom took the forms of tragedy wherein men pit their own freedom against fate and find their freedom entangled in a complex network of superior powers which baffles and often crushes them, or turn their purposes against themselves. In the philosophical field the tension of the will and causality leads to the burning intellectual question of determinism and free will. This question is articulated in terms of the will as one peculiar kind of cause—either with the determinists as one in a chain of causes, or with the free will believers as an uncaused cause.

Therefore, freedom has never been demonstrated in western thought, or in eastern, for it is a perpetual protest against necessity; only contingency can perhaps be demonstrated, and that is not the sphere of freedom. But when men have sought to demonstrate freedom—it has been in terms of

---

12. Hume, *Concerning Human Understanding*, 72.

free will which, though on one level is opposed to causation, has to be discussed as a certain kind of cause.

But now when we turn from the intellectual to the religious background of our culture we find this question started off in quite a different way. The influence of biblical religion is pointedly summarized in the work of the eminent historian Prof. Henri Frankfort and others in their work on Mesopotamia and Egypt.

> The monotheism of the Hebrews is a correlate of their insistence of the unconditioned nature of God. Only a God who transcends every phenomenon, who is not conditioned by any mode of manifestation—only an unqualified God can be the one and only ground of *all* existence . . . [but] Even the great conception of an only and transcendent God was not entirely free from myth, for it was not the fruit of detached speculation but of a passionate and dynamic experience . . . It created, in fact, a new "myth"—the myth of the Will of God. Although the great "Thou" which confronted the Hebrews transcended nature, it stood in a specific relationship to the people . . . It is a poignant myth, this Hebrew myth of a chosen people, of a divine promise made, of a terrifying moral burden imposed . . . Not cosmic phenomena, but history itself, had here become pregnant with meaning; history had become a revelation of the dynamic will of God . . . Man, according to Hebrew thought, was the interpreter and the servant of God: he was even honored with the task of bringing about the realization of God's will. Thus, man was condemned to unending efforts which were doomed to fail because of his inadequacy.[13]

"In the Old Testament we find man possessed of a new freedom (especially from the periodical of nature) and of a new burden of responsibility."[14] "With infinite moral courage the Hebrews worshipped an absolute God and accepted as a correlate of their faith the sacrifice of a harmonious existence,"[15] "a new and utter lack of *eudaimonia*, of harmony—whether with the world of reason or with the world of perception."[16]

When we turn to the New Testament the picture becomes complicated. There the question is not so much whether man has freedom over against the world—or even over against God—for it is evident that he does disobey the will of the Lord. The question here becomes can man do good

13. Frankfort, *Before Philosophy*, 369–70.
14. Ibid., 243ff.
15. Ibid., 370.
16. Ibid., 245.

in his own power. It is quite clear that he cannot claim merit for obedience or for exercise of response to God's command. But even so the parables are puzzling about this:

For instance, in the parables of The Sower and the Talents, some produce greater results than others. And in the Parable of the Talents it is apparent that these greater results occur because of greater or at least wiser effort. Though when all is said and done it is ultimately unprofitable. On the other hand, the parable of the Laborers in the Vineyard shows all being rewarded equally for different amounts of work.[17]

The gospels insist that God claims man as a whole, but he is free to respond or rebel—this in time with the prophetic tradition in which God is ethical will behind history. In St. Paul there is a formal (modern sense) similarity in his doctrine of the freedom of the Christian man in Christ and the Stoic teaching of inner freedom from the pressure of external events—as Rudolf Bultmann has shown. But for the Stoic this freedom is the reward of submitting the impulses and action to the reason—who is Plato's character in control of two houses. In St. Paul the problem of freedom comes in when man wants to do good, which is always the call of god, the self has a sort of self-defeating principle in it—though he does not use this language, the cause of it is a false self—*Le Moi Haissable* of Pascal—man is in radical bondage.

Not because he wills evil, but because when he wants the good his will is impotent. For St. Paul man is free when he has been made free by the grace of god—to whom he has surrendered—but the surrender is itself an act of divine grace in the believer—we can see that this paradoxical notion, if teased out into formal propositions, gives rise to the doctrine of predestination. But it is not my task to review the theological history of that controversy. I am recalling some of the origins in support of my thesis that the religious issues that cluster around the fact of human freedom helped to fasten attention to the fact of the will and its enigmatic character. We find as we take various jumps in the history of Christendom that in order to articulate the discussion more elaborate terminology is devised; the problem of freedom becomes the problem of free will and the relation of the will to other powers of the will becomes the subject of investigation. This is especially true as we move from the biblical climate and then from the Eastern Mediterranean world—westward to the Latin—which has always had a more psychological and moral taste than the mind of the Greek Christianity (more metaphysical).

17. This paragraph is an expansion by the editors of Demant's notes, which read:
"The Sower,
The Talents rewards, Labourers in the vineyard."

For example, in the fourth century Cyril of Jerusalem wrote some *Catechetical Discourses* in Greek. In a chapter on the soul, his description of freedom is simply to say "the soul is self-governed"—having its own power (this in a passage arguing with someone who might say his is overcome by the devil)—Cyril answers that the devil might suggest he has not the power to compel against the will. "The sheep is gentle, but never was it crowned for its gentleness: since its gentle quality belongs to it not from choice but by nature."[18]

When a translator rendered this document into Latin, the general term "self-governing" appeared to him too vague so he added with Latin precision to the words *Sui Potentatis* another two: *Liberaque arbitrium*, the general term for free will with a bias in the direction of making this freedom a liberty of choice.[19]

The story develops in both St. Augustine and Thomas Aquinas with increasing complexity. All this partly lies behind, yet contrasts with, our modern use of the word "will."[20]

To moderns, will suggests effort or resolve, to initiate or direct one's own powers. To scholastics, will is an appetite (as hunger is), but an intellectual rather than sensuous appetite. It is an appetite for something that presents itself to the mind as desirable; therefore we find two "intellectual natures": men and angels. An animal wants and does not wish. *Voluntas*, or will, makes us choose and appropriate to our affections something our intelligence presents to us as good: if choice is made soundly we rejoice in the attainment. Action of the will is a movement of all the powers, towards the chosen thing—king of love—love of the unpossessed is desire; love of the possessed is joy (fruition). The judgement may be swayed by the senses; and may present things as better than they are.

Just as object of the intellect is the *verum*, so object of the will is *bonum*. Human will is free in its *electio*, for though the *voluntas* is an appetite yet it is for the *bonum* at large; it chooses any concrete *bonum* or man or woman, or the unfortunate, by virtue of its participation in the nature of the *bonum perse*—the abstract or absolute good. Judgment (*arbitrium*) is needed to appraise several claimants;[21] *electio* between those two possibilities is free.

---

18. St. Cyril of Jerusalem, *Catechetical Discourse*, Lecture 4.21.

19. Demant ends this paragraph with the note: "Incidentally Cyril has already used term ... free will."

20. This is an expansion by the editors of Demant's notes which read: "GAP, Augustine 13th Century, GAP, Aquinas 13th Century: Voluntas, Electio, Arbitrium."

21. Here Demant includes a note which the editors believe was unfinished yet intended to be an example of such a judgment between several claimants: "what do with cool was in pool or saved up."

The choice may be wrong, but if the act is free, the object of desire has been chosen *sub specie boni*, it seemed good at the time to the corrupted will—corrupted by wrong judgement.

The will is bound as to *bonum*—free as to concrete embodiment of *bonum*.[22]

This makes freedom of will subject to correct judgment (intellectualist), though this does not explain freedom of will. *Other thinkers, though voluntarists, share this sense that free will is at least partly an act of intelligence. Augustine, Abelard, Occam, Luther, and Pascal see it as an interplay of knowledge and movement of the will.*[23]

For all their differences, medieval scholastics agreed that the will is "distinguished from sense appetite; they regarded it as a movement of the soul accepting or rejecting objects [or aims] without any intervention of external forces; they identified will and freedom; and they recognized that will apart from desire and knowledge is a psychological monster [chimera]." This meant that "freedom is not capriciousness."[24] Duns Scotus, the greatest of Scottish born medieval thinkers, pointed out:

> Freedom is not so much power of choice as action in accordance with the highest and most characteristic elements of the self . . . Secondly, if volition implies a known object and knowing is an activity of the intellect which, like will, is essentially one with the essence of the soul, then volition must be, to a certain extent, character—a thesis which as Bradley pointed out (*Ethical Studies*, 1st ed. London 1876, pa 46ff.) need not lead to the uncomfortable conclusion that all our volitions can be predicted, for character is what is being made out of our potentialities plus environment, and no one, not even the doer himself, can know all the potentialities, though as the self becomes a more unified whole, conduct becomes more predictable.[25]

Scotus, ever the subtle doctor, strikes a balance, "mindful on the one hand of the extreme intellectualism of Godfrey of Fontaines and on the other of the teaching of Augustine and Anselm that the will is the most fundamental faculty of the self, he endeavored to bring out the interdependence

---

22. After this sentence, Demant includes the note: "light—lights."
23. This is an expansion of Demant's note: "Other voluntarists: act of intelligence—knowing moved by will; Augustine, Abelard, Occam, Luther, Pascal."
24. Sharp, *Franciscan Philosophy at Oxford*, 397–8.
25. Ibid., 398.

of the intellect and the will. . . He thereby opposes both St. Thomas, who exalts the intellect, and Hugh of St. Victor who exalts the will."[26]

To turn back to Augustine, there is an interesting observation "that our will power and our responsibility are directly known to us [like time] and that only by free will can we deny the possibility of free will" (i.e., "the feeling of freedom and the idea of 'ought' could never have arisen if we were determined").[27]

Scotus was a careful student of Augustine, and followed him in a voluntarist doctrine of God—there can be no answer to the question why God does this or that—for that would posit a cause behind the divine will; but he cites other elements in Augustine where the apparent arbitrariness of the divine will "is modified by the directive influence of the Divine intellect."[28]

In Newman's seminal work, Grammar of Assent, *he considers how human beings come to beliefs about things that cannot be absolutely proven, or what he calls "real assent." Newman says of real assents that "they are of a personal character, each individual having his own, and being known by them. It is otherwise with notions; notional apprehension is in itself an ordinary act of our common nature."[29] Thus, notional apprehension belongs properly to the intellect, yet it seems that real assent involves not only the intellect but a voluntary element as well.[30]*

The Quietist Movement in 17th century France saw the will very differently.[31] Miguel de Molinos began this movement and in his work, Spiritual Guide, *he writes of how the will cannot possibly do any good. It is rather through annihilation of the soul and the will that the Christian approaches God. For instance, Molinos writes, "To be perfect in the soul, this annihilation must happen in your own judgment, in your will, in your affections, your inclinations, your desires, your thoughts, and in yourself, in such a way that you soul finds itself dead to wanting, desiring, obtaining, understanding, and thinking."[32]*

It may surprise you to be told of this voluntarist element in Augustine, because most theological students and others are only acquainted with him in connection with his controversy with Pelagius—where it appears that it was Pelagius who was over estimating the freedom and power of the

26. Ibid., 398–9.

27. Ibid., 399.

28. Ibid., 407.

29. Newman, *Grammar of Assent*, 63.

30. This paragraph is an expansion by the editors of Demant's notes which read: "Newman: Voluntary element in real assent. Grammar of Assent."

31. This paragraph is an expansion by the editors of Demant's notes, which read: "Quietists and Molinists in 17th Century French Catholicism."

32. Molinos, *Spiritual Guide*, 177.

human will; and Augustine as the champion of predestination. But it has to be remembered—Augustine's teaching is not that human will is bound by human circumstances (as he wrote in a letter in answer to one writer who interpreted him in this sense), but that man's will to good cannot act without God's grace because of original sin.[33] This is what Pelagius denied. *One can see a secular version of Pelagius's teaching in* The Impulses Behind Moral Re-Armament.[34]

The main trend of modern intellect development in West has been intellectualist, to exalt knowledge as the prime mover. Therefore education is the main force in making character. Often this leads to such abundance of knowledge and causes—and applied to human life and social sciences, leads to declaration of determinism. This sometimes was thought to be the Greek attitude where evil is ignorance and virtue is knowledge. [Here Demant references John Gould, the ornithologist who helped Darwin identify the species of birds he had collected. Gould's life and the contribution he made to the development of Darwin's theories could be seen as the pinnacle of such virtue.]

Even as development in the West has emphasized the intellect, there is also a voluntarist element, which entrusts power to the people. Since the breakup of the Middle Ages, there has been a separation. There is no longer any sense of the divine notion of a ruler. Indeed, there is no sense of a higher or Godly law that people should seek to follow. Instead, justice is whatever sovereign power decrees and political authority emanates from the will.[35]

We can see many examples of this emphasis on the will in recent history. For instance, in Goethe's Faust, the main character is disheartened by his quest for knowledge. He famously translates the beginning of the Gospel of John as saying "In the beginning was the act." Nietzsche also demonstrates this emphasis on force and deeds in his novel, Thus Spoke Zarathustra. The eponymous Zarathustra advises, "Ye say it is the good cause which halloweth even war? I say unto you: it is the good war which halloweth every cause."

In Johann Gottlieb Fichte, we find the following idea emerging: [the moral law] has a determinate (if never reachable) goal (absolute freedom from

---

33. Here Demant references Augustine's *Letter 214*.

34. This sentence is an expansion by the editors of Demant's notes, which read: "secular version of moral re-armament." Also, following this paragraph, Demant included note, which read: "Two different tempers: Souter. Heavenly Father. Concupuis sense—Freudian. Doctrine of Two Liberties in Augustine: (vad)."

35. This paragraph is an expansion by the editors of Demant's notes, which read: "But also a voluntarist element comes say. Since break up of Middle Ages—separated. Ruler and Law—divine notion of ruler. King or people. Nagum Taummunis—just is what sovereign power decrees."

all limitation); and a completely determinate way along which it leads us (the order of nature).[36] Fichte created his entire system on the pure "I." It was an embracing affirmation of subjectivity. Coupled with Hegel's emphasis on the processes of history expressing themselves in certain purposes, we can see the emergence of Hitler and the fascist vision of Giovanni Gentile.[37]

Sense of freedom under power does not lead to passivity.[38] It is ironic that most of the people who have made historic changes have been determinists of a sort. It is impressive how great geniuses of action speak of selves as docile to natural laws and elements of destiny. Take Napoleon—whose power intrigued L. Tolstoy in *War and Peace* and Thomas Hardy in *The Dynasts*—Tolstoy goes out of his way to show Napoleon was a slave of circumstances and only imagined himself to be master of them. I wonder whether he had read Napoleon's letter to Josephine, dated 3 Dec 1806: "The greater one is the less one needs the will; one depends on events and circumstances. . . I declare myself the most enslaved of men; my master has no human sympathies, and this master is the nature of things."[39]

FREEDOM AND ABILITY

The paradox of our present age is that political changes, commercial forces, industrialization, and technology, which are a result of human will and intellect, are making society an artifact. All this construction is a work of human freedom, yet it creates an environment harder and harder to shift and modify, like a second nature imposing its own determinism.[40]

Whatever philosophical understandings the west has inherited about free will, it is clear that our society is the result of the exertion of the will. And that movement of will has created a climate in which the extent of man's free will is impacted by the realities of our modern era: large-scale economic life, technology, and industrialization. The human will has created a climate in which the human will cannot move. This will be explored further in later lectures.

36. Fichte, 1971, IV: 166.

37. Preceding two paragraphs are an expansion of Demant's notes: "Also: Goethe In begin was act Nietzsche. Good war halloweth every cause. Fichte. Hegel. Hitler. Gentile: Supporter of Fascism."

38. Prior to this paragraph, Demant included the incomplete sentence: "Don't let this be a reason for democracies patting themselves on the back—for international will of people and other forms of it."

39. Quoted in Geer, *Napoleon and Josephine*.

40. Here Demant included the note to himself: "return to later."

Series I, Lecture V
Spirituality: Cultivation of the Inner Life[1]

WE COME NOW TO the key area of spirituality. This is the arena where the divine touches the human. It is the fundamental centering of the human life, where the soul touches the source of all our being. It is the most important aspect of being human.

The purpose of spirituality is to support the unaided will. By unaided will, we mean a will that seeks to constantly focus on God and live life conscious of the eternal context. It is a will in harmony with the Creator. In other words, it is a will not in constant conflict with the Creator—it is not given to constant sinful temptation. The result is a disposition. This is an outlook on life, which seeks to "do the right thing, simply because it is right." Internal conflict is at a minimum. There is not a struggle between human will and human action.[2]

Some see spirituality as primarily a way to increase morality in persons. However, Christian practices of prayer, asceticism, and mystical union do not have morality as their primary aim. Instead, these practices proceed from the desire to know and love God. Prayer, asceticism, and mystical union can and should lead to a moral life, but this is not the goal; holiness is the goal. Ethical insights and ability are a side-effect.[3]

Because Christian spirituality has no direct ethical purpose, and because it often seems to dispense with the Gospel facts of sin, redemption

---

1. This lecture was only one page of handwritten notes. Demant lectured from these notes for this Gifford. He did not develop the argument as he worked on the manuscript for publication.

2. This paragraph is an expansion by the editors of Demant's note that reads: "Serves to support unaided will—create a disposition."

3. This paragraph is an expansion by the editors of the notes that read: "Justify moral aims—but these practices. Prayer, Ascetism, and mystical union—have not primarily a moral aim but proceed from a root which may be described as a desire to know and love God. Many ethical insights and powers come in by the way."

and repentance, as well as with the concrete, historical work of Christ, many Christian theologians and teachers have warned us against some of the developments of "spirituality" as it is loosely called. It is important to attend to these critics, even if only to conclude that, if we followed them, we should be deprived of many of the most penetrating intimations of God and the soul of man.

The critics of "spirituality" have a strong case: [Here Demant references two works of P. T. Forsyth. One is *Faith, Freedom, and the Future* in which Forsyth argues for how the church can both confront and learn from what he calls the "Gnosticism of to-day."[4] The second is Forsyth's work, *The Justification of God*. Demant includes this quote:] "The first falsity was the substitution of religion for God, of spiritual attainment for searching humility; of an egoist piety for a sympathetic faith with the self-distrust of one whose foot nearly slips."[5]

[At this point, Demant has a reference to the article by D. M. Baille.[6] In this article Baille reflects on the complex relationship of the freedom of the will to human nature. He muses on the religious concerns of the Reformers, who felt that humans often want to do the right thing, but cannot do so. He concludes the article by identifying different meanings of freedom. Baille then suggests the following "simple truths" emerge. The first is that the "freedom of the will does not mean sheer indetermination."[7] The second is that the "freedom of the will which we all possess does not necessarily carry with it the *ability* to do or to be what we ought to do or to be."[8] The third is the need for grace. Grace is the vehicle that enables us to do what is right—to love our neighbor as ourselves. For Demant, this article captures much of the paradox of this lecture. We all struggle to do the right thing, but find it so difficult. With God's grace, we are able to be transformed such that we then learn how to do the right thing.]

[Demant here references H. A. Oberman's text on Archbishop Thomas Bradwardine.[9] One aspect of Bradwardine's views that Oberman analyzes is the topic of free will. Oberman argues that Bradwardine was not a determinist, however he also believed man's free will had been compromised by the fall. Thus, "the free will, for example, can be confused, confined, yes even

---

4. Forsyth, *Faith, Freedom and the Future*, 25.
5. Forsyth, *The Justification of God*, 115ff.
6. See Baille, "Philosophers & Theologians on the Freedom."
7. Ibid., 119.
8. Ibid., 120.
9. Oberman, *Archbishop Thomas Bradwardine*.

temporarily lost, when desire sends man into a rage."[10] At the same time, free will still remains as part of human nature. Now, though, "the Fall has so deeply cut into the structure of the human soul that God's aid is indispensable for the will to arrive at a right choice."[11] Similarly to the Baille article above, this text reflects Demant's argument that God's grace is necessary in the development of the unaided will.][12]

10. Ibid., 68.
11. Ibid.
12. Demant includes a final note to himself: "Further notes to be added."

Series I, Lecture VI
Secularization

WE WHO LIVE IN the West tend to take for granted that division of life into the religious and secular, which has marked out intellectual and spiritual history, and therefore assume that it is the normal condition confronting the human mind. The problems raised by this division have been so much part of the material on which the western mind has worked—wrestling with them has been almost the very stuff of Christianity, *in via*, that we cannot easily perceive it as the result of a very specialized historical development, a unique and peculiar phenomenon in man's career on earth, and what must appear like an aberration from the point of view of the wider religious life of the race.

This fact, that a division between the two parts of life can be accepted by us western minds without any sense of incongruity—with the idea that a religious view can, but need not, be added to a secular interpretation which would remain what it was if religion were eliminated—has struck certain historians of human culture and students of religion as something which requires accounting for. But it has not, so far as I am aware, received much attention from the theologian as such; and I wish here to indicate some of the questions which such a theological attempt would have to face.

We have to deal with two things. One is the fact, just noted, but only occasionally discerned, that a recognition of a secular order, with its own validity distinct from the religious, has been peculiar to Christendom. I use the word Christendom for all its ambiguity for a pattern of society, intellectual outlooks, and emotional dispositions formed by a culture in which the religious element has been Christian; I use the word Christendom in one of the two senses which Herbert Butterfield gives to Christianity, in the early part of his *Christianity in European History*. It is not to be equated with a morally perfect society or the redeemed community. Only in Christendom have we this phenomenon of a secular order recognized as having autonomy accorded to it by the theological as well as by the secular intellectual traditions.

The second thing to be considered is the rise of powerful and widespread accounts of man and the world since the seventeenth century which are avowedly secularist. Secularism in this sense is an omnibus term to describe movements of thought and philosophy which have been antireligious. They would account for all the facts of human existence and the world process, in terms of the secular order only. They deny the existence of a supernatural or eternal reality behind the temporal order—and they deny that any sphere of being has a sacred, mysterious and holy character. What is more, they often regard these marks of the religious outlook not only as illusory, but as harmful. This criticism takes two forms which have very often been allied together. In one, belief in a transcendent; divine or sacred reality is regarded as intellectually pernicious; in the other it is held to be an obstacle to good morals and to social betterment, a bulwark of reaction, especially in the matter of improving man's lot on earth. The outstanding expression of this criticism for a century has been the Marxist criticism of religion; but it was held, with more agnosticism than dogmatic atheism, by G. J. Holyoake, who in the following of Robert Owen, led the formation of a movement specifically known as Secularism in nineteenth-century England. Its passion was social rather than intellectual. Unconcerned with the unseen world rather than denying it, Holyoake put down both theism and atheism as "over-beliefs"—a term which is an almost exact rendering of what Tacitus called *superstitio*—a quite unnecessary and dissipating addition to *religio*—the social bond of the tribe.

This was a short lived form of secularism, though it survives in ethical humanists today. It is significant however as exemplifying a general truth, namely that secularism is never just a philosophy or theory of what is—with religion left out. It nearly always assumes the character of an alternative faith, geared to some notion of human or social salvation. Why this comes about is of interest to the theologian, for it could be included among the human movements, which a line of Christian teachers from Augustine to Bernard, Aquinas and Dante, have attributed to man's need of God in his being, operating as a tug upon him even when his consciousness is unaware of it. In this way, secularism in the end takes on a religious flavor.

Judged theologically, secularism has taken two forms of expression. It has meant an account of existence which dismisses any transcendent or eternal realm; this is a doctrine of pure immanence in the sense that all the forces of which it takes notice are forces immanent in the world process. But in the second place, the predominant emphasis in a secularist view has been a dismissal of any sacred element in existence, a sphere of reality which demands an approach of humility, penitence, awe, reverence for the mysterious and the holy. Although secularism in the second sense—regarding everything as profane, has nearly always gone hand in hand with secularism in the first sense—the doctrine of pure immanence—the two are not necessarily connected together; their relation is somewhat ambiguous and paradoxical. The effect, for instance, perhaps almost the motive—of the Reformation upon its adherent's outlook was to abolish the distinction between sacred and secular spheres of life and to make man's secular occupation as much a vocation under God as the practice of religion. But the Reformation held firmly and gave its own intransigent emphasis to the divine transcendence and grace. All that Calvin needs is logic and the divine omnipotence; all sins become crimes, and all crimes sins. The paradox is that this stalwart attempt to make the world *churchly* worked out in practice in making the church *worldly*. For in a night, as it were, a somersault was performed by many men of Calvinistic upbringing like Althusius, Grotius, and Locke—who woke up the next morning having dropped out the divine omnipotence as an effective factor in the affairs of men and proceeded to give birth to the greatest naturalist interpretations of existence in history.

But this is taking us too far afield. My point was that an overcoming of the tension between sacred and secular spheres did not at first, in this case, mean a denial of divine transcendence—whatever its ironical consequences may have been.

On the other hand, an outlook or doctrine which accepts only the temporal order as real, does not thereby get rid of the need for a sacred realm—in the end it gives a sacred value to some element in man's nature like his reason or vitality, or to some group consciousness or social program—hence the twentieth century pseudo-religions of a messianic state or race or class.

My thesis is that these things are bound to happen if the theological account of existence is the true one. In brief, just because in this account there is a transcendent divine being and only there is the sacred or holy to be found (and this is biblical religion), also because Christian theology with its Bible has served to give religious warrant to a secular sphere of life along with a sacred realm, therefore a doctrine of pure immanence (of the world process as total reality) is in a sense a Christian heresy. And, what is more, secularism is compelled by the nature of man to become at some point a pseudo-religion, giving sacred values to something creaturely, namely to become idolatrous.

THE EMERGENCE OF THE SECULAR

I have now to substantiate my statement that the duality of sacred and secular is, in its serious form, a phenomenon of Christendom. It is not an original discovery on my part and I have only to offer a number of spotlights on different phases of the history of Christian outlooks, and I use the word outlook rather than thought because we are concerned with dispositions and presuppositions which, while they give a bent to the mind, are not the result of its intellectual explorations alone. These spotlights are directed to elements in our religious and cultural tradition to which I have been directed by a number of writers, only a few of whom have had any direct theological interest. I confine myself to three main factors: the outlook expressed in the biblical doctrine of creation, the effect of Christianity in political and cultural history, and the effect of these two things upon spheres of knowledge.

It has been pointed out that the relation of God and the world implied in the Bible is a peculiar one among the religions of the world. The world is of God, but the world is not God. It is a creation and therefore significant, but the key to its significance is not in itself. The created order is not a regrettable lapse or an illusion or a bad joke, nor is it the expression of negation and evil. Aldous Huxley rejects biblical and Christian theology for this very reason and finds a more satisfying religion in the eastern systems. "Creation," he writes, "the incomprehensible passage from the unmanifested One into the manifest multiplicity of nature, from eternity into time, is not merely the prelude and necessary condition of the Fall; to some extent it is the Fall. This is clearly stated, he adds, in the Buddhist and Hindu renderings of the perennial philosophy."[1] Huxley has seen the point of biblical doctrine, if only to reject it; the Creation is a significant reality other than God.

But that is only the major premise, as it were, of the doctrine. The minor premise is stated for us by the late professor and Mrs. Frankfort in their description of the mental revolution brought about by the Greeks and Hebrews in comparison with the religion of the ancient empires. "The difference between the Egyptians and Mesopotamian manners of viewing the world are very far reaching. Yet the two peoples agreed in the fundamental assumptions that the individual is part of society, that society is embedded in nature, and that nature is but the manifestation of the divine. This doctrine was in fact universally accepted by the peoples of the ancient worlds with the single exception of the Hebrews."[2]

---

1. Taylor, *Faith of a Moralist*, 20.
2. Frankfort, *Before Philosophy*, 241.

"The dominant tenet of Hebrew thought is the absolute transcendence of God—the LORD is not in nature. Neither earth, nor sun, nor heaven is divine; even the most potent of natural phenomenon are but reflections of God's greatness."[3] It is in the light of this outlook, that we must give the emphasis an inference in the term "declare" of the Nineteenth Psalm: "the heavens *declare* the glory of God." "He is Holy . . . all values are attributable to God alone. Hence, all concrete phenomena are devaluated"—valueless before God.[4] The same goes for the social order as for nature. God created the existing social order, but this order does not derive any sacredness, any value from its divine origin and certainly no permanence. The Frankforts conclude: "Only a God who transcends every phenomenon, who is not conditioned by any mode of manifestation; only an unqualified God can be the one and only ground of *all* existence."[5] This view, they deduce, means that the Hebrew created the myth of all the will of God and the poignant doctrine of a chosen people, and history becomes a revelation of the dynamic will of God. "Man is possessed of a new freedom and a new burden" (and, we might add, a perpetual bad conscience).[6] "With infinite moral courage the Hebrews worshipped an absolute God and accepted as a correlate of this faith the sacrifice of an harmonious existence," *eudaimonia*.[7]

From another angle A. N. Whitehead, in *Adventures of Ideas*, saw that the doctrine of creation has a metaphysical effect. In contrast to Plato's view that the world contains only secondary substitutes or imitations, Christian theology with its Bible provided a doctrine of reality and significance for the plurality of created substances (though Whitehead somewhat misleadingly calls this a direct doctrine of immanence). And in the same vein the philosopher Collingwood, in what some have considered one of his most paradoxical utterances, has declared that the article of faith "God created the world" meant that the idea of a world of nature is an absolute presupposition of natural science, and that natural science would never have arisen on the scale and with the thoroughness which it has without an outlook represented in the presuppositions of the *Quinque Vult*. If I may venture an interpretation of this tantalizingly brief essay: it would mean that attention to the natural world is only possible on the fiduciary basis that the world is a universe, and that the principle of its unity is not in any of its constituent parts but transcends it. For if the principle of unity were in any of the

3. Ibid.
4. Ibid., 242.
5. Ibid., 369.
6. Ibid., 370.
7. Ibid., 373.

constituent parts then it would not be a world open to indefinite discovery. It is only thus open in an intellectual culture wherein the unity of things is taken for granted and therefore men can be chiefly interested in their manyness. This, Collingwood suggests, is our situation in the West; it is not natural to man or to philosophers; it is our situation because of the metaphysical revolution brought about by the outlook represented theologically in the Bible and Christian doctrine of creation.

This is jumping to conclusions, but conclusions about which I am sufficiently sure to wish that much more study could be given to this aspect of the fiduciary nature of the presuppositions of science, which apart from minor Chinese and Arabian developments, has been mainly a western affair. This however is only one aspect of the wider process which I am seeking to identify, the process which carried into the western mind outlooks congruous with, if not always derived from, the biblical doctrine of the nature of the world. This outlook gave religious and intellectual backing to the treatment of the secular order as something with its own validity and significance, a significance which could be explored without referring it at every point to its divine source.

The second main influence making in the same direction is the course of political and cultural history since the advent of Christianity. For one thing Christianity, along with the religion of the Hebrews, is the least cultural of all world religions, that is least tied to a particular social and cultural configuration; and it spread over various cultural groupings without being tied to any of them. This meant that the political and social life of communities in which the church ministered had to find their own principles of guidance not directly imposed from religious sanctions. In other words, Christianity encouraged the growth of secular spheres.

This has been most obvious in the political and social aspect. By its very nature as a supernatural and translocal religion, it served to make a bond of union between its members who belonged to a large variety of historical communities, political set-ups, and cultural backgrounds. These distinctions were never completely eliminated and Christianity could not ever inaugurate a totalitarian theocracy. While it provided a religious and ecclesiastical unity across natural and historically grown boundaries, by this very fact it brought about a duality within each social and cultural area, into the very substance of society. This is why Ernest Renan could say that European civilization has its key text in the distinction between the things that belong to God and the things that belong to Caesar; but of course, theology had to come to some doctrine which declared that the things of Caesar and other spheres of the secular order were also things of God, but in another mode than the religious. By and large this duality meant that a Christian who belongs, say to Corinth or Rome in the fourth century, or to Paris or Norwich in the fourteenth century had to maintain a link and allegiance both to his local community and government, and to a church which overarched all other divisions. I am not now recounting the interesting story of how this duality meant that man's obligations to his temporal community was not supreme and embracing. I am seeking to indicate the other side of this influence, how it made for an independent secular ordering of society. The tension of church and state is but one aspect of it; and Mr. Christopher Dawson has spent a lifetime showing that European society has been very deeply characterized by the fact that the religious, the political, and the cultural spheres of life have had to try to find a *modus vivendi* without being merged in a Unitarian sacred structure.

The secular part of life has perforce always had to be allowed for in Christian history, but not always consciously or theologically. But when the mood of a warfare between faith and the world expressed in the *Dies Irae*, "*solvet saeclum in favilla*," was displaced by the mood represented by St. Francis's *Hymn of Creation*, and when between about 1200 and 1500 the secular was pardoned, rediscovered, and restored, this was but the working out of the logic of Christian theology from the first. As soon as Christianity rejected the heathen idea of God as the soul of the world, you had an outlook which could give theological respectability to an autonomous secularity; and Christendom has had the recurring problem of retaining the duality without making two entirely different worlds; in other words, the problem of never confounding the powers nor dividing the substance of life.

One interesting phase of this story is the reality accorded by the scholastic to secondary causes. The thesis that natural things are not causes, writes Aquinas in *De Potentia*, implies that God effects everything by himself alone. This is clearly contrary to experience so that in *Contra Gentiles* he writes, "The causation of lower effects should not be attributed to divine power as to abolish the causality of lower causes."[8] This emphasis (with its battle against occasionalism, the doctrine that natural causes are not real causes but only occasions of divine causality) clearly supported the scientific enterprise which could not proceed if everything had to be referred to the first cause, God.

And then there is Berdyaev's insistence that that form of secularism which led to a mechanistic conception of nature was one of the secondary results of man's Christian liberation from demonolatry. "I am convinced," he writes, .

---

8. Aquinas, *Contra Gentiles* III.69.

that Christianity alone made possible both positive science and technique... When immersed in nature and communing with its inner life, and while living in fear of demons—man could neither apprehend the world scientifically nor master it technically. Christianity (by the discovery of the soul) had freed him from subjection to nature and has set him up spiritually in the centre of the created world. This anthropocentric feeling had been foreign to the man of classical activity... Christianity alone inspired man with the anthropocentric feeling which became the fundamental motivating power of modern times. It made modern history with all its contradictions possible.[9]

We might also consider Karl Jaspers guesses in his chapter on science and technology in *The Origin and Goal of History*.

I have spent some time in establishing the generalization that it is the doctrine and ethos of Christianity which has given rise to the idea of the secular—and of course always in a certain relation to its co-reality, the transcendent, the divine and the sacred realm. What then of "secularism," that group of anti-religious theories and movements which have deliberately attacked religious belief? It is the result of the mind giving exclusive reality to that part of life which Christianity has liberated from the sacred sphere. I have hinted that this process was not always just a piece of intellectual arrogance, it was often prompted by a spirit of revolt against the past for practical and humanitarian reasons. But secularism must be put down as a bastard and rebellious child of Christendom. It gets its name from a term which had been given a theological significance by ecclesiastical thought itself. The secular denoted that which belongs to this age, aeon, this *saeculum* as distinguished from that which is eternal and which makes its mark on the temporal order through a churchly and sacred order on earth. Secularism treats this temporal order as the whole of reality. Its name is legion for it has many forms. But let us glance at modern secularism.

I referred earlier to the fact that secularism is now acquiring religious overtones. Dictatorial regimes have all the formal characteristics of a totalitarian theocracy with God left out. They have their priesthoods, inquisitions, their holy of holies, and a messianic sense that they represent the one righteous people in an otherwise doomed world. Anglings for position and power have to be represented as battles of light against darkness, holiness against absolute evil, and the rules of morality do not apply. And no sphere of life, neither science nor art, nor education, nor literature, nor law, had

9. Berdyaev, *The Meaning of History*.

better be allowed its autonomy. Instead, these must serve the new secular priesthood.

We do not have it in this form in our country but there is a tendency in the same direction. Universal compulsory education cannot help inculcating some form of faith. Furthermore, political debates are less a business-like discussion of how to run a country and are becoming issues of moral judgement. Politicians tend to talk as at a prayer meeting. This general development in the twentieth century means that in one sense Christian history has come around a full circle. The last three centuries preached secularism by making absolute and exclusive and outlook that made room for and nourished a Christian ethos, while rejecting the sacred realms which were its counterweight in that tradition. But this modern period only for a short span got rid of the tension between these two realms. After three centuries, it has now transferred that tension to within the secular order itself.

Man's loss of religion has therefore been tragic, not because it was apostasy but because it was self-negation. He tried to get free from the problem of living in two worlds and from the wars of religion. He sought one world, safe, unfanatical, and scientific. And now he runs into the wards of the pseudo-religious, conflict between secular orders each claiming absolute and sacred pretensions. For human nature (if Christianity is true) needs a holy community and if man does not find it in God and the church, he will seek to fashion one that is wider than the sect and deeper and richer than the state.

What I mean by arriving full circle, I will describe by means of an analogy, which I will ask you not to treat too seriously. It is drawn from the relation of the sexes. There is a form of life in which there is no bi-sexuality (termites and what not).[10] So, there is a large part of human history covering both tribal and civilized cultures, where there is no difference between secular and religious spheres. That is the case in primitive peoples, in the Oriental societies, in the ancient empires, and in a less absolute form in the Hebrew church and state.

Christianity, with its supernaturally rooted and translocal church, and with its biblical doctrine, brought about a duality between religious and secular, analogous to that of female and male in bi-sexual situation of certain living things. This duality was not by any means a dualism, though at certain points there were open and deep clashes. In the first three centuries of the Christian era there was meeting and often conflict, but no agreements. Then perhaps the period from Constantine to the end of the eighth century is

---

10. Demant uses the term "bi-sexuality" to mean a situation or species in which there are two sexes.

like the period of engagement between a young woman and a young man. The epoch from Charlemagne to the fifteenth century is represented in my analogy by marriage, with its harmonies and strains, and the mutual interactions of the forces of unity keeping the couple together.

With the sixteenth century begins an era of divorce. Here, our analogy becomes confusing. For while the workaday world finds more purely secular modes of guidance, and spheres of knowledge acquire their independence from mother theology, religion becomes more inward and moralizing after the secular events instead of directing it, churches more introverted and apart. At the same time, there were moves to give the secular state some of the sacred and eternal attributes before belonging to the church. But on the whole the fruitful duality of religion and secular spheres gradually ceased to operate because of a divorce between them. This situation could go on so long as there was an underlying unity of social and spiritual culture. But when this had worn thin, mainly in the course of the nineteenth century, with the disintegrating effects of a complete divorce between the religious and moral traditions on the one hand and the secular and scientific on the other, the twentieth-century predicament was in the making. The soul of modern man seems unable to overcome that divorce by a recovery of the fruitful tension between religious and secular and has perforce to strive to reach an identification of the two. Hence the idolatries signified by the sacred value given to secular movements.

In other words, men today are seeking to return to the hermaphrodite condition. The whole span of Christian history has made a circle. Again, theology has the task of assessing this process, which seems to come to this. The contemporary mind knows no way of overcoming the dissociation of religious and secular, without reverting to the pre-Christian fusion of the two.

Series I, Lecture VII
Being and Becoming

When Christian worshippers sing hymns like, "Change and decay in all around I see, O Thou that changest not abide with me," or "A few more years shall roll," or "Time like an every rolling stream bears all its sons away," they are voicing one aspect of the consciousness of the deleterious nature of change and time, which in its own way the Christian gospel turns into a hope. It is to be found in the New Testament, not only in the Fourth Gospel, where "eternal life"—independent of time, becomes tacitly as the Johannine synonym for the Synoptic Kingdom of God—but also in other parts of the New Testament writings like 1 Peter—who closes his first chapter:

> You were not redeemed with corruptible things, but with the precious blood of Christ, He indeed was foreordained before the foundation of the world, but was manifest in these last times for you... Having been born again, not of corruptible seed, but of incorruptible, by the word of God, which liveth and abideth for ever. for [Isaiah] all flesh is as grass, and all the glory of man as the flower of grass. The grass withereth, and the flower thereof falleth away: But the word of the Lord endureth for ever. And this is the word which by the gospel is preached unto you.[1]

Thus, Christianity calls the eternal divine ground, to which the believer is linked in a bond of faith, by the personal name of God as Father of the Lord Jesus Christ. This identification of what the Greek mind called "eternity" and disfigured from time, marks off the Judaic Christian religion from all others, in that whatever there may be of "being" and "becoming" in the cosmic and historical order, the divine source is not namely one of them. He is the Lord of the being of things and of the becoming that makes them come into existence and pass away, and of the becoming that makes history

---

1. 1 Peter 1: 18–25.

a one dimensional movement never repeating itself—and moreover gave history a meaning in terms of an event, the Christ event, which cuts across the time dimension from another.[2]

The other world pictures either take becoming in endless cycles for granted—and ask to put men in touch with the religious source to escape from the unrealities of time; or conceive a timeless reality of eternal ideas as the sole reality of which the moving processes of nature and history are the moving image, to recall the famous platonic notion; or they hold with modern thought that there is nothing existent but the moving flux of history with no central measuring point anywhere to interpret the process, not beginning, or end, or middle.

The early religions are marked by rituals which express a movement in which men join themselves with the creative source of things—the chaos out of which the world was formed—they perform actions which re-enact creation; they endow buildings and places with "soul" that make them permanent. Acts and objects are real and enduring in so far as they initiate a divine archetype. Sacrifices are make for the abolition of time by repetition of paradigmatic actions in which profane time and duration are suspended; the New Year is a repetition of creation—a return to the beginning.

All this, described by Mircea Eliade in *The Myth of the Eternal Return* and *Trante de l'histoire des Religions*, is well known. In India this theory of the periodic destruction and creation of the universe has its most arduous form. Each sub-cycle is called a "yuga" preceded by a dawn and a dusk. A complete cycle Mahayuga is made up of the yugas, and the last sub-cycle is always marked by catastrophe. As Mahayuga lasts 12,000 years it might not seem to matter much, but the Hindu mind had a way of reconciling itself to this seeming futility of endless cycles in a way which the pridic myths (emanating from another branch of Indu-Sumerian stock) did not end by conflagration and incarnation. The reconciling principle was Karma, accounting for the individual in his successive life spans by a moral causality. This is found to be an unsupportable claim of existence, and the Buddhist and Jainist find a religion which breaks the claim of existences by the abolition of human existence and the achievement of Nirvana—undifferentiated being (not nothingness). "It is that wiser process, not the chain of activities

---

2. The editors believe this paragraph to be an expansion of Demant's note, which preceded it: "NOTE: overcoming—transience, false glories, sin who masters history, touch with eternal, enduring forever, How by fruits of his lover out of God and Jesus Christ. The Christ event. Preordained—now last times. New Creation. Date of new birth."

and events in the outside world, that constitutes the true history of the individual."[3]

Confucianism reconciles itself to time by stressing the importance of the unbroken family chain. But by the reincarnation of the ancestral family down through the ages the endless continuity of time is transcended by the fact that one and the same ancestral family is ever present. Chinese literature is replete with "annuals," but not history in our sense. The Taoist, has a more empirical philosophy than the Confucian—nearer to nature and less naturalistic. The Taoist sage penetrates the illusion a futility of all human doings which result from the interplay of opposites—they meet and cancel each other. To know this is to be united to the Tao. This means that doing is as not doing—the devotee operates without effort—good and bad, heavenly and ugliness, peace and war, every pair of opposites loses its meaning. Man rises above time disregarding it—he is thus in one sense outside time and outside impermanence—by not being involved in their demands. This Chinese thought neutralizes the lasting power of time.

The two great western contrasts to these Eastern attitudes are the Greek and the Christian, Judaic and Persian. Note that archaic man's aversion to time, meant aversion to nature time and historic time—that as to the impermanence of man's terrestrial participation in the cycle of nature—both growth, age and death—and the ruthless march of history especially its indifference to peoples upset or destroyed by conquests, migrations, empire building, colonization and political subservience and economic domination.

The Greeks were most concerned with the transience of nature and man's share in that transience. The Hebrews were interested in the baffling catastrophes of history. They were the people who set out to give value to history, and such a history—one should have perhaps some feeling for the multitude who felt that the prophets' message to accept that history came from the Lord was a steep and hard one. No wonder they hankered to return to Baal worship, which in tune with the older religious culture surrendered them to nature and nature time.

For the Hebrews every historic crisis, calamities especially, were acts of God connecting his people. They brought the people back to the true God—after peaceful times had tempted them back to the nature religions (negative theophanies). The prophets thus gave nature to history; events have a significance in the measure as they are determining the will of God. He is a personality who intervenes ceaselessly in history. History becomes an epiphany of the Lord and with this comes the dogma of the salvation of

---

3. Here Demant includes the note: "(Haas 4)."

time. The future regenerates time—it acquires an eschatological meaning. The Hebrew worldview sees the whole of history as having a beginning and an end. Instead of periodic act of overcoming faces of chaos and change, it posits one renewal in the end of the times. Historic events are accepted because, for one thing, they are evidence of God, for another because they are necessary for the final consummations.[4]

Notice, that while the Hebrew prophetic elite accepts the march of history as against repetitive and cyclical reason, it is in the end not a pure acceptance of history and time. While they do not seek to guide or abolish history periodically, they accept it in the hope that this will definitely cease some moment more or less distant. The irreversibility of historic events and of time is compensated by the limitations of history to time; in other words, the older periodic regeneration of creation is replaced by a unique regeneration which will take place in the time to come. But the acceptance of the end of history is still an anti-historic attitude in common with the older archaic conceptions.

In the Christian religion, which introduces another complication into these two traditions, the Adriatic and Judaic, there is still an adherence to repetitive religious acts. The Christian liturgical year is a periodic re-enactment of the nativity, passion, death and resurrection of Jesus, with all that this drama implies for the believer; it implies at least the personal and cosmic regeneration of the concrete re-actualization of the birth, death and resurrection of the Savior. But it is a unique once for all historic event that is there reenacted: and that event is somehow connected within the overcoming of time and history—it reenacts creation and anticipates the end of the world. It declares thereby that history and time are not the all in all—there is a para-temporal reality which gives history a meaning: and there is much theological discussion still going on about this.[5]

Let us consider two phases of this discussion. The early Christian theologians—forced to say something of the para-temporal transcendent nature of the Christian and biblical God who is Lord over but not involved in the vicissitudes of history—found the Greek conception of "eternity" a useful one, and were supported by many biblical phrases translated "eternal" in our

---

4. Following this paragraph, Demant includes the note: "Prophets and elite." This is developed in the next paragraph.

5. For instance, see the compilation of contemporary discussion in the pamphlet, Eschatology and Ethics, compiled A. Schweitzer, trans. R. H. Fuller (Ecumenical Studies No. A 3/4—November 1951).

English Bibles. For example, "Thou art the same and thy years shall not fail,"[6] and, "He sitteth between the Cherubim, be the earth never so unquiet."[7]

The Johannine doctrine of eternal life delineates the nature of God as a quality independent of time and circumstance, as well as the state of salvation for the believer who, in trust, can appropriate its quality. "The Realized Eschatology of Eastern Modern Theologies" is a statement of this faith. It was the primary interest of F. D. Maurice in the last century.[8] He was dismissed from Professorship of Pastoral Theology at Kings College London, for teaching that eternal and everlasting were not the same, and that after death man's existence is in a sense timeless. Therefore neither heaven or hell could be conceived as endless bliss or torment. It was especially its consequences for the doctrine of hell that concerned Maurice and his opponents. He believed in Hell as eternal loss of God, but not as unending fire.

[Niebuhr says of this, "With universality, Maurice mated the idea of eschatological immediacy. Eternity meant for him, as for John, the dimension of divine working, not the negation of time. As creation was the eternal, not the pretemporal work of God, so redemption also meant what God-in-Christ does in that eternal working that ever stands over against man's temporal action. The eternal does not cancel man's past, present, and future; neither is it dependent on one of these: God was and is and is to come; He reigns and He will reign."[9]][10]

You can read of this controversy in the *Life and Letters of F. D. Maurice*, edited by his son, and in the present Archbishop of York's book, *F. D. Maurice and the Conflicts of Modern Theology*.[11] His teaching was welcome to many. But now in this century comes Professor Oscar Cullmann telling us that there is no warrant in the Bible for eternity in the sense of timeless in God. Here is his own summary:

> The unique element in the Christian conception of time as the scene of redemptive history is of a two fold character . . . In the first place, salvation is bound to a continuous time process which embraces past, present, and future. Revelation and salvation take place along the course of an ascending time line.

---

6. Psalm 120:27, Coverdale trans.

7. Psalm 99:1, Coverdale trans.

8. Here Demant includes a note, developed by the editors in the next paragraph: "Richard Niebuhr Christ and Culture."

9. Niebuhr, *Christ and Culture*, 227.

10. This text is an expansion of Demant's reference to Niebuhr's *Christ and Culture*.

11. Cf. Maurice, *The Life of Frederick Denison Maurice*, and Ramsey, *F. D. Maurice and the Conflicts of Modern Theology*.

> Here the strictly straight-line conception of time in the New Testament must be defined as over against the Greek cyclical conception and over against all metaphysics in which salvation is always available in the "beyond," and we must show how according to the Primitive Christian view revelation and salvation actually "occur" in a connected manner during the continuous time process."[12]

In the second place, it is characteristic of this estimate of time as the scene of redemptive history that all points of this redemptive line are related to the one historical fact at the mid-point, a fact which precisely in its unrepeatable character, which marks all historical events, is decisive for salvation. This fact is the death and resurrection of Jesus Christ ... the different individual sections of the whole line are constantly determined from this mid-point, but yet have their own significance in time."[13]

Cullmann speaks of infinite time as God's time, distinguished from limited time which is man's time. We cannot pursue this debate any further, but I might indicate how I see a possible interpretation which allows for both the reality of history and time in Christian redemptive theology and a Christian usage of the conception of eternity which is above time.

[Here Demant references his own book, *The Religious Prospect*, in which he writes that there is eternity, meaning timelessness, in God. And the significance of the incarnation is that this eternity enters into time. "The dogma that God delivers His decisive word about the created human world in a concrete historic act of Incarnation gives each event of history a significance in relation to the Eternal, to its relation to that singular event."[14]

To illustrate what this timelessness of God means, Demant quotes Boethius's famous definition of the relationship between the eternal and the temporal:

> That which embraces and possesses the whole plenitude of unlimited life at once, from which nought of the future is absent, from which nought of the past has flowed away, that is rightly deemed eternal ... this unmoving present state of life is imitated by that infinite movement of the things of time; which, since it cannot express and equal the other, lapses from immobility into action, and from the simplicity of the present, tails off into an infinite quantity of future and past; and since it cannot possess the whole plenitude of its life at once, from the mere fact of, in a sort

---

12. Cullmann, *Christ and Time*, 32.
13. Ibid., 32–33.
14. Demant, *Religious Prospect*, 219.

of sense, never ceasing to be, seems in a way to rival that which it cannot fill out and express; binding itself to the presentness, such as it is, of this thin and fleeting moment, which presentness gives a semblance of being to such things as it attaches itself to. Since then it could not abide, it set out upon the infinite path of time, and so it came about that it stretched out by giving that life the plenitude of which it could not grasp by staying.[15]

This particular quality of eternity is evident in Dante's vision when he "sees all things in their relative differences, yet no longer as broken fragments but as forming together a single whole."[16]]

This understanding of God as being para-temporal and outside of time, while also entering into time and affecting temporal events is a unique element of Christian theology. For the Incarnation presupposed the doctrine of creation, which, on the one hand, forbids the eternal element in the Godhead being explained away in the process of mere becoming, and, on the other hand, insists that the concrete world process and each event in it are of divine significance and value.

15. Boethius, *Consolation of Philosophy*, Book V, quoted in *Religious Prospect*, 245–6.
16. Demant, *Religious Prospect*, 247.

Series I, Chapter VIII
Gender

THERE ARE FOUR MAIN reasons why I, as a Christian theologian, think it is high time to collect some considerations which may lead to the development of a doctrine of gender. By gender I mean that main divisions of things into masculine and feminine which has become so much part of our human thought and language. The four main reasons are these. First, not much has been contributed by the literature of Christian theology to an understanding of the place of gender in the created world, although much has been said about man and woman, and about the sexual nature of every human being. Only occasionally has devotion and speculation enquired how far this division into masculine and feminine runs in the universe, and whether in any sense it runs into the Godhead itself.

What is the significance of the almost exclusively masculine terminology of the Christian Trinity? How does Christianity stand in this in the light of other religious systems which the comparative studies of religion has disclosed? Why has the Christian priesthood been essentially a male vocation? And is there any genuine religious urge behind the pressure in the Roman Catholic world to push up the Virgin Mary to the very border-line between the Creator and Redeemer on the one hand and the creaturely existence which needs salvation on the other; a pressure which comes not from the authority at the top but from the worshipping multitude in the churches. In brief, how does the relation of God and the world look when we try to assess the enormous place which gender occupies in the created order-

The second reason, is that the relation of man and woman in the history of Christendom presents a number of puzzles and paradoxes which are interesting to explore. The same St. Paul who is often regarded as having a low estimate of woman, certainly said that in Christ there is neither male nor female,[1] while Christ had repeated the Genesis statement: male and female he created them. The same Christian religion which in many ways repressed natural relation of the sexes, makes marriage a sacrament. The same tradition which kept woman subordinate to man, has almost served to exalt women and make some pictures of sanctity almost over-feminine. The curious phenomenon of "courtly love" which introduces the romantic love into the man-woman relations, appeared in the Christian Middle Ages, and this romantic love was later introduced into the marriage ideal, and possibly overdone. And now we have recently had a big theological debate about two kinds of love, *agape* and *eros*, which has led religious thinkers to work out the possible connection between these two kinds of human love and the distinctive features of masculine and feminine love. These puzzles will occupy our second lecture.

The third reason for my concern with this question is that of course we have what is called a sex and marriage problem today. The traditional order in these matters is being seriously disturbed by the frequency of marriage breakdowns, changes in sex custom, and the suspicions of an increase in homosexuality (sexual attachment to persons of the same sex). The general bewilderment on these questions is due, in my opinion, to taking too narrow and isolated a view of the relation of men and women in sex, love, and marriage and not seeing these in the larger frame of gender. To examine the marriage problem as if it were merely a sex problem; or the love relation as if it were merely a romantic attachment, is to ignore the theological truth of each person's relation to God, society, and one's lifework.

In the fourth place, there are strong reasons for the guess that our western civilization is in danger of extinction from an overdevelopment of characteristics which have been, wisely or mistakenly attributed to male attitudes and outlooks, to the neglect of the feminine ones. And this question is mightily complicated by the suspicion that the so-called feminist movement is part of the masculine disease and not a counterweight to it. The psychologists have their say about this; and I shall try in the last lecture to relate it to a turning point in the career of Christendom, and by Christendom I do not mean the church, or a perfected society, or the redeemed community, but a culture running from the eighth century to the twentieth, in which the social pattern has been very deeply impressed by Christian outlooks, habits, and convictions.

---

1. Galatians 3:28.

THE POLARITY OF MASCULINE AND FEMININE

By gender, I mean that mysterious relation of powers, of which sex is the biological expression. The relation has often been described as one of polarity, like the positive and negative in electricity (positive and negative being quite conventional terms without any suggestion of relative value), or like the north and south poles of the earth's structure. The idea is that where there is one there must be the other like the two ends of a stick, which are on the same plane and yet are in a sense opposites. But where the poles are forces and not just positions, there is a tension which seems due to the fact that they can never be completely separated or completely fused in one.

Many thinkers, profound and superficial, have sought to find this principle of polarity at work through almost all levels of existence. Among the better superficial expressions of it we may take R. W. Emerson's essay on *Compensation*. In it he writes,

> Polarity, or action and reaction, we meet in every part of nature, in darkness and light; in male and female; in the inspiration and expiration of plants and animals; in the equation of quantity and quality in the fluids of the animal body; in the systole and diastole of the heart; in the undulations of fluids and of sound; in the centrifugal and centripetal gravity; in electricity, galvanism, and chemical affinity. Superinduce magnetism at one end of a needle; the opposite magnetism takes place at the other end. If the south attracts, the north repels. To empty here, you must condense there. An inevitable dualism bisects nature, so that each thing is a half, and suggests another thing to make it whole; as spirit, matter; man, woman; odd, even; subjective, objective; in, out; upper, under; motion, rest; yea, nay.[2]

There is some hit and miss in these pairs of Emerson. Let us list some of the polarities which have been considered by thinkers or assumed by others, before we enquire how this principle of polarity looks in the light of Christian theology. They fall into the two main groups: describing one, aspects of reality; two, powers or aspects of human nature. In each pair I shall name first the pole generally or often regarded as the feminine, and second the masculine, but I have to warn you that the first four pairs can be changed round from one gender to the other. You will find opposite positions taken by two recent writers on the subject: Geoffrey Sainsbury's *Theory of Polarity* and Lawrence Hyde's *An Introduction to Organic Philosophy* and "An Essay on the Reconciliation of the Masculine and Feminine Principles."

---

2. Emerson, *Essays*, 53.

Sainsbury puts under feminine and masculine such pairs as space, time; existence, change; substance, motion; base, acid; passivity, energy; economy, extravagance; intelligence, fanaticism; fact, ideal. Hyde, in some contradiction to this suggests this kind of pairing, again in the feminine masculine order, as becoming and being; change and permanence; feeling and thought; particular and universal. There is an apparent contradiction here between Sainsbury's attribution of permanence to the feminine principle and change to the masculine, Hyde's description of the acceptance of the concrete flux of existence as feminine, and the intellect's making of conceptions for grasping being behind becoming as masculine. I think they are not irreconcilable, but to go into that would take us into too deep waters. Here are some more pairs from the religious and philosophical literature with which I am acquainted: infinite and finite; being and becoming; eternity and time; universal and particular; and if you are philosophically interested, matter and form; potentiality and actuality; *eros* and *logos*. And we might add: life and consciousness; immediate awareness and inference; realist and idealist; wisdom and cleverness; acceptance and protest; conservation and creation-destruction.

We shall not at the moment try to sort these out; to some of them we shall return. They are enumerated here to indicate how the human mind has been inclined to find differences of gender far beyond the merely human and biological levels of existence. This is the point at which I should prevent you making a too easy equation between masculine and the human male, and feminine and the human female. However deep this contrast of gender goes in the universe, it is not to be found in its neat form in man and woman. For one thing, the male and female cell are not quite different in substance; both have the same structure composed of nucleus surrounded by cytoplasm; the male cell having a large nucleus with little cytoplasm; the female mostly cytoplasm with a relatively small nucleus. Then there is the well-known fact that each man has certain female characteristics in varying degrees, and vice versa. Moreover, as the psychologist Jung has so much insisted, every man has in his unconscious a female image, which he calls the *anima* (not an image projected outward, but an image or shadow of himself) and every woman a masculine image called the *animus*. So that when either is moved by his or her unconscious life they show some traits of the opposite sex.[3]

---

3. Cf. Jung's doctrine expounded by Gebhard Frei; in V. White, *God and the Unconscious*, "The anima (or animus) always has a complementary or compensatory function; this means that when consciousness tends in a particular direction, the unconscious tends in the opposite direction, thus balancing the inner forces. Thus for example the *anima* of an intellectual man often tends to be sentimental. "Anyone who

Bearing in mind, then, this mysterious meaning not to be identified with this man and this woman, let us consider its place in the scheme of things. The theologians asks questions about any important part of human existence. Does it belong to the order of creation, like matter and spirit, the family, race, and so on; or does it belong to the order of history like the state, nationality, civilization, science, and so one, things that are not found among men everywhere but arise under certain historical conditions. Thirdly, does it belong to the fallen nature of man, either as the working out of a sinful principle like cruelty, or as a device to curb the effects of egoism like coercive aspects of the state and lawful authority.

We can answer quite easily that gender belongs not to the order of history but to the order of creation, for it runs all through humanity and beyond. The other question is not so easy; does gender exist because of some kind of fall from true existence; this view has some able defenders, who are so impressed with the problems of bisexuality among humans, that they think man's spiritual and personal nature can only be tied up with biological urges by some original calamity. Notice, this is not the view often put forward, wrongly, in the name of Christianity, that the spirit of man is contaminated by its involvement with "the flesh"; it is the view that the innocent and neutral biological forces are corrupted by the egoisms of the sinful spirit.

The theory that the only true human being is androgyne man-woman, or rather a whole of which male and female are subsequent dissociations, is expounded at some length by Nicolas Berdyaev in several of his works.[4] He brings to his support Jacob Boëhme, in the seventeenth century, and other mystical writers as well as ancient writings like the *Zohar* of the Jewish Kabbalah, and many gnostic writings—all of which suggest that bisexuality is in some way a fall from the original Adam, a state which is androgynous. Though similar speculations are found in early Christian writers like Origen, Gregory of Nyssa,[5] and Maximus the Confessor, and John Scotus Eriugena, they are foreign to the main biblical and church tradition, and derive mostly from movements of pre-Christian origin in the Hellenistic world, especially that of gnostic speculation. The main Christian stream of

---

has recognized the image of the opposite sex in his own soul has thereby secured a considerable degree of control over his emotions and passions. This means the acquisition of real independence, but also of loneliness, the isolation of the inwardly free man who can no longer be held in chains by a love affair or a partnership; one for whom the opposite sex has lost its mystery because in his own soul he has discovered its essential features" (Jacobi, *The Psychology of C. J. Jung*, 112–13).

4. Berdyaev, *The Meaning of the Creative Act*, chs. ii, viii; *Slavery and Freedom*, 222; *The Destiny of Man*, Part I, ch. 3 § 3, Part II ch. 4 § 8.

5. Gregory of Nyssa, *De Opificio*, xxii, 4.

thought is closely geared to the Bible which insists that male and female are part of the creation as God wills it to be, and on which He looked and saw that it was good. And the line of thought which regards bisexuality as a fallen condition goes with the non-biblical view that the earthly material world is itself a fall from pure spirit, a view represented in the West today by Mr. Aldous Huxley and common to many Oriental religious systems.[6]

Having concluded that gender, or bisexuality is of the order of creation, we have to ask how deep does it go? Does it run into the Godhead itself? First of all, we observe that it does not run all through the created world. The stars have no gender, though they have male and female names; inanimate nature has no gender, though perhaps discoveries of negative and positive protons, on top of the more familiar negative and positive electrons, may be interpreted as a kind of polarity in matter, similar to gender. Anyhow, in its obvious form gender is confined to the biological world, but it does not spread all over that. There are lowly forms of life which multiply by division, and others which unite without propagation. The world of the amoeba, and such like, is full of virgin births.

Gender, then, does not mark the whole creative work of God. But, it certainly marks the human creation, and as man is, in Christian theology, the most significant part of creation, made in a unique sense in the image of God, it is legitimate to ask whether there is something in the divine origin corresponding to the gender in the human image, and of course whether the image has gender or is above or behind this kind of polarity.

We must not be misled into thinking that God as revealing Himself in the Bible has gender because his names and titles are masculine. *Elohim* is an abstract plural; the consonantal name, YHVH, corrupted to our Jehovah, is probably an extension of the word *Hu*, meaning he, has God is called by other Arab tribes at times of religious revival, the One Unnamable,[7] without suggestion of gender. And the answer transmitted through Moses to the Israelites question "What is His name?" is in the form of that cryptic evasion, "I am that I am," or I am he who is present with my people, as Buber, the distinguished Jewish scholar insists it should be taken,[8] implying the source of *being*, as such, or providential presence. And where the Lord is called "Father," as in Moses' words to Pharaoh, "Israel is my first-born son" or in Hosea's and Jeremiah's analogy of human fatherly love for God's divine love to Israel, the emphasis is not on fatherhood in contrast to motherhood or on

---

6. Huxley, *Perennial Philosophy*, 209.
7. Buber, *Moses*, 50.
8. Ibid., 51.

fatherhood as generative, but rather on the moral authority and lordship of history which later acquired benevolent attributes of loving care.

Nevertheless, in spite of the complete absence of the idea of God generating the world (the world is his creation not his offspring) and in spite of "fatherhood" having authoritative and providential rather than male meanings, there have been from time to time voices in Christian thought and devotion declaring that this imagery gave a masculine one-sidedness to the idea of God. A modern example is a beautiful book called *The Divine Motherhood* by Dom Abbot Vonier, OSB, of Buckfast. One of the best-known statements of this theme was made by the Dame Julian of Norwich in her *Revelations of Divine Love*. This fourteenth century English mystical writer, with considerable philosophical powers, subordinates theological precision in the requirements of her devotional insight. As we listen to a few passages from chapter fifty-eight and sixty-three of her *Revelations* we must remember she is using this gender imagery to convey the relation of God to man, and not formulating a gender theory of persons in the Trinity. I shall suggest later that if we were to attempt that we should have to come to a different way of speaking.

"In our making," she writes "God Almighty is our nature's Father; and God all-Wisdom is our nature's Mother; with the Love and Goodness of the Holy Ghost; which is all one God, one Lord. And in the knitting and the oneing He is our Very, True Spouse, and we his loved wife, His fair maiden." Note the sudden switch from the image of God as mother to the soul of man, to that of the husband to the wife. This latter is rare in Julian, though it is a very common form of symbolism elsewhere in Christian devotional writing. I continue the quotations, "In our Father Almighty we have our keeping and our bliss as anent our sense-soul; our restoring and our saving; for He is our Mother, Brother and Savior..."

> I understand that the High Might of the Trinity is our Father, and the deep Wisdom of the Trinity is our Mother, and the great Love of the Trinity is our Lord; and all this we have in Nature and in making of our Substance.
>
> And furthermore, I saw that the Second Person, which is our Mother as anent the substance, that dear worthy Person is become our Mother as anent the Sense-soul. For we are double by God's making; that is to say Substantial and Sensual. Our substance is the higher part, which we have in our Father, God Almighty; and the Second Person of the Trinity is our Mother in Nature, in making of our Substance: in whom we are grounded

and rooted. And He is our Mother in Mercy, in taking our sense part.

What are we to make of this language? Dame Julian is a sufficiently good theologian to realize that the second Person of the Trinity, the Word of God, the *Logos*, the Son, who took flesh in the man Jesus Christ, is the agent of creation, as well as the savior. The Father is the source of creation for He is the unmanifest origin, in the Son He manifests Himself, first in creation then in redemption. Along with the prologue of St. John, "all things were made by Him," and along with the same idea in St. Peter's first Epistle; St. Paul's Colossians and the Epistle to the Hebrews. The Word is the Creator *ad extra* (a note much lost in modern Christian teaching). All things are made in the configuration of the Christ, and man especially, "He is the light that lightest every man" and if you look at a likeness of the sculpture of the creation of Adam on Chartres Cathedral, you will see that the Creator is the Christ. Only because He is the fashioner of nature is He also the restorer of nature by redemption.

Dame Julian speaks of man as created in terms of substance and sense-soul. Substance means that man is made in some way out of the divine undifferentiated substance—spirit; and this takes a specific form or structure in the creature; in man, it is the combination of flesh and spirit, or soul; the first being sensitive to the self. If we imagine the structure of man to be represented by a circle, the circumference is the body with contact to the external world; the center is the spirit of man—the self—the ultimate subject, and between circumference and center is the whole inner life, which, if we were speaking precisely, is the soul. The phrase "sense-soul" is Dame Julian's way of expressing the fact that man is an incarnate spirit, or as we put it more loosely, composed of soul and body. It is this double nature which, as she says, is especially the work of the Son, who Himself becomes incarnate God. Julian's attempt to make the Son feminine is debatable, and I shall later put forward a different view. But we can see why, it is because the tender, healing and forgiving action of God seems especially a feminine characteristic. Further, it is in the Son that redemptive suffering takes place, and the Son is the one person of the Trinity to take human flesh.

There is a very widespread use of the idea that God's care for His creation is like that of a mother for her young. He is likened to an eagle in her nest (Deut 12:11). His care for Israel is likened to a woman bearing a child (Isa 66:3). He does not forget Israel as a woman cannot forget her suckling child (Isa 64:15). He comforts His people as a mother (Isa 66:13). Christ's lament over Jerusalem is that of a hen who would have gathered her chickens under her wings (Matt 23:37). And in much of the Wisdom literature the Divine Wisdom is feminine though feminine gifts of nourishing and suckling are also attributed to the Father (Odes Sol 19:1). Augustine speaks of "*sapientia dei, mater nostra.*"[9] All this is gender symbolism for God's relation to man, and is not the same as finding some principle in the Godhead which we can call motherhood alongside of fatherhood, as Dame Julian undoubtedly does.

Let us now turn from these speculations about the nature of God to his creative work. We have noticed that gender covers part of the created world but not all of it; it covers all but the most rudimentary forms of life. Gender covers all human existence, and that is much more than a biological fact, though it is always rooted in the life stream. Gender colors man's psyche or soul, and as we shall observe soon, gender symbolism, even sex symbolism, is used to express religious relationship, involving God, man, the church, and the soul. But, just now, let us look at the Genesis story and see whether this great myth suggests anything about the connection between gender in mankind and the image of God in man.

There are two narratives. In the priestly document (Gen 1–2 4a, and continued in 5) we have the creation of man mentioned twice (Gen 1:27 and 5:2) where the phrase, "in the image of God created he him" is immediately followed by "male and female created he them." In the other document (Gen 2:4b-4) there is no mention of the image; instead we have the procedure described. "The Lord God formed man of the dust of the ground, and breathed into his nostrils the breath of life; and man became a living soul" (2:7). Then follow the prohibition of eating the tree of knowledge of good and evil; then the formation of Eve out of a rib of the man; the temptation by the serpent; the eating of the forbidden fruit; and the expulsion from Eden.

The first question which arises is whether the mention of the image with immediately "male and female he created them" means that the image does not belong to each separately but to the two together. Those that have thought that neither man nor woman is a complete human; but that only the androgyne is perfectly human, give this interpretation to the text. I do not think it can carry that weight. Karl Barth in his *Dogmatik iii* in the section on the doctrine of Man, does consider "male and female he created them" as a statement about the image. He will not have anything to do with man confronting God, as an I with a thou, in a full personal sense, except in Christ. But he has to find some meaning for man's creation in the image of God. Apart from redemption in Christ, there is in man's very being as created something analogous to—or reflecting—an I-Thou relationship, namely in the individual man's relation to his fellow human beings. The most

---

9. Augustine, *Questionum Evangelium*, 1.36.

searching and testing of the relationship of the human being to a neighbor is the man-woman relationship. Though sin corrupts humanity, and God's restoring love is necessary to restore and complete human nature—and this is life in Christ—yet even in our fallen state in the relationship of man to woman, and man to man, there is a replica of the image of God in man functioning in ordinary living. Here are a few of Barth's own words: "Man is alone among animals and in the whole creation in this, that he stands continually and will stand in his life in relationship (as man and woman) before God." "A human being will in any case only be such before God and among his kind upon these conditions, that it is as a man in relationship to the woman, or woman in relationship to the man."[10] This seems to say that the man-woman relation, given in nature, is an analogue of the man-God relationship which is only made explicit in grace. For Karl Barth the image of God in man is purely man's power to enter into personal relations, as one self-confronting another. But this analogue—of one self-confronting an-other—exists in many human relationships besides that of man and woman in love or in marriage. It forms the network of all neighborly meeting. It constitutes the kind of bond which makes us neighbors to a great number of other persons, a bond that is often the meat of conflict and rivalry as well as of harmony and cooperation. Any two personal selves meeting one another would do as an analogue in nature for the personal meeting of man and God in the realm of Grace. There must be something special about the man-woman relation which makes Barth fasten on this gender relation as the most telling form of interpersonal contact. I do not think the fact that man is only man in personal relations contains the whole meaning of the divine image in him. I shall expound in my third lecture a doctrine of marriage which assumes that in the relation of man and wife we have to do with that of two neighbors bound together by several bonds, which make marriage the type and test of what life with a neighbor means. Anyhow, the Genesis account of the image with the male and female human being; suggests at least that they are complementary parts of human existence by the will of the Creator.

To turn now to the Fall story, there is nothing in the place taken by Eve in that story that is of material importance for our theme. Only in a negative sense can we use it as a denial of certain false views. It denies too that woman is the principle which causes the Fall, (though there is a human touch, in that Adam implies he has slipped into disobedience because Eve tempted him, as if she had done so deliberately; but she too had slipped because of the deception of the serpent). The order of events is suggestive,

---

10. Barth, *Church Dogmatics* III.2, 286.

but of what is often a mystery. The prohibition is told to Adam before the creation of Eve; the serpent lies to her "you may not eat of any of the trees" and puts her in a position to correct him (always a dangerous position). No, we may eat of all the trees except one, she answers—and adds words which God had not spoken "touch it not, else you must die."

The thing taken is not anything wrong, evil, or morally bad; it is fruit of a tree. "Good to look at and to eat." (As G. K. Chesterton observes, not even "apple" is mentioned. The apple that Eve ate was an orange and the peel has been lying about ever since). It was the fruit of the tree of knowledge of good and evil and for the ancients this meant not so much moral good and evil, as pleasure and pain, joy and misery, and fortune and ill-fortune. Martin Buber, in *Images of Good and Evil*, knowing the finer shades of meaning of Hebrew scriptures, dismisses three common interpretations of eating of the tree of knowledge of good and evil.

> One, which refers to the acquisition of sexual desire, is precluded by the fact of the creation of man and woman as sexually mature beings and by the concept of "becoming like God" which is coupled with the knowledge of good and evil; this God is supra-sexual. The other interpretation, relating to the acquisition of moral consciousness, is no less contrary to the nature of this God: we have only to thing of the declaration in His mouth that man, now he has acquired moral consciousness, must not be allowed to attain aeonian life as well![11]

They are turned out of Eden lest they pluck of the Tree of Life, and live forever, which fruit presumably they may have taken with impunity before plucking the tree of knowledge of good and evil. (I am prepared to defend this second view that moral consciousness is a consequence of the Fall). "According to the third interpretation, the meaning of this knowledge of good and evil is nothing else than: cognition in general, cognizance of the world, knowledge of all the good and bad things there are. But this interpretation . . . is also unfounded."[12]

But now,[13] in place of these three interpretations Buber expounds his own:

11. Buber, *Good and Evil, Two Interpretations*, 70.
12. Ibid.
13. Preceding this paragraph, Demant includes the note: I must put in here that those writers like D. H. Lawrence and others who have felt that knowledge was a disaster have something to be said for them. What bliss it would be if there were only existence and no doubling of it in consciousness, dividing life into subject and object, with questions of the validity of this or that process of knowing; and all the problems of mind versus life.

> Knowledge of good and evil means nothing else than cognizance of the two opposites which the early literature of mankind designated by these two terms; they still include the fortune and misfortune or the order and disorder that is experienced by a person... God knows the opposites of being... He encompasses them, untouched by them... A superior-familiar encompassing of opposites is denied to him who, despite his likeness to God, has a part only in that which is created and not in creation... He knows oppositeness only by his situation within it.[14]

And one of the forms of this oppositeness is that of masculine and feminine; "they knew that they were naked." We might say that one consequence of the Fall is to turn complementary different things, or polar complements, into opposites and contradictions.[15]

We must now glance at the various expressions of tender symbolism in the language of the church and the minds of its writers. The first that comes to mind perhaps is the figure of husband and wife as symbols of the relation of Christ and his church. This has the authority of the Epistle to the Ephesians 5:22–23, but it runs through a great deal of the liturgical and informal piety as well as the thought of Christian devotion. The Ephesian's passage is not an illustration of Christ's bond with His church, in terms of the bond of husband and wife. It is the other way about. Husbands and wives are to live in the same kind of relationship that Christ bears to his church. "Husbands love your wives, even as Christ also loved the church and gave Himself up for it" (5:25). They are one flesh, and "no man ever hated his own flesh; but nourisheth and cherisheth it, even as Christ also the church" (5:29). And they shall cleave to one another for the twain shall become one flesh. "This mystery is great; but I speak in regard of Christ and of the church" (5:32), mystery here meaning that it has a significance in the framework of the divine plan which is made known only be revelation. This image has been used from the time of Hosea (Hos 2:19ff; Isa 54:5; Ezek 16) where the nature of God and his attitude to Israel had been expressed in terms of marriage. Our Lord transfers this metaphor to Christ and his church. Christ is the bridegroom (Mark 2:18–20); the kingdom is likened to a marriage feast (Matt 22:2–12; 25:1–13; Luke 12:35ff.) In Revelation the church is the bride (19:2ff; 21:2–9; 22:17), "The Spirit and the Bride say: Come." And in another passage St. Paul speaks of the church as presented to Christ as a pure virgin (II Cor 11:2). One of the most interesting much later commentaries on this theme is to be found in the work of a seventeenth-century Christian

---

14. Buber, *Good and Evil, Two Interpretations*, 70–74.
15. cf. Nicholas of Cusa on the coincidence of opposites.

Platonist, Ralph Cudworth. In a writing called *The Union of Christ and the Church; in a Shadow*, Cudworth asserts that the union of man and woman is not a mere metaphor or symbol, but is a divinely appointed copy or image of Christ's unity with the church. Husband and wife are the type of which Christ and the church are the archetype. Dr. Thornton has summarized this whole teaching in the words: "the divine human *koinonia* of God and man in Christ. It (marriage) is to be the 'effectual sign' of that divine human *koinonia*, the earth by union being engraced with the graces which abound in the heavenly union."[16]

The Incarnation is often likened to the marriage union. Dr. Sherwin Bailey has collected a number of passages from the church fathers which illustrate this.[17] Origen wrote, "More truly indeed of this (the union of the Word with human nature) than of any other (union) can the statement be affirmed. 'They shall both be one flesh, and are no longer two, but one flesh.' For the Word of God is to be considered as being more in one flesh with the soul (of Jesus) than man with his wife.[18] Again referring to the union of the Word with human nature, he writes, "the sacred language of Holy Scripture knows of other things also which, although 'dual' in their own nature, are considered to be, and really are 'one' in respect to one another. It is said of husband and wife, 'they are no longer two but one flesh.'"[19] Jeremy Taylor in the seventeenth century uses similar language, "Christ descended from His Father's bosom, and contracted his divinity with flesh and blood, and married our nature, and are become a Church, the spouse of the Bridegroom."[20]

There had been attempts among some early Christian speculators to liken the relation of persons in the Trinity to partners in marriage. Augustine discusses these views in his treatise *De Trinitate*. He says it is a faulty analogy but makes some interesting contribution of his own. "The text in Genesis, dealing with the image, and male and female says that human nature itself, which is complete only in both sexes, was made in the image of God, and it does not separate the woman from the image of God which it signifies."[21] But marriage is no analogue to the eternal generation of the Son, nor to the eternal procession of the Holy Spirit. Only in the most general way could the two persons in one flesh, of marriage, be a metaphor for the distinction of persons in the divine unity.

16. Thornton, *Common Life in the Body of Christ*, 225.
17. Bailey, *Mystery of Love and Marriage*, 113.
18. Origen, *De Principiis*, ii.6.
19. Origen, *Contra Celsum*, vi.47.
20. Taylor, *Marriage Ring*, 22.
21. Augustine, *De Trinitate*, XII.5–8.

To complete the account of gender symbolism, we must look at one more example. The most frequent is the idea that in some way the human creature is feminine to God. This sometimes, in the mystics, takes the form of seeing God or Christ as the spouse of the soul. In the case of women, mystics like St. Teresa and Angela of Foligno. The distinctly erotic language has shocked people who misunderstand the symbolism; or it has been used to support the theory that all desire for mystical union is due to thwarted sex life. But, the answer to this has been well given by Simone de Beauvoir.

> It would be false to interpret her emotions as a simple "sublimation of sex; there is not first an unavowed desire that later takes the form of divine love. The amoureuse herself is not at first the prey of a desire without object which is later to become fixed in an individual man; it is the presence of the lover that arouses in her a desire directly oriented to him. Similarly, St. Teresa in a single process seeks to be united with God, and lives out this union in her body; she is not the slave of her nerves and her hormones; one must admire, rather, the intensity of a faith that penetrates to the most intimate regions of her flesh . . . She poses in a most intellectual fashion the dramatic problem of the relation between the individual and the transcendent being; she lived out, as a woman, an experience whose meaning goes far beyond the fact of her sex.[22]

I will now take as an outstanding example of this symbolism of the soul and God, under the image of the beloved and the lover, the sermons of St. Bernard on the *Song of Songs*. I must leave on one side the beautiful work of Ramon Llull, *The Book of the Lover and the Beloved*. St. Bernard, who had written another treatise on the four stages in which man passes in learning to love God, *De Diligendo Deo*, in his sermons the Song of Songs takes the love of the bride for her bridegroom as the human type of the soul's pure love of God. By conversion the soul is reformed and rendered comfortable to the Word in love.

> Such conformity marries the soul to the Word, when she shows herself like by will to Him to whom she is like by nature, loving as she is loved . . . A great thing is love, but there are degrees in it. The bride stands in the highest. For sons love, but think of their inheritance, and, while they fear in some way to lose this, they reverence more but love less, Him from whom the heritage is expected. I hold in suspicion the love which the hope of acquiring something seems to support. It is weak if perchance, should

---

22. Beauvoir, *The Second Sex*, 674.

the hope be withdrawn, it is either quenched or diminished. It is impure if it desires ought else. Pure love is not mercenary. Pure love gathers no strength from hope, nor suffers loss through distrust. This love the bride hath, because it is all that the bride is . . . In this the bride abounds, with this bridegroom is content. He seeks nought else; nor hath she ought else.[23]

We have looked at four ways in which the man-woman relation has been thought of as a symbol of theological mysteries: of the bond of Christ and the church; of the divine and human natures in Christ; of the Father and Son and Holy Ghost in the Trinity; of the soul's unity with God. If these are at all equally inspired insights they tell in the direction of supposing the gender relation to be one of a number of polarities which are not themselves of the order of gender, but which can be likened to the polarity of male and female.

To extend the account of gender symbolism, we should have to add at least two more forms of it, namely the doctrine of the two Eves, Adam's Eve and Mary, the Mother of Jesus; and secondly, the widespread acceptance of feminine gender to the Wisdom of God. But these must be left out at present.

Now, for comparison, and to help in interpreting the masculine and feminine polarity in Christian terms, we must see how it is handled in other religions and in some of the heretical movements which invaded the Christian consciousness. Here we are in a veritable jungle of beliefs and only the most significant ones can be selected. And we must remember that in many primitive and advanced religions the gods and goddesses are not supreme beings, but creations or emanations of an ultimate reality which may or may not be a personal deity. We shall not pay attention to these intermediate beings, and confine ourselves to ideas of gender in the ultimate divine source of all things, and of gender in archetypal man.

In many religions there are male and female cosmic powers, but they are usually regarded as split off from a unity which lies behind their differentiation.[24] In the old Iranian religion of Persia, the two ultimate male divinities of Ormuzd and Ahriman, the good and evil powers in the active godhead are both masculine, the offspring of one Zervan—often translated Chronos. And in most of the pantheons of the ancient near East supreme divinities are impersonal, beyond gender, or they are both sexes or, as in tantric Hinduism, male and female in a cosmic embrace. This widespread theme of the deity as androgyne—or ante-gender—but giving rise to masculine

---

23. St. Clairvaux, *Saint Bernard on the Song of Songs*, 257.
24. Cf. Bertholet, *Das Geschlecht der Gottheit*.

and feminine powers has its more philosophical and theological form in a highly developed doctrine that God resides in the coincidence of opposites. Heraclitus was the earliest Greek exponent of it; there are elements in Plato suggesting the same; in Christian thought the coincidence of opposites was a favorite line of speculation in Pseudo-Denys, Meister Eckhardt and the great Cardinal Nicholas of Cusa, whose *The Vision of God* is a profoundly interesting work.

As widespread nearly is a doctrine that primordial man is bisexual, sometimes conceived as a sphere or an egg. This is to be found among Australian stone age people, in Iranian tribes; in China and in popular Greek religion. Very often this primordial man-woman gives rise to the two worlds of the sky and the earth—and in this division sky is generally masculine and earth is generally feminine. It is found in the gnostic movements of antiquity and in Rabbinical Judaism. And in many rituals, men and women change garments as if to suggest that regeneration, somehow means, the believer identifying himself or herself with the opposite sex, a return to the origin as it were.

But to turn to more philosophical expressions of the idea; we have an interesting version of it in the Vedanta teaching of Hinduism. It is a primary tenet of this school that Atma (the little self) is identical with Brahma (the big cosmic self). This identity is the only reality—all that seems to separate the little self from the big self is illusory and a kind of Fall. Brahma within man is called Purusha. It is not seen or felt or known because it is the ultimate subject, and all else is known by it. By it man is linked with universal being, we might call it spirit. But this Parusha must enter into relation with another principle Prakriti to give rise to separate, concrete and individual things and persons. This pair of Parusha and Prakriti corresponds roughly to Aristotle's substance and form, or essence. Parusha is masculine and Prakriti, feminine; the one active, the other passive. The interaction of these two gives rise to the world though they are themselves unmanifested. All manifested things are produced by Prakriti, but without the presence of Parusha these productions would be deprived of all reality. Parusha is a sort of universal undifferentiated energy, unknown in itself; Prakriti impelled by Parusha gives rise to the manifold existence of our world.[25] It is plastic in relation to Parusha but the world is plastic to it. I mention this doctrine for I shall later suggest that these two are something like the Father and the Son of Christian theology.

There are, however, other quite different strands in Hindu religion. The Indian theory of government is that of a marriage between the priesthood

---

25. Cf. Guénon, *Man & His Becoming.*

and the civil ruler. The Brahman priest, the Purohita addresses the King, "I am that, thou art this; I am sky thou art earth;" and in this whole universe of discourse the priesthood is masculine and the civil ruler is feminine; sky is masculine and earth feminine. Their union is affected with a marriage formula, "Be ye united of one intention, loving one another." But while the sky is masculine to the earth, it is feminine to the sun. But it is stated over and over again that the worlds of celestial and terrestrial, essential and natural, were originally one. Creation however is feminine to Brahma. The King is feminine to the Priest; but masculine to this own realm. In general, this theme is that the outer world is feminine, the inner is masculine. In the marriage ceremony the man addresses the woman with the words: "I am He, thou art she; I am the harmony, thou the words; I am sky thou art earth. Let us twain here become one."

In an early Chinese document, *The Ching*, or *Book of Changes*, which Confucius later took up and rationalized into a system of morals, we have a similar, though really different scheme. The two basic principles are called *yin* and *yang*, the dark and the light principles; earth and sky. But this set of opposites are bound up with other pairs: heat and cold; moist and dry; female and male; soft and hard; passive and active; round and square. These opposites are in a state of balance and when the balance is upset it must be restored or they must alternate like the coiling up and straightening out of a caterpillar. In the words of Ching, "When the *yang* has reached its greatest strength, the dark power of *yin* is born within its depths; night begins at midday, when *yang* breaks up and begins to change into *yin*." Or to put it into more familiar terms, the conscious, clear determined active masculine will has its limits and its disasters; there is needed the intuitive, accepting, instinctive, and make-do, cosmic feminine principle. Goodness and knowledge of the goodness in Tao consists in the complementary balance of *yin* and *yang*.[26][27] This insight is of much value in assessing our western civilization, which for the Taoist is definitely a *yang* society.

---

26. The Valley Spirit never dies. / It is named the mysterious female. / And the Doorway of the mysterious female / Is the base from which Heaven and Earth spring / It is there within us all the while; / Draws upon is as you will, it never runs dry.

27. Estate and Waley, *Chinese Poems*.

Series I, Lecture IX
Eastern and Western Religion

IN OUR DAY THE meeting of East and West means in the main certain external happenings: these comprise the freeing of nations from the dominance of the West; the appropriation by Oriental peoples of western political intellectual and scientific methods, and a weakening of the West's confidence in the strength of its own culture. The history of these tendencies is somewhat confused and paradoxical. The development of the modern west seems to have sent it on a course which differentiated it more and more from the common pattern of traditional civilizations which began to form about the period 800 to 200 BC. In various places such as China, India, Prussia, Palestine, and Greece. On top of what may be called a Promethean Age making the use of language, the invention of tools, and the use of fire; on top of the period of the ancient civilizations of Egypt, Mesopotania and North India and China; we seem to have in this period, around 500 BC, a new set of forces which gave a character to life in East and West. Some spiritual, intellectual, and cultural elements appeared which constitute roughly what we call civilization.

> Confucius and Lao-tse were living in China, all the schools of Chinese philosophy came into being, including those of Mo-Ti, Chuang Tse, Lieh-Tzu and a host of others; India produced the Upanishads and Buddha and, like China, ran the whole gamut of philosophical possibilities down to skepticism, to materialism, to sophism and nihilism; in Iran Zarathustra taught a challenging view of the world as a struggle between good and evil; in Palestine the prophets made their appearance, from Elijah, by way of Isaiah and Jeremiah to Deutero-Isaiah; Greece witnessed the appearance of Homer, of the philosophers—Parmenides, Heraclitus, and Plato . . . man becomes conscious of Being as a whole, of himself and his limitations. He experiences the terror

of the world and his own powerlessness. He asks radical questions. Face to face with the void he strives for liberation and redemption. By consciously recognizing his limits he sets himself the highest goals. He experiences absoluteness in the depths of selfhood and in the lucidity of transcendence . . . Man proved capable of contrasting himself inwardly with the entire universe. He discovered within himself the origin from which to raise himself above his own self and the world.[1]

It was the use of consciousness—intellectual and moral—the Dawn of Philosophy as Georg Misch calls it, the origin of civilization in traditional religious cultures.

Regarding relativity in civilizations, the westerner finds a bewildering variety of cultures in the East. One cannot speak of one culture. The easterner finds more ideological, spiritual, and cultural conflict with the West than he knows of in his own Orient. From the point of view of any broad survey of human history, civilization is one thing, from 500 BC onward. The West causes further separations therein, namely separating man from cosmos. In comparison, the East has a customary unity in spite of wide variety of cultures.

Moreover—the modern West from the fifteenth century onward has distanced itself from the traditional West, which was marked by a certain pattern of life, outlook, existence—not nearly so unlike Oriental pattern. And the modern West has been quite different in the post-Renaissance world in Europe and America. So far as there is antithesis between the East or modern West, its more thorough form is the antithesis within the West between its modern form and its traditional past. Yet in its traditional past one finds elements already differentiating it from cultures in the East. These elements, once emancipated from tradition, made the modern West. They led to religious and intellectual changes in the fifteenth and seventeenth centuries and technical and economic changes in the nineteenth and twentieth centuries. This modern western development achieved differentiation (and powers) at a cost of unity. Against this background appear the facts of our day: the east's resistance to domination by the West; the East's imitation of the end-products of western culture—while critical of that culture; the predisposition in the east to welcome movements like Communism which, though having western origins, have sprung from attempts in the west to recover from some of the worst of western dissociations; and lastly a crop of movements and impulses in the West to seek in Eastern Yoga or Wisdoms, the kind of force which might unify inner and outer life, the economic and

---

1. Jaspers, *The Origin and Goal of History*, 2–3.

the practical, religious and empirical—aspects of western life which have been more and more falling apart since the seventeenth century.[2]

---

2. Here Demant includes the note: "V. Social evolution."

Series I, Lecture X
The Christian Revolution

BY REVOLUTION HERE I do not mean the fundamental upheaval of society, which normally goes by that name, but the complete turn of a wheel. I have said enough in previous lectures, I hope, to convey a sense that the appearance of Christianity with one route in Judaism and the other in a new revelation, the unique Christ event, did serve to bring about a revolution, in the sense of innovation, in the consciousness of mankind; and that the impregnation of Greek thought and this new religious fact was a union of two things in the sense dissimilar, but in another a meeting of two forces which were congruous to one another as compared with the mentality of the ancient civilizations and the Eastern religions.

I have also hinted that this combination, spreading over the field of Roman imperialism, gave a peculiar character to western society; politics and thought. Further, that in the course of centuries outlooks, attitudes, mental tools, brought into play by this innovation by stages lost their dependence on religion and produced the modern secular world. Then, covertly in the nineteenth and overtly in the twentieth centuries, there have appeared movements, philosophies, and literature which seek in various ways to overcome the disassociations in human living and the schisms in the human soul which this career has brought about. Lastly, that this attempt to recover some sort of unity, where there has been division and conflict in the life and thought of western man, naturally looks to the eastern religious traditions for a principle of healing, and movements which uncontrollably base themselves on instructive urges, the wild dark "telluric" forces which "Logos" religion had tamed, or rightly ensuring that reason and ideas cannot control instinct or the hidden emotions, intend to order life at a deeper level than the conscious intellect. Marxism was the biggest of these, appealing behind its social conscious aims to a stream of process which it called the dialectic of history, couched in terms of the conflict of common powers.

Modernity is rebelling against the parent. Modernity was birthed by a Christian worldview. But as modernity decides that belief in God is implausible and unlikely, our culture is in trouble. Idealism that always postulated the primacy of mind over matter is increasingly replaced by materialism.[1] *Modernity in its rebellion is not happy. There have been a variety of responses to its torment. Freud, for example, seeks to create a unity of personhood, despite his lack of belief in a soul.*[2]

Three other reactions are worth noting. Nietzsche can be read as a materialist response to the crisis of modernity by simply asserting human will and power. The novelist D.H. Lawrence talks of "pulsating life streams." And Goethe's famous play "Faust" is a perfect exploration of human anguish, as the pact with the devil leads, ultimately, to mayhem. In all cases we have the anguish of modernity captured.[3]

---

1. This opening section is an expansion of Demant's note on the "Curtain of Idealism."

2. Demant has a note here: "Freud. Conscience and Id, Ego, Super-ego."

3. This paragraph is an expansion of the following notes: "Nietzsche. Will and Power; D H Lawrence. Pulsating life stream. Gothe. Dead. Vitalists. Faust. Ethics of salvation." Demant has in the text the following concluding remark, "There are more notes which will be added to this section."

Series II

The Moral Career of Christendom

Series II, Lecture I
The Place of Ethics in Our Culture

FOR MY SECOND SERIES of Gifford Lectures I have chosen as my title "The Moral Career of Christendom." To have done so implies certain assumptions which I will briefly lay out without seeking to establish them, in the hope that my treatment in this series will show that they are valid assumptions. In the first place, my title presupposes that there is some kind of an entity denoted by the term "Christendom." What I mean by it was stated in the opening lecture of my first series in these words, "I am not using the term as the designation of a Christian society, or the redeemed community, or of the church, or a realm under the hibilage of theology or of an ideal brotherhood. I am using it for the society and culture of the western world, where Christianity along with a number of factors of different origin and some rival ones, has been the dominant religion." In the second place, this culture or society has a certain moral complexion, which gives it a character and a certain uniqueness throughout, a large number of moral conflicts and oppositions within its bosom. This character has a history; it is not the result of any natural development of the human mind, but the outcome of very definite religious, intellectual and social forces. How these forces were set in motion is hidden from us, but we can know much about their beginnings. In the first series of these lectures I dealt with the religious climate in which some of them were nurtured. The origins of religions are new facts, though they take hold of what is already in the field of history; as Christianity, a new fact, took hold of the Jewish and Zoroastrian material. We shall within these lectures be looking at a few of the "new facts" behind the moral career of Christendom. I am at the moment trying to stress the overwhelming importance of trying to set that career and the situation of the present forces which have only one history. If they had not occurred there would have been no history of Christendom and no modern world and these things would not have occurred at any other place or time. We may not understand very much about our place at the end of this story, with the poor equipment of our minds for assessing past human movements in action or in thought. But we shall understand nothing at all about our inheritance or our present problems, if we think in terms of the natural development of the human mind. In fact, we shall get a completely misleading and dangerous picture of things as they have happened and as they are, if for instance, we cling to this disastrous dogma of the recent past in the west, namely the inherent march of man's mind—not only do we overlook that we really mean a development towards what we are—here in the western world—and that is rather conceited of us, we also put down other human contributions, civilizations, religions, ethics which do not have our achievements or problems—such things as the significance of the individual or the institution of parliamentary government. We shall put down these differences from other cultures as due to their "lagging behind" in the evolutionary race, atavistic, undeveloped, or endowed with an extra dose of original sin. And we shall hang onto the illusion that if only other people had a good look at us then this is what they would want to be like—when they do not want it—we regard it as blindness or further evidence of their perversity.

It is not my theme here to explain the damage done to human relations by the dogma of the "natural development of the human mind"; it is however, my theme that the moral and ethical situation at this or any other time (and indeed any cultural situations and its problems), can only be understood and, if the Lord will—handled, when one sees it as one part of a definite culture.

In the third place, I have used the term "career" to designate the course of this culture. That sounds disrespectful; careerism is not an admissible way of life; it suggests an unscrupulous activity for gain, pleasure, or power in disregard for integrity, means or for persons affected. Like the *carrus* (racing carriage car) from which the word career derived—when in its modern form is moved by petrol, it is regarded as the norm of transport and everything that hinders it is an obstruction. "Career" however has the meaning of "swift course"—and that is exactly what I wish to convey as a characteristic of the history of Christendom as a culture with its ethics, morals and its other ingredients. Its religion but 2000 years old, incorporating and transforming more ancient material, seems to us ever so aged. But as a culture, Christendom is a late comer in the history of civilization and its vitality has indeed been a swift and perhaps reckless course. You can draw two different conclusions from this fact: either it is too young that we must not make premature predictions about its possible long future; or it is quickly coming to an end. This however is not our concern now.

In the first series on the religious climate I sought to show that everything that has happened within the human field where Christianity has been the dominant religion, even the revolts against it, is conditioned by that religion. I developed the argument that the emergence of secular spheres of knowledge and activity was a working out of certain outlooks inherent in Christian theology and attitudes to the nature of things.

We are now to consider that Christian faith is not one aspect of a total culture, but retains an independence of it and allows it a certain autonomy. It has to minister to moral situations created by social, intellectual, and moral forces in the secular process itself. The Christian religion has not been a pure "catalyst" to use the chemical term for a substance which produces effects outside it without itself undergoing permanent change.[1]

The moral and ethical problems of this culture are not set by Christianity only, any more than its intellectual ones. It is unclear the extent to which the religion and the thought produced by it have made the questions and the answers, or have transformed those set to it by social influences which would have been there anyway. But some sort of enquiry is what we are all about.[2]

There is this peculiarity about the relation of religion and the rest of the culture of Christendom, that it has preserved a fundamental Christian foundation underneath a great variety of cultural diversity, without making the whole into a close, compact, tribal sort of unitarian society. The complication arising out of this characteristic gave a unique and puzzling character to the ethics of Christendom. The peculiarity of a diversity of mores, some of religious others of secular descent, and one underlying ethical temper withal, does not come out of the blue sky. It is a special Christian case of a tension between religious and social ethics, of which adumbrations can be identified behind and outside the Christian ethos.

Before we come to that, I should perhaps say what is involved in speaking of the culture of Christendom. It is not a Christian culture, but one formed by the meeting of the Christian spirit with the economic, social, and racial traits brought into the field by material changes and the mores of invading peoples, changes in the status and kind of leadership at different

---

1. Here Demant includes the note: "It is possible that this is an out of date analogy, for it is hard to keep up with the rapid switches of theory in recent chemistry and physics."

2. Here Demant includes the note: "(Cf. Hodges Middle Ages). He is perhaps thinking of the way in which Christian ideas overtly infused the thinking of the Middle Ages. In the essay, 'Our Culture: its Thought,' Hodges writes how for Anselm, 'Metaphysics as an incident in the course of a religious meditation: philosophy springing from worship and returning to it, with no sense of any barrier or boundary between the two—that is the spirit of medieval thinking.'" Hodges in *Our Culture* (London: SPCK, 1947), 22.

periods. Yet there is something distinctive which comes out of this melee, and as the temper, thought and impulses of it all have been so largely directed and colored by the Christian spirit, we can call it the culture of Christendom.

In this context, the term culture is used in the sense in which the anthropologist uses it, to describe a certain pattern of life which influences the aims and habits of men. As we might speak of the culture of the Hebrides, or as W. H. Rivers wrote of the culture of Melanesia, so we speak of the culture of the European West to describe a set of outlooks, aims, and ways of life, which has a history and has spread to activities known as culture in the narrower sense; the arts, sciences, education, and religion of a community—they largely adorn and invade life, and do not merely preserve or increase it. It comprises also the unofficial societies and associations which exist for some interest in which men may engage but which are not vital to their physical and political existence.

Attending Gifford Lectures is a cultural activity in this narrower sense. But in the wider meaning in which I am using it, the culture of a people or groups of people is concerned with the relation of all its functions and dreams; it includes its organized activities in politics, economic behavior, and the naturally given forms of community like the family, the nation, as well as free associations of those who are bound by social allegiances such as trade unions and religious profession. Now this whole pattern of life, which has a definite character, is very near to what we call civilization. It is the inner side of civilization. But civilization also includes the outward instruments and organizations of a culture, like the stone and the bronze which give their names to historic ages, the crafts and cathedrals of the middle ages; modern commercial Anglo-Saxon conceptions of economic purposes; the peculiar power of the modern state over all other social groupings and activities. All this is part of civilization. We are concerned, however, mainly with its inner side, the aims, assumptions, and habitual modes of life which have given rise to it, that inner side which I have called our culture. In my first lecture of series one, I pointed out that the ethics of a culture are only the clearest part of it around which operate a number of more obscure forces which I called the penumbra; and that ethics represent only the conscious body of thought about how men should live; morals or mores inform people's lives very much without thought about their ground or nature. Moreover, the culture of a people, a region, a period enable people to live a great deal of their lives in accordance with it, without at every point having to make intellectual judgements and moral decisions. It decides much for men, and we can say that to that extent it determines their lives; but on the other hand, it is a power for freedom, for if everyone had at all times to act only after wisdom and will had been used to the full, men would be theoretically free but practically dead—for human powers are limited.

This freedom is what William James writes of in his work on psychology when he says that "Habit is thus the enormous fly-wheel of society, its most precious conservative agent.[3] *James notes the necessity of acting out of habit, so that one doesn't have to think about every action.*[4]

A culture is recognized as one recognizes a face. Sir Harold Nicholson spoke the other day on the wireless on the "Values of Europe." "Why," he asked "when Ireland or Brindisi or Marseilles, which superficially are far more alien to me than Massachusetts or Illinois, should I feel that I have recovered my identity? It is because I have again found myself within a civilization formed and conditioned by traditions that I understand and share. In other words I have recovered my European values."[5] When we hear a phrase like "European Values" it is important to understand that it is not the equivalent of Christian values in the religious sense, but the kind of life, felt rather than thought, to be of worth in that social milieu of the western world, formed by the meeting of Christian outlooks with others, like the classical inheritance and the contributing of new races, the results of social, political, and economic changes. Prof. H. Butterfield has recalled a judgement of the historian Freeman to the effect that Christianity has to be understood in two senses.[6]

In the one it is a religion, a gospel, a faith, and a church. In this sense it is not tied to any culture or region. In the second sense, it may mean a pattern of society and culture, such as I have denoted by the term Christendom. Freeman had said it was doubtful whether Christianity in this sense would appear anywhere else but in the area once covered by the Graeco-Roman culture—and this is Sir Harold Nicholson's view of the provenance of what he calls "European Values." There has been a reoccurring strain between the two: men of faith and movements have repeatedly protested and combatted what they consider to be conventional and socializing stifling of the authentic religious force of the Gospel by its social and cultural integuments.[7]

---

3. James, *Principles of Psychology*, 121.

4. This paragraph is an expansion of Demant's note: "see Habit William James Principles of Psychology (1980) Chapter 4 Fly Wheel of Society. 'Habit economics energy.'"

5. Reprinted in *The Listener*, Jan 2, 1958.

6. Following this paragraph, Demant includes the note: "vad note; (Why concerned with them? VAD'S Europe paper) (Christianity in European History)." The editors suspect that this is a reference to Demant's essay in Oldham, *The Church Looks Ahead*. The editors did not expand on the latter as Demant does so himself in the following paragraphs.

7. Following this paragraph, Demant includes a note giving examples of such

Morals and ethics are one layer of a culture, which includes many other layers. The most obvious of these other layers are custom, authority, belief, rituals. These operate widely and strongly without any moral awareness, they provide norms of action which only become material of moral and ethical treatment at certain stages. In Christian history, for example, ethics only became differentiated from theology in the thirteenth century.

There are however certain steps (not stages) taken by the human race which mark a new kind of awareness and bring about problems which later form the subject of ethical enquiry. It is now well known that in primitive or tribal society mores or morality have a vital place, but it is customary rather than consciously ethical and rulers are as much under the sway of custom as their dependents.[8] Foreigners were feared because of their strange mores. Savage is conformist. Novelty is fearful; the tribal head is not the author of discipline, he is its subordinate; if he broke it he often ended his life! [Demant references a particular page of Edward Westermarck's *Origin and Development of the Moral Ideas*.[9] Westermarck notes different culture's practices of sacrifice (animal or human) to propitiate the gods, particularly as a way to atone for transgressions.][10]

The discipline is not consciously recognized as ethical, though it is practiced inculcation to the rapturous and sacred powers surrounding and permeating the practical life. A break is made with this morally innocent tradition by the appearance of some element of civilization. It is marked by a conscious impulse to make a pattern of life, the discovery of natural laws, co-operation and control of the power of nature, and a view of reality

---

thinkers: "(R Niebuhr: Christ and Culture) Tertullian, Samardu, Kierkegaard."

8. Here Demant includes the note: "cf. A Lang: *Custom and Myth*." This work explores customs and folklore from many societies. The bull-roarer is but one example of the way in which ethics operate. Lang writes, "Among the Kurnai. . . when boys go through the mystic ceremony of initiation they are shown turnduns or bull-roarers, and made to listen to their hideous din. They are then told that if ever a woman is allowed to see a turndun, the earth will open, and water will cover the globe" (p. 34). Here tradition is a matter of life and death and cannot be bent to accommodate those of high position.

9. Westermarck, Edward. *The Origin and Development of the Moral Ideas*, vol. 1 (London: Macmillan and Co., 1906) p. 62

10. Following this reference, Demant includes the note: "cf. MacIver: Society: wherever differentiation of social function: domestic, economic, authority, recreative—bound to be some clash of mores which later give rise to moral and ethical questioning. MacIver wrote under the same document as Spencer that religiously based morals are recalcitrant to change. and that human morals in demanding change are opposed to religious foundations. 'religion seems to confirm established moralities, and new moralities seek to modify religion.' *Society*, 326. 377ff. This is an error, as a generalization, due to a purely modern perspective."

greater than the tribal whole. Food-producing, conquest, and empire, early laws and the idea of a representative kingship, writing, calendars, commerce, industry, early astronomical calculations come in here. It is represented by the civilizations of Slavs, Babylonia, and Egypt. The men of this kind of civilization viewed their task "as a religious rite by which they co-operated as priests or hierophants in the great cosmic mystery."[11] The priest or priest-king "represented the god himself and stood between the goddess and her people, interpreting to them the divine will, and sometimes even offering up his own life for them in a solemn ritual ceremony."[12] You may read about it in detail in Frankfort's *Before Philosophy*, an account of the religion, society, ethics of Babylon and Egypt.[13] Throughout man is felt to be part of society, society part of nature, and nature as divine. It is fairly obvious that this kind of civilization was bound to bring about some oppositions in behavior and purposes, between the official religion and the element of tribal and local populace which were gathered under its sway: a schism has begun to develop in the soul of man, which requires an adjustment of loyalties—and this encouraged the raising of ethical questions: for instance,

> while the conception of the cosmic state remained relatively stable throughout the third millennium, the actual human state developed considerably. The central power grew stronger, the machinery of justice became more efficient, punishment followed crime with ever greater regularity. The idea that justice was something to which man had a right began slowly to take form, and in the second millennium—appropriately the millennium of the famous Code of Hammurabi—justice as right rather than justice as favor seems to have become the general conception.[14]

From this stage we have the earliest moral codes like the Laws of Mann, the Code of Hammurabi, and the Egyptian moral precepts. This idea, however, could not but conflict violently with the established view of the world. There emerged fundamental problems, such as the justification of death and the problem of the righteous suffers. And in Egypt of the old kingdom, there appeared a "youthful and self reliant arrogance" in the successful makers of civilization. "The gods? Yes, they were off there somewhere, and they had

---

11. Dawson, *Dynamics of World History*, 113.
12. Ibid.
13. Frankfort, *Before Philosophy*.
14. Ibid. 223.

made this good world, to be sure; but the world was good because man was himself master, without need for the constant support of the gods."[15]

The Greek city state, should perhaps be included in this picture of archaic civilization; transcended by fifth-century philosophers and later by Stoic universalism. [Gilbert Murray writes of how Greek confidence was dashed after the defeat of Athens in 404. "The city state, the Polis, had concentrated upon itself almost all the loyalty and the aspirations of the Greek mind. It gave security to life. It gave meaning to religion. And in the fall of Athens it had failed."[16] This shows the extent to which the power of the city state created new loyalties.][17]

WORLD RELIGIONS AND PHILOSOPHIES

Now, however, we have to note the most momentous movement before the advent of Christianity, a movement which carried man's intellectual and moral consciousness to a new and different perspective, which supervened upon the world of trial cultures and archaic civilizations. It is the rise of what we called the world religions or philosophies. "World" here has not a geographical sense, for the movement did not cover the globe; but it has a sense of "the Humanicum," man universally considered apart from his local habitat and minor allegiances. Karl Jaspers has delineated it in *The Origin and Goal of History*.

> The most extraordinary events are concentrated in this period. [between 800 to 200 BC] Confucius and Lao-tse were living in China, all the schools of Chinese philosophy came into being, including those of Mo-ti, Chuang-tse, Lieh-tsu and a host of others; India produced the Upanishads and Buddha and, like China, ran the whole gamut of philosophical possibilities down to skepticism, to materialism, to sophism and nihilism; in Iran Zarathustra taught a challenging view of the world as a

---

15. Ibid. 106.

16. Murray, *Five Stages of Greek Religion*, 106.

17. This paragraph is an expansion of the first of three notes Demant included here. The notes in their entirety read: "(G Murray on Greek City State) (T S Fregan, pg 36 to 40) (cf. Toynbee, T S Fregay 'Toynbee's account of these archaic civilization is well known. In chapter V of the Study of History he suggests that it was achieved not as a result of superior biological endowment or geographical environment but as a response to a challenge in a situation of special difficulty, which rouses him to make a hitherto unprecedented effort" The Sumeric, Syriac, Mayau, Minoan civilization came out of man fitting his miner powers over the challenge of geographical and social forces. (Spiritual) Egypt seems to have no predecessor and successor.)"

struggle between good and evil; in Palestine the prophets made their appearance, from Elijah, by way of Isaiah and Jeremiah to Deutero-Isaiah; Greece witnessed the appearance of Homer, of the philosophers—Parmenides, Heraclitus, and Plato—of the tragedians, Thucydides and Archimedes. Everything implied by these names developed during these few centuries almost simultaneously in China, India, and the West . . . man becomes conscious of Being as a whole. . . Spiritual conflicts arose, accompanied by attempts to convince others through the communication of thoughts, reasons and experiences . . . In this age were born the fundamental categories within which we still think today, and the beginnings of the world religions . . . The step into universality was taken in every sense."[18]

The world religions here referred to are Christianity, Islam, Hinduism and Mahayana Buddhism.[19] It is in the East that they appeared first: Christianity and Islam are later. In brief their characteristic was belief in a world of absolute and unchangeable reality, while the world of appearances and of earthly life became illusory or harmful. "They attained the two fundamental concepts of metaphysical being and ethical order . . . some of these movements of thought, such as Brahmanism, Taoism, and the Eleatic philosophy, concentrated their attention on the idea of Being, while others, such as Buddhism, Confucianism, Zoroastrianism and the philosophy of Heraclitus, emphasized the idea of moral order; but all of them agreed in identifying the cosmic principle, the power behind the world, with a spiritual principle, conceived either as the source of being or as the source of ethical order."[20]

(Though some Buddhisms did not identify this principle with a deity.) They "found it in thought as the supreme Reality and in ethics as the Eternal Law."[21] The new world religions were "liberated from the power of the nature demons and the dark forces of magic."[22] The religious life was not

18. Jaspers, *Origin and Goal of History*, 2.
19. Here Demant includes the note: "NOTE This period (the Axial, Joysen) does not represent a universal stage in human evolution but a singular ramified of a tribal process. Alfred Weber attributes it to the effects of the Suth European horseman which had penetrated Europe and the Mediterranean by the end of the third millennium, and then went Eastward as far as Iran and India about 1200BC, while other bands reached China by the end of the 2nd Millennium BC. 'History became a conflict between these two forces: the old stable, unawakened matriarchal powers against the new, mobile, liberating tendencies of the equestrian peoples which were rising into consciousness.' JOYCE." [quote from Jaspers, 16.]
20. Dawson, *Dynamics*, 177.
21. Ibid., 178.
22. Ibid.

submitting to a dark fate, "it was a process of spiritual discipline directed towards the purification of the mind and will."[23] "Alike in India and in Greece we can trace a striving towards the conception of an invisible underlying cosmic cause or essence—Atman, Logos, the One [the Father]—and of the unreality [absolute or comparative] of the continual flux which makes up the phenomenal world."[24]

Thus the cosmic principle or source is expressed differently in the various religious traditions that emerge in this period. In Judaism and Islam, one can see the emphasis on a moral order, with God as the Lawgiver. In Taoism and parts of Confucianism, the goal is the harmony of human action with the cosmic process. And in Buddhism and the Vedanta tradition, one seeks to be freed from illusion and led to reality.[25]

The world religions had some characteristic effects upon ethics. Their members and adepts had to deal with one overall problem: "how to reconcile the new attitude to life (individual salvation by unity with the being behind the world) with the old civilization that they inherited, a civilization that had been built up so laboriously by the worship and cultivation of the powers of nature."[26] These world religions were not themselves productive of new material civilizations (Toynbee says they occur because of decline); their whole tendency was away from the (social) material and economic idea to life towards the life of pure spirit. But in India especially the archaic culture remained intact as we see in the temple cites of Dravidian India—or the great palaces of Knossos from the Hycencecus age.[27] The main cultural contributions were in literature and art (not tied to a palace). The result of all this was a tension and often a conflict between the ways of life of the representatives of the new religions and the old civilizations. This was the field for moral and ethical discussion. In Islam, there was little of this tension.

It was the element of transcendence in the world religions that gave them a new ethical temper. No longer was conduct dictated by the earthly community, it was exercised in obedience to a super-terrestrial principle. Their moral systems therefore often (except in China) show a tendency of hostility to the actual social groups, and established themselves in a super social sphere. The man has thereby a dual citizenship, and in this the idea

23. Ibid.

24. Ibid., 118.

25. This is an expansion by the editors of Demant's notes, which read: "NOTE: (Ethics Lawgiver: Judaism and Islam; Harmony of human action with cosmic process Taoism Partly in Confus individual freedom from illusion and led to reality (Budd&vedanta)."

26. Dawson, *Dynamics*, 121.

27. Ibid.

of the "individual" has its germ. But neither Buddhism nor Plato showed any concern for the common need of humanity.[28] Then also this individualist religious climate demanded a spirit of asceticism, intelectual ascesis or bodily, to enable the soul to be free of determination by the world. No wonder that in the East there appeared a certain lessening of the civilizing process and some deterioration; where these universal religions appeared, there is a disentangling of the soul from the life of society and its material substation; and often to a decline in the earthly benefits of civilization.[29]

These characteristics of the world religions stand out. The first is the belief in a transcendent principle overarching the separate culture of civilization. It means that the individual believer has a link with the ultimate source of truth and goodness—apart from and often in contrast with his loyalties to the earthly community. Then two further characteristics follow from this first one. The second is a universalist ethic (for all men) which is usually connected with religious actions and practice for deliverance—deliverance not only from the dark evil forces of human existence, but also from the stifling ties of family, profession and state. The ethics of the world religions have therefore a measure of asceticism in them, whether it be intellectual or subjugation of the body. The third characteristic has been the power of the world religions to overstep the boundaries of the culture which gave it birth—this is part of their disentanglement from specific cultural communities. I need not mention the spread of Buddhism from India to China, of Islam over the near East; or the Syriac cultural influences upon the Persians, that Indo European people—who delivered one Syriac people, the Hebrews, from the yoke of another; or the Hellenizing thought which colored later Judaism.

The most momentous leap over cultural borders was, however that of the Christian faith. True, there were two trans-local forces already at work: the spread of Greek thought over the ancient world and the sway of the Roman dominion, with its inevitable idea of universal justice. But these do not go deep enough to account for a new sect of the Syriacs that would take possession of the Graeco-Roman culture in so short a time. The beginnings of that unique conquest can be read in the New Testament. Dom Gregory Dix has recently given a most vivid picture of what is involved in his posthumous and unrevised little book, *Jew and Greek*.

"The Jewish Christians at the Council of Jerusalem in AD 49 finally accepted the fact that the Old Israel as such had lost its Covenant and in the pathetic phrase of the Epistle to the Hebrews, 'They went forth unto Jesus

---

28. Here Demant included the note: "181.2."
29. Here Demant included the note: "Toynbee."

without the camp, bearing His reproach"[30] (Heb 13:13). This was St. Paul's great achievement.

> Jesus of Nazareth Himself springs from, indeed is, the very heart of the whole Syriac World, now preparing for its own Thermopylae against the Greeks. In ten short years His Syriac "Gospel" is forcing the gates of the Greek world at Antioch. Ten more, and it has followed Xerxes into Athens itself, in a victorious thrust that would meet no Salamis (Acts 17). Only ten more and it is already so deeply planted in the whole Hellenic world that all the struggles of the Hellenistic Empire for three centuries to eradicate this Syriac thing from its own vitals will fail. There was need of swiftness! The Syriac roots of "the Gospel" were about to be cut by the collapse of the Jewish forlorn-hope of Syriacism in AD 66–70. If "the Gospel" was to survive, it must be rooted afresh before that happened. The astonishing "leap" of Christianity from one world to the other between AD 50 and 60 was made only just in time. After that the pace is much slower for more than a century. Christianity is out of the deadly historical trap formed by the clash of the two great cultures now represented by the Empire and the Jews. But after that pause for breath Christianity will be ready to advance again to the conquest—of the Greek mind this time, by its own alien Syriac conceptions.[31]

(I must refer you to the second lecture of series one for a development of that theme).

I have already run a bit ahead of my argument: by pursuing the account of world religions over leaping cultural boundaries. In the Far Eastern world religions, however, Hinduism and Buddhism are passive with regard to the world and deny the significance of history. Judaism, Christianity and Mohammedism of the West are historical religions, in that they give crucial importance to the historical existence of their founders, and have a unique relation between God and his people. But neither Judaism nor Islam has produced a common way of life for people of entirely different cultures in the way Christianity has. The appearance of Christianity seems to me the one big religious event since the rise of the world religions. What does it signify? Let me remind you that the Hebrew faith made the Lord Jehovah, the supreme and overriding deity—behind and in phenomena but not conditioned by them. The personal Lord takes here the place of impersonal fate, or destiny which in Greek literature and thought was alone above the

---

30. Dix, *Jew and Greek*, 54.
31. Ibid., 54–55.

Gods. And it made the world more accountable than in the systems where there is one immanent principle of which all things are derivative. Its ethics become personally determined, because the Lord leaves so much of his purpose and motives unexpressed. Abraham, David, Job, the prophets wrestle with God: and represent not historical cultures but universal history in religious terms—from the beginning of things with the creation of the world, and will end with the last few days, the fulfilling of the Covenant. The Old Testament stories represent an unbroken relation—tested in infidelities and conflicts—to a single hidden God, who yet shows himself and who guides universal history by promise and exaction; but behind the daily life which is the context of O.T. ethics, there is no source of stability short of doing the Lord's will. So, said Alfred Zimmern, comparing the Jews with the Greek, "The Greeks, unlike the Jews, have nothing quixotic in their nature. They never lead a forlorn hope, unless they can persuade themselves that it is not forlorn."[32] The Jews had never been allowed to seek *sophrosune* safe mindedness.[33]

Compare for instance the temper of this passage from Sophocles's *Antigone* (332):

> Many mighty works there are;
> None mightier than man;
> He sails beyond the sea, lashed white by winter wind,
> Pursing the waters that soar around
> He furrows unwithered earth, greatest of immortal divinity
> From Year to Year, with horses and curling plough he knows the Lord
> Light winged kinds he snared, wild beasts and fishes of the sea;
> Wild horse, untamed mountain bull he tames and yokes;
> He taught himself speech also and wisdom,
> And customs of law whereby men live in cities,
> In all things he findeth a way.
> Death is too great for him, yet he deviseth healing of sickness.
> He hath art and skill to invent?

And in the Eighth Psalm,[34]

> When I consider thy heavens, the works of thy fingers
> The moon and the stars which thou hast ordained,

---

32. Zimmern, *Greek Commonwealth*, 78.

33. Here Demant includes the note: "(Footnote: Cambala Ancient History V p. 127) For this contrast between Jew and Greek: see further Murray, *The Rise of the Greek Cynic*, 78—9; Taylor, *Faith of a Moralist*, 2, 325."

34. Psalm 8:3–6.

> What is man that thou art mindful of him?
> And the son of Man that thou visitest him?
> For thou hast made him a little lower than the angels
> And hast crowned him with glory and honor
> Thou madest him to have dominion over the works of thy hands,
> And hast put all things under his feet.

In the Greek drama man's authority over nature, to build a city of sophistication, is attributed to the wisdom and might of man; in the Hebrew poem it is a gift of God, "man is what he is and does what he does only by divine creation and permission." It is an apparent paradox that the Hebrew consciousness, with its intense sense of the divine otherness, and its ritual sense of partaking in the march towards the fulfillment of history, served when it was transformed into an incarnational religion in Christianity, to set going the world's transforming phase of human history. It is the impulse perhaps more than the ability to fashion life that needs explaining.

The important stress is that in Hebrew religion phenomena are not appearances of God—he can be inferred from them. . "The heavens declare the glory of God and the firmament sheweth his handywork." "The pillars of the earth are the Lord's and he hath set the world upon them."[35] God created the existing order but it derived no sacredness from its divine source. This kind of monotheism devalued all phenomena of nature and the achievement of man—art, virtue, and social order. "Only a God who transcends every phenomenon, who is not conditioned by any mode of manifestation—only an unqualified God can be the one and only ground of all existence."[36] A new "myth" arose the myth of the will of God—and the people chosen to be tied to that will. Man is the interpreter, a servant of God. History is a "revelation of the dynamic will of God . . . man was condemned to unending efforts which were doomed to fail because of his inadequacy. In the Old Testament we find man possessed of a new freedom and of a new burden of responsibility."[37] "With infinite moral courage the Hebrews worshipped an absolute God and accepted as the correlate of that faith the sacrifice of an harmonized existence."[38]

There is something of this spirit in Christendom, which informed the other moral and intellectual factors and which made up vigorous variety of European culture.

---

35. 1 Samuel 2:8.
36. Frankfort, *Before Philosophy*, 243.
37. Ibid., 245.
38. Ibid., 370.

How did it come about, that a small group of peoples in Western Europe should in a relatively short space of time acquire the power to transform the world and to emancipate themselves from man's age-long dependence on the forces of nature... Why is it that Europe... has been continually shaken and transformed by an energy of spiritual unrest that refuses to be content with the unchanging law of social traditions which rules oriental cultures? It is because its religious ideal has not been the worship of timeless and changeless perfection but a spirit that strives to incorporate itself in humanity and to change the world."[39]

There is no Prometheus myth in the Bible; there is the story of the Fall in Eden and of the Tower of Babel. *"Man has his peculiar significance from the fact that he is in a unique relation to the eternal, while at the same time he is in the process of the earth's life and the sweep of human history."*[40]

I showed in a lecture of series one, that the idea of a secular order with its own warrant from God independently of the sacred order, is a product of Christendom. In the eighteenth century this secular order produced a religious body of thought known as "natural theology" in a new sense—product of reason only, as if reason started with no presuppositions. We know now, that the reason of the modern world, presupposed much of the natural, moral, and social texture of European man. I would refer you to C. Dawson's first Gifford Lectures at Edinburg, "Religion and Culture," for evidence of his statement that "positive, historic religion is always primary, and philosophical or theological religion is the result of a secondary reflective activity."[41] As Leslie Stephen wrote, "The vigor of English Theology at this period, and it was the golden period of English Theology—is due to the fact that, for the time, reason and Christian theology were in spontaneous alliance. The theologians of the middle and end of the seventeenth century... were anxious to construct a philosophical religion, and they were not alive to the possibility that such a religion might cease to be Christian."[42]

What was happening from say Descartes and Spinoza to Tillotson and beyond was an external joining of faith and reason, like (to borrow Francis Bacon's telling image) "the iron and clay in the toes of Nebuchadnezzar's image—they may cleave" but they will not incorporate.[43] It is a precarious thing, holding side by side of what had been a dynamic intervening of faith

39. Dawson, *Religion and the Rise of Western Culture*, 8.
40. Here Demant included the notes: "(Not one sided) (Culture Paper pp. 9—14)." The quote is from his book, *Our Culture*, 13.
41. Dawson, *Religion and Culture*, 43.
42. Stephen, *English Thought in the Eighteenth Century*, 79.
43. Bacon, *Bacon's Essays*, 23.

and reason throughout the Middle Ages. Natural theology, natural ethics, and natural science soon lost their religious connections, and it was to this situation that Newman addressed himself in an essay which denied that the basis of the Enlightenment were really using the term "natural religion" in the right way.

Newman said that there are three main channels which nature furnishes us with the Knowledge of God, of his will, and of our duties towards him: via our own minds, the voice of mankind, and the course of the world, that is of human life and human affairs. In our own minds, Newman finds the central testimony in conscience—and it is an [unreadable] conscience. "The special Attribute under which it brings Him before us, to which it subordinate all other Attributes, is that of justice—retributive justice."[44] (And Newman anticipates the necessary warning made by Mr. C. A. Pierce in his study, *Conscience in the New Testament*, that in St. Paul conscience always occurs—and is not all infallible facts in the box appearing when wanted to settle any moral perplexity.)[45] Newman writes:

> Wherever Religion exists in a popular shape, it has almost invariably worn its dark side outwards. Of these distinct rites and doctrines embodying the severe side of Natural Religion, the most remarkable is that of atonement, that is, "a substitution of something offered, for a penalty which would otherwise be exacted" . . . In the oldest books of the Hebrew scriptures. . . by means of the heathen records, we meet with the same notion of atonement. If we pursue our inquiries through the accounts left us by the Greek and Roman writers of the barbarous nations with which they were acquainted, from India to Britain. . . among the various tribes of Africa, the islanders of the South Seas, and even that most peculiar race, the natives of Australia.

We have a witness that need for atonement is part of natural religion.[46] There is a brighter side, but,

> In thus making it a necessary point to adjust the religions of the world with the intimations of our conscience, I am suggesting the reason why I confine myself to such religions as have had their rise in barbarous times, and do not recognize the religion of what is called civilization . . . such religion does but contradict the religion of barbarism; and since this civilization itself is not a development of man's whole nature, but mainly of the

---

44. Newman, *Grammar of Assent*, 390–91.
45. Pierce, *Conscience in the New Testament*.
46. Newman, 392–3.

intellect, recognizing indeed the moral sense, but ignoring the conscience, no wonder that the religion in which it issues has no sympathy either with the hopes and fears of the awakened soul, or with those frightful presentiments which are expressed in the worship and traditions of the heathen. This artificial religion [the natural theology of the Enlightenment] then, has no place in the inquiry, because it comes of a one-sided progress of mind."[47]

[Such a perspective is in line with William James's emphasis on religious experience, rather than theology or ecclesiastical structure.]

There is some narrowing of religious history in this account of Newman's for the idea of atonement, though widespread and deep rooted, does not feature in all religious climates. But his general theme stands. The natural religion and ethics of the modern world, is the least natural thing of all; it is the product of a definite piece of cultural, intellectual and spiritual history. And I indicated in my first lecture of series one, that it survived into the nineteenth century by getting attached to another dogma "that of evolutionary naturalism" which in ethics gave us in England of the early twentieth century such works as *The Origin and Development of the Moral Ideas* and Professor Hobhouse's *Morals in Evolution*.

The following lectures will, I hope support my statement that our modern situation, however much it appears thus to be a revolt from its past, is linked inextricably with one piece of cultural and religious history.

[This[48] link is to the "conception of history as a whole with real significance" grounded in the "Jewish and Christian Scriptures, with their doctrine of the redemptive purpose of God in history."[49] Such an understanding is not shared by other cultures or eras, even the greatest of them. For instance, Thucydides may be the "noblest and austerest moralist who has ever written history," but he does not "see the struggle of which he is the historian as an act in a drama which has significance as a whole."[50] This understanding of history as being the site of redemption leads away from interest in repeated cycles and patterns or static perfection, as can be seen in William Blake's concern for "individual historical reality, the 'minute particular,' as he repeatedly calls it."[51] In addition, this interest in history and in

47. Ibid., 395–6.
48. Here Demant references Taylor's *Faith of a Moralist*, vol. 2, page 327 along with several incomplete quotations from that work. The quotations have been completed with the editors adding the additional notes.
49. Taylor, *Faith of a Moralist*, 327.
50. Ibid.
51. Ibid., 360.

the particularities of the world leads to ever more sophisticated questioning of a priori assumptions, as exemplified in the words of Hume's Philo, "To be a philosophical sceptic is, in a man of letters, the first and most essential step towards being a sound, believing Christian."[52]

This understanding of history and this push toward inquiry contribute to form the culture of Christendom.

---

52. Hume, *Dialogues Concerning Natural Religion*, 130.

Series II, Lecture II
Not of This World

WHEN BERTRAND RUSSELL WROTE his *History of Western Philosophy* he had the distinction of being the first modern historian of thought in the West to include a large section on the church from Moses to the fifteenth century. Most others had skipped from the ancients to Descartes or thereabouts. And when he wrote "The Church brought philosophic beliefs into a closer relation to social and political circumstances than they have ever had before or since the medieval period."[1] He realized that this period which he too narrowly interpreted in terms of philosophical beliefs has brought ultimate views of reality to bear upon history and worldly affairs—more thoroughly than before or after. This is a magnificent admission from one who thinks that the alleged other-worldliness of Christianity has been a menace to mankind, and who does not believe a word of Christian dogma. But perhaps he is like the late Sir James Frazer who wrote *Psyche's Task* to show that superstition, which was untrue, contributed greatly to the formation of morals in respect of domestic life, authority of rulers, and respect for property.

There is in this widespread idea that "the other-worldly" element in Christianity is inimical to its effect upon world history, a number of unfounded assumptions. What is usually meant is that there is much evil in earthly societies and Christianity does not put its weight against them. There is also an ignorance of what is meant by the "world" which has to be opposed by the Christian; and a blindness to the staring fact that in order to be deeply concerned with the life of other men in this world it is not sufficient to disbelieve in another world. A sub-human view of existence does not by any means generate social reform or revolutionary zeal.[2]

---

1. Russell, *History of Western Philosophy*, 247.

2. Following this paragraph, Demant included this note: "cf. VAD's Difficulties article."

[Demant references here his *Religion and the Decline of Capitalism*, in which he demonstrates how liberalism emerges from Christian roots, but often with a rejection of the idea of the existence of two worlds. Capitalism, as part of this growth of liberalism, assumes that there is an inherent "harmony of interests" which can be "recovered by human nature."[3] In reality, though, capitalism proved a force which too often not only failed to generate social reform, but caused harm to many through unsafe working conditions, child labor, and other results of economic life being an autonomous activity.

P. T. Forsyth in his work, *The Church, Gospel, and Society*, notes some of the challenges workers face in a largely unregulated capitalist system and calls upon the church to respond. "Christian ethics cannot be satisfied with calling on such people to glorify God in their station. It must go on to promote such a reorganization of industry as may give the worker freedom to live and hope as a man should."[4]]

In my first series I tried to expound the reasons why the peculiar twist given by its doctrine of God and the transcendent and of the incarnation of the Divine word in the flesh of one concrete man, has given the religious basis to a world transforming disposition. It shares with other world religious belief in that divine source of things as being over and not in nature and society, yet active in them. But their "other-worldly" element, if that is the right word, never penetrates history and cuts into it as the living God who is manifest in the historic Christ has done, in the mind of Christendom. It is a characteristic of the world religions that their ethic is concerned with a way of life distinct from the bond of the tribe, measures for survival or instruments of social cohesion. These forms of purely societal ethic are always under a certain judgment as misleading or perverted from the perspective of the true life.

This transcendent ethic of the world religions becomes, however, embodied as concrete historical facts and institutions with the history of Israel and the church as the new Israel. In the Old Testament the duality between the pure spiritual ethic and the working ethic of actual societies in the world religions is replaced by a duality between the people of the covenant and the outsiders. A recent writer, The Rev. Martin Thornton, has made a rather breathless plea for a recovery of the Remnant theory of the church, as an essential for a vital pastoral ministry. He discusses very fully but untidily the history and present-day necessity for this extension of the Covenant relationship. It involves, he points out,

---

3. Demant, *Religion and the Decline of Capitalism*, 37.
4. Forsyth, *The Church, The Gospel, and Society*, 54.

(1) Yahweh is majestically transcendent yet majestically personal; he is the Father—creator of all things whose ultimate concern can be limited to nothing less than all; all nations, ages and even creeds. But (2) Israel is his chosen race, the peculiar people, the elect, the priestly caste; set over against the Gentile world. yet through sin and apostasy, its mission and even salvation is delegated to, and depends upon, the faithful Remnant, and the faithful Remnant is typified by purity in worship and loyalty in faith: religious or ascetical, rather than directly ethical, qualities. Thus (3) the salvation of the world depends upon the faith of Israel, the chosen instrument, which in turn revolves around the faithful Remnant. We are faced with the tremendous implications of (4) the vicarious principle; epitomized in the Servant poems (of the second Isaiah) and prophetic of the Cross. The Remnant, far from being an amputated segment—the clique detached from the whole—is at the center of the parochial organism and of power extending beyond it.[5]

I do not believe this to be the right Christian church pattern; for it has been a special feature of Christianity to minister to a world with its own secular pattern, and yet to influence that pattern secularly. This has been regarded by many as an apostasy (constructive). But calls for "a church of the remnant" are an essential part of Christian history; they too however, as we shall see, have influenced the secular career of Christendom.

This lecture is about the Christian community in its contrast to the world. "Other-worldliness" is not the best term for denoting this kind of opposition in Judaism and Christianity, though it is good enough for the other world religions. The tension is between societies as they are, with not only their evils but also their institutions for the provision of order, and a sort of foreign body within societies overlapping them often, with roots in the forces of the internal world or the powers of the world to come. "Christians are those who "have tasted the good word of God, and the powers of the world to come."[6]

Already the fact of the Covenant people in the Old Testament exemplifies this. They are separate from mankind, yet in a way representative. Covenant is not a most favored nation clause, in the religious history of man; it is a tie, and therefore a challenge.[7] It is necessary to notice that while the Covenant relationship between the Chosen people and the Lord is the central fact of Hebrew religion, it does not occupy the whole picture. And

5. Thornton, *Pastoral Theology,* 22–23.
6. Hebrews 6:5b.
7. See Demant on the myth of the will of God from Series 2, Lecture 1.

then we see that the Covenant, a sort of contract between the Lord and his People, is not unrelated to another kind of relationship, which by contrast we call status, and in considering this we shall see something of the thread which links the Old Testament with the New Testament.

[Here Demant references his work, *Christian Polity*.

> The Bible begins with a status between man and God. A natural connection bound Jehovah and his people. There was no reason behind it; God and man were linked to each other by their very nature and existence... It was a relationship of status, and sprang from a natural tie, forged in what man and God were rather than upon what they did for each other. This had its limitations, and as we trace the exaltation of Jehovah into the one and only true God, the relationship between him and his people becomes more and more one of contract instead of status, based not upon nature but upon what each was prepared to do for the other . . . And this movement from an ethic of status to one of contract has been held to mark a great advance. It led to the breakdown of tribal national exclusiveness; the relationship was the reward of a free act, of deliberate moral choice . . . But it should be noticed that its superiority to the other conception does not lie in the fact that a relationship of contract, of a quid pro quo, is higher than a relationship of status, of beings bound together by their very nature. On the contrary, the most perfect form of relationship between God and man, and between man and man, is always that status which is the bond of beings truly personal . . . This is surely the purpose of our blessed Lord's atoning work . . . He enters into this contractual world, pays a price, meets a cost, earns a salvation, so that once and for all the whole sorry business of contract can begin to be superseded through the leaven of a new history beside the old . . . The language of the Kingdom, the language of family, of sonship, and fatherhood and membership, and also the language of friendship, is the language of status and not of a bargain or contract.][8]

It is from within this renewed status that Christian man saw himself as no longer bound exclusively to the requirements of his earthly communities. This produced a sense of his individual significance and a strain between his two loyalties—that is his earthly and heavenly citizenship. This sense was fortified by the actual process by which the church encountered the world. The sense of individuality, a tension between two loyalties, and an impulse to make history, all go together. We have now to see how they

---

8. Demant, *Christian Polity*, 32–35.

reinforced one another, and how the Christian outlook is one of the major facts behind them.

[From the early days of the Christian church, there was a clear sense that fidelity to God was more important than following the law; "there are some spheres of life in which the writ of Caesar does not run."][9]

It is apparent I think, that here was enough for ferment of moral and ethical speculation, with the possibly conflicting claims of local custom, rulers, ways of life, surviving ancient cults, imperial politics, and the new translocal church. But for some centuries the church was not much interested in general ethics. It has enough on hand to preserve the fidelity of its own members, to voice disgust at the vices of a degenerate and waning pagan culture, and to defend itself against the frequent accusations of undermining the security of civil society.

In the fourth century with the baptism of the Emperor Constantine and the ensuing conversion such as it was of the Roman Legions, and of a wider populace a new situation arose. Conventional Christianity came into being—joining the church because it was done by multitudes, or because of authoritative pressure, without fundamental change of belief or heart. No wonder many have regarded this event as a disaster, a secularizing of the church. And there was naturally a revolt within the Christian community; it took two forms; one a rigorism which led to controversy over readmission of the lapsed—lapsed in faith or morals: and a sharpening of opposition to all that was meant by the world. Already in the previous century Tertullian had thundered against assimilation to heathen thought and social conformity. "Away" he exclaims "with all attempts to produce a mottled Christianity of Stoic, Platonic, and dialectical composition. We want no curious disputation after possessing Christ Jesus."[10] And the Christian believer has to combat not only the natural impulses but the snare of the social order. Christ came not to bring "boars and savages ... with some civilization, but as one who aimed to enlighten men already civilized and under illusions from their very culture."[11] And Tertullian had followers in this strain later.[12]

The other great movement, counteracting the tendency to make the church assimilated to the world, was the flight to the desert. It is an error to regard this as a form of escapism. It was a genuine protest and a nursery of forces needed later to handle the world! [As Charles Norris Cochrane writes,

---

9. Here Demant included the note: "Our Culture Paper 9–12." Quote is from *Our Culture*, 11.

10. Tertullian, *Apologetical and Practical Treatises*, 442.

11. Ibid., 53.

12. Here Demant includes the note: "De Spectailis."

"monasticism contained no message for the man who, while impressed by the salutary character of Christian teaching, sought in any way to reconcile it with the battered ideals of Classicism."[13] There are some extravagances and some infiltration of Manichean influences in this movement—but as a whole it cradled a spirit of discipline and independence of the world's life, which later under monasticism nurtured a new intellectual and social culture after the complete debacle of the Roman civilization.

[To explore this period further, one can look to Louis Bouyer's work on Athanasius and his biography of St. Anthony. In addition, Owen Chadwick writes of how John Cassian took these ideals to Provence and began the tradition of monasticism in the West. And Marjorie Strachey offers a different perspective with her collection of early Christian sources, *The Fathers without Theology*.]

It is not possible here to describe all the phases of this kind of distinctiveness from the world and Christian in the world; exercises in the ascetic and contemplative life as a counter weight to natural impulses and worldly entanglements, and the rise of mystical schools of prayer seeking spiritual status from beyond the flux of time and history. They are all part of a current running throughout the course of Christendom which stands in a sort of judgment upon accommodation to worldly history and the church's attempts to be influential in it.

Besides these endeavors there appears also throughout Christian history movements which await "the new age" or seek to bring it about. These too operate as a kind of protest against a church too implicated in the present world. These movements fasten on the eschatological element in the original Christian teaching and in the earlier Jewish apocalypses. They are not other-worldly but assume the arrival of a pure state of world history, in society as a whole or in a new elect within it.

[As Jacob Taubes has noted, Joachim of Fiore believed in this sort of immanentized eschatology. But the Joachists were not alone. The variety and abundance of similar millenarian movements in the middle ages is outlined by Norman Cohn's *Pursuit of the Millennium*. And this impulse has not disappeared. Bultmann has shown how the eschatological emphasis of Christianity brought about a teleological understanding of history that is still influencing even intentionally secular belief systems.]

Harnack, the great church historian of the liberal school, appreciated the force of this element which continually disturbed the regular ministry to men settled in their settled communities. "The dual concepts of Christianity dominate the whole evangelical story down to present days Eschatological

---

13. Cochrane, *Christianity and Classical Culture*, 339.

considerations are strongly suppressed, but keep breaking through and venture to project spiritual values against the worldly ways by whom they are threatened."[14] Eschatology in the East never became the impetus of historical movements; in the West it takes the form of a consummation, after the Thousand Years Rule of Messiah. Quite early in Eusebius we find men thinking of four realms of the world, and of six ages, or four world empires; Assyria, Persia, Macedon, and home—these had to arrive before history was closed. The world of the time was in the fourth world empire and the sixth age. By contrast the main Christian tradition thought of deliverance from the burden of history as coming from above (realized eschatology). This idea is found in Augustine and the mediaeval church teaching. But the chiliastic movements looked forward not upwards; thus history gains absolute significance.

The twelfth and thirteenth centuries witnessed on the one hand the great power of the church over society, but also the two most interesting representatives of the new age. One Joachim of Flora, Abbot of Calabria, put down the whole ecclesiastical history up to his time as of the old world, to be succeeded by political spiritual and cultural millennium. This was the spiritual ancestor of modern radicalism. History in Joachim's view has these ages: that of the Father, from Adam to Christ; that of the Son, parting from the Incarnation to the year 1260. Thereafter is the age of the Holy Ghost, going on until the end of the world and having in it the thousand years realm. This, I am sure, is one of the genius of the dynamic optimism of modern Europe.

The other force of the same kind, that of gentler and more paradoxical temper, was the Franciscan movement. The Friars Minor of St. Francis of Assisi were a new thing in Christendom: lay preachers mostly without ties. St. Francis was a rich young man of knightly education who dreamt of a crusade; he hurried back and conceived a new form of life to replace the Crusades. The church had become wealthy. Francis's ideal was poverty; it is the gospel of the migrant orders. Yet this poverty was not just a protest—it was a means or sanctifying the temporal. "The people" wrote a chronicler "seemed to fear a visitation of God in 1260, the year forecast for Joachism as the beginning of the last age. Suddenly in Perugia, the first of the Friars raised his voice and the inhabitants marched, headed by bishops and clergy, in a long train as far as the next city. Peace, charity, mercy were the words they uttered with signs."[15] The Franciscan movement became involved in politics and in the ideas of Joachim of Flora, and by the Ghibellines. The

---

14. Source of quotation unknown.
15. Source of quotation unknown.

Ghibellines, Dante's own party, regarded the emperor as the righteous ruler of the new age; against the Pope who was upheld for this role by the Guelphs. But Francis himself was a Papist; he was also the greatest force in turning the fire of love upon God's creation. Man is a flower, the world, a garden in which he is planted. He discovered a new world both in the old world of monasteries, emperors and monks. In vision Christ came to redeem not mankind only but all creation. The heart of man moves towards creation. For the first time the walls of a house were felt to be hostile to the reconciliation of man and nature. You know the hymn of Creation, "Praised to Thou, my Lord with all thy creatures."

FRANCIS IN A TWO WORLD RELIGION

The history of the Franciscan movement is a fine example of the way a movement, counter to the main center of church and civic life, was created to leaven it and in the end got caught in it. St. Francis is the favorite saint of sentimental unbelievers, and that popularity is based on a mistake. People feel sympathy for one who deserted houses and cities for the open road and the sun and the air; and they admire the courage to own nothing. Especially, they are attracted by St. Francis's love of his fellow creature: then they wrongly regard him as a Nature lover—an emancipated soul who escaped from an ecclesiastical straight jacket. In the end they tend to view St. Francis as part of those who hold the slogan, "the more I see of men the more I like dogs!"

But this is all wrong. St. Francis did not find God in his fellow creatures: he loved and respected them as creatures and servants of God. Therefore, he met his fellow creatures with a love and courtesy which is so appealing, the birds, the wolf of Gubbio, the leper, brother sun, and also the fire that was to cauterize his eyes. The secret is, of course, that he could love disinterestedly because he wanted nothing; he had overcome the hold men and things had on him. And this was such a spiritual revolution in him, and such a close union with the suffering Christ that Francis carried about in his own hands and feet the scars of the crucifixion.

I will mention one other movement, with perhaps even greater influence, in preventing any acquiescence in the present state of church and world. It is the Cathar Movement, "Catharoi," the purified—an ancient sect, with ties behind Christianity in Mithraism, and then associated with Manichaeus's denial of this world and Gnostic esoteric presumptions. It spread from the East along the trade routes and from the Byzantine enclaves of Italy, and thence pressed forward into the Albigensian territories. It was not

Christian in origin, nor influenced by Christian eschatology—and contrary to Franciscanism—it rejected the world and its doctrine was a Manichaean dualism for which the cast of the flesh were evil. The movement however was violently anticlerical—and it intermingled with a number of chiliastic Christian forces—to preserve the notion of an "Illuminati" in an otherwise doomed world and church. [In his preface to Ross Williamson's book about the Cathar movement, Demant notes how this belief system is "one representative of a very deep rooted and recurring religious force."][16]

This brief account of chiliastic trends has been given in support of my thesis that attitudes and outlooks which seem part of the essential furniture of human consciousness have, on the contrary, roots in phases of religious or intellectual history.[17] In this case, it is the radical, unreforming, revolutionary propensities of modern man from the Renaissance onwards, with a revival in the eighteenth century after Post Renaissance disillusionment and despondency, which would never have informed the human race, without this current of eschatology transferred from religious to temporal affairs. In place of the duality of "this age" and the heavenly, or "world to come," it takes the form of a duality between past and present deformity of life on the one hand—and a fulfillment at some point or condition, or a vaguer millennium without a date, which is the doctrine of Progress. "One far-off divine event to which the whole creation moves."[18] "The kingdom of Man"; Bacon's faith in the supreme saving efficacy of knowledge; Sprat's "all millenniums have been completed, for perfection of life"; Royal Society; Leibniz; Hegel's intellectual realm in the history of philosophy; the kingdom of God in the philosophy of Religion, in which in the end the Prussian King takes the place of the Pope in the ecclesial spirituality of John of Olivi—These are examples of the eschatological hope in modern thinkers. In the makers of history, the French Revolution had its own chiliastic spirit; Rousseau had given a romantic turn to this trend by pitting nature against society and civilization. By doing so he gave to the third Estate ideas which flared up in the Revolution.

16. Demant, in preface to Williamson's *The Arrow and the Sword*, xiv.
17. Demant included a note preceding this paragraph that indicates the rest of the text was not part of his of his original lectures: "NOT DELIVERED 11 to 16 in exercise book, i.e. from here to end."
18. Tennyson, "In Memoriam," CXXI.

SOCIAL EVOLUTION

Social unrest is no new thing; it is as old as civilization. As Dawson notes in his *Progress and Religion,*

> In every age misgovernment and oppression has been met by violence and disorder, but it is a new thing, and perhaps a phenomenon peculiar to our modern western civilization, that men should work and think and agitate for the complete remodeling of society according to some ideal of social perfection. It belongs to the order of religion, rather than to that of politics, as politics were formerly understood. It finds its only parallel in the past in movements of the most extreme religious type, like that of the Anabaptists in sixteenth-century Germany and the Levellers and Fifth Monarchy Men of Puritan England. And when we study the lives of the founders of modern socialism, the great Anarchists, and even some of the apostles of the Nationalist Liberalism, like Mazzini, we feel at once that we are in the presence of religious leaders, whether prophets or heresiarchs, saints or fanatics. Behind the hard rational surface of Karl Marx' materialist and socialist interpretation of history, there burns the flame of an apocalyptic vision. For what was that social revolution in which he put his hope but a nineteenth-century version of the Day of Lord, in which the rich and powerful of the earth should be consumed and the princes of the Gentiles brought low, and the poor and disinherited should reign in a regenerated universe?[19]

I would fill this picture of modern radicalism as the terrestrial version of "not of this age" religious impulses. *For instance, one might also add the example of Auguste Comte who created his Religion of Humanity based on positivist philosophy in the nineteenth century.*[20] But even before the nineteenth century when these movements reached a turning point and almost an end, with the human Revolution and Nazi chiliasm, men had voiced their pessimism about a future millennium. Goethe wrote, "People will be clever and more penetrating but not better, not happier, not more energetic."[21] Chateaubriand, de Maistre, and Lamennais, in France; Burke, Coleridge and Matthew Arnold in England—represent disillusion with these hopes. And then with Nietzsche, Spengler, and Toynbee we have a complete dismissal

---

19. Dawson, *Progress and Religion,* 177.

20. This sentence is an expansion by the editors of Demant's note which reads: "Comte."

21. Attributed to Goethe in Nock, *Memoirs of a Superflous Man,* 214.

of eschatological thinking. This thinking survives only in underground or dissipated sects like Jehovah Witnesses.

This piece of history, which I have sketched, is the coming out of the duality of the two worlds, inherent in the Christians's outlooks. That outlook produced several kinds of tension, between supernatural and mundane ethics, eschatological and day to day ethics for actual living, and between millennial and stable society or church ethics. The Christian community has thereby been recurringly prompted to stand over against, if not always in opposition to established orders and the ethics society makes for its own stability. The point I now wish to make is that this detachment from communal moral patterns and often disturbance of them, has made on the one hand for a withdrawal from society and on the other for a world changing impulse. And these twin manifestations of the original duality between the realm of the spirit and the present state of human history. It is therefore quite mistaken to believe that the "other-worldly" roots of Christian life and thought always make for a passive acceptance of things as they are; it has often engendered the most violent impulses to change things as they are. The world changing impulse is a consequence of the world withdrawing impulse.

This has much to do with the growth of science in the modern West. This movement is a result of a peculiar combination of events is not an accident. But as a world movement it is much more than a set of aptitudes for comprehending and controlling the physical and theological world. It has been a crusading enterprise, and its high priests and political dupes talk in terms of eschatological salvation of science. As a technique western thought goes back to the Ionian philosophers—"Stand back and ask reason why." But as a crusade modern scientific assessment is an heir of the messianic expectation I have mentioned.

And what is more important to understand is that scientific handling of the world, involves detachment from it. (The birds do not write PhD treatises on ornithology; nor do active and busy people in society make theories of public seminars). The natural social sciences are the result of an inner refusal to be immersed in nature or society. Several philosophers of human activities have realized this. Jaspers, in his *Origin and Goal of History*, traces the impulse (not ability, for that occurs elsewhere) to comprehend and contrive to the peculiar religious and intellectual temper of Christendom.[22] And N. Berdyaev writes, "However paradoxical it may seem, I am convinced that Christianity alone made possible both positive science and technique. As long as man found himself in communion with nature and had based his

---

22. Jaspers, *Origin and Goal of History*.

life upon mythology, he could not raise himself above nature through an act of apprehension by means of the natural sciences or technique. Christianity has freed him from subjection to nature (and history) and has set him up spiritually in the centre of the created world."[23]

In spite of severe conflicts between the dogmas of science and the dogmas of Christianity; the impulse to do science is of the same kind as the ascetic's impulse to master nature in himself. They are both on the same side against immersion in the community as it is and the stream of natural life. The withdrawal from the world of the hermits and monks, was a retirement into an inner spiritual world and involved a struggle to overcome subjection to nature and the current social order. It dammed up man's inner powers, which in a way could then spill over at the Renaissance for the political and scientific enterprises of the modern world. The negative attitude to nature and society of the Middle Ages, became a positive in the seventeenth century. But both mark a phase of man's history in which he stands over against his earthly communities and his natural setting, and makes objects of them instead of living blandly as part of their existence.

We shall have to see also that the great conceptions of law in Christendom is the fruit of the same spirit of interested detachment.

---

23. Berdyaev, *Meaning of History*, 117.

Series II, Lecture III
The Field is the World[1]

READERS OF ERNST TROELTSCH great work on *The Social Teaching of the Christian Churches* will notice that he said:

> Medieval Christianity produced two great types of social doctrine: first, the relative type of the idea of Christian Society which is represented by Thomism; and, secondly, the radical idea of Christian Society which was evolved by the sects ... the Church ... takes up into its own life the secular institutions, groups and values which ... are adapted to the conditions of the fallen state; the whole of the secular life, therefore, is summed up under the conception of a natural stage in human life, which prepares the way for the higher supernatural stage, for the ethic of grace and miracle ... [In the second type] the religious community has evolved its social ideal purely from the Gospel and from the Law of Christ ... the Christian character and holiness of this ideal should be proved by the unity reigning within the group ... Therefore, either it does not recognize the institutions, groups, or values which exist outside of Christianity at all, or in a quietly tolerant spirit of detachment from the world it avoids them, or under the influence of an "enthusiastic" eschatology it attacks these institutions and replaces them by a purely Christian order of society.[2]

For the first, "the Church-type, its doctrine of sin facilitated the acceptance of the existing social order ... this social order, therefore, must be in a way accepted and tolerated ... in the case of the sect-type ... [its doctrine of sin is] an argument for the radical rejection by Christians of the secular life

---

1. Demant begins with the note: "Possible end of lecture 2."
2. Troeltsch, *Social Teaching of the Christian Churches*, 461.

and all its works, and as a challenge to create a social order which is based purely upon the principles of the Gospel."[3]

This generalization of Troeltsch has been frequently criticized; but in spite of its over simplification of the effect of the two types, it rightly calls attention to a double strand in the meeting of church and world, which goes back to the early centuries of Christendom. In the last lecture I described earlier phases of thought and movements which emphasized contact between the life of the spirit and that of society with the regular church ministry which accepts its main structure. In this lecture, we shall look at some of the ways in which this regular ministry and some of its powerful thought movements, penetrated and leavened, without downright opposition, the secular order in which it worked. There were forces making for stability; they exist in two main periods in the early history of Christendom, one when the church was faced with the task of cradling a new frame of civilized living and breakup of the Empire; the other of Christianizing the Barbarian invaders and incorporating their social structure into the remnants of the older culture. These endeavors were imbued with the need to find a workable social bond for communities concerned, which also protected and encouraged the specific significance of the individual and the idea of the solidarity of mankind behind historically grown decisions, two axioms which were implicit in the Christian mind.

Some sets of norms were necessary in a society enduring despondency in the crumbling fabric of Roman civilization, with the decline of personal and civic virtue. After the disillusion with that ancient form of moral rearmament attempted by the Emperor Augustine, Christians as well as pagans recognized what the Empire had done. *St. Paul's missionary work was successful in part because of the ease of travel and quality of communication across the Roman Empire.*[4] Lactantius wrote, "When Rome the head of the world shall have fallen, who can doubt that the end is come of human things, aye, of the earth itself. She, she alone is the state by which all things are upheld even until now."[5] Tertullian and Clement of Rome wrote in the same strain of gratitude to the Emperor. And Jerome when he heard at his monastery at Bethlehem of the sack of Rome by Alaric in 410 cried, "The human race is included in the ruins, my tongue cleaves to the roof of my mouth, and sobs choke my words, to which that the city is captive which led captive the whole world." St. Augustine wrote his last words on the Psalms in

---

3. Ibid., 462.

4. This is an expansion by the editors of Demant's note which reads: "St Paul's Roman Citizenship."

5. Lactantius, quoted in Bryce, *Holy Roman Empire*, 21.

Hippo with the sounds of vandals sounding at the gates. It was an appalling moment in the world's history.

When Julius Caesar lay dead at the foot of Pompey's statue four centuries earlier, the decline had started. Different ways of recovery—Now, when the end was near in the 4th century, an unexpected source of renewed order was operative—a religious awakening and a moral regeneration began. The church men had now the task of deriving from the ethics of covenant and of grace, a system of ethics for masses of men, not only by any means inwardly changed by the grace of God from the rules of their societies to the freedom of the Christian man. This task largely took the form of using and reinterpreting the personal and civic virtues of the old world. The church had already her teaching of the theological virtues for those within the covenant of Grace, Faith, Hope and Agape, fruits of the life in Christ, with which St. Paul summed up his hymn to charity in 1 Corinthians 13, and which create an inclination to seek God, our true end analogous to our seeking our natural wellbeing in the created order. They are theological because directed primarily to God, but also and more deeply, because they originate in God's action appropriated by faith. *As the words of the spiritual put it,*[6]

> Ezekiel saw a wheel,
> Way up in the middle of the air. (sky)
> Little wheel run by faith
> Big wheel run by the grace of God—
> A wheel in the middle of the air!

Many have been the commentaries and expositions of these theological virtues, making them correspond to e.g., Faith, Repentance, and Zeal in the requirements made of Christ in his disciples, then linking them with the Beatitudes; the Gifts of the Spirit in Isaiah 11, and the fruits of the spirit in Galatians 5. *Thomas Aquinas explores the concepts of virtues, beatitudes and gifts in great detail in* The Summa. *And these ideas are developed further in Richard Hooker's writing as well as the manuals for the laity written by Jeremy Taylor and others. Vladimir Solovyov's* Justification of the Good *similarly roots human action in a desire to participate in God's goodness.*

St. Paul's virtues of Faith, Hope, and Love provided the framework for believers. Faith rooted life in the act of believing and the object of belief. Hope guards against the sin of despair and presumption. And finally, Caritas.[7] Not

---

6. Italicized text added for clarification.

7. This is an expansion by the editors of Demant's notes: "Thomas Aquinas summa Prima Secondae Commented only by Jeremy Talyor, Richard Hooker and many more. (Manuals)"

Solovyer; Justification of the Good 5.4.10; Faith: act of Believing, and object of

any kind of love, but love of God whereby he is loved as the object of beatitude to which we are ordained. *Dante's* Paradiso *contains such a vision of all things participating in the Divine essence:*[8] "Within its depths I saw contained, bound by love into one volume what is dispersed in leaves throughout the universe"[9] "The truth doth he make plain to my understanding who demonstrated love the primal love of the eternal beings is their Maker."[10]

These theological virtues, however were part of the spiritual sustenances of the holiness within the church, (and there was throughout much else besides holiness and much that seemed opposed to it). Something else was needed for guidance in the current ethics of day to day living, when the older bonds of community and civic loyalty were weakened. It is mainly to the Latin fathers that we owe an endeavor to provide this. The Greek theologians were more concerned to refute errors about the nature of man, errors which enfeebled the moral faculty of Christians. So we have Cyril of Jerusalem of the 4th century writing his Catechetical discourses.[11]

It was however St. Ambrose, whose sermons at Milan had quite an effect on Augustine, who began the task of laying out an ethic for the life of men and society, whether fully converted or not. This took the form of examining the four classical virtues to be found in Plato, Aristotle, and Cicero. Prudence (or wisdom) fortitude, temperance, and the servant of these three, justice (to which Aristotle devotes a whole book of his *Nichomachean Ethics*). Ambrose's *On the Duties of the Clergy* has been called "the first great Western textbook of Christian Ethics"; he writes on honesty in business, generosity to the unfortunate, on the need for fair play and the evil of fraud, he speaks strongly on the vice of lying and duplicity, and is critical of the profit motive. Ambrose by adding the three theological to the four cardinal virtues started a tradition of the seven virtues, which were set out against the seven deadly sins: pride, envy, anger, despair(dejection), avarice, lust, and gluttony.

---

belief; Hope—sin against: despair and presumption (le Bon Dieu), accidie (unreadable); Caritas:"

8. This is an expansion by the editors of Demant's notes: "Aq. Dante: Par 33 In Vision of all things in Divine essence."

9. Dante, *Paradiso,* 33.86.

10. Ibid., 26.37

11. Here the editors removed some of Demant's writing that was incomplete or unreadable: "in which inter alia he discovers the soul x . . . x faculties: the will is antagonize self-governed (not stars), sin is not bought into the world (v. haisumpiation?) The Devil tempts (need of repentance Luke 11 v5 incipient plagiarizing?) A lot the body and its desires but though movements of the spirit all the source of evil (very Manichean and Gnostic)

(Clement of Alexandria Paridagogns)"

The cardinal virtues, taken over from the Greek philosophies and the Romans, have a parallel in the Wisdom literature: In Wisdom of Solomon 8.7 we read, "If a man loveth righteousness [the fruits of wisdom's labors are virtues]. For she teacheth soberness [temperance] and understanding [prudence], righteousness [justice] and courage [fortitude]; and there is nothing in life for men more profitable than these." In their Aristotelian clarification these four moral or civic virtues were brought into use by the Christian moralists—all but the Doctrine of the Mean in which Aristotle comprehended them—This view not be expounded here, but it is worth noting that Aristotle excepted the supreme virtue of justice from the Doctrine of the Mean, and that he also placed prudence in a category by itself. Prudence, which as a virtue, is the habit of finding and pursing the right means for a desired end; and even *sapientia*, cleverness, wisdom schematizing. Anyone can know how; a prudent one judges the particular circumstances in which a thing is best done. Therefore, says Aristotle, it is not a moral but an intellectual virtue; it can be misused. That is to say while justice, courage, and temperance, are not capable of misuse (in that they are always of moral worth in themselves), prudence can be and often is an instrument of virtue, in the service of base ends, or merely flat ones. Now the Christian teachers, arrived with their depository of revealed moral law in the Bible and with their faith in the freely given grace of God which alone makes a man justified before Him; and finding the cardinal virtues just what was wanted in a semi-Christianized social order, set about re-interpreting them and giving them a theological setting.

So, we find Augustine of the fifth century, in his *De Moribus Ecclesiae Catholicae*, interpreting them as variations of Christian man's love of God.

> As to virtue leading to a happy life, I hold virtue to be nothing else than perfect love of God. For the fourfold division of virtue I regard as taken from four forms of love. For these four virtues (would that all felt their influence in their minds as they have their names in their mouths) I should have no hesitation in defining them: that temperance is love giving itself entirely to that which is loved; fortitude is love readily bearing all things for the sake of the loved object; justice is serving only the loved object; and therefore ruling rightly (within and without); prudence is love distinguishing with sagacity between what hinders and what helps it. The object of this love is not anything but only God, the chief good, the highest wisdom, the perfect harmony.[12]

---

12. Augustine, *De Moribus Ecclesiae Catholicae*, XV.25.

We could spend a lot of time tracing the development of expositions of virtues and their opposing vices. It set going an intensification of introspection and a discovery of the inner world of man, in all its complications. It gave rise to the minute examinations of movements of the soul, as well as of the refinements of outward acts as matters for moral judgement. The Celtic Penitentials, for instance, are as bold as Dr. Kinsey about sexual aberrations. While all this had often an artificial, and perverse effect of over-refinement, as well as putting things into peoples' heads. This whole trend of sustained soul training gave rise to individual counseling, both within and without the confessional, which has produced a vast literature, from [unreadable] up to Wycliffe, St. Francis of Sales's *Introduction to the Devout Life*, the spiritual letters of John Knox, and the pastoral correspondence of Thomas Chalmers of Glasgow in the last century.

Two new spiritual issues emerged from the attempt to found the Christian life on the seven virtues, which were not explicit at the first. One was the realization that the salt of humility had to season the practice of all the more obvious virtues; this came to mean that pride is the root sin;[13] and distinction had to be elaborated to make clear what pride is, and why it is sinful; whereas vainglory and conceit are only silly. Pride is the movement of the created spirit which refuses to acknowledge its dependence.

The other new insight which came out of the training of the soul in the virtues, was the need for purity of motive, which had come from the gospel promise of blessedness for the pure in heart, it is one thing however to retain the innocence of childhood before the moral struggle has arisen, and when once lost can never be recovered; it is another to acquire some replica of it after struggling in the moral turmoil of life. In the spiritual tradition this recovered ability was called "disinterestedness" or indifference to consequences or the "*amor castus*," pure love of God and of[14] creatures for his sake. From this we get the insistence upon "motive" as in a way the deepest quality in the moral value of an act. It is the parentage of what is called *Gesinnungsethik* as distinguished from *Verantwortungsethik*, or the ethic of consequences; modern moral systems have divided into opposing camps on this question—Kant standing for *Gesinnungsethik* and the utilitarians for *Verantwortungsethik*. This split had been in the making since the end of the Middle Ages, where an elaborate moral analysis in St. Thomas Aquinas had required four conditions for an act to be morally virtuous; it must be well done, technically as it were, no [unreadable]; its object must be good, the

---

13. Here Demant includes the note: "cf. St Bernard's Twelve steps of humility and pride, twelfth century."

14. Here Demant includes the note: "St. Bernard—Indifference Ignatius Loyola."

circumstances, manner time and degree; and the end too must be good. If an act fails in one of these four ways, it is morally defective.

Take the case cited by Mark Twain; man gave his car fare away to a poor woman and had to walk miles home in the cold. The nature of the act was good technically; he did it; the object was to help the women; the circumstances did not cause any unseen consequences; but says Mark Twain; when he comes to the motive; he gained a whole night's sleep all for twenty-five cents. For Mark Twain had a theory that all actions are in the end self-regarding. What a man! This motive, however falsely the writer describes it, is what the scholastics called "the end" of an action.

This same sort of thinking about the genuineness of motive, led to the doctrine of conscience, which already in the thirteenth century was in the air. A man is morally bound to obey his conscience, even if the outside judge knows that it is giving a false decision. Aquinas discusses it under the God question, does an erring conscience bind and does an erring conscience excuse? He answers "Yes," it does for "all that is not of faith is sin" and even if the light that is in thee be darkness you must follow your light. But then he asks, "Does an erring conscience excuse?" The answer is sometimes it does; at other times, it does not. It does not excuse in two cases; one when a man does evil, believing that it is good and commanded by God, when such a thing is forbidden by God's law, which a man is bound to know; or when he has not taken the opportunities he has really had to know what the right and wrong is, in other words when his ignorance was variable, could be overcome with trouble. If his ignorance that his act is wrong, is invariable; his blindness could not be removed, his will is still good because it voluntarily follows what he believes to be the right moral dictate of conscience; hence the doctrine of "invincible ignorance." Without going into the consequences of all this; we should note how this trend of moral thinking led to recognition of the inwardness of the moral principle—which in recent times has got to the point of ignoring all other aspects of the nature of a moral act, but only the motive.

To come now to another set of questions which this history of moral thinking within the church raises. It naturally led at an early stage, when pre-Christian ethics were found serviceable, to a working out of the relation between the revealed moral law of the Old and New Testaments to the general moral sense of mankind. Why were the Ten Commandments necessary, if their content was given to man in creation by a natural light? This is a kind of question which engaged the attention of theologians from the second century onwards. It concerns the relation of revealed law and what has been called natural law in the field of morals—more of this in the next lecture. There are two kinds of law, natural, or rationally apprehended (nomos) and positive, propagated by a law giver. In theology these are called natural divine law, and revealed divine law. It did not escape the earlier church moralists that while the Bible has at its moral center, the revealed law of God and the covenant of grace, there are many passages which, incidentally and casually as it were, admit a reliable moral sense in the heathen, apart from those bound by the covenant who have had specifically revealed commandments.

Speculating on this question; in Mosaic law, and in Christ more fully, mankind is confronted with the original law of his creation; and in a way this would apprehend it by reason—or *synteresis intellectualis* not *ratio*.[15]

Demant writes in another work on A. N. Whitehead's understanding of rationality and the order of the world. "Whitehead, in Adventures of Ideas, makes plain that this rationalism, as it affects Europe, came from the medieval scholastics' refurbishing of Greek rationality. Because this rational handling of life at first made obeisance to the organic, non-rational, super-rational realities it could win many triumphs. When it took over the field, or sought to do so—and did this under the banner of freedom—then it was found that this freedom gave rein not only to reason but also to the dark forces in man and community."[16] *Here is highlighted the problems arising from looking to natural law solely and rejecting the idea of positive law.*[17]

[The place of natural law[18] is important, though. Richard Hooker writes of how, "The Law of Nature, meaning thereby the law which human nature knoweth itself in reason universally bound unto, which also for that cause may be termed fitly the law of reason. This law I say comprehendeth all those things which men by the light of this natural understanding evidently know, to be becoming or unbecoming, virtuous or vicious, good or evil for them to do."[19] Bishop Sanderson spoke of the positive, revealed law, saying "the second light, which we call infused or imparted, comes into the mind from without, and proceeds from Divine Revelation. . . it directs our good actions to a nobler end, above the dictates of the Natural Light."[20] Jeremy Taylor wrote of the relationship between the two, saying "nature and her laws have both the same author, and are relative to each other, and these

---

15. Following this paragraph, Demant included the following sentence, which he had crossed out: Whitehead has discussed the relation of the two sources of law in human life in a way which is illuminating as well as entertaining.

16. Demant, *Decline of Capitalism*, 57.

17. This paragraph is an expansion of Demant's note: "Classical, Christian, Modern."

18. Here Demant included the references: "Nat Law, Sanderson, Taylor Hooker, Calvin."

19. Hooker, *Ecclesiastical Polity*, Book I, viii, 9.

20. Sanderson, *Bishop Sanderson's Lectures*, 111.

as necessary to the support and improvement of human nature, as nourishment to the support of human bodies."[21] Calvin, in Book 2 of his *Institutes* upholds the idea that knowledge of right and wrong has been written on the human heart.]

Besides the theological interest of these questions, there were practical reasons for teachers of revealed moral law and of the gift of grace to the Christian man in his freedom from the bondage of law. There was a reoccurring temptation to use this religious liberty for disregarding or disobeying the laws of moral and civic duty. Luther and Wesley had to dispel or crush these antimonial tendencies in some of their followers.[22]

Such an impulse comes to the fore dramatically in the trial of Charles I for treason.[23] Charles I, at trial said, "It is not my case alone; it is the freedom and liberty of the people of England . . . for if power without law can make laws, may alter the fundamental laws of the kingdom, I do not know what subject he is in England that can be sure of his life, or anything he calls his own."

The Tudors and his own father had already undermined this theory and the growing absoluteness of the state. Aided in different ways by the Renaissance and the Reformation, they had tended to put the ruling power above the law. We may say that Charles held a view of kingship he was no longer able to embody.

> Scot and Jesuit hand in hand
> first taught the world to say
> That subjects ought to have command
> and monarchs to obey.[24]

[As we can see, all of this is a result of a particular history. This perspective on morality was not inevitable. And this is apparent when one considers the literature from other cultures outside of the modern West. Monica Wilson's book has traced the impact of changes in scale on persons in Bantu Africa and shown that magical thinking and the idea of there being two

---

21. Taylor, *The Whole Works of the Right Rev. Jeremy Taylor*, 270.

22. Here Demant included the note: "Wesley Sermons and F. D. Maurice. Inaugural 13."

23. The italicized text was added to address a gap in the notes

24. Here Demant includes this Book list: "Monica Wison: *Religion and the Transformation of Society*,
Mary Douglas, *Natural Symbols*, Cresset Press (1970),
cf. Rachel Levy (Faber 1947),
Dorothy Emmet, *Rules, Roles, and Relation* (Macmillian 1966),
D. M. Mackinnon, *Study of Ethical Theory*,
Berdyaev, *Solitude and Society*, pp. 87ff."

worlds still remains in that context. Mary Douglas's work, *Natural Symbols*, makes clear that no such "natural" symbols exist. Every society understands the world via symbols, but they are particular to the social makeup of the culture, the axioms and aims of that community. And these underlying cultural norms are reinforced through social relationships.]

The moral career of Christendom leaves us noting, along with Mackinnon that "rational benevolence must be taken very seriously indeed. But is it the whole of virtue?"[25] Berdyaev has written of the great challenge of solitude. "Communism eliminates this problem by identifying the Ego with the social collective . . . The erotic aspect of human life is sacrificed to the economic and technical aspects. The same tendency is apparent in the German racial doctrine."[26] But for the Christian, neither option will do. The relationship with God is the only solution to solitude. "Religion not only binds and unites man to God, but it is also the essential bond between man and his fellow-beings; it is both community and communion. This union is consummated on an extranatural plane wherein each man, as well as God Himself, is a Thou, and not an object."[27]

---

25. MacKinnon, *Study in Ethical Theory*, 280.
26. Berdyaev, *Solitude and Society*, 90.
27. Ibid., 92.

Series II, Lecture IV
Natural Law Doctrine

IN ITS ATTEMPT TO provide a foundation of morals and law for the secular world, after the influx of the barbarians and their taking over much of the structures left by Roman Imperialism, the church set about enquiring into the nature of justice and righteousness, which could stand on its own feet without the sanction of revealed religion. And then to define the relation of what the Christian man knew from the law of Moses, the precepts of Christ and the ethic of grace in the church, to a general conception of right and wrong and good law, which was obviously at work in people who had not been touched by Christianity. After Charlemagne's short-lived experiment to build a political structure entirely under the domain of church and theology—a totalitarian theocracy—church leaders and theologians were pressed to discover a basis of ethics and law-making which had an authority of universal application, and by which custom in moral conduct and in government could be tested and judged.

Such a basis would have to satisfy three conditions if it was to become part of the philosophy of Christian ethics. First, it would have to be as securely grounded in the communal existence, as was the moral law promulgated by the Lord of History, and of Creation, and of the Redeemer and Judge of all things. Its warrant must be more illuminating than the fluctuating mores of historical communities, or the preservative measures of groups, or the decisions of temporal rulers. Secondly, a basis for a universal secular ethic must be found not to contradict the religious moral claims of divine ordinance and life of grace and love known to the Christian. Thirdly, such a foundation must be the source of both public law and private morals, in different ways. Otherwise, there would be only these possibilities: 1) law having no relation to the moral sense of the community (in which case it would fall into disarray and disrespect, or alternatively be imposed in spite of persistence by the central power); or 2) law becoming merely a reflection of morality, with the state concerning itself with the private lives of citizens (whether their behavior violates public order or not). The third course, which can be conceived if there is no source of authority in law or morals open to men in their secular convocations, is of course a theocratic church state in which the ecclesiastical power determines both public law and personal behavior.

Now the church fathers, looking for a basis in the constitution of things, independent of revealed law which was accepted only by believers, found it in the doctrine of the Law of Nature as it was called: Natural Law, *Ius Naturale* or *Lex Naturae*. The term is confusing today, because we understand "Law" only in two senses—the laws of nature (*nomos*) or the laws of the land (positive law). In the natural law tradition, "law" did indeed convey the idea of a *nomos*—a principle running through all things, which included a moral principle inherent in reality, which is the warrant for the moral standards and codes of men. That is the first spirit of the doctrine.

The doctrine did place the foundation of ethics beyond the changing flux of custom; it did recognize an objective norm of right and wrong as against theories which regarded these terms as projections of subjective desires or interests: (Freud, Nietzsche, Marx); and it did insist that moral distinctions and legal enactment had a basis behind the capricious rulers. If you need convincing that some objective basis is necessary for morals—and indeed for any value judgement—whether you are seeking it in natural law doctrine or elsewhere you can find it discussed in relation to education and literature in Mr. C. S. Lewis's lecture, "The Abolition of Man," when he criticized some writers of educational textbooks who have said when Coleridge called the waterfall "sublime," he was talking not about it but his own feelings. He shows that writers who attack the traditional body of teaching on values—which Lewis calls the Tao they are in fact using some of it against other parts of it; (posterity v respect for parents). Mr. Lewis lists at the end a number of quotations from eastern religions, the ancient civilization of the Bible, to show that there is a great deal in common about the basic virtues; he uses the Chinese term Tao for what the western writers called the natural law.

Then, of course, the term "natural" requires some explanation. It is perhaps the most ambiguous term in the language, and it requires some investigation into the universe of discourse of earlier periods to grasp that it there meant what belongs to the true essence or *naturae* of things and of man in particular, and not what we mean by nature; the sub-human world of physics and biology, and our participation in it. We sometimes in ordinary language catch an element of the older idea when we say, e.g., "It is unnatural" and we mean it's not the sort of thing a human being is expected to do. "Nature" said Leslie Stephen, "is a word contrived in order to introduce as many equivocations as possible into all theories, political, legal, artistic or literary into which it enters."[1] You can pursue the story of this equivocation on the term "nature" with such works as; J. S. Mill, the first of his *Three Essays On Religion*; C. C. J. Webb's *Introduction to Studies in the History of Natural Theology* (where the term "natural" means "open to reason and is contrasted with theology of Revelation"); and Collingwood's *The Sea of Nature*. The idea of nature is not part of nature but part of human history. *David George Ritchie identifies further concepts of Natural Rights in his book.*[2] In the doctrine of natural law, "natural" denotes what is interior to all lawgiving and enactment; it is thereby contrasted with positive law— revealed or civil; and it is something laid up in the nature of things—and for the Christian thinkers who used the conception it meant, of course, the pattern which the Creator gave to his creation and especially the pattern of human existence which was in a special way "made in his own image." The feature of the natural law which became most important for political theory and the system of law, was that it represented a principle above the law giver, to which he was subject and unless he was answerable to it, his authority was invalid. Mr. Bertrand de Jouvenel has written two recent books, *Power* and *Sovereignty* to show that for want of some such accepted conception, authority seems to us in the modern West merely a form of despotism, and that authority in the past hadn't always carried with it the ideas of "authorization"; it limited power, and this is what made the doctrine of natural law welcome to the jurists.

In brief, natural law doctrine served to make the law of communities answerable to a higher law, and while preserving the connection between law and morals, it maintained a distinction between them.

What then was this doctrine? There were two forms of it in pre-Christian times. A glimpse of it, in a religious context without the idea of a rationally apprehended moral principle in the universe, is found in the *Tragedy of Antigone*. In Aeschylus and Sophocles the idea of an unusual divine moral law is presupposed. And in *Antigone* Sophocles writes of a girl who dies for obeying the gods rather than men. She has claimed the unconditional right to fulfill her duty of piety and sisterly love. In this case, it was to give honorable burial to her dead brother who could receive it from no one but her. She had no enmity against the city state, but the diktat of the ruler Creon, who forbade the burial was not absolute, it was limited by the law of religion, and

---

1. See Stephen, *Hobbes*, 173.

2. At this point, Demant has the following reference "(Birds) and Ritchie Natural Rights." The phrase "Birds" is puzzling. However, the reference to Ritchie is clear. This is a reference to his book: Ritchie, *Natural Rights*.

so she could say to Creon, who maintains against her the law and order of the state, "I owe a longer allegiance to the dead than the living: and in that world I shall abide forever. But if thou wilt be guilty of dishonoring the laws which the gods have established in honor, then I disobey." Antigone is there referring to an eternal moral order which cannot be cancelled by a civil enactment.

The stoic Roman moralists held a view of a universal moral law which was rational rather than religious. But Cicero in the *De Republica* says:

> The true law is right reason in accordance with nature, spread abroad among all men, stable and eternal . . . this law may not be amended, nor are we allowed to restrict its application, nor can it be altogether repealed; nor can senate or people free us from this law . . . There is not one law at Rome and another at Athens, nor one now and there hereafter, but for all time one eternal unchangeable law will bind all peoples, and there will be one common master and commander of all, god who drew up, spoke for, and put forward this law.[3]

When we read the classical authors who use the word "natural" it is well to remember that to the Greek the natural apple was not the wild one from which our cultivated apple has been grown, but rather the golden apple of the Hesperidia. The natural object was that which perfectly expressed the idea of a thing. It was the perfect object.[4]

Dante, in the second book of *the Divine Comedy, Purgatorio, also explores the issue of natural love and the love that can err. So Dante writes:*

> Natural and rational ture?
> Lo naturale è sempre sanza errore,
> ma l'altro puote errar per malo obietto
> o per troppo o per poco di vigore. (Purg. 17.94–96)[5]
> [The natural is always without error, but
> the other may err through an evil object, or,
> or err through too much or too little vigor.]

I will pass over much in the Roman Jurists and Stoic philosophies and the early Christian fathers, except to note Irenaeus *believed that the patriarchs had the Decalogue written on their hearts.*[6] Also, idea patriarchs

3. Cicero, *De Republica*, III.22.33.

4. Here Demant includes the note, "Pound, *Introduction to the Philosophy of Law*, 32."

5. Demant introduces this section on Dante with the following notes: "Also Dante the natural countess? only the rational community."

6. Demant's note seems to read "Irenaeus Dally 10."

stood in a kind of natural covenant with the Lord. This was expressed in the Promise to Noah. Later [writers] like St. Hugh of Victor were fond of referring to the Noachide (Covenant); as preceding the Mosaic.

The story of natural law continues. A key person was Isidore of Seville, which divided natural law into three, which includes: the divine law grounded in nature, and the human law grounded on custom.[7]

[What follows is a set of notes, which starts with a list of books that he wants to discuss with short comments. We have expanded his list with full citation. The books are:]

R. W. Carlyle and A. J. Carlyle, *History of Mediaeval Political Theory in the West* (Edinburgh and London: W. Blackwood, 1903).

Ernst Troeltsch, *The Social Teaching of the Christian Churches* (London: George Allen and Unwin, 1951).

George H. Sabine, *A History of Political Theory*, 4th edition (Dryden Press, 1973).

A. P. D'Entreves, *Natural Law: Introduction to Legal Philosophy*, 2nd edition (London: HarperCollins, 1970).

[Next there is a set of notes about possible themes. At certain points, a page number is indicated. We have included the page number in the footnotes.]

It is important to discuss the following:

Jus gentium and the civil law.[8]

The role natural law plays in providing a check on government, see Troeltsch.[9]

Augustine's concept of the Two Cities, especially the themes of the unity of the human race and the sociability of man.[10]

Natural law is an empirical law, even if it is acquired through transcendent means.[11]

---

7. Demant's note here is: "12. Isidore of Seville 7th century: three parts natural law, law of nature."

8. *Jus gentium* is Latin for the "law of nations," which was developed in the Roman empire. He notes p.13.

9. Demant actually writes, "19. Relative Nat. Law Troeltsch. 19. Governments dyke again sin."

10. Demant's note is: "Augustine Two Cities Not touch yet the unity of the human race, the sociability of man."

11. After this note, Demant then writes, "31. is a sign of wretchedness and 31.34–36 Aquinas, 46. Property ownership and use." It is clear that he is citing a book, but it is not clear which book he is citing.

There are limits to the state. Natural Law creates moral parameters, but it does not necessarily make men good. Instead it provides order and punishment.[12]

The principles of natural law extend to money, just price, interest, and work.[13]

Natural law is linked to the Roman concept of *jus gentium* and that idea is linked to Just War. The Just War principles include:

1. the need to redress an injustice,
2. war to be invoked when all efforts at arbitration fail,
3. war is never an end in itself, it is always a means to a just peace,
4. the harm of war does not exceed the good (in particular by damaging civil life),
5. and there needs to be some type of clear—curtailment of war.[14]

[Demant then returns to the list of books with comments.]

Grotius, 1625, *The Rights of War and Peace, including the Law of Nature and of Nations*, (New York and London: M.Walter Dunne, 1901).

Important to discuss the priority of family. See my Theology of Society.[15] *Francisco Suarez (1548-1617) is important to mention.*

Turning next to the Reformers. John Calvin wrote about the "threefold use of the law"; the law is to be a mirror, a restraint on evil, and to reveal what is pleasing to God.[16]

We do not get with Protestantism a violent break from natural law, instead there is a voluntarist tendency. And slowly we get shift from natural law to, on the one hand, the divine law of the Bible and on the other hand, the

---

12. Demant's actual note is "State limits not make men good—order and punishment."

13. Demant's note is "Money Just Price Interest Work."

14. Demant's note is: "Just War 1. redress injustice, 2. all efforts arbitration fail, 3. Means not an end in itself, 4. Harm done not exceed good (civil life), 5. curtailment. problem of winning."

15. Demant's note is: "One fact not special stated; Priority of Family VAD Theo of Soc."

16. Demant's note is: "Calvin. Institutes 3 users of law."

positive law of the state, which is grounded in the will of God. At this point we are near to the "Divine rights of Kings and Governments."[17]

The non-conformists sometimes used the language of natural law to oppose papal authority. The concept of the Chancellor in legal terms was a recognition of an authority above ruling power.[18]

In philosophy and political theory, we see a shift in Kant. Natural law turns inward. In Hegel, the absolute ethical totality is willing but ein volk, a people or a nation.[19] The State is the ethical whole, the incarnation of God in history. In Hobbs, it "is the power of reason actualizing itself as will." And in Rousseau, "who ever refuses to obey the General will shall be compelled to do so by the whole body."

In Hobbes, there is no distinction between society and state; except there be legitimate Government, individual with power to enforce their will: there is neither state nor society. For Hobbes, the law of nature is descriptive. Each thing preserves its own existence in a scramble for secular power. For Hobbes, all give up to Leviathan Mortal God, who is the guardian of law and order.

Secular versions of Natural Law

The Declaration des Droits de l'Homme et du Citoyen was adopted by French National Assembly August 1789, and proclaimed the natural inalienable and sacred rights of man, single and indisputable principles. *Rousseau and Locke are both key Enlightenment thinkers that attempted to create a version of Natural Law and Natural Rights not grounded in religion.*

The result swept away institutions over individuals; and the victor was not in a strong position. Concepts such as dynasty, confessions, and creedal bonds—which in earlier times had kept the supreme ruler in check—were no

---

17. Demant's note is: "Protestantism not violent break: voluntarist bent discouragement of Natural Law in favour of divine Law of Bible, on the one hand, and positive law of state, grounded in the will of God on the other. 'Divine rights of Kings and Governments.'"

18. Demant's note, "Non Conformity—stood for what popes, nat law, Chancellor had stood for—an authority above ruling power."

19. Demant's note, "Kant lead? Nat Law inward. Hegel; The absolute ethical totality is willing but ein volk a people or nation." Demant goes on to note, "Scientific treatment of N.L. 1802."

longer available. Claims of natural rights, which were separated from the religious sanction, were damaged.[20]

There were two periods: the first was the period of the unlimited sovereignty of King; then, the absolutism of the people.[21]

[Demant then turns to the criticisms of natural law. He titled this section number 3.]

3. Criticisms:
The first set were theological: Luther and Calvin believed that God was not constrained by a natural law.[22] *Voluntarism develops in the work of Abelard and Ockham. Pufendorf's Law of Nature and Nations in the seventeenth century is part of the narrative.*

Leibniz attacked voluntarism in his *Essais de Theodicée: Réflexions su l'Ouvrage de M. Hobbes,*

> The justice of God, says Mr. Hobbes, is merely the power which he has and exercises of bestowing blessings and misfortunes. This definition surprises me; it is not the power of bestowing them but in the will to bestow them reasonably—in, that is to say, goodness guided by reason, that the justice of God consists. But, says he, justice is not with God what it is with man, who is made just only by observance of the laws made by his superior. Mr. Hobbes is wrong there too, as is Mr. Pufendorf who has followed him. Justice turns not on the arbitrary laws of superiors, but on the eternal ordinances of wisdom and goodness, in men as much as in God.[23]

20. This is an expansion of Demant's notes: "Mod hat paw? a sartorial construction assertion of the value of the individual. Rousseau and Locke. Natural Rights

Swept away institutions over individuals; had to make others; and also weakened VICTOR? faity, dynasty. quils, confessions, credal bonds which in earlier times had kept the supreme ruler in check. In claims of nat rights now loosen the religious sanction. Retained Nat Law New elites; Hegel saw Tew and poper? (scientists)."

21. This sentence is an expansion of Demant's notes, which read: "Periods unlimited sovereignty first of King then of people absolutism."

22. This paragraph is an expansion of Demant's notes, which read: "Theological: Luther and Calvin might of God's will exalt over
    quality of goodness: dependence
    voluntarists Abelard Ockham
    Pufendorf Law of Nature and Peoples (17 Century)
    a Calvinist"

23. Leibniz, *Theodicy.*

Nominalism and voluntarism in theology is an attack on natural law. An action is not good because of its suitableness to the essential nature of man but because God so willed. This view is traceable to Duns Scotus in the thirteenth century and with William Ockham in the fourteenth century.

Volition of moral law as expression of the bare will of God passed over from the nominalists to the reformers such as Wycliffe and later to Luther and Calvin.[24]

The second set of criticisms were more philosophical.[25] In philosophy David Hume spent many pages of his *Treatise of Human Nature* in demolishing not only theological natural law but also that secular form of it which had inspired the French and American Revolution, Locke and Rousseau, and Utilitarians. In morals and in politics, since values depend upon human progress then it is impossible that reason should create itself as obligation. Consequently virtue is merely a quality or action of mind that is generally approved; in other words, a convention.[26]

*The third set of criticisms are t*he *attacks by jurists Austin and Ritchie. David Ritchie's views are found in his book,* Natural Rights.[27] *The result is only positive law. But in recent years, there has been a revival as seen in the work of C. S. Lewis and Charles Grove Haines's* The Revival of Natural Law Concepts.[28]

A key text[29] is Otto Gierke, *Natural Law and the Theory of Society 1500–1800.*

Professor A. P. D'Entreves is correct, when he writes,[30] "but for natural Law the petty laws of a small peasant community of peninsular Italy would

---

24. Here Demant included the note: "Barth? marriage became of & commandment."

25. The italicized text was added to address a gap in the notes.

26. Demant then has some very incomplete notes. These are: "(Earlier critics of positivists school wrong whail? my father not done in my society)
Pascal Pesees id 92 (163)– quotation in French Look up reference
Pascal like Hume Revealed religion on faith no relation to Reason or Nature; two worlds. Thomas Aquinas Goucher."

27. Richie, (New York: Macmillian, 1895).

28. This paragraph is a clarification of Demant's notes: "Attack by jurists Austin and Ritche Natural rights
only positive law
But Revival; Hamies C. S. The revival of Natural Law Concepts
Law Case
Dual State Errant Frankenstal Law of Contract."

29. The italicized text was added to address a gap in the notes.

30. The italicized text was added to address a gap in the notes.

never have become the universal law of an international civilization. But for natural law the great medieval synthesis of godly and worldly wisdom would not have been possible. But for natural law there would probably have been no American and no French Revolution, nor would the great ideals of freedom and equality have found their way in to the law books after having found it in the hearts of men!"[31]

[Demant then has some concluding notes that seem to stress the horrendous consequences of a world without natural law. He notes Nietzsche and Hitler, and a "church troubled by tendencies which put fact of power over ethics and laws."][32]

The Ideas of Natural Law And Humanity in World Politics.

It is enough to show that this highly controversial doctrine was after all one of the most constructive elements of our culture and civilization, and that without it, or something equivalent to it, we cannot escape the scramble for power, or totalitarian dictatorships, or equation of law and morals; or confusion of the two—in other words we should not have our nations culture with a libertarian society on top of a cultural unity.[33]

---

31. D'Entreves, *Natural Law: An Introduction to Legal Philosophy*, 13.

32. Notes are: "Burst Toeschsch German sitz will over reason; power over ethics
Faust Heaseen _ Nietsche a good war
Hitler entscheiding
Church Troubled by tendencies which put fact of power over ethics and Law."

33. It is not clear whether this is Demant finishing his lecture or whether this is a quote from another source. Right at the end, there are the following notes, which seem to be unrelated to the earlier argument. "5. Totalitarianism v a law above state. Justice is that art of ruling power. Russia Decrees nothing else. Hegel Volk."

Series II, Lecture V
Is Man a "Real Kind"?

THE DOCTRINE OF "NATURAL law" which I outlined in the last lecture did attempt to provide a basis for personal morals, social behavior and law, a basis which was not shifting and fluctuating with the histories of communities, groups and interests, and it claimed an authority from the nature of man himself—his *essentia* (form)—which could be apprehended by the human mind, without the revealed truth of the Christian tradition. It reached its greatest refinement, and theological warrant in the work of St. Thomas Aquinas. In his treatment, the eternal law is identical with the reason of God, the eternal plan of divine wisdom by which the whole creation is ordered. In itself this eternal law is above the physical nature of man and its entirety is beyond human comprehension (my thoughts are not your thoughts), though it is not on this account contrary to human reason. So far as his finite nature permits, man has a real participation in the wisdom of God; these are reflected in him though his nature reproduces only a distorted image. This image of the eternal law in man (seen though a glass darkly) is natural law, a reflection of divine reason in created things. It is manifest in the inclination which nature implants in all beings to seek their good and avow their evil, to preserve themselves, and to live as perfectly as possible the kind of life suitable to their natural endowments (degrees of perfection). In the case of mankind this means, as Aristotle had taught, the desire for a life in which the rational nature may be realized. Thomas mentions as examples, the inherent inclinations of men to order society, to preserve their lives, to beget and educate children, to talk of the truth and develop intelligence. Natural law enjoins all that is implied to give their human inclination their widest scope.

But besides the human natural law there was another mode of operation in the divine law, this is revelation; such as the special code of laws which God gave to the Jews as the chosen people or the special rule of Christian morals or legislation, given though scripture or the church. Divine revealed law is a gift of God's grace, rather than a discovery of natural reason. Revelation adds to reason but never destroys it. Reason and faith were however points of one structure, a universe created by the source God. Natural law, because it is grasped by the unaided reason, is common to all men, both Christian and pagan, hence morals and government do not in general depend upon Christianity.[1] *Robert Sanderson shares Richard Hooker's view that such natural law exists and that not all laws need be laid out in scripture.*[2] *Jeremy Taylor on the other hand, is more skeptical about the idea of a universal natural law and says of such instances, "they are prepared by nature, but completed by God in other ways than by our nature and creation."*[3]

Reason; *intellectus*; man is a rational soul—reason includes all that lifts man out of the stream of nature—not only by his power of discursive reason—arguing from premises to conclusions, tracing causes and effects, but also his will and purposes, and the emotional forces that make him attached to things of beauty, and the kind of love which is given freely and not just a desire for what is attractive. Greeks are not such rationalists as supposed.

Before we go on to the consequences of change in the idea of natural law—from a being geared to a system of revealed morality, and its secularization, and then its temporary disappearance—let us just recap the main features of the doctrine. First, it meant that man is by creation a creature with a definite structure—the *natura* of man; secondly, that it stands for a universal character in human beings, behind the special characteristics of persons and communities; third, it represents the freedom or rational character of mankind; fourthly, it posits that there is a gulf between what a man essentially is and what he is actually. Man does not follow his true nature in practice; for the Christian this gulf is called the Fall of man; for others it is his failure to be a truly rational being; fifthly; all human behavior and institutions like moral codes, civil law, and government are only valid and can claim authority so far as they reflect the natural law.

It is not difficult to see how this doctrine could be used politically as well as morally. In Locke and Rousseau it became the foundation of the liberal or democratic movement—of natural rights against the powers that be; of equality before the law and of government by consent. And further, in the modern period, the idea of natural law was separated from any notion

---

1. Here Demant includes the note "Precepts and Counsels." He perhaps considered contrasting natural law with the precepts or divine commands and the counsels of perfection suggested by the writings of Paul and others.

2. These sentences are an expansion by the editors of Demant's note, which reads: "Sanderson J. Taylor, Hooker."

3. Taylor, *The Whole Works of the Right Rev. Jeremy Taylor*, 283.

of it being but a human version of divine law, and that it must be congruous with what was revealed of divine law in the Christian revelation. Further, the faculty by which natural law was apprehended became narrowed; no longer the mind as a whole, by intuition of man's own being (*synteresis*), but that part of it which we call the intellect, the scholastics called *sapio*, became the power of taking hold of the truth about man. The reason of the modern rationalist was regarded as acting without any presuppositions, whereas in fact Rousseau, Locke, Spencer, Hill, Montesqueue, took for granted as the discoveries of reason what European man had by that time imbibed from the older tradition of Christian ethics and natural law.

Revolts against any idea of man as a real kind. *There emerged a relativism in morals and positivism in legal theory. Thus the only source of law was the decision of the community (either the decision of the monarch or the decision of the voters. The idea of natural responsibilities or duties faded from popular consciousness. In addition, there was a separation of civil power from ecclesiastical power, which meant that no outside authority could be brought to bear on monarchs who had overstepped their authority.*[4]

"And so it follows of necessity, that kings were the authors and makers of the laws, and not the laws of the kings."[5] The later radical doctrine of the sovereignty of the people is of the same species.

WILL OVER LAW—CREATES LAW AND RIGHT

This can be seen in the Levellers of Cromwell's time, such as John Lilburne. Lilburne advocated for people's "freeborn rights" and appealed to popular sentiment rather than the court, parliament, or monarchy.[6]

What is common to the last three centuries is that public philosophy is a scramble of rights without any source of right behind the claimants—either religious or natural law. An era of absolutism—will of rulers, people, sections of society—and each discipline its own law. Education, science, politics, business—nothing gives them a unity of aim, but tattered remnants

---

4. These sentences are an expansion of Demant's notes: "relativism in morals. positivism in legal theory. source only in communities decision, either royal sovereign or popular sovereignty. Natural Rights—and Divine Rights of Rulers. Separating of civil and Ecclesiastical power. indirect power of church; civil rulers not be bought to book by a law above them; James V1 Fries Law of Free Monarchies Kings existed before there were estates or courts of men, before parliaments were held or laws made, and that called? property in land existed only by the grant of the king."

5. Willson, David Harris. *King James the VI and I* (New York: Holt, 1956),t 123.

6. This paragraph is an expansion of Demant's note: "e.g., Levellers of Cromwell time, John Lilhouse natural right appealed to popular sentiment overhead of court."

of the European tradition. *This lack of framework outside human life creates the tendency towards absolute interpretations of individual and collective life. This leads to the breakdown of liberal values because liberal values require a religious framework. Nineteenth-century reactions include both Auguste Comte and Bertrand Russell's theories suggesting that science could provide all the answers to humanity's problems.*[7]

Similarly,

> *Totalitarianism sought to reach the truth of being in terms of becoming and we saw the most recent expression of Totalitarianism accorded basic significance to the irrational, biological elements of existence. . . Because rationalistic Liberalism has ignored or suppressed these irrational elements in its dogma, reality has taken its revenge in the political vitalism of totalitarian movements, as well as in the literary vitalism of writers like D. H. Lawrence, the irrational art of the Surrealists, sensuous dynamic rhythms in music, and the libido-gnosticism of psycho-analysis. Ernst Troeltsch, the great historian of culture and religion, has shown that the Germanic mind tends to explain existence in terms of this irrational, energetic side of life, whereas the western, Latin, classical tradition is logocentric.*[8]

Thus eighteenth-century Rationalism leads to nineteenth-century Romanticism.[9] In the modern age rational and irrational accounts of existence are in conflict. "Rationalism abstracts from the concrete process its universal forms and calls these the essence of reality; irrationalism sees that this desiccates life, gives up the attempt to find any super-temporal element in existence, and throw itself into the flux of becoming in order to apprehend the world as a whole. The former makes for form without energy; the latter for energy without form."[10]

[There is a gap now in the handwritten manuscript. It is clear, however, that Demant wanted to progress the argument that the social sciences need to take the Christian frame of natural law seriously. This is the

---

7. This is an expansion of Demant's examples: "Comte, B. Russell."

8. Demant, *Religious Prospect*, 124-6.

9. This paragraph and the next are an expansion by the editors of Demant's notes: "absolute interpretations individual and collective life
liberal doctrine Religious Prospect 124 134 Rational and Vitalist
18th century Rationalism 19th romanticism
Technical = blood
Rational and irrational manifestation
The Idea of the Natural Order."

10. Ibid., 127-8.

whole concept of Christian Sociology. Demant then notes Philip Mairet. Mairet was a supporter of Social Credit, part of the Chandos Group, and editor of the *New English Weekly*. Demant then develops in note form the idea that any assessment of society must take into account natural law.]

It is the hope of social science that the formation of societies will one day be fully comprehended.[11]

If we study societies descriptively, without endeavoring to discover law or system, we become aware of a vast movement of a timeless stream of human activity, that underlies our consciousness of it, both present and historical. There appears a stream of mere human procreation and community flowing on while dynasties rise and fall, whilst religions come and go, and whilst our technical powers develop and disintegrate. It has a certain independence of all these conscious creations. It is as if there were a vegetative substation of humanity, upon which all that we call the historical process feeds and lives and changes, we see it has its own laws, its metabolism, its migrations and development, but of all of this we in the social sciences know less than we care to think.

This hidden social metabolism, however, has produced things we can see, and in various branches of the Judeo-European civilizations, we find a recurring pattern emerging. (Whether we can take this pattern as evidence of the humaniaum as such, and its consciousness social pattern forming, depends upon what may be an act of faith, that in this civilization, mankind finds most fully its essential being.)

[Demant at this point wants to develop the argument that the idea of a spiritual center to a healthy civilization is found in a whole range of cultures. From India, where the Brahman is the highest caste, to *The Republic* of Plato, to Christendom in the Middle Ages, the spiritual needs to be central. These are mainly notes.]

Same pattern in India, in Plato and Middle Ages, and a turning to something of the sort in modern prophets who suspect the abstract nature of democracy—liberated individual—in theory responsible for everything through delegation to parliament and in practice able to affect nothing. *This can be seen in Comte's positivist philosophy and Rudolf Steiner's interest in a scientific spirituality.*[12]

We may be regretful of or oblivious to the Indian caste system, but we should study the Laws of Manu and the Brahmanic sociology as one of the supreme schools of racial education. Four castes; manual workers,

---

11. Here Demant includes the note: "Reinhold Niebuhr The Self." Demant is perhaps thinking of Niebuhr's description of the challenge of understanding history in chapter 11 of his book, *The Self and the Dramas of History*.

12. This sentence is an expansion of Demant's note: "Comte—Steiner."

commercial organizers, rulers, and teachers—and the last highest only because their work to teach the nature of man and society.

Every individual is born into one of these classes—but all low functions are discharged by each individual in the course of a normal life.

1. Childhood and youth, up to marriage and a separate household—attitude of manual worker, obedience to education and efficiency.

2. from marriage of man to marriage of first born son. responsibilities of ordering household and family—commercial virtues—"economy"—household—best use of resources.

3. achieve freedom from family cases, acquisition of virtue, and exercise of social authority = imposition.

4. Withdrawal from human affairs concentration of mind upon truth of whole.

Teacher Brahman. Teachers higher can be than kings, rulers, military leaders that make up the

Kshatriya caste.

The Merchant class; regulated finance and distribution. Wealth of the whole state depended upon their faithfulness to social nature of their function. Vaishyas.

Manual worker or Shudras—thoughts once born was also Brahmin; sustaining the fabric of society.

It is not a mere rationalization of the power of rulers—like the dangers of Dante's *Paradiso*. *Instead the spiritual center provides for contentment* and makes for organic unity. The work of a humble craftsman could become an art illuminated with some spirit of creation as sublime as a temple, or tapestry of a palace.

The fourfold order—reappears in the West in the Periclean period of Athens—but this time in the realm of pure theory. Plato's *Republic*—not pretend to have direct communal wills, practical politics of his time, idea of perfect state—in contradiction to the democratic city state. Everyone knows the philosopher king from this society should be shaped by those who know archetypal realities of ideas. This knowledge compels them to take place in politics and act as guardians of the community. Plato recognizes that there are four classes of men; for the merchants and manual workers appeared grouped as one—though manual workers were often slaves.

In both the *Republic* and the *Laws*, it is recognized that what is indisputable is general social fact, namely that the purpose of manual work (if not to make employment) does (in other than tribal society) in fact depend upon enterprise, mastery and exchange. But the *manual work is only possible—it only supports social confidence, and political order, and good government—when it is part of a society that is expressing the ultimate spiritual goals.*[13]

[Demant concludes his notes by offering a brief history of how Christianity modified ancient cultures to create the achievement of Christendom in the Middle Ages. The notes are very unclear, what follows is a summary.]

Christian society was built by quarrying in ruins of several previous civilizations from Rome and others. Here fundamental motive of power of the father and notion of equality and law (common) Christianity took the universal Roman civilization, parasites of capital, and power of the mob and tried to direct them. Christianity offered a yet higher standard of living, idea of new justice, and wider view of the world. As the Roman Empire went into decay, Christianity arose with its new worship of the son—equal with God, and yet a man with a reachability. It then dealt with the consequences listed above. With the adherence to new faith; then the rescue of society after Rome's downfall and confusion of barbarian's invasion. Then the secular state was the organ of territorial chiefs under the king—ruler class (numerous) protection of localities—Christianity organized their social order of chivalry. So orders of religion and orders of chivalry become two upper classes. The third class decided its organization from crofts, guilds, merchants—in defense of their work quality and ensuring members against destitution; powerless, charters 4th class agricultural labors, who only emerged from serfdom in late Middle Ages—yet serfdom more secure than the lot of the poor in the nineteenth century.[14]

---

13. The actual text reads: "are possible only account to social confidence and political order, which belongs to sphere of government—of Government; this depends for its efficiency and authority upon the most spiritually expressive actually of the whole people." Demant clearly wanted to continue this contrast, but the notes are very unclear.

14. This is a summary of Demant's notes, which read: Therefore two orders of dependence; spatiality?: workers on viganic?, viganic on rulers, rulers on chafer? thinkers on the Idea. But materially condemned order is reversed, whole sapiers histue? is reared on heavily basis of labourers, and each of the other functions on that which is next below it.

Christian society was built by quarrying in ruins of several previous civilization. manual Rome and quite different. Here fundamental motive of power of the father (poxcheic mann?) and notion of equality and law (common) Then Euguor worklops (in decline) then universal roman civilization, megatpolitan parasites of capital, and power of the mob. Yet higher standard of living, idea of new justice, and wider view of the world. In decay, Christianity arose with its new worship of the son—equal with God one, and get a man with a realichebilizizty?. Dealt with omit queeces? first above. adherence to new faith; then rescue of society after Rome's downfall and confusion of barbarians invasion. then Secular state was organ of territorial chiefs under the king—ruler class (numerous) protection of localities—Christianity organized their cuts sort of order of chivalry. so orders of religion and orders of chivalry become two upper

[**Demant concludes the lecture with some musings on the breakdown in modernity of this spiritual hierarchy. He talks about this as the fourth period.**]

The fourth period begins with French and Indian Revolution. Any idea of a social order came to an end under democracy and capitalism—its heir and opponent, all four classes of men: thinkers, rulers, organization, and workers became merged in a single confusion—social consciousness separated from social functions. Citizen of the state only and lords of selling. The remnant of older functions of *the spiritual* idea was left in the rituals of Government.

The coronation assumes that the nation over whom a monarch rules is an organized society with religion, State, and people in a blessed and fruitful alliance. It embodies the idea of the State as a holy community, and conception of rulership as a sacred God given office, which is above the kind of utilitarianism and sectional interests, and which binds man in the earthly enterprise to the order of heaven.

Of course, in Britain society is not what that ceremony assesses it to be. But we express in figures sentimental which are not part of our present condition—and sometimes people do become what they keep saying that they are.

However these examples of a similar structure of society do perhaps suggest that it represents an order of human living in society, in accordance with the nature of man.

---

classes, which and manor?. Third class decided its organization from crofts guilds, merchants—in defense of their work quality? and in surviving members against destitution; powerless, charters 4th class agricultural labors, who only emerged from serfdom in late middle ages—yet serfdom more secure and tot state that ages cult lab rat time between Renaissance 19th century yeoman freeman certainly much better. semi of freedom

3rd period mod period Viesliyn merchanted and understood claims rise to power fusion

Series II, Lecture VI
Society

SOCIETY, WORK, AND LOVE are those realities with which every human being has to come to terms. In favorable conditions this happens without much thought and effort. But when it goes badly these realities draw attention to themselves; then they become problems; and coping with the problems makes them into tasks or "adult responsibilities."[1] That is why humankind in the modern West gives inordinate attention to social life, to work and wages, to love and marriage.

In this lecture we are looking at the relation of persons to their corporate milieu, which we call society. In the modern west we enquire about the place of the individual in society, about society's effect upon him, about the influence of his actions upon the social whole, and about the ways social organization divests or distorts the individual's aims. And if morality comes into question, it takes the form of enquiring how men and women can or ought to contribute to the wellbeing of society. It is these questions themselves, and not the answer to them which identify our current problem as belonging not to humankind as a whole, but as characteristic of our own historically limited culture. We formulate our problem as that of individual and society and assume this to be an essential feature of human existence. But mankind has not always been bothered with it.

Man is a social being by his very nature as human; it is the supervening of individuals which calls for an account of itself. This is largely ignored today because we inherit from the seventeenth century a belief that primitive man is an aggressive individualist who has to be tamed in order to become a good cooperative-operative creature. This was the unquestioned and unformulated presupposition of the idea of progress. Social anthropologists and

---

1. Demant's footnote: "I owe the term 'adult responsibilities' to Alfred Adler, the Viennese teacher of Individual Psychology. He coined the phrase 'the inferiority feeling,' popularly miscalled 'the inferiority complex.'"

students of early societies, however have completely demolished the notion of man as the original self-regarding individualist. And too often Christian prophets who share this assumption regard as their message the offer of religion to act as a social cement which will counteract the fissiparous forces of human egoism.

We tend to read back into earlier periods the tensions we meet in our recent history. For three centuries individual development has been the conscious aim of western peoples; they had to struggle with older corporate accounts of human life in which "society" was taken for granted as the basis of living. But by the nineteenth century society itself had become a problem. This was predominantly the result of the two great cataclysms of the French Revolution and the Industrial Revolution which shocked thinkers into asking: What is this thing called society? Thus was sociology born; it is a clinical subject, much as pulmonary medicine deals with the respiratory disorder, and digestive restoration is called for when the digestion does not function well. Besides the sprouting of the social sciences the century was also marked by powerful propaganda for socialism, and among religious prophets, for "The Idea of a Christian Society," to use the title of T. S. Eliot's famous essay. By the turn of the century however, there emerged strong currents of thought and feeling running counter to the stifling of the individual by the steam-rollering campaign for social cohesion. A plaintive cry was raised for I-Thou relationship. Contestants for the individual appeared, like Max Steiner pleading "Self-Revelation of the Individual"; Nietzsche, "The Superman"; and Kierkegaard, "The Single One." Many of the existentialists represented this wave of conviction, notably Nicolas Berdyaev in *Solitude and Society*. All three voice a revolt against the mass man of the bourgeois age becoming collectivized.

I have jumped to the nineteenth-century version of the dialectic between individual and society. Can we guess how it ever began? The prehistoric evidence from the Old and New Stone ages indicate that the earliest group relation among humans that we know anything about was not the nuclear family of parents and offspring like that of the animal world. It exhibited a social dilution of this blood relationship by a wider kinship where the physical father and nuclear family are merged in a wider social parenthood and brotherhood, and where children were as dependent on their age mates as on kin. Sir James Frazer showed that the totem bond is stronger than the bond of blood and family.[2] The evidence, largely derived from dying primitive peoples by modern ethnologists is aptly summarized by Rachel Levy who speaks of such primitive organization as "a willed par-

---

2. Frazer, *Totemism and Exogany*.

ticipation in a life both physical and non-physical, which stretched through time to include the dead and the unborn." And it included a bond with the animal and vegetable world, a bond kept curiously alive ceremonially by ritual and art.[3]

"Willed participation" indicates an area of life where social bonds become deliberate; for they can be endangered. The [unreadable] become purposive, being favorable or inimical to the tribal whole. Commands and sanction become necessary. The further human existence transcends its vegetable and animal matrix, the more social living needs attention and becomes the field of civic and moral obligation. What belongs to nature needs no command. "The good God gave us a command that children should honor and love their parents," said a wily Frenchman, "for it is not natural for children to love their parents. He gave no command that parents should love their children, for that is natural; therefore, no command is necessary."[4] In tribal society no command is necessary for social cohesion. Certainly, in tribal society men often have to fight for food, for mates and for territory when these needs are threatened. But there is no need to manufacture internal unities. There is a layer of human consciousness in every stage of history, however submerged it becomes by more sophisticated and contrived social realities and problems. This tribal consciousness could be called the soul life of society. Its existence has commonly been ignored since the Enlightenment with its emphasis on will and reason. Man is only a critic, a political and economic animal on top of this soul life. Though he learns by practice to be a member of social groups based on common interests of security, protection and trade, he is in origin a tribal or gregarious creature living in a milieu to which he is bound by common ancestry history, habitat, and shared emotions. In each new generation, he begins again as a being whose relations with others are a family affair. A recent professor of Greek has put it this way: "We think that it is normal to regard society as an aggregate of individuals. This is not normal from the historical point of view; it is a local development. The normal view is that society is an aggregation of families, each having its own responsible leader. This conception is not Greek only; it is also Roman, Indian, Chinese, Teutonic."[5]

We in the modern West have been led to think of the tension between individual and society mainly in terms of single citizen in relation to the state, to civil society, and industry. But this peculiar form of the problem derives from asking what is the nature of social bonds after several waves of

---

3. Levy, *The Gate of Horn*.
4. Saurat, Introduction to *The End of Fear*.
5. Kitto, *The Greeks*, 226.

individualism had monopolized the modern mind, and when movements for social change were seeking to overcome the disruptive effects of unrestrictive free enterprise in the economic life and to correct what appeared the abstract unreal protection of human needs by the representation of the individual atoms in parliamentary democracy. One unfortunate result is that we tend to envisage society entirely in terms of individualism or collectivism, free enterprise or planned economy, the single person or the state. The sociologists of course know better, but the average voter, news reader, and school teacher is mentally conditioned to regard the state as the counter weight to the individual. The bare dichotomy of man and the state is a peculiar result of the specific course of western history and does not occur elsewhere except where westernizing hence has penetrated.

We have now to see that attention to social living comes about as a result of the same follies which have brought about the emergence of the individual. I have insisted that social bonds are inherent in human existence, the family, kinship groups, racial unities, associations for the division of labor, exchange, and the distribution of acquired wealth. These occur in primitive communities and in non-European civilizations. What really needs accounting for are the forces which break up these elemental unities, and then the measures for recovering a replica of the broken unity. This is the deliberate activity which we call politics, both the genuine and the counterfeit. Political entities are thus erected on top of tribal unities and of their disruptions. That is the long story which runs from the empires of the ancient world to the most recent conflicts of governments. The consciousness of the individual has a much more limited career in mankind's history.

"What we actually see in the world," wrote J. N. Figgis, "is not on the one hand the State, and on the other a mass of unrelated individuals, but a vast complex of gathered unions, in which alone we find individuals, families, clubs, trade unions, colleges, professions, and so forth."[6] Moreover, the modern state is not the result of the extension of these bonds; it is something super added over them, and this is possible because of a previous disentangling of the individual from these inherent social unions. Over half a century ago, Edward Jenks wrote of this in his *Law and Politics in the Middle Ages*. He showed how the disentangling of the individual from the clan is one side of the same process that makes the state supersede the clan. The state in not an enlargement of the clan; there is no identity of principle between the two; the success of the state means the destruction of the clan. The clan is a community of groups; the state is an association of individuals. He adds, "in the long run, as we have seen, the state is victorious all along

---

6. Figgis, *Churches in the Modern State*, 70.

the line. . . gentile [i.e. clannish][7] ideas spring from instincts deep-rooted in humanity, and they cannot be entirely neglected. No doubt that, so far as efficiency, pure and simple, is concerned, the principles of the state are sounder than the principles of the clan . . . if gentile ideas do not make for efficiency, at least they make for stability."[8]

Jenks, I believe, was correct, but we should have to add to the clan other social bonds which form the social tissue underneath the state principle, such as neighborhood, natural sentiment, and spontaneous association for common purposes. The modern state is the product of migration and warfare and gives social association primarily a territorial character. Its tendency, from its very inception, was to break down all the intermediate barriers between itself and its individual subjects. Jenks adds that the feudal polity of medieval Europe represented the old patriarchal organization of groups within groups, but differed in principle, in that rights of the individual were no longer birthrights, but the grant of a superior in return for service, military support, money, labor, and prayer.[9] Feudalism was thus the connecting link between patriarchal and purely political society.[10] In the following section of this chapter we shall note the paradoxical consequences of Christianity's universal character breaking down tribal prejudice and thereby contributing to the growth of great political communities.

In sum, the state becomes the most obvious expression of social solidarity in so far as individuals are loosened from the ties of those pre-political groupings in their every day awareness. The modern state has acquired enormous powers because it seems the only source of cohesion after the free market economy and its theoretical justification has weakened the bonds of family, dynasty, space, nationality, and locality. In the second hand world of mass communication the individual has perforce to see himself primarily as a citizen or an economic functionary, joined to his fellows as a voter, as a vendor of labor or a buying utility. But as a man does not act responsibly because he has roots in society and then seeks a political co-ordination of his purposes with those of others. Neither the isolated individuals nor the political state is natural to man.

Consciousness of individuality is a historical product and does not occur everywhere. There have been many accounts of its emergence. The early Greek experience is well known and it provides us with an archetype of the recurring problem of the individual in society. The ancient city state

7. The bracketed portion is Demant's parenthetical addition to the quote.
8. Jenks, *Law and Politics in the Middle Ages*, 311ff.
9. Here Demant includes the note: "contract theories."
10. Jenks, *A History of Politics*.

was composed of families. Then, so runs the pattern the state subordinated the family to itself by calling in the aid of the emancipated individuals; these powerful personalities tended to run riot, and consequent civic deterioration accompanied the formation of larger state units. State power and personal accomplishment grew side by side, each supporting each other. "At one blow the family system was shattered, undermined at its very foundation. The State was placed in direct contact with individuals."[11] The *phratry* and the *deme* ceased to be the realm of *idiotes*. In Aeschylus's *Prometheus Vinctus* the contrast is made:

> The sore estate of man, how witless once
> And weak they were, until I lodged in them
> Reason, and gave them beasts to understand[12]

Yes, The Greeks of the Imperial period were pressed to find bonds between men more far reaching than kinship and inheritance. This they found in reason; and the whole intellectual and moral philosophy of the West was born. Plato found domestic and regional ties a nuisance. And after the failure of the corporate spirit which accompanied the disruption of the empire, the ancient world endured "The Age of Anxiety," marked by weakening of the corporate spirit and the rising of a cosmopolitan and individualistic temper. One need produced by this situation was Plato's totalitarian reaction; the other was represented by the proliferation of voluntary and unofficial bodies or clubs. The collapse of the Greek state sent people to find social salvation in a re-awakening of the elemental forces earlier manifest in family and tribal tissue.[13] State and family belong to separate and unreconciled traditions. Jacob Burckhardt noted the fascinating and perplexing interaction between the three realities of society, individual and state in the early Greek situation. In the *polis* the state dominated culture. Yet, "in the colonies culture (trade, industry, free philosophy, etc.) was from the outset the dominating factor... since the colonists eluded the rigorous political law of the mother country... with the fervor of civic life the individual too was unchained... And thus there developed that indescribable life of the fifth century. Individuals could maintain their position only by unprecedented

---

11. Glotz, *The Greek City and its Institutions*, 107. Demant here also referenced two additional texts: "Barber, *Problems of Historical Psychology*, 160; and Zimmern, *The Greek Commonwealth*, 71ff.

12. Aeschylus. *Prometheus Vinctus*, Lines 44.3. Translation unknown. Perhaps Demant's own translation.

13. Demant's footnote: "Tod, *Side Lights on Greek History*, especially the chapter on "Societies in the Greek World." cf. de Grazia, *The Political Community*, 134ff. for modern equivalents."

services to the city (Pericles) or by crime (Alcibiades). This atmosphere of perpetual tension plunged Athens into a terrible life-struggle, in which it succumbed."[14]

I have attended to this account of Athens because it offers a splendid paradigm of the forces which recur in western social history, with an emphasis of my own upon the priority and pervasiveness of pure sociability which underlies all individual development and all collective constructions. This pervasive substratum of human societies is largely ignored by the planners, reformers and revolutionaries, for theirs is the [unreadable] for [unreadable] inoculations. But pure sociality breaks through all the organization and seeps through its crannies from the depth of the human soul. We could aptly call it conviviality, if it were not for the riotous complexion the term has popularly acquired. We do not need an account of its origin, for it belongs to human nature. But we certainly need to understand its radical originality and then the forces which dissolve, destroy, or smother it.

A phenomenon similar to the upsurge of spontaneous mutuality in primitive and classical culture, has been identified in the appearance of club-matiness in modern business, laboring, and administrative circles of Britain and America. Office and factory workers, managers and party members and politicians, build up, out of hours, friendly gathering for social and other 'do it together' movements, for food and drink parties which break through status and wealth symbols. Socialist MP's sing "Auld Lang Syne" at party meetings; directors stop directing forms and play games. Conviviality insists on breaking through.

So far, I have tried to elucidate the tension between individual and society as a purely human phenomenon without recourse to religious belief and practice. We cannot however, overlook the presence of moral factors in their purely human setting. How then, we may ask, does the relation between the single individual and the social order raise the moral questions with which these lectures are concerned? I have already indicated that strong ethical impulses are to be detected, competing with one another, namely the need for social solidarity and the ache for free personal fulfillment. Both these drives have moral incentives, and their contrast makes a fine mess of attempts to give social living a neat moral interpretation. Man and society therefore, present in acute form what in my general title I have called The Penumbra of Ethics, that indefinite realm surrounding the clearly defined affirmations of recognized moral and social systems. Is society a moral agent at all, in the same sense as the single human being? Before elaborating that question (later in this lecture), I have three puzzles curiously

---

14. Burckhardt, *Reflections on History*, 212–4.

to present, to which society gives rise and baffles ethical judgements. They are first, organized society acquires a direction and momentum of its own; second, society takes away from individuals the results of their acts; thirdly society itself has influenced many thinkers as the source of man's alienation from himself. These three puzzles contradict the assumption, dear to men in the seventeenth and eighteenth centuries, that society is the individual writ large.

Puzzle number one is that the consequences of the mercantile desires of men become congealed into a historical complex which acquires its own inherent drift and cannot be forced against the current of its own direction. This is of course most evident in modern commercial and technical civilization. In earlier societies men have grown food to feed themselves; they have made clothes to warm their bodies, they have gathered in the market place to settle the price of the room. But when these needs are organized in larger social units, a secondary set of aims become uppermost and rapidly become primary. This is compulsion to keep the vast machinery of production and trade in commission. Trade boards are set up, unions for protection of employment arise, products are birth controlled or destroyed when over abundant. A large network of contracts for safeguarding opportunities of gainful employment becomes imperative. The bigger the organization the more difficult it is to recover the primary purposes of human effort, and this accounts for the difficulty of redirecting large scale social organization.

The same kind of social determinism which comes with increasing scale, is operative in other spheres. Government arises for the maintenance of law and order, then the enlargement of its powers becomes a profession. The human space began education by initiating the young into the mores of family and tribe: today keeping school and university well primed is a major propaganda issue. Reformers by inclination and profession thrive on having evils to combat. Moralists need vice on which to sharpen their knives. Philosophers become expert in delineating intellectual dilemmas and would be mentally on the dole if men lived like cats. In general, we get a vested interest in our problems occupationally, financially, and psychologically, and the larger the scale of organized occupations the narrower become the grooves in which corporate living runs. The benefits of large scale organization are many, but we pay for them at the price of rigidity. This intractability of the social organism, so resistant to the fluctuating desires of individuals, gives it a paradoxical character. On the one hand, it can save the public from arbitrary tyrannical interference, but it can also be a menace like Mrs. Shelley's Frankenstein, a creature which becomes formidable to those who made it. In as far as organized society is in some way a tool surreptitiously devised by humanity it tends to become the master of its inventors. This is the familiar predicament of the tyranny of tools, dramatized in Macbeth confronted by the air drawn dagger.

> Is this a dagger that I see before me.
> The handle towards my hand? Come let me clutch thee.
> Thou marshall'st me the way that I was going;
> And such an instrument I was to use.[15]

Not only daggers, however, also newspapers asking to be picked up in idle moments, also attractive shop displays, also armaments. The handy presence of the instrument invites its use.

When the instrument is a highly efficient social organization it not only rejects all guidance alien to its own structure, like a cybernetic piece of machinery, if feeds on itself and exhibits the social equivalent of hypertrophy. It over-rides or sucks in the lesser loyalties and commitments of citizens. When its inherent momentum becomes intolerable, revolution is inevitable, and then the new construction too often is but the mirror image of what it replaces. The refractoriness of long standing social ordering to a change of direction has certain consequences for human consciousness. It cramps the fulfillment of many desired moral and political achievements. Ignorance of its over-mastering power leads to a delusive assumption that if a problem is intractable it will become manageable by enlarging the area of its operation. The obstinate refusal of long standing organization to be led by current ideals, has prompted the pseudo diagnosis which attributes it to technical and scientific developments outrunning the scope of morality, as if the two progressions were of the same order, and in spite of reformers enduring a good deal of moral pain at their own powerlessness.

Mankind's inherent sociability does not spread with widening the scope of its operation. The welfare state of modern Britain does not seem to have increased the population's sense of civic obligation. It is doubtful whether Alexander Pope was correct in picturing sociability as expanding from familial affection to the world. "Friend, parent, neighbor, first it will embrace, his country next, and next all human race."[16] For the realization of long term social excellence men cannot count on support merely from tendencies which close up the networks of human togetherness. Such tendencies run away in lines of their own, independently of individual purposes, and constrain them.

A second puzzle to which "society" gives rise, for weal or for woe, concerns the ineptitude of many human intentions for the public sphere.

---

15. Shakespeare, *The Tragedy of Macbeth*, Act 2 Scene 1.
16. Pope, "An Essay on Man, Epistle IV," lines 367–68.

Collective living has a baffling effect in both serving and frustrating mankind's hopes for its future.[17] "Society" exhibits a complex variant of the enigma of the individual's failure to carry out his intentions, which we confronted in our first series of lectures.[18]

Here are a few examples within my cognizance and according to my estimate, of society taking men's aims away from them. Julius Caesar did not intend the creation of the Roman Empire but his management of the far-flung legions made it inevitable. Later on, the Empire, through administrative necessity, brought about a society with a new characteristic, namely a common law for all its members whatever their local customs, language, and rulers.

Protestantism in its earlier and official form was the arch enemy of civil liberty, but on breaking up into sects it contributed in point of fact to the emergence of liberty. Oliver Cromwell did not believe in toleration, but he brought it about by splitting loyalties as between established church and denominations.

After the First World War, President Woodrow Wilson was so sure that the European dynasties were undemocratic and divisive, that his influence at the peace conferences made for their abolition, and we got Adolf Hitler instead. Liberal reformers hoped that the end of Colonialism would inaugurate an era of sweetness and light. In its place populations freed from Imperial rule became torn through regional and tribal animosities. Voltaire's sanguine confidence in the triumph of satirical philosophy was noted in his 1765 letter to Helvetius. "During the first twelve years there has been a perceptible revolution in men's minds. The light is certainly spreading in all directions."[19] But Voltaire then neither desired nor foresaw the dynamic impulse of the Revolution of 1789. I can now adduce a recent historian's account of the way wide dissemination of information about world happenings through newspapers, broadcasting and television, produces instead of hoped for conviviality, growing personal isolation of readers and listeners who are thereby deprived of what he calls the "therapy of distance."[20]

On a wider canvas, the last phase of liberal humanism in Europe and its offshoots was marked by the triple hope of material prosperity, international peace, and democratic progress. The theory and madness for these

---

17. Demant's note: "The phenomenon has been discussed in Professor Emmet, *Rules, Roles and Relations*, 126ff., 192. Especially, her reference to R. K. Merton 'The Unanticipated Consequences of Purposive Social Action.'"

18. See Series I, Lecture Four, "The Mystery of The Will."

19. Demant's note: "Letters vi 10. I owe this reference to Dawson, *The Movement of World Revolution*, Chapter 3."

20. Boorstin, *Exploring Spirit*.

things have been developed in abundance. In the event, the very success of large scale production is now the occasion for restricting its output in order that men may satisfy the conventional conditions of acquiring it. The interdependence of states, which Richard Cooper and Herbert Spencer believed would prove to be an international cement, has sharpened rivalry all along the line, and then concealed it under the league and covenant labels. Further, the democratic idea is so emptied of the vital content it had in the Greek polis and in eighteenth-century Europe, that it has become a flag of moral appropriation for any person with a grievance; a banner waved to indicate a program, which all disaffected factions can be induced to put their last shirt on. But what is the use of a password applied to all conflicting factions, especially when it suggests that citizens can influence everything, but in practice they can affect nothing.

In countless ways the twentieth century does not exhibit the character that men of the nineteenth century believed they were making for. This aspect of social history, by which men appear to be cheated of their goals, creates a dire problem for the moralist, for he is inclined to attribute results to the direction and force of ideals. Secular and religious prophets, who offer theory and practice for firmer associative tissue, tend to suppose that failures in achievement could be cured by more intense and higher ideals. I revert therefore again to the presuppositions of these lectures namely that effective pursuit of good aims require life to be purged of a self defeating principle.

Puzzle number three in the problem of man and society makes its most tantalizing appearance in the minds of western thinkers from the seventeenth to the nineteenth centuries. It concerns not the force of this or that influence which makes for enhancement or destruction of human society, altruism or egoism, and liable to moral judgement. It poses the question how far society itself is anti-human and the root of dissociation within man himself. On such an estimate the single human being is in fact a divided creature, and this conflict is somehow due to his immersion in society. Four great names, among the lesser ones, denote discoveries of this riddle. They are Rousseau, Hegel, Marx, and Nietzsche, with overlaps in Goethe beforehand and Kierkegaard afterwards.[21] Like all thinkers they tend to see the whole of mankind's social enterprise through the spectacles of their own period. The perspectives set up by a particular historical phase become misleading and identified with the bedrock humanism as such.

21. Demant's note: "A masterly study of these four figures and others is to be found in Karl Lowith *Von Hegel zu Nietzsche*, English Translation *From Hegel to Nietzsche*. For a more literary and [unreadable] estimate, see Lionel Trilling, *The Opposing Self* and *Sincerity and Authenticity*."

Rousseau was the most perceptive and the most self-contradictory worrier about the problem of man in society. In his first Discourse[22] he called on every individual to renounce himself on behalf of the community. In *Emile* he declared that society enchained man. In *Confessions* he saluted the single man's personal identity, after the manner of St. Augustine. In his second Discourse[23] he refers to the Christian realm of Paradise as the archetypal condition of the true man. In one breath, he posits a universal brotherhood; in another he preaches a firm natural religion. Rousseau is thus the prophet of both the Jacobian and of the revived priest-emperor of a [unreadable] type. Anarchist communism and totalitarian despotism are the twin brood of his protean and tormented genius.

It is therefore only one half of Rousseau which discusses how society crushes the individual. The other half assigns him with the building of the omnicompetent political state. Because he sets out the question as one of the naked individual confronting the naked state, finding only a historical interest in the multitude of gathered unions as in ancient Sparta or the conviviality of the Geneva clubs, he was driven to propound the device of the social contract. In this device, the human individual is conceived as the source of the impulse to be himself and also his readiness to subordinate himself to the constraints of the social whole. This puzzle led him to the subtle contrast between the general will and the will of all. That chasm yawns over all attempts to derive society from an act of the corporate will.

In *The Social Contract*, trying to find a way back to social reality from the perspective of the individual, Rousseau complains that it is the gospel which "separating the theological system from the political system, made the state no longer one, and caused the internal divisions which have continually disturbed the Christian peoples." Rousseau wants a return of the ancient system to re-unite "the two heads of the eagle."[24]

In him we find the torn consciousness of modern western man, "*une aime declinée*," torn between hope and despair. So, while Rousseau feared the coming revolution he felt doomed to share it. When Napoleon created the first Empire to restore order, he could exclaim "*C'est la faute de Rousseau.*"

---

22. Rousseau, *Discours sur les Sciences et les Arts (Discourse on the Sciences and Arts)*.

23. Rousseau, *Discours sur l'origine et les fondments de l'inegalite (Discourse on the Origin and Foundations of Inequality)*.

24. Rousseau, *The Social Contract*, IV.8.

Series II, Lecture VII
Work

"CHAOS IN THE ETHICS OF WORK" MAY, 1964

MEMBERS OF THE HOUSE of Lords have been voicing their alarm at what is supposed to be a coming age of leisure.[1] This gave rise to frivolity on this part by journalists and commentators and to questioning whether the prophecy of much less work in industry is well founded. Our newspaper gave us quaint pictures of men with so much time on their hands that they got in the way mainly of their wives. "Work" was once a music hall joke along with mothers-in-law; now it looks as if "leisure" for multitudes will arouse similar affectionate cynicism. "I love work" wrote the author of *Three Men in a Boat*, "It is not that I object to work mind you; I like work; it fascinated me. I can sit and look at it for hours. I love to keep it by me; the idea of getting rid of it nearly breaks my heart."[2] This typically English remark, occurs in a page or two of banter in which Sales berates his companions for shirking.

But to return to the House of Lords: Lord Milverton said the possibility existed of a world in which any minority needed to work to keep the majority in luxury. Soon that minority might be so small that it would be recruited from the most gifted part of the population. The question was whether, deprived of economic necessity, the human character would collapse. Lord Shackleton said it was likely that enforced idle luxury would come, the most privileged people being allowed to work perhaps four hours a week, and the less privileged two hours. The rest would just have to make do with golf or galaxy hopping.

1. *Times of London*, May 14th, 1964.
2. Jerome, *Three Men in a Boat*, chapter 15.

Of course, their Lordships have been taken to task on two grounds. It has been retorted that such an age of leisure for most people is not imminent—considering the enormous needs of the world as a whole. And secondly, these alarmist prophets are accused of snobbery for suggesting that with little or nothing to do in the way of gainful employment, the mass of mankind will degenerate—though there have been workless classes with wealth enough in the past who if not always inspiring were at least not culturally or morally debased, and often examples of the art of being leisured. It is however easy to ridicule this talk of coming leisure when we are confronted with the spectacle of people clamoring for industries to be sent their way—not because they particularly want the product but because they want employment, and no industrialized society has yet in any regulated way found a method of paying people except though wages or salaries—or unemployment benefit or now redundancies bonuses. No economic thinker has yet earned his keep by advising government how to distribute throughout the community the increasing product which requires less labor to make—the energy coming from tapping its economic sources than human agency. In spite of the real human demand for more employment, for income, not for productive reasons, which disguises the problem and makes talk of a leisure age seem fantastic. The House of Lords was not silly. They have been reading the scientists, the technologists and perhaps some of them had read Keynes, who in 1930 put out an essay called "Economic Possibilities for our Grandchildren."

> I think with dread of the readjustment of the habits and instincts of the ordinary man, bred into him for countless generations, which he may be asked to discard within a few decades . . . must we not expect a general "nervous breakdown"? We have already a little experience of what I mean—a nervous breakdown of the sort which is already common enough in England and the United States amongst the wives of the well-to-do classes . . . who have been deprived by their wealth of their traditional tasks and occupations . . . To these who sweat for their daily bread leisure is a longed-for sweet—until they get it.[3]

One more quotation, earlier still in the pessimistic vein, from C. E. M. Joad: "Work is the only occupation yet invented which mankind has been able to endure in any but the smallest doses."[4] There are dangers in the future of leisure. Since Aldous Huxley's *Brave New World*, there have been

---

3. Keynes, *Essays in Persuasion*, 366–67.

4. Joad, C. E .M. quoted in *Inventing the Future* by Dennis Gabor (London: Penguin, 1964).

no more utopias. But Berdyaev, quoted by Huxley, had written: "Utopias now appear much more realizable than one used to think. We are now faced with a very different worry: How to prevent their realization."[5]

The counter-optimism is to be found in the scientific experts and their popularizers—and in one kind of science fiction. Many of them, just in order to reconcile men to the triumphs of science and technology, have to posit a race of technically, socially, and morally perfect beings in some cosmic Ark upon Simon among the [unreadable].[6] I have only been able to scan a tiny fraction of the cheerful prophecies based upon the diminution of necessary labor by technologies, automation, cybernetics, synthetic foods, communities across space, automatic accountancy, and so on.

[It appears as if Demant started to cross this passage out, however it remains essential for the sense of the rest of the article.] They are all vitiated by the prevalent dogma that it is a moral duty to be optimistic. Yet I cannot avoid the conclusion that if the scientific world survives, labor will take a smaller and smaller part in it, because of the new techniques and when, to this, the displacement of men by non-human power sources is added.

With the possible and (as I would say) necessary disappearance of deliberate obsolescence—things made to wear out, and elimination of work done for employment and not for obviously required output, then the labor-saving process will go on at a frightening pace. But why frightening? It is not only peers of the realm who are alarmed and bewildered; the philosophers of the technical development are also confused, but they are comforted by a prevalent assumption that technical ways of doing things are bound to be the best way.

[Again an attempt to cross it out] All are not as wise as Carl Friedrich von Weizsäcker, a German physicist who attacked as childish the view that it was proof of progress to carry out all that became technically possible—a view encouraged by the fascination exercised by modern techniques.[7] For the most part the prophets of what they call the neo-technical age, talk in terms of adapting human beings to it. Here is a paradox, indeed which might prove fascinating or daunting to the theologian and moralist—quite apart from the effect upon the ethics of work. The paradox, as it seems to me, is disclosed in the double aspect of the neo-technical development so far as I can glean its significance. On the one hand, we have the powers by which the brain taps cosmic energy for what has historically been done by human and

---

5. Berdyaev, quoted in Huxley, *Brave New World*.
6. Here Demant includes the note: "new messianicism."
7. Speech in Frankfurt on receiving German Peace Prize, October 13, 1963.

animal muscle, or primitive power and [unreadable] waterfalls, and now making mechanical processes so nearly self-governing, that the element of human attention is reduced to a minimum. (This is what is known as Cybernetics). On the other hand, as one expert Sir William Puckey puts it, "The more we are able to delegate control of machines, the more responsibility is vested in us, as members of the community, to develop better control over ourselves."[8] Note the vagueness of the pronouns "us," which may conceal a threat that men must be changed in order that applied science may do its job.[9] The machine is to serve human beings but human beings altered to accommodate the machine, and of course what is not openly admitted is that initiatives will rest with the few who are technically adroit, by scrapping multitudes with the dangers usually from human nature not being cooperative enough.[10] It sounds as this consummation may well be the devil's work.

But let us give it the benefit of the doubt and attend to its effect on the ethics of work. By that I mean the ethical status of work in employment—not questions of what is good or bad work—is it justly allocated, should work be distributed by the freeplay of supply and demand or socially controlled—questions which have played an important part in social and moral thought.

How much does the ethical status of work require re-examination in the light of these disturbing possibilities? John Maynard Keynes based his dread of the future upon the enormity of the task of changing men's age-long attitude to work. Whether Keynes, after his famous thesis that one could always have full employment by varying this ratio of investment to saving, did not go on to enquire how much employment was necessary and where, and what sort for full production because of his alarm or because he died too soon, I do not know. But he certainly faced a real problem, which I will now try to unfold in my own way, in order to see how the tradition about the status of work in Christendom is affected by the new situation.

Instead of a cumbrous and wearisome survey of all that biblical and Christian societies have said about work—daily work, I will list what I think are the main conceptions.

---

8. Quoted in *The Listener,* February 26, 1959.

9. Here the transcriber was unsure of Demant's note: "(Actual word cutuiest?) Here Demant was perhaps referencing William Cubitt and his invention of the 'treadwheel,' a technological development that came to be used as a way of punishing prisoners."

10. Here Demant includes the note: "Tomato growers."

WORK AS NECESSITY

This seems to be the basic biblical view, held without much conscious attention. Certainly M. J. Oldham said in his pamphlet, "Work in Modern Society," "Work in the Bible is not presented as a problem. It is taken for granted as part of the order of the created world. 'Man goeth forth unto his work and to his labor until the evening.' 'Six days shalt thou labor and do all thy work.'"[11] Work belongs to the stuff of life, and in this the Bible view is not very different from that of the old world generally. Except Troeltsch in *Social Teaching of the Christian Churches*, rightly warns against the extravagance of attributing to early Christianity the idea of consecration of work. This is the modern mystique of work, but it appears that it had a pre-Christian version in the widespread notion of work as a priestly activity, in which no thing or action is valid and real unless it is part of the sacred ritual of perpetual renewal.[12] In the Bible life was sacred as God given, but labor, work, and action were equally subject to the necessity of present life. Nor does it appear that glorification of labor—or romantic conceptions of work—occurs in early Christian writers.[13] What can be said however is that Christianity did free the laboring activity from the contempt in which some phases of antiquity had held it—but interest for work in antiquity has often been exaggerated by exclusive allusion to the eighth-century Athens—and the prevalence of slavery. St. Paul's epistle hardly glorified labor in the modern romantic sense. First Thessalonians 4:9–12, and Second Thessalonians 3:8–12 enjoins work upon those who from laziness "eat other men's bread," or command "it as a good means of keeping out of trouble, and minding ones own business." Tertullian makes the appeal that Christians must appear respectable therefore they are to work like other people.[14] There is little about work in Aquinas, but what there is in the *Contra Gentiles* asserts that only the necessity to keep alive compels to do manual labor. "*Sola enim necessitas victus cogit manibus operari.*"[15] The Pauline "if a man does not work neither does he eat," explains the ethic of labor as a necessity; unless you are producing some equivalent of "what you are consuming you are robbing your brother." It is fairly obvious that this equation is quite upset by the scientific age where a man can produce a tremendous multiple of what he consumes.

---

11. Oldham, *Work in Modern Society*, 49.
12. Here Demant references Mircea Eliade's work, *Patterns in Comparative Religion*.
13. Here Demant included the note: "Against Borne *Le Travail et L'homme*. Jacques Leclerq (Lecours du droit habitude)."
14. Tertullian, Apologetics, 42.
15. Aquinas, *Contra Gentiles*, III.135.

Closely linked to this evaluation of work as a necessity is its application to the community of brethren; work becomes also a labor of love for those in need. From St. Paul onwards there is plenty of exhortation in the early writers of work in order to devote the fruit of labor to the relief of need—one aspect of this service is the ideal of [unreadable], for it is better for a man or a fraternity to be self sufficient than to be dependent outside support.[16]

But now compare this duty of work for giving to a modern situation described by Matthew Arnold in an essay on Tolstoy; "I do not know how it is in Russia, but in an English village the determination of 'our circle' to earn their bread by the work of their hands would produce only dismay, not fraternal joy, amongst that 'majority' who are so earning it already. 'There are plenty of us to compete as things stand' the gardeners, carpenters, and smiths would say; 'pray stick to your articles, your poetry, and nonsense; in manual labor you will interfere with us, and be taking the bread out of our mouths.'"[17] Already by 1888 the non-laboring rich men were performing a neighboring service by keeping out of the labor market. A fortiori, in a neo-technic age he serves best who will use up most without insisting on the privilege of being employed.

WORK AS A CURSE, OR ASCETIC DISCIPLINE

The pain of labor as a curse and as punishment for original sin does not seem to have been a prominent conception in the church fathers. The religious significance of work had some early exponent in Ambrose, and of course in Augustine. Augustine's scheme was that activity in paradise was a sort of effortless bliss. But with Adam's sin the order of creation is upset; "the [unreadable] of order" is lost and toil, the penalty of sin, takes its place.[18] "We are born to labor, and then reborn to rest." It seems that for Augustine labor belongs neither to man archetypal nor to his fully eschatological structure. It is a discipline, an *askesis,* but one of growth rather than of purification and purgation.

Of course, the Christians shared with the older known moralists the commendation of labor as an antidote to otiosity, a means of keeping out of trouble. This conception is close to the idea of work as a mortification of the flesh which played a prominent part in monasticism. Chapter 48 of the Benedictine Rule enjoins labor as a prophylaxis against the idle body.

16. Clement of Alexandria, *Paedagogus,* III.
17. Arnold, *Essays in Criticism,* 298.
18. Augustine, *City of God.*

The formula *ora et labora* of St. Benedict soon became sentimentalized into "*laborare est orare!*" The medieval church seems to have contained two lines of thought about work in some unstable tension; on the one hand it contested two older ideas of work as expiation for Adam's fall, as charity towards the brethren and (primarily in the religious rituals) as purification through [unreadable]. On the other hand the doctrine of work as necessity allows place for no more of it is required, than is physically necessary, when work is a kind of desperate last resort, the fulfillment of duty. In many places Augustine adumbrates the priority or superiority of contemplation which was more systematically stated by Aquinas. This stream of thought uses the famous distinction between "*uti*" and "*frui*"—the things to be enjoyed are good in themselves there to be used, only for what they lead on to. This enabled Aquinas to put play in a superior category of human activity than work.[19]

The Reformation and post-Reformation period seem likewise to have contained two strands: one is a newer version of the older disciplinary vindication of work; the other is a relatively fresh doctrine of work as a vocation. It is this doctrine of work as vocation that we now attend. Luther is often, and I think rightly, credited with assigning an unknown dignity to manual labor; it was a way of serving God, and his ideas spread throughout Protestant communities and their hermeneutics of the Bible. "A cobbler, a smith, a farmer, each has the work of his trade, and yet they are all alike consecrated priests and bishops."[20] "As has been said Luther placed a scepter in the horny hands of labor,"[21] (perhaps miter on its head would be a better simile). Luther seems however to leave out of his teaching of vocation in daily work all elements of production and making—it is confined to finding the heavenliness God put into the earth.[22] There is an aspect of the Lutheran version of this dependence of man as a vessel of the Lord. For Calvin man is a tool of the Lord, remolding this world, in a common and spirit-led attempt to build the Holy community. Lutherans suffered the world, but Calvinism sought to master it. In Calvinism there is another note, namely work as an antidote for anxiety over salvation; this activity of work dissipates religious doubt and then this brings conviction of God's grace.[23]

19. cf. Gavin, F. "The Catholic Doctrine of Work and Play," *Theology*, XXI (1930) 14–40.

20. Luther, *Works of Martin Luther*, 69.

21. de Grazia, *The Political Community*, 61.

22. Here Demant's notes are incomplete: "'Golt miss es dalin legen, rolles diedibert funden.' (Weche cd Valch v 1873.)"

23. Demant concludes this paragraph with a sentence perhaps giving a humorous example of how work can diminish or replace concerns about salvation: "'Man Part?

I find in John Wesley, what I consider a wholesome rejection of the puritan notion that it was the interior affects of work that mattered. In [unreadable] and Calvinism work itself as an activity was sanctified; in Wesley's leading, work was the Fruits of Salvation which were the sign of salvation. "Render unto God, not a tenth, not a third not a half, but all that is God's, be it more or less, by employing all on yourself, your household, the household of faith, and all mankind, in such a manner that you may give account of your stewardship."[24]

The idea of work as a vocation was revived during the last war when church leaders in England had down five points for a recovery of social health. The fourth of those points stated that every man should be able to consider his work as a divine vocation. What is involved in this fairly recent idea? Initially one may say that a vocation is a work to which a man is called by God. But the fourth point of these prelates was both narrower and wider than this general conception. It was first of all concerned with that form of work in which men are employed for their own livelihood and in providing things and services for which the community pays them. Secondly, the criterion was clearly meant to be a list of conditions which affect not only Christian workers but all men, including many who have no religious commitments which would lead them to put the questions in terms of a divine call to their work. It is of use only in a derivative or analogical sense that we can use this specifically Christian idea of vocation as a test of value in the work of which men get their living. In its strict theological meaning the "calling" according to 1 Thessalonians 2:12 is to membership, of the kingdom of God and is part of the doctrine of justification. Such a call induces a certain indifference to one's state in the Kingdom of the world (1 Cor 7:20-24). For the most part however, the New Testament, like the Old, uses the term more widely for a summons to the individual man, or people, or church to a particular duty which carries its own privilege and responsibility. But whether used in its purely soteriological sense, or in that of a life task, vocation is held to proceed from God's eternal purpose. It has the hold of divine authority and is independent of, and often opposed to, the person's sense of fitness or inclination for the task to which he is called; it has nothing to do with what is congenial or with what one is good at. It is no doubt because vocation has its origin in the unfathomable decree of God that the church has never been able to lay down an unmistakable criterion of a vocation and that there is little guidance for finding one in the teaching of moral theology. Although the church has rightly been shy of

---

now is a man in meeting. Are you saved—I don't have to be I'm a reporter.'"

24. Wesley, John. "The Use of Money," Sermon 50.

defining a vocation by any human tests, there has been a general Christian understanding of certain states of life as "vocation," such as life in a religious order, or the priesthood, and the idea has then been more generally applied, for example, to celibacy, to marriage or to some occupation requiring special renunciations, such as the mission field, nursing, or dangerous public services. These vocations represent not a call from idleness or evil doing to work and well doing, but the call from a normal good state of life to a special task that involves a restriction of valid satisfactions.

It is therefore a far cry from the idea of vocation as used in the Bible and in early Christendom to the requirement that daily work should be considered as divine vocation. I am not condemning this modern usage. But I consider that nothing but harm and confusion and fantasy can follow a neglect to appreciate that we are now stretching the idea of vocation to include something which Christian thought has not succeeded in competently handling under the heading. The attempt to give significance to work by calling it a vocation must be saluted, but it has put us in something of a muddle. However much Max Weber and R. H. Tawney have had to be corrected, largely for reading into the first Calvinists economic development and exaggerated motive of "monetary acquisitiveness," they were right to see as a peculiar historical phenomenon the close connection between the forces which made for the growth of industrial commercialist civilization and interior disposition carried with the idea of work as a calling. And Troeltsch's conclusion, that the contribution of Calvinism's habits of thought to the problem of the commercial era is only indirect and consequently an involuntary one, leaves the important point obscured. The point is that reliance upon a purely subjective principle, namely the calling to man to be active in a process, without enough attention to the object of the process, leaves men with the impulse to intensify his activity as a pledged sign of grace without regard to the objective nature of the result. Naturally, when this intense religious faith that marked the foundation of the doctrines faded, men retained the dispositions associated with it and unconsciously held on to a belief in salvation by activity—and this seems to have produced a world where masses of men find no significance in their work, even a human significance. No wonder the cry arose for recovering the idea of vocation in work.

And when this trend consecrated economic activity as an interior activity, as an interior discipline, the facts of modern world history turn it into a self-defeating principle. For when success in labor of hand and brain has made human expenditure of energy less and less necessary to produce a unit of result, mankind is steadily deprived of the spiritual medicine he has relied upon.[25] An unsolicited ally of such a religiously formed habit of mind could be identified in the conception of labor as almost the essence of humanism. "The creation of man through human labor was one of Marx's persistent ideas"[26] (*Jugendschriften*) and Engels observed labor as marking the transition from ape to man (*Ursprung der Familie*), etc. Both men were determined that the unconditional definition of man as *animal rationale* should be replaced by defining him as *animal laborans*. And Adam Smith's contempt for those who consumed without leaving an equivalent behind them would be regarded as another side of the same coin. One must not of course attribute the mental habits of the public to the explicit tradings of the prominent leaders of thought.

For completeness, I have called attention to religious treatments of the status of work, which glorify it under the heading of a creative act or of material for a liturgical offering. Etienne Borne's *Le Travail et L'homme* was a notable example and many more recent writers who expand a romantic view of the creature in which it is man's calling to share the activity of the creator by changing and improving everything. Borne wrote,"It is a metaphysical dignity which gives to the humble activity of the workers the rank of a secondary cause and makes them collaborators in the development of creation."[27] Then came the Dominican M. D. Chenu, with his *Pour une Theologie du Travail,* in the same vein arguing that just as God is creative in making the universe, so humans made in the image of God are called to creative in their labor.[28] Chenu can certainly find precedents for this creature interpretation of work in the Christian tradition; there is some of it in Augustine, and Chenu uses a text of Maximus the Confessor on the Relation of Man to Nature.

It is not difficult to see how this "creature" conception of work provides strong encouragement to those aspects of liturgical reform which insists on the offering of work-products as part of the Eucharistic pattern. I do not wish to be in the least scathing about this doctrine of daily work as part of a delegated act of creation. It has I think acquired a welcome amongst Christians as a way of giving significance to work after the proletarianization of the worker rendered obsolete the world of small masters and its valid assumption that work would always guarantee bread and honor. But the acceptance of such vindication of work tends to regard any activity in

25. Here Demant includes the note: "making working destincts and wash?"
26. Arendt, *The Human Condition*, 86.
27. Borne, *Le Travail et L'homme*. (Demant's translation.)
28. Chenu, *Pour une theologie du travail.* Demant did quote from the text here; however, it is difficult to tell from the handwritten script precisely the location of the quote. We have provided a summary of the quotation.

production as susceptible of it. Whether it be redundant, or made up to keep people busy, or sheer waste, or if not economically ridiculous perhaps had better be lessened because its benefits show diminishing returns in comparisons with disruptive effects. (Hard to stop something if it is shown to employ a population.)

I conclude by asking which of these conceptions of work will have any sense if our scientific prophets are correct in envisaging a world of laborees largely without labor. If most men apart from technicals and intellectuals are at leisure most of their lives; the conception of work as necessity becomes less real; that of survival will still have some validity, although the stage may be reached when the best service is to keep out of way. As for the discipline function of employment, clearly sales tactics for it will be required. The same applies to vocation and offering, their place in life for Christians will not vanish but their spheres will be more a matter of choice than of compulsion. Perhaps in the end the only doctrine that will stand up to all these possible changes is that work is the result of a curse, a necessary consequence of the Fall, and this civilization might be supported by the difficulty of envisaging a healthy society without a good lot of it. That is why all the professed solutions offered for the alleged leisure age look so ridiculous to us. Here is one courageous and honest man, Gabor in *Inventing the Future*. Some people will ask, "Is it really so difficult to break man of his habit of keeping his equilibrium by hard work that we must steel him by hardship courses against leisure? Have the Eastern peoples not set an example and shown that one need not get into mischief when doing nothing?"[29] One must admit that they appear to have found a short cut to dignified leisure. It is said that the Balinese think nothing of sitting cross—legged for hours, without smoking, without thinking. An old Turkish *affendi*, smoking his hookah, who had neither home nor work during his whole life, had a dignity unequalled by any western professor emeritus or elder statesman. The perpetual Oriental siesta, which is not rest after work but blissful repose, appears so alien to us western work addicts, that one might believe that we could never find our way to it. But an eccentric Englishman of a hundred years ago, Mansfield Parkyns, has found a way to the Egyptian brand of siesta, called "Keyef" and has left a masterful description of it.[30] He succeeds at it incomparably better than all those modern authors who have tried to convey, for instance, the mindless mediations of Zen Buddhism.

Does this look terrifying, or comic, or fantastic? Well there is worse to come. Maybe men will pay to be allowed to work, as they will perhaps have

29. Gabor, *Inventing the Future*.
30. Parkyns, *Life in Abyssinia*.

to wait to get rich before they can enjoy food from the castle and the cooking pot, the masses being nourished chemically—just as we now have to pay highly if we do not want things like noise, or petrol fumes, or provided education. It is all very daunting. I am only sure about two things. Firstly, it would be theologically wrong to condemn the machine and applied science. (There is a real but somewhat obscure connection between the growth and the ethos of Christendom.) But it is also theologically and humanly false to assume that whatever can be done technically had better be done that way. I shall not have any responsibility for the age of leisure as it is promised, except I hope in paradoxical intercession. And of course, it may never happen—though I'm afraid it will.

Series II, Lecture IX[1]
Enterprise and Establishment

WHEN THE OLD GREEK, Archimedes, discovered the principle of the lever, which as you know is a means by which you could lift a weight much greater than you could with your unaided muscles, he was so excited about it that he exclaimed: "Give me whereon to stand and I will move the world." Of course, he had nowhere to stand except on the world, and a very few square inches of that.

This tale about the early history of mechanics provides a useful simile for the power of the human spirit. It can do mighty things, for in some ways it is more powerful than the whole physical and natural creation; it can detach itself from it, reach a supremacy over its determinism, and also turn around upon it to refashion it. That is the spring of religions, cultures, civilizations, and science. (I had better here recall, what I developed in the first series, that in using the phrase "the human spirit" I am not referring to anything religious or godly. Man has inner powers which enable him to confront his world instead of being merely immersed in it. He can see it and not merely experience it—think of it, will to act in it, master it by concepts and experiment, and formulate his feelings about it in art and literature. This he does whether he is godly or an unbeliever. Religion does not make man a spirit-centered creature, he is that as human. Religious faith is that movement by which he submits himself, and through his spiritual obeisance, brings also his mental, willing, feeling, and creative life into voluntary unity with the gods, or the one God.)

When Pascal called man a reed, but a thinking reed; he expressed the truth that man is limited and creaturely, bent by the winds of outside reality, but also not passive in this world because he has this power of handling it by that layer of his spirit which we call thought.

---

1. Demant's notes for Lecture XVIII are missing.

In the simile of Archimedes's lever, you have the two things; one, man's power of thought, construction and ability to move things which his physical organism is not able by itself to do; but also his dependence on the laws of gravity and a point of support both for his lever and his own body. Now I have attempted to describe the history of Christendom as a growing impact of the human spirit upon its physical and social environment. First, in the world religions the human spirit transcended the boundaries of the closed communities of tribe and people—and saw itself as universal. The idea of man arose, and the task of reconciling the universal and particular aspects of each man or people—and the moral or spiritual struggle appeared which gave a universality to the notions of the good life which now became a personal destiny and not only a social bond. Deity in Hebrew and Christian religion was revealed as Lord of Creation and not the soul of the world; there man, linked directly with this transcendent source of being and not merely through the creation, is able to confront the created order. Meeting the Greek invention of the concept or idea, behind the concrete and temporal items in the created order, the dynamic Hebrew Christian impulse, combined with the Hellenic intellectual form of transcendence, to provide the impulse and mentality of Christendom. The really hard task of Christian thought, was to fit into it the unprecedented fact of the "Word made flesh" wherein that which is above the waterfloods of earthly history, enters into world history, indeed starts a new history, in the manger child and the crucified Jesus. Both the birth and the death are historical and public events; but that here it is the transcendent Creator who is making a new creation, is hidden from public knowledge and is disclosed only to believers. The resurrection and ascension at the right hand of God are the secrets of the church. But what became public was the effect of this church, its beliefs and outlooks, its spur to world changing, the enormous responsibility it placed upon man with its teaching of sin and repentance and the last judgement. Every moment is a moment of crisis or judgment. And even where this faith has become a minority movement, leaving a secularized world dominant on the scene, the dispositions remain, especially the disposition representing European man's recurrent effort to bend history towards a recovery of original perfection—effort sometimes called progress and often revolution.

I cannot go over the material, which these lectures have tried to summarize, showing the element of colossal enterprise in the disposition of Christendom. (For modern insights into this read Karl Jaspers's *Origin and Goal of History*; C. Dawson's *Christianity and the Rise of European Culture*; Berdyaev's *Meaning of History*; or Albert Camus' *L'Homme Revolte*.)

In this lecture I am calling attention to the serious situation which has arisen at our end of the story, through the emancipated spirit forgetting its dependence. At the religious level it is the sin of Lucifer, a spirit, an archangel—presuming because he is pure spirit assuming the predisposition of the Creator spirit, and ignoring that though spirit he is created and therefore dependent. What a beacon that it is Lucifer who becomes Satan. But on the level of history, society, and culture the same fall occurs, it is not a fall from spirit into matter; but a turning of creative into destructive spirit—adumbrated in the classical myths of Icarus and Prometheus. There is no Prometheus myth in the Bible, it is not sin but responsibility to subdue the land with the powers given to man in his image of the divine; but there are the myths of the fall of Lucifer, the disobedience of Eden, and the Tower of Babel: and supremely the death of Christ brought about by the good powers of the world and church arrogating to their justice and holiness an absolute righteousness in place of a due recognition of their relative and delegated righteousness.

This is to say theologically what I will now try to say sociologically. For the Christian man his freedom is a dependent freedom, a delegated power of enterprise, which becomes destructive and damned if asserted in its own right. Man is a physical animal and a community fellow as well as an enterprising spirit; Christian and secular man (not heathen but post-Christian man) have this dependence in common. They can only examine their enterprises from a base in nature and community. The Christian impulse served to liberate western man from their limited and conflicting bonds; but at the end of this history it is possibly the specific mission of the Christian teaching to recall mankind to the fact that the modern mind has carried on its enterprise in fashioning the world and society in culpable ignorance of the need for a foundation; (it suggests a picture of Archimedes without a fulcrum, in mid-air on the long end of his lever, no longer moving but being lifted by the weight at the far end). While the church had to emphasize that man was a spirit-centered creature and not only a drop in the stream of nature and an item in the social whole, I think it must now remind him that he is an animal and a community fellow by origin, and not a mechanism or an angel, not completely free to disregard his roots in the natural life process, in the elemental social loyalties, in the blood and the feelings, as if he were an angel, nor a mechanism completely adaptable to any technical or scientific utopia developed by the physical or social scientists. Reinhold Niebuhr's recent work, *The Self and the Dramas of History*, posits this lesson—in a different way from mine).[2] Man being a human creature and not an angel,[3] it must be that only when men are settled in some part of their existence are they able to be free and fashion existence in other parts of their life.

It is this settled part of human life which I have called "establishment." (The house of Archimedes's fulcrum and his patch of the earth's surface; or to vary the metaphor, a tree as it grows higher in the air must also put down its roots deeper or it will be blown over.)

In my last three lectures I dealt with three basic realities of all human terrestrial existence which for countless ages were part of the establishment of life, and in which in the West men retained a base in their lives, out of which they proceeded to intellectual, political, and technical constructions. The government must rely upon the health of the societies or communities that precede it. For government cannot create the social tissue; it can only organize it into political patterns. The work life in which men for generations have had the economic task of transforming material into means of livelihood and of culture is a task given by man's existence itself, and on top of which can be erected specialized manufacture, industry and exchange, commerce, and finance. Yet this work life can be neglected and too easily assumed to be looking after itself, so that today we are mastering nature at the cost of weakening or destroying the source of economic life. We are subduing the earth but neglecting to replenish it, and having to be worried about the volume of employment, instead of what it produces. And then the love life between the sexes and the family, which until the nineteenth century was a refuge and place of recovery from the contractual, economic, and impersonal relationships of civilization, has now become an achievement requiring education, technical information, marriage guidance, child clinics, and a vast legal machinery to preserve it. In other words community, work, and love—instead of underlying enterprise as a foundation of establishment—have become the objects of highly skillful enterprise in government, economics, and education. This has a great deal to do with what Karl Mannheim calls the "crisis in valuation" in his useful study, *Diagnosis of Our Time*, setting out the problem without, I think, questioning deeply enough

---

2. Niebuhr, Reinhold. *The Self and the Dramas of History* (London: Faber and Faber, 1956). Demant then includes the note: "organism and artifact." He is perhaps thinking of Niebuhr's understanding of community as both organism and artifact. Which is to say that communities develop organically to some extent, but also that they are always created with human thought and intention and thus are also artifacts.

3. Here Demant includes the note: "Mae West. . ." He may be thinking of West's movie, *I'm No Angel*, in which West's character must deal with the many complications that come from her aiding a thief, who is also her boyfriend at the beginning of the film.

the assumptions which make us acquiesce in them in their modern form.[4] One of the bases of establishment in the past has been acceptance of authority in some parts of life. Mannheim writes,

> When society was more homogeneous the religious and political authorities coincided at many points, or else there was a violent conflict to define the spheres of religious and political authorities. But now we are faced with a variety of religious denominations and the disagreement between various political philosophies which, as all of them act at the same time, only succeed in neutralizing each other's influence upon the minds of the people.[5]

And again,

> An even worse predicament of our age is caused by the fact that whereas the most important values governing a society based upon the rule of custom were blindly accepted, the creation of specifically new values and their acceptance is to a large extent based upon conscious and rational value appreciation. Whether one should love one's neighbor and hate one's enemy is based, as we have seen, upon the belief that there is either a demand of God or a part of our ancient traditions, but whether the democratic organization is preferable to a dictatorial one, or whether our educational system should pay more attention to the study of the classics or to further specialization, these are decisions which have to be argued . . . Although this process leading to a greater consciousness and deliberation is in itself a great advance, yet when it is brought into the existing social context it completely upsets the balance between conscious and unconscious forces operating in our society.[6]

The question so well posed by Mannheim raises the one I am concerned with, and about which I think he is too optimistic: whether the human being can live responsibly when nearly every movement of his life has to be the result of deliberate and conscious choice. Where there is no establishment, no tradition, or only a very weak one, which looks after and provides values for our living and relationship, too much is put upon the individual conscience—quite apart from the query where he gets his criteria of valuation from, if not from a tradition of some sort. The philosopher Bergson, in his *Two Sources of Morality and Religion,* and a contemporary philosopher Karl

4. Mannheim, Karl. *Diagnosis of Our Time.*
5. Ibid., 21.
6. Ibid., 22.

Popper, in his work *The Open Society and Its Enemies*, have in quite different ways proclaimed the need to cultivate and defend an open society. Popper is particularly concerned to combat philosophies and political regimes which restrict human freedom. But I would say to him that a completely open society, one in which nothing is settled, accepted, and everything has to be decided on and voluntarily done, is one which so mistakes human for angelic nature, that it sends men in panic back to the herd—and that is part of the tendency toward totalitarian societies and a mass society today. Only with a proper balance of establishment and enterprise can freedom of enterprise be maintained. This is quite beside the more logical point that even a free society is not an open society, but one committed to a certain set of beliefs and to that extent is closed—a point made by Professor Michael Polanyi in his *Logic of Liberty*.

To turn to the economic aspects of the problem I am raising, the late Professor Elton Mayo who has studied the effect upon social loyalties of the American factory system had results in giving advice to management as to how to foster cooperative attitudes therein. Having put himself to school with the sociologists like Le Play, Durkheim and Christopher Dawson, he has shown how rapid industrial and technical development, quite apart from economic rewards and penalties, has undermined spontaneous social cooperation, such as is universal in pre-industrialist society. He gave us this important dictum "they have relapsed upon self interest when social association has failed them"—in other words the alleged "economic man," whose only incentive is gain, is a product of industrial society.[7] Incidentally, he discovered though his studies of earlier cultures that both the hypothesis of a rabble of unrelated individuals (as the state of primitive man who had to be bribed into being cooperative pointedly argued by the champions of *laissez faire* economics) and the conception of a powerful state, which arises to order the rabble (as in Rousseau and Hobbes), have the same roots—namely a weakening of all the natural associative forms of human grouping, the family, the church, the clan, the club, the guild, and the university—in my terminology, the organs of establishment. Mayo says there are two principles of social organization; that of established society and that of adaptive society. Established societies are those which obtain everywhere before the industrial era, represented by the primitive tribe, "the early industries of New England, or of the small Australian city of the 1880s."[8] He points out that most revolutionary movements are impelled by a desire, largely

---

7. Mayo, *Social Problems of an Industrial Civilization*, 39.
8. Ibid., 11.

unconscious, "to return from present uncertainty to established certainty."⁹ Adaptive society is the one made necessary by the transcending of local economies, by specialization in production and by large scale industrial and urban centers. Mayo hopes for an increase in human adaptiveness to social change, for the alternative is, he would claim, a loss of the benefits of modern technique. I mention this interesting contribution without accepting the latter conclusion. I think a different conclusion must be drawn. His studies certainly suggest that men can be adaptive in some activities in a society which is established in respect of other and more fundamental activities. But, inconsistently I think, he counts too much upon an unlimited power of adaption to any change of social structure which diminishes its established elements. For man cannot be adaptive all along the line, his life must be established somewhere. Then he is free to adapt himself in other respects. In my Holland Lectures, *Religion and the Decline of Capitalism*, I sought to show that the economic freedom of capitalism was possible so long as it did not occupy the whole field; that is so long as there was underneath the market economy, a sound social tissue in which the bases of life, such as land, labor, and money, and the social units of family, neighborhood, crafts, and culture were not marketable.

It is interesting that the nineteenth-century economic writer Walter Bagehot, whose *Physics and Politics* is still worth reading, realized this necessary basis in establishment for enterprise of freedom of social and political construction—yet about the economic life he wrote there had once been "a sort of 'pre-economic age' when the very assumptions of political economy did not exist, when its precepts would have been ruinous, and when the very contrary precepts were requisite and wise."¹⁰ And with regard to the whole movement of liberation from tradition, marked so violently by the French Revolution, he wrote

> In 1789 when the great men of the Constituent Assembly looked on the long past, they hardly saw anything in it which could be praised, or admired or imitated: all seemed a blunder—a complex error to be got rid off as soon as might be. But that error had made themselves. On their very physical organization the hereditary mark of old times was fixed; their brains were hardened and their nerves were steadied by the transmitted results of tedious images. The ages of monotony had their use, for they trained men for ages when they need not be monotonous.[11]

9. Ibid., 10.
10. Bagehot, *Physics and Politics*, 7.
11. Ibid., 19.

This is of course a bit short sighted. Previous ages were not so monotonous and the modern period not so varied as it seemed to the men of the Victorian age. But it is the same point, men cannot be on the stretch all the time—and if the layer of customs grows thin, the spirit of man wilts under the burden of incessant adaption and activity. Civilization is a superstructure; it must stand on a more elemental foundation than itself if it is to survive. Power to erect civilization over the sources of life, biological, social, and spiritual sources, is a great achievement but it requires that those sources are still there and robust enough to produce new vitalities when the pattern of civilization needs renewing. I am not advocating a renunciation of the powers of mind over the stream of life, but that its achievements must not make the economic so big that it crushes the life out of its bases in nature and community, and the pay due relation of men with men and of men and women, and the linch between men and the hidden spiritual realm. It means that there can be relations of contract of some part of life if marked by statues, the capacities of intellect are limited by the vitality underneath, you can make an artifact of society by manning at one level if it leaves enough of society in organic relationships, and spirituality—in the sense of man's using powers wisely over the stream of life, if there remains enough piety to recognize the dependence of those powers upon what is given in existence.[12]

In my view, the strength of Communist Russia and China rests not on their Marxist pattern of government nor upon their westernization in industry and technique, but upon their being in the stage which we were in during the early nineteenth century, with a moderate amount of political organization and industrialization on top of a deep rooted folk life from which it gets its vitality and toughness. (Quite apart from the simple separation of the evanescent illusion, which in this case takes the form of placing vast hopes on such things as national sovereignty, technical advance, and political democracy in the Eastern and African peoples, because they have just started in the road after them. Progress doesn't look the same to us—because we have had it!)

I have to pass over much which my syllabus has indicated under this head. But I should like to call your attention to the place of authority in the course of European history and its relation to moral values and the change from a largely established society to an almost exclusively enterprising one. Bertrand de Jouvenel, in his books *Power* and *Sovereignty,* calls attention to the fact that authority vested in rulers, priesthood, and parents was in

---

12. Here Demant includes the note: "Santayana Vol Religion; Life of Reason. quoted Holland p190."

earlier days a limitation of power, limited by institutions, in the moral sense and so was never so absolute and without reason, as it became in the sixteenth century. And when the supreme authority of the ruling disposition was overthrown, there was also overthrown the natural authority of the institutions that had made Europe a civilized unity in variety, and which had kept the ruling power in check. The revolutionary era really left social life a scramble for power between different powerful interests political, economic, and intellectual with no generally accepted standards of value for the mass of people to judge between them.[13]

[Peter Drucker speaks of how limitation of power is created through a balance between the social and governmental sphere. "There has to be a competing ethical principle for the power in the socially constitutive sphere. And this power in the socially constitutive sphere had to be limited by a competing principle in political government."][14]

There is no tradition by which power can be morally assessed. And the young are expected to pick up a code of values and standards of judgement which their parents or teachers are incapable of giving them. When a culture is in the growing creative stage, youth knows itself as immaterial and as in a condition of discipleship; when culture is no longer formative but is merely a withering survival and regarded as self-perpetuating, or a hindrance to the creation of political and technical enterprise, youth is regarded by its elders as having a value in itself.[15]

It is as if a poor youth is expected to discover a way of life which its parents' time already lost. Education doesn't solve this problem because education is the transmitting of a tradition—and now it has become a training in technical and intellectual aptitudes.

[Here Demant includes incomplete notes about ideas he considered developing further. He references his lecture "The School and the Churches" in which he notes how much the educational institutions are taking on in the work of forming young people. "The School in the modern West has inherited the educational functions which in earlier periods were performed by other agencies, mainly the family or domestic tradition, the church and the apprenticeship system." He also raises the question of a Christian understanding of the development of politics and government. Both of these ideas fit into his overarching point about the human need for something that is consistent, a tradition or custom that underlies life such that every part of existence is not a conscious

---

13. de Jouvenel, *Sovereignty* and de Jouvenel, *Power*.
14. Drucker, Peter. *Future of Industrial Man*, 134.
15. Here Demant includes the note: "Youth Movements, Public Schools."

and voluntary choice. Demant then goes on to write of Cabeza de Vaca, whose life shows man's ability to adapt to new situations when there is some sort of firm foundation.][16]

---

16. Demant's notes: "School and the Churches p6&7
Christian Interpretation of History Bible begins with Garden. Closes with a city
The Power Within Us Story of Cabeza de Vaca
By Haniel Long in which he retells the Remarkable experience of the Spanish Cabeza de Vaca whose shipwreck expedition to America was a disaster in Spanish Colonial history, but a branch? in the history of man."

Series II, Lecture X
How Adaptable is Christian Ethics?

IN THE YEAR 1873, John Stuart Mill published an essay on "The Utility of Religion" in which he wrote, "When we consider how ardent a sentiment, in favorable circumstances of education, the love of country has become, we cannot judge it impossible that the love of that larger country, the world, may be nursed into similar strength, both as a source of elevated emotion and as a principle of duty."[1] The theory of this great and good mind has been shared by many others, the theory namely that man's devotion to his fellows and the morality in which that devotion is codified, spreads from small groups like his family and clan, to the wider unit of the nation and state, and in a continuous movement with proper educational guidance may become a devotion and an ethic embracing all mankind.

It is however a serious error that love of man and ethics of justice for them spreads in this way. For one thing the nation or state is not an extension of the clan, but an association of individuals, with a different origin, which may exist on top of a lot of clannish groupings. A new principle has intervened. And it has become abundantly clear, from the work of Reinhold Niebuhr, *Moral Man and Society*, that loyalty to groups such as class, nations, and profession often show more unscrupulousness and enmity towards other groups than individuals in personal confrontation do to one another. And now it has to be realized that love for all men, in all situations, is not a growth of the same sentiment as love for these with whom we are in personal contact.[2] It comes as a new jump in consciousness. This has taken two forms: one was the appearance of the world religions, the Greek concept of man, as distinct from these men; and then the need for a

---

1. Mill, *Nature and Utility of Religion*.
2. Here Demant references his radio talk in which this idea is expanded further, *Two Way Religion*.

system of justice for people of different origins, the creation of which was imposed on the philosopher and jurists of Imperial Rome by its practical faith of administering a vast territory. The other source was the religious impulse of Christianity with its Bible. This is not unique by virtue of its universalism, or its apprehension of man ("the humanism"), but it is unique in the religious and cultural vitality in which its universalism is reared. To repeat some truisms: In place of the classical argument for humanism; in place of the Buddhist compassion for man tied to his wheel of re-birth: we have love, as the attitude of Christianity to man as ends, (a delighted *agape* from the redeeming *agape* of God and Christ); and coupled with it, indeed part of its texture, an active world transforming spirit. I hope these lectures have done something to elucidate the connection between the Christian disposition towards universalism and this activistic, interfering, constructing disposition. Both dispositions stem from the freeing of the spirit from its immersion in nature and the bonds of simple communities. The great biblical figures, though speaking out of their Hebrew or Gentile context, are not representatives of that context, in the way the heroes of Greek tragedy are. Abraham, Job, Elijah, David, St. Peter (denial), and St. Paul stand for the universal assertion of man, in any social, cultural, and political context. And the Christ himself, though incarnate as patriarchical-man, is as such the archetype of man himself. "Behold the Man," was truth declared through the error of the Roman governor.[3]

It is this universal, or existential, basis of this Christian ethics that makes it infinitely adaptable. The theological ethics of Christianity are applicable no matter what state of culture or civilization, social or national grouping, political system or economic pattern. On this level what the church has to teach applies to all times and all places and is not part of any cultural tradition; nor is it permanently identified with the moral injunctions, required at a secondary level, to minister to the needs of men in each social or cultural pattern. In this sense the language of theological ethics is universal, in a way in which the cultural ethics of Christendom is not universal but relative. The roots of theological ethics in the theological virtues of Faith, Hope, and Charity, live in the deepest foundation of human existence, where the spirit of man is linked with the transcendent divine sense of all existence. Therefore, they move men to confident and humble practice of good works in any situation and in social order or disorder, without demanding that the world's pattern should be any better than it is. It steers clear of the attitude: "if only things were different in the world we could practice the Christian virtues." No, the power of theological ethics lies

---

3. Here Demant includes the note: "Pope and Saint Joseph."

just in the fact that the church thought Christian men can help to change the world just because they can spiritually afford not to have it changed. This is scarcely part of the freedom of the Christian man of whom St. Paul speaks. He can seek to address wrong ways and injustices, without regarding this as bringing in the Kingdom of God. He can bring good out of evil by a delegated participation in the redeeming work of Christ, who did not overpower the evil of men outwardly but rose from the dead, thereby refusing to vanish independence.

(The Old Testament model of this is in the story of Joseph.)

All this however is the witness of the saints and martyrs. They testify to the power of God unto salvation in any or every social situation. If these lectures have caused any [unreadable], however we cannot leave matters there. For the historical career of Christendom has produced a particular kind of earlier culture which has taken root in Europe and has given to its society some distinctive pattern of thought, structure, and disposition which are tied up with its Christian alliance. And like every other culture it is a life in which sinners have to live their natural lives and pursue their valid secular aims; secular living has been in some ways made more difficult and not easier by the influence of Christianity. On the other hand, Christendom has therefore, excogitated a greater variety of ethical philosophies and moral systems to deal with changing situations and mentalities than any other human culture; it has sharpened the moral conscience sometimes almost to breaking point, and has demanded increasingly a moral effort to create social harmonies which in other cultures come more naturally. Social order becomes a moral construction whereas elsewhere, it is a basis which personal morals can presuppose. The fact is that mankind is in a precarious condition when society needs an awful lot of morals to keep it in being, and I could say too, when it needs a vast apparatus of education. You wouldn't estimate the health of a distant land very highly if you found a large minority of its population having turned into medical and physical therapist experts in order to teach the rest how to breath; nor could you judge a region particularly sane if you found every fourth building was a mental hospital. Similarly, I judge a culture very bad if the normal living of its inhabitants requires a degree of moral insight and vigor to be expected only of saints. I have drawn a picture of the moral career of Christendom in which it appears that in it the spirit of man has so dissociated itself from the stream of life, and man's past, and from the closed communities of tribes, localities, and spontaneous hierarchical structures—that on top of these, or displacing them it has developed a system of rights, laws, and patterns of social behavior that cut right across the units of unsophisticated mankind. This has complicated men's loyalties and purposes. In its latest phase, moreover, this emancipation of the spirit of man, and of his mind from the rest of his will, has brought about a vast technical civilization, clearly geared to an expanding economy—which is so well symbolized by the airplane, which must go on or it drops. This acquires a momentum of its own which imposes limits on man's moral initiative and political choice, producing a form of social determinism in place of the physical necessity earlier imposed by marked dependence on nature, which in civilized history it has in large measure surmounted. "The technical age" begets a second nature, as Paul Tillich calls it, which narrows the area of moral maneuver, which calls for too many choices to be made by mankind, not in order to live the good life but to exist at all. And this I believe is the reason of the moral frustration on the present day West, and it results in either moral apathy or moral irresponsibility. "Technical reason" writes Tillich, "subjected man to the blind and cruel laws of a 'second nature' completely alien to him and far more impenetrable than the laws of nature itself proved to be in the age of science."[4]

To repeat,[5] man has escaped from dependence upon nature to dependence upon the artificial world of his own creation and finds himself under the same kind of compulsion as primitive man.[6]

I have repeated perhaps to one's weariness, that this technical, organized, and self-propelling civilization would never have arisen without the freeing of the human spirit withdrawing from nature and then conforming it as its master. And I am now asserting the tremendous paradox that this has at last put western man in a cage of his own fabrication. Other parts of the world can perhaps escape this fate, if they are not too anxious to become like us. The crucial turn happened, as I think when the spirit of man in the West threw over the religious, dependent, and pious mood and identified the spirit with only one of its functions, the extraverted intellect, as Jung has repeatedly pointed out.

The conclusion I draw from this cycle, is that the Christian moral consciousness cannot assert that it is only concerned with theological ethics. True, that is the source of its love for man and of the moral systems it elaborates for each situation. But it cannot without infidelity renounce concern for the present predicament of man in his human and social situation, for that situation is the end product of Christendom's own career. One false way of evading this responsibility for the life of natural man in this age is to say Christians know that human imperfection is due to sin—radical

---

4. Tillich, "The World Situation" in *Christian Answer*.

5. This paragraph is preceded by the note: "Californian Tomatoes."

6. Here Demant references two works by Nikolai Berdyaev, *Meaning of History* and *Freedom and the Spirit*.

evil—therefore all societies and cultures are in the same boat; and that therefore the Christian mind has no responsibility for judging differences between varying social structures. As I pointed out in the very first lecture, this leaves out the fact that cultures and social mores are positive attempts of sinful wants to counteract or transform life so that it is more than a struggle of egoisms—a positive work of the human spirit—and in spite of invading our culture, politics, and economics—they are not all equally under sin. Martin Buber puts it correctly in these words:

> Nor do I see how the concept of being evil can be translated from the realm of being "before God" into that of being before earthly authorities, and yet retain its radical nature. In the sight of God a state of radical evil can be ascribed to man because God is God and man is man, and the distance between them is absolute, and because precisely in this distance and in virtue of it God's redeeming deed is done. In the sight of his fellow-men, of human groups and orders, man, it seems to me, cannot be properly described as simply sinful, because the distance is lacking which alone is able to establish the unconditional ... Hence no legitimate use can be made in politics or political theory of the concept of human sinfulness.[7]

We can get from theological ethics, which is independent of any social situation, to a sociological ethic which compares and evaluates different social situations. But before we get to that we must beware some insidious pieces of soporific magic which are currently offered to us. "Technical power is neutral; results depend on what we make of it." The error is concealed in the ambiguity of the term "we." The technical case is not only the use of machines and applied science, it contains a form of social organization, and a philosophy which takes for granted that if a thing can be done technically; that is the best way of doing it, and will certainly be in the human interest. This ignores that it may destroy the very creative power of renewal which has made this civilization possible. And what is more—it is not the case that man in general has mastered nature. As Mr. C. S. Lewis in *The Abolition of Man* points out, "there is therefore no question of a power vested in the race as a whole steadily growing as long as the race survives."[8] Each new power won by man is a power by some men over others. As regards, for example, the powers manifested in the airplane and the wireless, man is as much the patient or the subject as the possessor, since he is the target

---

7. Buber, *Between Man and Man*, 90–91.
8. Lewis, *Abolition of Man*, 87.

both for bombs and for propaganda!⁹ Another slogan which has become one of the most faded flowers of platform and pulpit oratory is that "man's moral development has not kept pace with his intellectual advance." This answers a natural intellectual progression which has taken us to where we are, and an ethical progression which depends entirely on the moral will, and this ethical progression, says the slogan, has slowed up. This is the view of Bertrand Russell in his Reith Lectures, *Authority and the Individual*.[10] This view advises us to adapt our ethics to our technics; adaption however is a tricky word. There are two forms of adaption necessary in life: ethics and the technical revolution.

This brings us again to the relation between morals and civilization. When ethics, whether religious or secular, operate in a social milieu where consequences of action can be foreseen, that is where the milieu has a fairly unified culture pattern, as for example in a primitive tribe, or city state, a feudal region, even Victorian Britain, then the task of ethics is to proclaim the nature of the good life, identify and oppose the morally hostile acts of people in it. The task is intellectually simple, namely to expose the acts and habits of egoism, pride, power, striving, self-deception and so on: however difficult it may be practically to convert the sinful will into the good will. But when the culture becomes confused and the consequences of human actions are not morally foreseeable, where men do not know whether this or that action is morally beneficial, then there is added a problem of intellectual bafflement.

For instance, where there is a general agreement in a society as to what is in the best interest of men, a morality embedded in the culture, then how to love one's neighbor is fairly obvious, though to practice it may be hard. But where the only criterion is what the neighbor wants—where he or she is ignorant of any doctrine of the true needs of man—to love one's neighbor is a baffling problem. Many people have a sense of injustice; they say they are not given their rights; they complain that they do not have a fair share of the gifts of their civilization. The cause of these complaints is very often not in the greed and power of others, not in any defective political systems, but in the kind of civilization that nearly everybody wants. Today many people are unhappy and thwarted and they attribute it to social injustice. But much of it is due to the kind of life fostered by the relentless pursuit of technical progress, to minds fed on the newspapers, to the endless stream of words on the wireless, to standardized amusements. Moreover, a civilization often

---

9. Here Demant includes the note: "Experts clear distinction not on a stack of Bibles Moraca?"

10. Russell, *Authority and the Individual*.

induces in men a deceptive idea of what their real selves really want. I have often heard it said "I'm fed up with the pictures but I keep going!" And I find myself reading trivial bits of the papers—just because they are there and handy. Civilization induces certain habits and desires, which we do not positively will to follow. They are part of the climate in which we live, they cling round our senses as a sort of bogus good we had better not miss. Does love for the neighbor then mean wishing for him what he actually wants, with his desires and ideas of the good insinuated into his mind by what his civilization induces at present (e.g., to be a large-scale buyer, user, and consumer of mass produced goods), or does it mean judging—against the stream—what he really needs in the truly human interest? If you know what is really your neighbor's good—does he know it too? If not, your morality will look like tyranny. For these reasons—the over-complication of moral issues, and the restricting of the area of moral maneuver, which the technical age and planned society have bought about—the Christian moral consciousness cannot throw up the sponge and say the structural and culture of this age is of no Christian concern. Let us just seek to purify men's motives within it.

One theme running through these lectures is that the modern situation, with this bewilderment of the moral consciousness, is not due to a number of outright unbelieving or anti-Christian forces having produced a secular Christendom, but that the secular age with its tremendous power over creation which Christendom has fostered, even though by a colossal paradox has built up a structure which in the end restricts freedom. I have analyzed the process as one which has formed human disposition of mastery, and there departing when cut away from the sense of dependence and need of redemption, from piety and godliness, became in their secularized form a social poison. If this society is to find criteria for judging not only the actions of men in our conviction, but also the ends to which the civilization pre-disposes man, it will be some sort of public philosophy comparable to the ethics of stoicism, or habitual law or the morals of Utilitarianism, or Marxism—comparable in the sense that all these not only lay down the goal of human effort, but base them upon a teaching of what man essentially is—and a culture which supports their aims. This is not to Christianize society but to humanize it, in such a way as to make it the field on which the Christian community can proclaim the salvation of the gospel and the ethics of the faith. The Christian believer knows that good aims are not enough. The freedom of the Christian man is won by that surrender to God which life in Christ makes possible. It is the freedom in which he is delivered from feeling inwardly crushed by being involved in the social disorder. He accepts that as a fact of existence and can take up an attitude which is capable of using the disorder as the very context in which he really may seek to do the will of God. That is theological ethics. But he also knows that short of the kingdom of God that inner freedom is always being lost unless he uses his initial gifts to build up a culture of the soul by prayer and worship, by inwardness and love within the shoddy membership of that disfigured part of Christ's church which is his own local church life, and by identification with the drama of the redeeming agony and risen life of Christ. He knows that he obtained this freedom only because God knows he could do nothing to gain it—solely by virtue of God's love which asks for no *quid pro quo*. Basic willing is not enough.

But this is not all, for when the Christian makes the jump from theological ethics to an ethics for society, he who knows what his salvation means, however knows that there is a good kind of natural life and that some societies are better than others in fostering to it. He sees in the repeated efforts of man in society to find and build a perfect frame for his existence: naturalism or vitalism, liberalism, or communism. All delusive though they might be, he sees in there the manifestation of a noumenal reality which tugs at man all the time seeking to overcome the defects in each phenomenal social community. It represents a pull of man's true being, away from the definition of his being in the actual society, an alienation, for the human race ever tries again after each failure. A society which reflected in its culture something of the natural good of man would not ensure his moral perfection, let alone his salvation, but it would free his mind from confusions and his will from frustrations which come from mistaking a conflict of human purposes, for a defect in the nature of things or for the effects of conscious human egoism.

I do not think we can preach Christian ethics without making criticism of the cross purposes of our secular civilization. Its contradictions bedevil the moral conscience. But where Christian ethics have to be preached, the Christian mind is always aware that when ethics have been strong and influential they have never been just a set of ideas serviceable to living; they have derived their force from connection with a realm of the holy, the sacred, the divine—the religious penumbra of ethics. Even so, the Christian believer does not despise secular attempts at social ethics, they may lack force but they testify to the moral nature of man who lives in dissociation between the Is and the Ought, and seeks to overcome that dissociation. We must not snap our religious fingers at the weakness of this ethic; or its fragility when not underpinned by the holy, or when we are aware that rational morality cannot curb the irrational, instructive, and destructive forces of the hidden man (the *Id* of Freud), but that only religious forces can curb them. For the secular, post-Christian world lacks not moral will but enlightenment. Let us whose morality flows from our faith, not go about nagging our secular fellows into religion; let us show if we can, what is baffling their moral ideas and efforts.

Ethics are only the clear part of man's purposive actuality, and behind them is the realm of divine power; before them is the baffling confusion of social, political, and economic life. I believe ethics can only succor society when it puts down its roots again into the realm of the holy.

END OF THE WORLD

And the end of the world—on earth—may come not from warfare, but just the wilting of the natural bases of life—in the land, the community, and the human spirit. These may wilt under the automatic spread of the technical equipment of civilization.

SECTION THREE

Assessment and Critique

Assessment and Critique

DEMANT TRIED TO SHOW how Christendom, with its distinctive two-worlds emphasis, modified by subsequent secularizing elements, brought about the modern culture. Running parallel with this development is the ethical dialogue between the church and the world, and this dialogue is the subject of this chapter. Demant believed that the moral development of humankind took a distinctive step in Christianity, involving a universal ethic not dependent upon revelation, namely, natural law. This chapter will briefly outline this development, before proceeding to examine Demant's application of the natural law model to three problematic areas within our culture: society, work, and love.

According to Demant, there are four identifiable steps in the moral development of human society. The first step is seen in the integration of morality with custom in the tribal or primitive societies. Morality in these societies is not conscious but a question of habit and belief. Demant writes, "It is now well known that in primitive or tribal society, mores or morality has a vital place, but it is customary rather than consciously ethical and rulers are as much under the sway of custom as their dependants."[1] Demant is writing with some authority here, for his early book was on the subject of myth in primitive societies. He cites with approval the work of A. Lang who also argues for this unconscious moral structure which everyone in a tribal society is compelled to recognize.

The second stage is the start of a conscious awareness of moral obligation. This arose in parallel with the rise of civilization. Demant puts it like this: "A break is made with the morally innocent tradition by the appearance of some element of civilisation. It is marked by a conscious impulse to make a pattern of life, the discovery of natural laws, co-operation and control of the power of nature, and a view of reality greater than the tribal whole."[2]

1. Demant, Gifford Lectures. Series 2. Lecture 1. University Summaries.
2. Ibid.

He believes these developments can be traced in the study of ancient Mesopotamia and Egypt by the Frankforts. Their book, *Before Philosophy*, was clearly very important for Demant. The study is a serious examination of the nature of these ancient societies, focussing on the importance within them of their myths. In the concluding chapter, the Frankforts argue that the Hebrews reduced the mythical to an absolute minimum. They write, "The doctrine of a single, unconditioned, transcendent God rejected time-honoured values, proclaimed new ones, and postulated a metaphysical significance for history and for humanity's actions. With infinite moral courage the Hebrews worshipped an absolute God and accepted as the correlate of their faith the sacrifice of an harmonious existence. In transcending the Near Eastern myths of immanent godhead, they created, as we have seen, the new myth of the will of God. It remained for the Greeks, with their peculiar intellectual courage, to discover a form of speculative thought in which myth is entirely overcome."[3] It is the linking of the Greek and Hebrew traditions which created Christianity (one of several world religions), but this is to move the story on too rapidly.

The third stage is the development of world religions. Demant means by this the development of religions which claimed certain insights as universally true. The Mesopotamian civilization had certain conscious moral obligations, but these were not intended to apply to all men everywhere. This development arose with the world religions, which involved metaphysical claims applicable to everyone. Their emergence produced movements which could embrace not just one tribe, but numerous different nations, and perhaps, even cultures. Demant's source for this stage is in the work of Christopher Dawson, especially in his Gifford Lectures of 1947–48. Dawson writes of the "teaching of the world religions, like Buddhism and Christianity and Islam," that "though they all asserted the necessity of a supernatural revelation, they regard it as transcending human culture and universal to all men and all peoples. Thus the great world religions of the past actually created spiritual unities which transcended the limits of culture and brought together peoples of diverse origin and alien ways of life—Indians and Tibetans, Greeks and Abyssinians, Latins and Scandinavians, Arabs and Malays and negroes—in common allegiance to a spiritual law and an eternal truth."[4]

The point that Demant is making is that one of the features of the moral way of life is the principle of universalizability. So what is right for one person in a situation is also right for anyone else in that situation. This

---

3. Frankfort, *Before Philosophy*, 247ff.
4. Dawson, *Religion and Culture*, 211.

principle arose with the concept of universal metaphysical beliefs applicable to all people everywhere, a key feature of the world religions.

The fourth stage in the moral development of mankind is the rise of Christianity. The difference between Christianity and the other world religions seems mainly to be one of degree. The impact which each religion had upon moral development is heightened with Christianity. Demant writes:

> In the Far Eastern world religions, Hinduism and Buddhism are passive with regard to the world and deny the significance of history. Judaism, Christianity, and Mohammedanism of the West are historical religions, in that they give crucial importance to the historical existence of their founders, and have a unique relation between God and his people. But neither Judaism nor Islam has produced a common way of life for people of entirely different cultures in the way Christianity has. The appearance of Christianity seems to me, the one big religious event since the rise of the world religions.[5]

Christianity was exceptionally adaptable and able to encompass several very different cultural outlooks. It needed a universal ethic which could accommodate this variety. This ethic presupposed a fundamental distinction between God and the world, and therefore between the church and the world. Yet despite this distinction there was also a need for the world to recognize its dependency on God and the church. Christian ethics arose as a result of these two factors, the distinction yet the dependence. This double aspect gave rise to a universal ethic which was not dependent upon revelation. This is the doctrine of natural law. The modern world view, which separates religion from morality, is a result of taking the universal ethic but denying its dependence on God. Demant wants the church to promote the recovery of this dependence. It should retain the natural law system; if it did so, it would be able to understand and interpret the world with power.

NATURAL LAW

Demant's natural law system has already been discussed in earlier chapters. However, the earlier discussion was more descriptive than evaluative. Here, we shall outline the essence of his argument, as it is found in the Giffords (which is broadly the same as in his early work), and we will proceed to evaluate the merits of his system.

---

5. Demant, Gifford Lectures. Series 2. Lecture 1. University Summaries.

Demant rehearses the main features of a natural law doctrine when he writes,

> First, it meant that man is by creation a creature with a definite structure—the nature of man; secondly, that it stands for a universal character in human beings, behind the special characteristics of persons and communities; third, it represents the freedom or rational character of mankind; fourthly, it posits that there is a gulf between what man essentially is and what he is actually. Man does not follow his true nature in practice; for the Christian this gulf is called the Fall of man; for others it is his failure to a be a truely rational being; fifthly, all human behaviour and institutions—like moral codes, civil law and government—are only valid and can claim authority in so far as they reflect the natural law.[6]

Demant's summary focuses on two elements in a very varied natural law tradition. The first is the historical function of natural law in the development of law and politics. The second is an emphasis upon the creatureliness of humankind, the objective character of ethical injunctions, and a rationalist epistemology.

The problems with all natural law accounts are: first, their justification in nature, which seems to presuppose an Aristotelian scientific framework, where the idea of purpose in nature is legitimized; and secondly, by the identifying of the actual prescriptions which come from the system. For example, the Roman Catholic Church has decided that the primary purpose of human sexual activity is procreation, and anything which does not enable this purpose to be fulfilled must be condemned. Thus, contraception, homosexuality, artificial birth techniques, and masturbation are all condemned on this account. As Keith Ward remarks, "it is, to say the least, ironic that a methodology meant to secure the agreement of all people of good will is now the greatest stumbling block for a great many people to acceptance of the moral teaching of the Catholic Church."[7] How does Demant's system overcome these two objections?

In the Giffords, Demant makes much of the positive contribution natural law has made in the history of ideas. This is what impressed A. P. D'Entreves at the end of his brief study of the concept. In it he commends the natural law theorists for being the first to explore "the ambiguous borderland between law and morals. They were the first to secure the comparative independence of the law-giver as well as the inviolable rights of the

---

6. Ibid.
7. Ward, "Christian Ethics," 226.

individual conscience. They were the first to analyze the complex interplay of legal and moral obligation, the mysterious process by which the truly honest man abides by the law and yet is free from its bondage. We must be careful before we reject their eloquent plea that law is part of ethics."[8] Demant too makes much of considerations of this sort.

Demant wishes to retain the role that natural law has played because he is convinced that the alternative could be some sort of totalitarianism. It is grounded in the creation of humanity and denotes the manner of life intended for him by God. It satisfies humanity's fundamental needs, and applies to all universally. It conforms to the essence of humanity.

In Lecture Five, which is called "Is Man a 'Real Kind'?" he seeks to identify this human essence. He gives two arguments for the existence of a human essence. The first is one which occurs elsewhere in his work, namely, that to posit the existence of a real essence alone explains the constant dissatisfaction of the human spirit as it swings from one layer to another. The hypothesis of a natural life ultimately needing to be grounded in God explains the constant swings from individualism to collectivism, or from the market principle to the state principle, or from rationalism to romanticism. In the University Summaries, Demant puts it this way, "These movements and counter-movements can be taken as outward signs of a 'noumenal' structure of human existence which is never seen phenomenally but which alone accounts for the historical and intellectual phenomena."[9] The inaccessible noumenon (or human essence) is posited because it makes sense of the historical and intellectual phenomena (i.e., the swings from one extreme to another).

The second argument is derived from a cross-cultural comparison of India, Plato's *Republic*, and the Middle Ages. Demant argues that a scale is identifiable in these different systems which may reflect the human essence and the appropriate priorities. In all three the priority lies with the cultural, (i.e., religion, art, philosophy and meditation). It reflects the human capacity to transcend nature to the greatest degree. The second emphasis falls on the political and organizing skills of the human creature; and the third is the economic. Production, trading, and purchasing are the most dependent upon nature and therefore the least important. It is true that broadly these three societies did grade these three activities in this way. In the Indian caste system there are four castes; priests, rulers and teachers, commercial organizers, and manual workers. In Plato's *Republic*, the philosopher rulers are those who have meditated upon the Forms, and such men are the most

---

8. D'Entreves, *Natural Law,* 121.
9. Demant, Gifford Lectures. Series 2. Lecture 5. University Summaries.

important class, the Guardians. The second class is the Auxiliaries, who assist the rulers in the execution of their duties, and the third class is all those engaged in economic activity—farmers, manufactures, and traders. Finally, Demant suggests, feudal medieval Europe reflects a similar structure, with economic activity considered the least important, after the cultural and political activities of man. He concludes by writing: "these examples of a similar structure of society do perhaps suggest that it represents an order of human living in society, in accordance with the nature of man."[10]

One could very easily reject Demant's arguments. There are many unanswered questions. Why pick these three traditions out of the great number of human social arrangements? And can one really argue that the Indian Caste system represents the ideal balance? But Demant protects himself against some of these objections. He is only suggesting that his broad pattern of priorities can be adduced from this elevation of the cultural over the economic to be seen in three very diverse cultures. Despite these and other difficulties, some elements of Demant's natural law system are very strong.

Demant's achievement is that his natural law system is not dependent upon an Aristotelian science. It is not a system which is found in the biology of nature, so one is not involved in seeking the purposes of nature. This, Keith Ward feels, is a consistent position. He writes, "One can quite consistently say that God has a purpose in creating the universe, and that God has specific purposes for parts of nature, without being committed to the essentially Aristotelian belief that the structures of nature are of themselves purposive."[11] By its reliance on the observation of cultures, it overcomes the first objection, which I noted above to natural law systems.

A further achievement is that Demant's system can be flexible. His system is not involved in the detailed biological claims of the Roman Catholic Church. He devotes his book on *Christian Sex Ethics* to sustaining the Christian view of marriage as "continence outside marriage and fidelity within marriage."[12] He does not even mention contraception. He believes that the natural setting for human life is a family and therefore wants to sustain the Christian conception of marriage. He does not consider whether his view can extend to include polygamy, which within certain cultures might fulfil his requirements of natural law. He does not write much about homosexuality. Although as a member of the Wolfenden Committee, he did accept without objection all the conclusions of that report.[13] Again, having

10. Ibid., Series 2. Lecture 5, p. 256.
11. Ward "Christian Ethics," 226ff.
12. Demant, *Christian Sex Ethics*, 11.
13. The Report of the Committee on Homosexual Offences and Prostitution,

rejected the biological basis of the older natural law systems, he is free to accept the possibility that two people of the same sex should be allowed to express their love physically. These two achievements are considerable and offered at that time a very distinctive approach to natural law.

Demant went on to apply his model of natural law to certain problems which, he felt, reflected the cultural crisis. It is to these three problems of society, work, and love, that I now turn.

SOCIETY, WORK, AND LOVE

As we have seen, one of the most important concepts Demant formulates in the Giffords is the idea of the penumbra. It is worth recalling that the discussion of these three topics is not simply an examination of the issues they raise in the abstract, but as they actually present themselves within the inner life of a culture. So, Demant starts his lecture on society by complaining of the manner in which this topic is conventionally handled. "In the modern West," writes Demant, "we enquire about the place of the individual in society, about society's effect upon him, about the influence of his actions upon the social whole, and about the ways social organization divests or distorts the individual's aims. And if morality comes into question, it takes the form of enquiring how men and women can, or ought to, contribute to the well being of society. It is these questions themselves, and not the answers to them which identify our current problem as belonging not to humankind as a whole, but as characteristic of our historically limited culture. We formulate our problem as that of individual and society and assume this to be an essential feature of human existence. But mankind has not always been bothered with it."[14] These questions reflect part of the problem within the penumbra. The presupposition behind them is the individualistic, liberal tradition derived largely from John Locke and, in some respects, from Thomas Hobbes.

Demant believes that the individualistic conception of society is completely mistaken. To understand the problems confronting our fragmented society we require an understanding of the mistakes in liberal political theory. He rejects an individualistic account and opts for an account of the "organic" type.[15] The origin of society does not rest in the social contract,

---

otherwise known as the Wolfenden Committee Report published September 1957.

14. Demant, Gifford Lectures. Series 2. Lecture 6, p. 257.

15. The term "organic" is not actually used by Demant. However, this is undoubtedly what he means. His concept also correspondends with the term popular in the United States (i.e., communitarian). See for example, Stout, *Ethics After Babel*.

as proposed in classical liberal theory. Primitive men were not aggressive individuals who opted for the benefits of government and therefore gave up some of their rights to live under law. Instead, human creatures are born into families, and families have always been linked to each other in communities and tribes. Demant claims that primitive societies "exhibited a social dilution of the blood relationship by a wider kinship where the physical father and nuclear family are merged in a wider parenthood and brotherhood, and where children were as dependent on their age mates as on kin."[16] There bodes a strong sense of custom, tribal loyalty and obligation which made commands unnecessary. There was no need to manufacture internal unities; these already existed and were accepted simply by being born into the society. This is the natural foundation of society. It is a base comprising families, communities, natural associations formed around pleasure, work, and religion.

Demant believes that the doctrine of individualism which has arisen chiefly since the Enlightenment represents a destructive shift in outlook that is responsible for the problems of our modern society. The doctrine of individualism has found expression in the modern scientific and technological society, which has destroyed the deep foundations of our culture. In brief, modern society has destroyed the elementary unities.

This requires some elaboration. Demant believes that inherent in the modern conception of the state is power, and state control has meant that all natural associations tend to be stripped away, leaving only the State and the individual. Demant puts it like this: "The modern state is the product of migration and warfare and this gives social association primarily a territorial character. Its tendency from its inception was to break down all the intermediate barriers between itself and its individual subjects."[17] This powerful institution, which was so destructive of the natural associations which should be the basis for society, ran parallel with other forces imposed by technological and industrial success. Demant writes, "In a world of mass communication the individual has perforce to see himself primarily as a citizen or an economic functionary, joined to his fellows as a voter, as a vendor of labour or a buying utility."[18] This is an unnatural self-perception of the human creature, argues Demant. Such a conception of the State has led to three puzzles which are indicative of an unbalanced state of affairs. First, there is the manner in which the economy has become an entity in its own right, beyond the control of anyone. Even things which are not needed

---

16. Demant, Gifford Lectures. Series 2. Lecture 6, p. 258.
17. Ibid.
18. Ibid.

are made, simply to generate economic activity. Secondly, there is the constant conflict which can be traced between the aims and intentions of men. Demant gives several examples. Just to take one, he cites the Reformers' opposition to civil liberties; yet their activities in fact made toleration necessary. Thirdly, he cites the development of thinking in the West which thinks of society as in opposition to the individual. Such ideas are developed in different ways in the thought of Rousseau, Hegel, Marx, and Nietzsche. If society were based upon the natural foundation of human activity, then, of course, such an opposition would be virtually impossible.

The economic dislocation is one which has already been discussed elsewhere, and will come up again with the problem of work. The conflict between aims and intentions is a matter of some importance to Demant. He believes that the conflict of St. Paul, described in Romans 7, represents a crisis between conscious intentions and subconscious attitudes, and has a cultural parallel in our society in the conscious talk of shared human rights running alongside the subconscious moral attitudes of a subjective kind. It is true that a comparable contradiction between stated beliefs and actions can be seen in the Reformers. This is an interesting problem which Demant has identified. It is highly likely that similar ironies can be seen elsewhere in different cultures and before the modern world; but Demant wants to claim that the importance of these discrepancies in the modern world is exceptional. Unfortunately, he does not give many illustrations. The final claim, that opposition between humanity and society which can be found in the work of Rousseau and others, is interesting. Demant is correct to point out that presupposed in this talk of a conflict between society and the individual is the idea of society as an entity which can be set against the individual. If society is viewed instead as a natural development of certain localized loyalties, then such talk becomes unintelligible.

Demant's argument here is very strong. His claim is that, viewed in the light of his model and his language, modern society is unnatural and unbalanced. He writes that "neither the isolated individual nor the political state is natural to man."[19] Michael Taylor is correct to commend Demant on his distinctive conception of society, when he writes, "Demant's most helpful contributions have arisen out of his conception of an 'organic' society . . . It is this 'organic' view which is a useful supplement to the proximate norms of equality, liberty, order and justice, which deal more with structure of social relationships than with the elements of a balanced context for human living in its political and economic, spiritual and cultural aspects."[20]

19. Ibid.
20. Taylor, *The Christian Social Thinking of V. A. Demant*, 123.

The second problem area which Demant discusses in detail is that of work. The problem that has arisen is a result of a certain attitude to work resulting from conceptions engendered at the Reformation. There work was seen supremely significant in terms of value and self-worth. The success of this attitude has in fact made work ultimately less and less important. Demant assumes that the problem of production has been solved. Modern technological industry relies less and less on human labor, and it is this which is posing the problem for our culture. Demant writes, "It seems that, in this complicated situation, the modern West has got itself into a position where work can no longer be thought of in the traditional terms of necessity, duty, service, offering, vocation, personal fulfilment, and has to be regarded primarily as a condition of a claim to share in the community's wealth."[21] He gives several examples of the problems which have already arisen, and which are going to get worse. He believes that the appeal for the government to generate employment, not with the production of specific goods in view but simply to keep the men in work, is a good example. Things are no longer made to last, but to wear out, thereby ensuring ongoing economic activity. More generally, he draws attention to the generation of goods and services which no one needs and which must then be advertised in such a way as to generate the need for them.

Demant's argument can be set down thus:

> The problem of production has been solved. Machines have made people unnecessary.

This leads to two consequences:

I. It creates the problem of distributing rewards to those who are not working.

II. It gives rise to the problem of leisure in a work-obsessed culture.

Demant's argument has been proved false by events since the late fifties. The actual position is much more complicated than he envisaged. The idea that the problem of production is about to be solved and then the problem will be one of coping with leisure has a perennial fascination. Demant is even able to cite Keynes who in the 1930s envisaged these problems arising in the next half-century.[22] However, despite Keynes, what has happened has not been quite so straightforward.

It is since the fifties, and since Demant produced his analysis, that the really significant economic technological revolution has happened. Ronald

21. Demant, Gifford Lectures. Series 2. Lecture 7. University Summaries.

22. Demant, Gifford Lectures. Series 2. Lecture 7, 270; And for Keynes see "Economic Possibilities for Our Grandchildren" reprinted in Essays in *Persuasion*.

Preston believes that the problems this has generated appears to be faced largely by the unskilled workers in large, labor-intensive industry.[23] In agriculture, for example, a work force of 3 percent supplies 50 percent of British food needs, largely as a result of a technological revolution in an area formerly very labor-intensive. Elsewhere, there is a skills shortage. The dramatic expansion of goods and services requires more and better trained people.

Moreover, it is not true that modern industrial society is simply satisfying artificial demands. Although a dishwasher might not be essential, it is a luxury which can improve significantly the quality of life. So the problem becomes two-fold: first, to improve the training and educational opportunities for more people; and secondly, to open up other service areas to employ unskilled school-leavers. It does not take very much reflection to think of numerous needs which could be satisfied by the work of school-leavers, in areas such as, child care, domestic services, and environmental care. Demant could not argue that any of these jobs are artificially generated.

Underlying Demant's chapter on work are social credit presuppositions. To put this simply (and rather crudely), economics makes the assumption that the problem with which economists must grapple is one of unlimited needs and scarce resources. Thus, a central difficulty for an economist is the concept of "opportunity cost." For every purchase, which involves the allocation of limited resources satisfying certain needs, there is the further cost of other needs which could have been satisfied by those resources if the initial purchase had not been made. These other potential needs which could have been satisfied constitute the opportunity cost. Social Credit assumes that this central problem of economics is now solved. The problem is now a financial and purchasing one. Demant's discussion of work fits into this framework of assumptions.

This is clearly Demant's weakest area. It is very difficult to sustain the view that there are no more legitimate needs which economic resources could satisfy. Although Social Credit is understandable in the context of the 1930s, and although it was correct in certain very limited respects, the manner in which it continues to affect Demant's thinking even in the fifties reflects a fairly major error of judgment. His reflections on work are of very limited value. At best, one could argue that he rightly draws attention to the manner in which work—for so many in the West—has become an end in itself, rather than part of a well-balanced life. The life of the business person, commuting by train, working six days a week, leaving very little time for his or her family, let alone any cultural and religious pursuits, is unbalanced. Demant is right to draw attention to this. Further, the market forces which

---

23. Preston, Interview, 16.2.88.

value the work of a broker on the stock exchange so much more than the nurse or the teacher, must make one wonder whether our society is natural and balanced. It is here that the value of Demant's insights is to be found.

The third problem area for our culture is the phenomenon of love. Demant starts by drawing attention to the unusual preoccupation with partners and sex in our society. If Demant was weak on work, when he writes on love he is at his most powerful. Drawing from his *Christian Sex Ethics* which largely repeats his Gifford argument, he identifies three main reasons for the sexual obsession of the twentieth century.

The first is that:

> people are unknowingly driven to venereal experience, and hope for a great sense of fulfilment in it, as a refuge from or compensation for a sense of deprivation elsewhere. The crudest form of this is just a resort to sexual activity as a kind of narcotic. . . And sex is an even more cogent relief from the pain of individuality and its problems. It is commonplace that sexual desires arise not from natural passion for union with one of the opposite sex, but from a demand to escape from anxiety, however temporarily. Economic anxieties, worries about esteem and status, intolerable personal relations, hating one's work or despising it, general feelings of failure or cowardice—all this sort of anxiety can be momentarily shed in the sexual embrace.[24]

Demant is arguing that the pressures placed upon men and women within our modern culture go far to explain the compulsive resort to sexual activity. He cites various studies, for example, T. M. Newcomb, "Recent Changes in Attitude to Sex and Marriage," American Sociological Review, 1937. It is worth noting that this is a very charitable interpretation of sexual promiscuity.

The second reason is that our culture has made the demands of marriage difficult to sustain. Demant writes,

> I pointed out that in marriage one is dethroned from a position of superiority and has to live together with husband and wife as equals—all defences and disguises are down; all masks are stripped off. To anyone with a painful feeling of inner poverty in himself or herself this is a great trial. And when men are given little significance in monotonous work, are easily replaceable and have no sense of responsible citizenship or powers of skill, then they expect tributes to their significance beyond what they

---

24. Demant, *Christian Sex Ethics*, 116.

earn as a human being. Not getting it in the family, as indeed they should not, sexual irregularity is a great temptation.[25]

Demant believes that someone with a weak ego will find the attraction of breaking the rules very alluring. Our culture generates such a sense of worthlessness, so that the marriage institution is difficult to maintain.

The third reason sums up the first two. Demant writes, "Sexual adventure outside the bonds of marriage is sought after, mostly quite unconsciously, as a counterweight to the rackets of modern life ... There is no home for the soul. However, much egoism and emulation enter into sexual adventure, sexual intercourse does penetrate to the biological and pre-conscious level, and even when least enriched by personal affection, it provides moments of intimacy and tenderness."[26] Sex and love are the only access to the spiritual and natural roots of human life. Sex is attempting to satisfy the same need as the interest in Eastern religions. Both reflect an attempt to return to nature. The urban, mechanical, atomized society with a predominantly intellectual culture, without robust communities and without much contact with nature, starves the emotional life elsewhere. Therefore, argues Demant, too much emotional capital is locked up in the love and marriage relationship which finds it hard to bear the weight. This pressure has led to the situation where people continue to get married but find it difficult to remain faithful and committed. It is in this way that the problems facing marriage can be shown to reflect the crisis of our culture.

One further difficulty needs to be mentioned. Demant believed that a culture which has undermined the traditional assumptions about an institution such as marriage has placed further anxieties and pressures on the individuals within it. In other words, when a culture assumed monogamy and made divorce very difficult, then married people were genuinely inaccessible. There was little point in trying to forge a long-term relationship with a married person; it was always bound to finish with the person outside the institution failing in the attempt. However, this is no longer the case. Within a year a person can be divorced and available for remarriage. Thus, commitment to the institution requires a much more conscious resisting of temptation. The penumbra has changed the climate and is leaving more and more to the conscious decision of the individual.

As an analysis this is very perceptive. It is not at all judgmental, rather it outlines the various cultural pressures which have generated the contemporary problem. What precisely it implies in terms of policy is, however, not made clear. Although Demant was worried about the significance of

25. Ibid., 119.
26. Ibid., 120.

relaxing divorce laws, we have not found any evidence of him opposing these changes.

In sum, Demant wants to see a revitalized culture, with a shift in priorities away from an obsession with the market or State planning to an organic, environmentally concerned, cultural, and ultimately a religious society. He concludes the Giffords by appealing for a public philosophy "comparable with the ethics of stoicism, or natural law or the morals of Utilitarianism, or Marxism—comparable in the sense that all these not only lay down the goal of human effort, but base them upon a teaching of what man essentially is—a culture which supports their aims. This is not to Christianize society but to humanize it, in such a way as to make it the field on which the Christian community can proclaim the salvation of the gospel and the ethics of the faith."[27] This reminds one of T. S. Eliot's plea for a Christian Idea to underlie our culture.[28] As with Eliot, one can identify the broad outlines but not always the details.

CONCLUSIONS

Demant's Gifford Lectures have provided an insight into the scale of his interests. To identify him simply with Christian sociology and certain economic fallacies is extremely unfair. Demant wanted to be known as a "historian of cultures," and the Giffords are his most systematic attempt to provide such a survey. Legitimate questions can be raised about the attempt to show that everything in our modern society is either a result of or a reaction to certain dispositions which are inherent in the Christian religion. Furthermore, we have been critical of the unsystematic and the selective use of sources in his argument. Inconsistencies have been noted. However, this critical examination of the Giffords has brought to light four concrete achievements.

1) He has shown that the Christian religion was a significant influence on certain key elements in our modern world.

2) His concept of the penumbra has been shown to be very fruitful. To concentrate upon the explicit ideas, and imagine that will lead to an understanding of a culture, is very misleading.

---

27. Demant, Gifford Lectures. Series 2. Lecture 10, p. 297.

28. See Eliot, *The Idea of a Christian Society*. David Edwards in his introduction underestimates the influence of Demant in this essay. He reduces it simply to the mistaken economic input (See p. 11–13). It seems very likely that the themes in these lectures were clearly the subject of many discussions between the two men.

3) He has provided a basis for a natural law system which overcomes some of the standard objections.

4) He has provided us with a penetrating discussion of society and love.

Bibliography for Section Two, The Giffords

Arnold, Matthew. *Essays in Criticism by Matthew Arnold.* Leipzig: B. Tauchnitz, 1887.
Bacon, Francis. *The Two Bookes of Sr. Francis Bacon: Of the Proficience and Advancement of Learning, Divine and Humane.* London: Printed for William Washington, 1629.
Bagehot, Walter. *Physics and Politics or Thoughts on the Application of the Principles of "Natural Selections" and "Inheritance" to Political Society.* London: Putnam Sons, 1885.
Bailey, Derrick Sherwin. *The Mystery of Love and Marriage; a Study in the Theology of Sexual Relation.* London: SCM, 1952.
Baille, D. M. "Philosophers & Theologians on the Freedom." *Scottish Journal of Theology* 4 (June 1951) 113–122.
Barbu, Zevedei. *Problems of Historical Psychology.* Westport, CT: Greenwood, 1976.
Barth, Karl. *Church Dogmatics.* Edinburgh: T. & T. Clark, 1977.
Beauvoir, Simone de. *The Second Sex.* New York: Vintage, 2011.
Berdyaev, Nikolaj Aleksandrovic. *The Meaning of History.* New York: Meridian, 1962.
Berlin, Isaiah. *The Hedgehog and the Fox; an essay on Tolstoy's view of history.* New York: Simon and Schuster, 1953.
Bernard, of Clairvaux, Saint. *Saint Bernard on the Song of Songs: Sermones in Cantica Canticorum.* London: A. R. Mowbray, 1952.
Bertholet, Alfred. *Das Geschlecht der Gottheit.* Tübingen: Mohr, 1934.
Bonhoeffer, Dietrich, *Ethics.* Edited by Eberhard Bethge. Translated by Neville Horton Smith. Second Impression. London: SCM, 1971.
Boorstin, Daniel Joseph. *The Exploring Spirit: America and the World Experience.* London: BBC, 1976.
Borne, Etienne, and François Henry. *Le travail et l'homme.* Paris: Desclée de Brouwer, 1937.
Boyd, Andrew Kennedy Hutchinson. *Twenty-Five Years of St. Andrews: Sept. 1865 to Sept. 1890.* London: Longmans, 1893.
Bryce, James. *The Holy Roman Empire.* New York: Macmillan, 1877.
Buber, Martin. *Between Man and Man.* Theology and Philosophy. Place of publication not identified: Collins/Fontana, 1947.
———. *Good and Evil, Two Interpretations: I. Right and Wrong.* New York: Scribner, 1953.
———. *Moses.* Oxford: East and West Library, 1946.
Bultmann, Rudolf, and Reginald Horace Fuller. *Primitive Christianity: In Its Contemporary Setting.* New York: The World, 1966.

Burckhardt, Jacob. *Reflections on History.* London: Allen and Unwin, 1943.
Bury, J. B, and Charles A. Peard. *The Idea of Progress: An Inquiry into Its Origin and Growth.* New York: Dover, 1955.
Butler, Joseph. *Bishop Butler's Analogy of Religion, Natural and Revealed.* New York: Harper, 1852.
Calvin, Jean. *Institutes of the Christian Religion.* London: James Clarke, 1949.
Chenu, Marie-Dominique. *Pour une théologie du travail.* Paris: Éditions du Seuil, 1965.
Cochrane, Charles Norris. *Christianity and Classical Culture: A Study of Thought and Action from Augustus to Augustine.* Indianapolis: Liberty Fund, 2003.
Coleridge, Samuel Taylor. *Aids to Reflection in the Formation of a Manly Character on the Several Grounds of Prudence, Morality, and Religion: Illustrated by Select Passages from Our Elder Divines, Especially from Archbishop Leighton.* London: Taylor and Hessey, 1825.
Collingwood, Robin George. *An Essay on Metaphysics.* Oxford: Clarendon, 1940.
Cullmann, Oscar. *Christ and Time: The Primitive Christian Concept of Time and History.* Philadelphia: Westminster, 1950.
Daking, D. C. *Jungian Psychology and Modern Spiritual Thought.* London: Anglo-Eastern, 1933.
David-Neel, Alexandra. *Magic and Mystery in Tibet.* Introduction by A. d'Arsonval. New York: C. Kendall, 1933.
Dawson, Christopher. *Religion and the Rise of Western Culture: Gifford Lectures Delivered in the University of Edinburgh 1948–1949.* London: Sheed and Ward, 1951.
Dawson, Christopher, and John J. Mulloy. *The Dynamics of World History.* Mentor Omega, 378. New York: New American Library, 1962.
De Grazia, Sebastian. *The Political Community: A Study of Anomie.* Chicago: University of Chicago Press, 1948.
Demant, Vigo Auguste. *Christian Polity.* London: Faber & Faber, 1946.
———. *Religion and the Decline of Capitalism.* London: Faber and Faber, 1952.
———. *The Religious Prospect.* London: F. Muller, 1941.
———. *Theology of Society: More Essays in Christian Polity.* London: Faber and Faber, 1947.
D'Entreves, Alessandro Passerin. *Natural Law.* London: Hutchinson University Library, 1951.
Descartes, René. *The Method, Meditations and Philosophy of Descartes.* London: M. Walter Dunner, 1901.
Dix, Gregory. *Jew and Greek: a Study in the Primitive Church.* London: Dacre, 1955.
Dodds, Eric Robertson. *The Greek and the Irrational.* Berkeley: University of California Press, 1963.
Drucker, Peter F. *The Future of Industrial Man: A Conservative Approach.* New York: New American Library, 1992.
Dryden, John. *Religio Laici or A Layman's Faith: A Poem.* London: Printed for Jacob Tonson at the Judge's Head in Chancery-lane, near Fleet Street, 1682.
Eliade, Mircea. *The Myth of the Eternal Return.* London: Routledge & Kegan Paul, 1955.
Emerson, Ralph Waldo. *Essays.* Philadelphia: Henry Altemus, 1895.
Emmet, Dorothy M. *Rules, Roles, and Relations.* New York: Macmillan, 1975.
Engels, Friedrich. *Anti-Duhring; Herr Eugen Duhrings Revolution in Science.* English Translation. London: Lawrence & Wishart, 1934.

Evans-Pritchard, E. E. (Edward Evan). *Theories of Primitive Religion*. Oxford: Clarendon, 1965.
Fichte, J. G. *Fichtes Werke, Vol. IV*. Edited by Immanuel Hermann Fichte. Berlin: de Gruyter, 1971.
Figgis, John Neville. *Churches in the Modern State*. New York: Longmans, Green, 1914.
Forsyth, Peter Taylor. *The Church, the Gospel and Society*. London: Independent, 1962.
———. *The Justification of God: Lectures for War-Time on a Christian Theodicy*. London: Duckworth, 1916.
Forsyth, P. T., and Jessie Forsyth Andrews. *Faith, Freedom and the Future*. London: Independent, 1955.
Frankfort, Henri, et al. *The Intellectual Adventure of Ancient Man: An Essay of Speculative Thought in the Ancient Near East*. Chicago: University of Chicago Press, 2013.
Frazer, James George. *Totemism and Exogany: A Treatise on Certain Early Forms of Superstition and Society*. London: Macmillan, 1910.
Gabor, Dennis. *Inventing the Future*. London: Secker & Warburg, 1963.
Geer, Walter, and Napoléon I. Kaiser von Frankreich. *Napoleon and Josephine*. New York: Brentano, 1924.
Glotz, Gustave, and Nora Mallison. *The Greek City and Its Institutions*. Translated by N. Mallinson. London: Kegan Paul, 1929.
Goethe, Johann Wolfgang von. *Poetry & Truth: From My Own Life*. Bohn's Popular Library. London: Bell, 1913.
Guénon, René. *Man & His Becoming: According to the Vêdânta*. London: Rider, 1928.
Haas, William S. *The Destiny of the Mind: East and West*. London: Faber and Faber, 1956.
Halévy, Elie. *The Growth of Philosophic Radicalism*. London: Faber and Faber, 1928.
Hartmann, Nicolai, and Stanton Coit. *Ethics*. New York: Macmillan, 1932.
Hodges, H. A. "Languages, Standpoints, and Attitudes." In *Riddell Memorial Lectures*. New York: Oxford University Press, 1953.
Hooker, Richard. *Ecclesiastical Polity, Books I-V*. London: Dutton, 1925.
Hume, David. *Dialogues Concerning Natural Religion*. 2nd ed. London: London and Co., 1779.
———. *An Enquiry Concerning Human Understanding*. Indianapolis, IN: Hackett, 1977.
———. *A Treatise of Human Nature*. London: printed for John Noon, 1739.
Huntington, J. F, and Bertrand de Jouvenel. *Sovereignty: An Inquiry into the Political Good*. Cambridge: Cambridge University Press, 1957.
Huxley, Aldous. *Brave New World*. New York: Bantam, 1970.
———. *The Perennial Philosophy*. London: Harper & Brothers, 1945.
James, William. *The Principles of Psychology*. New York: Holt, 1890.
———. *The Varieties of Religious Experience*. Mineola, NY: Dover, 2013.
Jaspers, Karl, and Michael Bullock. *The Origin and Goal of History*. New Haven: Yale University Press, 1953.
Jenks, Edward. *A History of Politics*. London: Macmillan, 1900.
———. *Law and Politics in the Middle Ages*. London: Murray, 1898.
Jerome, Jerome K. *Three Men in a Boat: (To Say Nothing of the Dog)*. Illustrated by A. Frederics. Bristol: J.W. Arrowsmith, 1889.
Jouvenel, Bertrand de, and J. F Huntington. *Power: The Natural History of Its Growth*. London: Hutchinson, 1982.

Jung, Carl Gustav. *The Secret of the Golden Flower: A Chinese Book of Life.* New York: Houghton Mifflin Harcourt, 1962.
Kant, Immanuel. *Religion within the Limits of Reason Alone.* Chicago: Open Court, 1934.
Keynes, John Maynard. *Essays in Persuasion.* London: Macmillan, 1931.
———. *Two Memoirs: Dr. Melchior: A Defeated Enemy and My Early Beliefs.* Edited by David Garnett. London: Rupert Hart-Davis, 1949.
Kitto, H. D. F. *The Greeks.* Harmondsworth: Penguin, 1966.
Knight, Margaret. *Morals without Religion, and Other Essays.* London: Dobson, 1955.
Leibniz, Gottfried Wilhelm Freiherr von. *Theodicy: Essays on the Goodness of God, the Freedom of Man and the Origin of Evil.* London: Routledge and K. Paul, 1952.
Lessing, Gotthold Ephraim. *Lessing's Theological Writings: Selections in Translation; with an Introductory Essay.* Library of Modern Religious Thought. London: A. & C. Black, 1956.
Levy, G. Rachel. *The Gate of Horn.* London: Faber, 1948.
Lewis, C. S. *The Great Divorce: A Dream, Etc.* London: Geoffrey Bles, Centenary, 1945.
Lewis, Hywel David. *Morals and Revelation.* London: Allen and Unwin, 1951.
Llull, Ramon. *The Book of the Lover and the Beloved.* London: SPCK, 1923.
Lovejoy, Arthur O. *The Great Chain of Being: A Study of the History of an Idea.* Cambridge: Harvard University Press, 2009.
Löwith, Karl. *From Hegel to Nietzsche: The Revolution in Nineteenth Century Thought.* New York: Columbia University Press, 1991.
Luther, Martin. *Works of Martin Luther: With Introductions and Notes, Volume II.* Philadelphia: A. J. Holman, 1915.
MacKinnon, Donald Mackenzie. *A Study in Ethical Theory.* London: A. & C. Black, 1957.
Mannheim, Karl. *Collected Works: Wartime Essays of a Sociologist Volume Three,* 1943. http://librarytitles.ebrary.com/id/10782724.
Maurice, Frederick Denison, and John Frederick Maurice. *The Life of Frederick Denison Maurice: Chiefly Told in His Own Letters; Edited by His Son Frederick Maurice.* London: Macmillan, 1884.
Mayo, Elton. *Social Problems of an Industrial Civilization.* London: Routledge, 1949.
Mayo, Elton, and Piet Rademakers. *The Political Problem of Industrial Civilization; The Modernization of a Primitive Community; Change and Its Social Consequences.* Cambridge: Harvard University, Graduate School of Business Administration, 1947.
Mill, John Stuart, George Nakhnikian, and John Stuart Mill. *Nature: And; Utility of Religion.* Indianapolis: Bobbs-Merrill, 1958.
Molinos, Miguel de, Robert P Baird, and Bernard McGinn. *The Spiritual Guide.* New York: Paulist, 2010.
Murray, Gilbert. *Four Stages of Greek Religion: Studies Based on a Course of Lectures.* London: Oxford University Press for the Columbia University Press, 1912.
Newman, John Henry, and Charles Frederick Harrold. *A Grammar of Assent, by John Henry Newman.* New York: Longmans, Green, 1947.
Niebuhr, Reinhold. *Christ and Culture.* New York: Harper Torch, 1951.
Nock, Albert Jay. *Memoirs of a Superfluous Man.* Harper, 1947.

Oberman, Heiko Augustinus. *Archbishop Thomas Bradwardine a Fourteenth Century Augustinian: A Study of His Theology in Its Historical Context.* Utrecht: Kemink, 1958.
Oldham, Joseph Houldsworth. *Work in Modern Society.* London: SCM, 1950.
Otto, Rudolf, and John W Harvey. *The Idea of the Holy: An Inquiry into the Non-Rational Factor in the Idea of the Divine and Its Relation to the Rational.* London: Oxford University Press, 1931.
Parkyns, Mansfield. *Life in Abyssinia, Being Notes Collected during Three Years' Residence and Travels in That Country, by Mansfield Parkyns.* London: J. Murray, 1853.
Pascal, Blaise. *Pensées, D'après L'éd. de M. Brunschvigg.* Coll. Gallia 4. London: London & Co., 1913.
Pierce, C.A. *Conscience in the New Testament.* London: SCM, 1958.
Plato. *Plato's Phaedrus.* Translated by Reginald Hackforth. Cambridge: Cambridge University Press, 1996.
———. *The Republic of Plato, Translated into English, with an Introduction, Analysis, and Notes. By J. L. Davies and D. J. Vaughan.* Cambridge: Macmillan, 1866.
Polanyi, Michael. *Beyond Nihilism.* Cambridge: Cambridge University Press, 1960.
———. "Beyond Nihilism." *Encounter* 78 (March 1960) 34–43.
Pope, Alexander. *An Essay on Man: In Epistles to a Friend. Epistle IV.* London: Printed for J. Wilford, 1734; 61–80.
Pound, Roscoe (Jurist). *An Introduction to the Philosophy of Law.* New Haven: Yale University Press, 1971.
Ramsey, Michael. *F. D. Maurice and the Conflicts of Modern Theology.* Cambridge: Cambridge University Press, 1951.
Reavey, George, and Nicolas (Nikolai Aleksandrovitch) Berdyaev. *Solitude and Society.* London: G. Bles, the Centenary, 1938.
Ritchie, A. D. "The Christian Religion and Contemporary Thought." *The Modern Churchman* (September 1950) 203.
Ritchie, David G. *Natural Rights: A Criticism of Some Political and Ethical Conceptions.* London: Macmillan, 1903.
Rousseau, Jean-Jacques. *Discours sur les sciences et les arts. Discours sur l'origine de l'inégalité. Rêveries du promeneur solitaire.* Paris: E. Flammarion, 1938.
———. *Discours sur l'origine et des fondments de l'inégalité parmi les hommes.* New York: Oxford University Press, 1922.
———. *Du Contrat social.* Genève: C. Bourquin, 1947.
Russell, Bertrand. *Authority and the Individual.* Boston: Beacon, 1968.
———. *History of Western Philosophy.* London: Routledge Classics, 2004.
Sabunde, Raymond of. *La theologie naturelle de dom Raymon Sebon.* Paris: De l'imprimerie de Vascosan, 1551.
Sanderson, Robert, and Christopher Wordsworth. *Bishop Sanderson's Lectures on Conscience and Human Law, Delivered in the Divinity School at Oxford. Edited, in an English Translation, with a Preface by Chr. Wordsworth, D.D., Bishop of Lincoln.* Lincoln: J. Williamson, 1877.
Saurat, Denis. *The End of Fear.* London: Faber and Faber, 1938.
———. *Regeneration.* New York: E. P. Dutton, 1941.
Schleiermacher, Friedrich. *On Religion: Speeches to Its Cultured Despisers.* New York: Ungar, 1955.
Schuon, Frithjof. *The Transcendent Unity of Religions.* London: Faber and Faber, 1953.

Schweitzer, Albert. *The Philosophy of Civilization*. New York: Macmillan, 1949.
Shakespeare, William. *The Plays of Shakespeare: The Tragedy of Macbeth*. Introduction by Frederick Henry Sykes. New York: C. Scribner, 1910.
Sharp, D. E. *Franciscan Philosophy at Oxford in the Thirteenth Century*. Oxford: Oxford University Press, 1930.
Spencer, Herbert. *Various Fragments*. New York: D. Appleton, 1898.
Stephen, Leslie. *History of English Thought in the Eighteenth Century: In Two Volumes*. London: Smith, Elder, 1876.
———. *The Science of Ethics*. London: Smith, Edler, 1882.
Taylor, Alfred Edward. *The Faith of a Moralist. Gifford Lectures; 1926-1928*. London: Macmillan, 1931.
Taylor, Jeremy. *The Marriage Ring; Or, The Mysteriousness & Duties of Marriage [a Repr. of the 1651 Ed., Edited by J.A. Kerr]*. London: London and Co., 1883.
Taylor, Jeremy, and Reginald Heber. *The Whole Works of the Right Rev. Jeremy Taylor, D.D., Lord Bishop of Down, Connor, and Dromore: With a Life of the Author, and a Critical Examination of His Writings*. London: Ogle, Duncan, 1822.
Tertullian. *Apologetic and Practical Treatises*. Translated by C. Dodgson. Oxford: Parker, 1842.
Thibon, Gustave. *Retour au réel*. Lyon: H. Lardanchet, 1946.
Thornton, Lionel Spencer. *The Common Life in the Body of Christ*. Westminster: Dacre, 1942.
Thornton, Martin. *Pastoral Theology: A Reorientation*. London: SPCK, 1964.
———. *Pastoral Theology: A Reorientation*. London: SPCK, 1964.
Tillich, Paul, Theodore Meyer Greene, and George Finger Thomas. *The Christian Answer*. New York: Scribner's, 1945.
Tod, Marcus Niebuhr. *Sidelights on Greek History; Three Lectures on the Light Thrown by Greek Inscriptions on the Life and Thought of the Ancient World*. Oxford: B. Blackwell, 1932.
Trilling, Lionel. *The Opposing Self: Nine Essays in Criticism*. New York: Harcourt, 1979.
———. *Sincerity and Authenticity*. Cambridge: Harvard University Press, 2009.
Troeltsch, Ernst. *The Absoluteness of Christianity and the History of Religions*. Library of Philosophy and Theology. London: SCM, 1972.
———. *The Social Teaching of the Christian Churches*. Louisville, KY: Westminster John Knox, 1992.
Waley, Arthur, and The Arthur Waley Estate. *Chinese Poems*. New York: Routledge, 2012.
Weber, Max. *From Max Weber: Essays in Sociology*. London: Routledge, 2009.
Westermarck, Edward. *The Origin and Development of the Moral Ideas*, vol. 1. London: Macmillan, 1906.
Wicksteed, Philip H. *The Religion of Time and the Religion of Eternity: Being a Study of Certain Relations between Mediaeval and Modern Thought*. London: P. Green, 1899.
Williams, Charles. *He Came down from Heaven*. London: Faber & Faber, 1956.
Williamson, Hugh Ross. *The Arrow and the Sword: An Essay in Detection*. London: Faber & Faber, 1947.
Zimmern, Alfred Eckhard. *The Greek Commonwealth*. New York: Random House, 1956.
Zouboff, Peter, and Vladimir Sergeyevich Solovyov. *Godmanhood as the Main Idea of the Philosophy of Vladimir Solovyev*. New York: International University Press, 1944.

Bibliography for Sections One and Three

Adamthwaite, Anthony P. *The Making of the Second World War*. London: Allen and Unwin, 1977.
Allen, Diogenes. *Philosophy for Understanding Theology*. London: SCM, 1985.
Atkinson, R. F. *Knowledge and Explanation in History. An Introduction to the Philosophy of History*. London: Macmillan, 1978.
Barth, Karl. *Church Dogmatics*. Edinburgh: T. & T. Clark, 1977.
Berdyaev, Nikolaj Aleksandrovic. *The Bourgeois Mind, and Other Essays* London: Sheed and Ward, 1934.
———. *The Meaning of History*. New York: Meridian, 1962.
Bonhoeffer, Dietrich, *Ethics*. Edited by Eberhard Bethge. Translated by Neville Horton Smith. Second Impression. London: SCM, 1971.
Brunner, Emil. *The Divine Imperative: A Study in Christian Ethics*. Philadelphia: Westminster, 1947.
———. *The Word and the World*. London: SCM, 1931.
Carmody, D. L. *How To Live Well: Ethics in the World Religions*. Belmont, CA: Wadsworth, 1988.
Cataldo, P. J., ed. *The Dynamic Character of Christian Culture. Essays on Dawsonian Themes*. Lanham: University Press of America, 1984.
Chadwick, Owen. *Britain and the Vatican during the Second World War*. Cambridge: Cambridge University Press, 1986
Collingwood, Robin George. *An Essay on Metaphysics*. Oxford, Clarendon, 1940.
Cooper, John W. *The Theology of Freedom. The Legacy of Jacques Maritain and Reinhold Niebuhr*. Macon: Mercer University Press, 1985.
Cox, Harvey. *The Secular City*. London: SCM, 1965.
Cross, F. L. "The New Orthodoxy." *Christendom* (September 1939).
Cupitt, Don. *The Sea of Faith*. London: BBC, 1984.
———. *Taking Leave of God*. London: SCM, 1980.
Daking, D. C. *Jungian Psychology and Modern Spiritual Thought*. London: Anglo-Eastern, 1933.
David-Neel, Alexandra. *Magic and Mystery in Tibet*. Introduction by A. d'Arsonval. New York: Claude Kendall, 1933.
Dawson, Christopher. *Beyond Politics* London: Sheed and Ward, 1939.
———. *The Historic Reality of Christian Culture*. London: Sheed and Ward, 1961.
———. *Religion and the Rise of Western Culture: Gifford Lectures Delivered in the University of Edinburgh 1948–1949*. London: Sheed and Ward, 1951.

D'Entreves, Alessandro Passerin. *Natural Law*. London: Hutchinson University Library, 1951.
Descartes, René. *The Method, Meditations and Philosophy of Descartes*. London: M. Walter Dunner, 1901.
Dix, Gregory. *Jew and Greek a Study in the Primitive Church*. London: Dacre, 1955; pp21.
Dodds, Eric Robertson. *The Greek and the Irrational*. Berkeley: University of California Press, 1963; 327.
Douglas, C. H. *Social Credit*. London: Cecil Palmer, 1924.
Dunstan, G. R. *The Artifice of Ethics*. London: SCM, 1974.
Durkheim, Emile. *The Elementary Forms of Religious Life*. Translated by J. Swaine. London: Allen and Unwin, 1976.
Durkin, Kenneth. *Reinhold Niebuhr*. London: Geoffrey Chapman, 1989.
Edwards, David L., ed. *The Honest to God Debate*. London: SCM, 1963.
Eliot, T. S. *The Idea of a Christian Society*. London: Faber and Faber, 1982.
Evans, Stanley G. *The Social Hope of the Christian Church*. London: Hodder and Stoughton, 1965.
Evans-Pritchard, E. E. (Edward Evan). *Theories of Primitive Religion*. Oxford: Clarendon, 1965.
Foster, M. B. "Christian Theology and Modern Science of Nature." *Mind* 44 (1935) 439–66.
———. "Doctrine of Creation and Modern Science." *Mind* 43 (1934) 446–68.
Frankfort, Henri, et al. *The Intellectual Adventure of Ancient Man: An Essay of Speculative Thought in the Ancient Near East*. Chicago: University of Chicago Press, 2013.
Gaitskell, H. "Four Monetary Heretics." In G.D.H. Cole, *What Everybody Wants to Know about Money*. London: Victor Gollancz, 1933; 58–59.
Gogarten, Friedrich. *Verhangnis und Hoffnug der Neuerzeit*. Stuggart: Friedrich Vorwerek Verlag, 1953.
Gore, Charles. and a group of Churchmen. *The Return of Christendom*. London: Macmillan, 1922; 251.
Green, Ronald M. "Religion and Morality." In *The Encyclopedia of Religion*, edited by Mircea Eliade. New York: Macmillan, 1987; 100.
Harries, Richard, ed. *Reinhold Niebuhr and the Issues of Our Time*. London: Mowbrays, 1986.
Hastings, Adrian. *A History of English Christianity 1920-1985*. London: Collins, 1986.
Hodge, A. "The Art of Living Together: Niebuhr, The Statists and the International Order." PhD diss., Georgetown University Law Center, 1988.
Hodson, Harry V. *The Diseconomies of Growth*. London: Pan/Ballantine, 1972.
Hughes, Gerald J. *Authority in Morals*. London: SCM, 1978.
Hulme, T. E. *Speculations*. London: Kegan, 1924.
Jaki, Stanley L. *Lord Gifford and his Lectures: A Centenary Retrospect*. Edinburgh: Scottish Academic, 1986.
James, William. *The Will To Believe and Other Essays*. New York: Longmans, Green, 1897.
Kegley, Charles W. and R. W. Bretall. *Reinhold Niebuhr: His Religious, Social and Political Thought*. New York: Macmillan, 1961.
Keynes, John Maynard. *Essays in Persuasion*. London: Macmillan, 1931.

———. *The General Theory of Employment, Interest and Money*. London: MacMillan, 1941.
Kojecky, Roger. *T. S. Eliot's Social Criticism*. London: Faber and Faber, 1971.
Lampert, Eugueny. *Nicolas Berdyaev and the New Middle Ages*. London: James Clarke, 1941.
Lang, Andrew. *Custom and Myth*. Wakefield: EP Publishing, 1974.
Laski, Harold J. *A Grammar of Politics*. London: Allen and Unwin, 1925.
———. *Liberty in the Modern State*. London: Allen and Unwin, 1930.
Long, Edward LeRoy. *A Survey of Christian Ethics*. New York: Oxford University Press, 1967.
Lewis, Hywel David. *Morals and Revelation*. London: Allen and Unwin, 1951.
Lewis, J. Douglas. *Fallacies—A Critique of Social Credit*. London: Chapman and Hall, 1935.
Lloyd, Roger. *The Church of England 1900–1965*. London: SCM, 1966.
MacIntyre, A. *After Virtue*. London: Duckworth, 1985.
———. *Whose Justice? Which Rationality?* London: Duckworth, 1988.
Mackie, J. L. *Ethics*. London: Penguin, 1977.
MacKinnon, Donald Mackenzie. *The Church of God*. London: Dacre, 1940.
———. *God the Living and the True*. London: Dacre, 1940.
———. *A Study in Ethical Theory*. London: A. & C. Black, 1957.
Macmurray, John. *Freedom in the Modern World*. London: Faber and Faber, 1932.
———. *Twentieth-Century Religious Thought*. London: SCM, 1981.
Macquarrie, John and James F. Childress. *A New Dictionary of Christian Ethics*. London: SCM, 1986.
Mannheim, Karl. *Collected Works: Wartime Essays of a Sociologist, Volume Three*, 1943. http://librarytitles.ebrary.com/id/10782724.
———. *Diagnosis of Our Time: Wartime Essays of a Sociologist*. London: Kegan Paul, 1974.
Markham, Ian S. "Faith and Reason: Reflections on MacIntyre's 'Tradition-Constituted Enquiry.'" *Religious Studies*. Forthcoming.
Maritain, Jacques. *True Humanism*. London: Geofrey Bles, 1938.
———. *Three Reformers, Luther, Descartes and Rousseau*. London: Kegan Paul, 1943.
Martin, David. *The Religious and the Secular*. London: Routledge and Kegan Paul, 1969.
Matthews, W. R. et al. *William Temple: An Estimate and an Appreciation*. London: James and Clark, 1946.
Mayhew, Peter. "The Christendom Group: A History and an Assessment." BLitt thesis, University of Oxford, 1977.
McCann, Dennis. *Christian Realism and Liberation Theology: Practical Theologies in Creative Conflict*. Maryknoll: Orbis, 1981.
Milbank, John. "A Socialist Economic Order." *Theology* (September 1988) 412-13.
Mink, Louis O. *Mind, History, and Dialectic: The Philosophy of R.G. Collingwood*. Bloomington: Indiana University Press, 1969.
Minnema, Theodore. *The Social Ethics of Reinhold Niebuhr*. Amsterdam: Kampen, 1958.
Mishan, Ezra J. *The Costs of Economic Growth*. London: Staples, 1967.
———. *Growth: the Price We Pay*. London: Staples, 1969.
Mitchell, Basil. *Morality: Religious and Secular*. Oxford: Clarendon, 1980.
Munby, D. L. *Christianity and Economic Problems*. London: Macmillan, 1956.
———. *Essays in Anglican Self-Criticism*. London: SCM, 1958.

———. *God and The Rich Society*. London: Oxford University Press, 1961.
———. *The Idea of a Secular Society*. Oxford: Oxford University Press, 1963.
Needham, Joseph. *Science and Civilization in China. Volume 2. History of Scientific Thought*. Cambridge: Cambridge University Press, 1956.
Neuhaus, R. J. *The Naked Public Square*. Michigan: Eerdmans, 1984.
Newman, John Henry. *Sermons and Discourses 1825–1839*. New York: Longmans, Green, 1949.
Niebuhr, Reinhold. *Beyond Tragedy*. New York: Scribner's, 1937.
———. *The Children of Light and the Children of Darkness*. London: Nisbet, 1945.
———. *Christian Realism and Political Problems*. London: Faber and Faber, 1954.
———. *Faith and History*. London: Nisbet, 1949.
———. *An Interpretation of Christian Ethics*. London: SCM, 1937.
———. *Moral Man and Immoral Society*. London: Mowbrays, 1963.
———. *The Nature and Destiny of Man. Volume 1*. London: Nisbet, 1941.
———. *The Nature and Destiny of Man. Volume 2*. London: Nisbet, 1943.
Norman, Edward R. *Christianity and the World Order*. Oxford: Oxford University Press 1979.
———. *Church and Society in England 1770–1970*. Oxford: Clarendon, 1976.
———. *The Victorian Christian Socialists*. Cambridge: Cambridge University Press, 1987.
Oldham, Joseph Houldsworth. *The Churches Survey Their Task*. The Report of the Oxford Conference on Church, Community and State, 1937.
Oldham, Joseph Houldsworth, et al. *The Church Looks Ahead*. London: Faber and Faber, 1941.
Oliver, John. *The Church and Social Order: Social Thought in the Church of England. 1918–1939*. London: Mowbrays, 1968.
Ortega y Gasset, Jose. *The Revolt of the Masses*. London: Allen and Unwin, 1932.
Peart-Binns, John S. *Maurice B. Reckitt: A Life*. Basingstoke, UK: Bowerdean, 1988.
Penty, A. J. "Has Machinery Causal Importance?" *Christendom* (October 1925) 272.
Plato, *The Republic of Plato, Translated into English, with an Introduction, Analysis, and Notes. By J. L. Davies and D. J. Vaughan*. Cambridge: Macmillan, 1866.
Polanyi, Michael. *Beyond Nihilism*. Cambridge: Cambridge University Press, 1960.
Preston, Ronald H. "Christian Socialism Becalmed." *Theology* (January 1988) 24–32.
———. *Church and Society in the late Twentieth Century: The Economic and Political Task*. London: SCM, 1983.
———. *Explorations in Theology*. London: SCM, 1981.
———. *The Future of Christian Ethics*. London: SCM, 1987.
———. "The Malvern Conference." *The Modern Churchman* (April 1942) 15-22.
———. *Religion and the Persistence of Capitalism*. London: SCM, 1979.
———. "The Theology of the Malvern Conference." *Christianity and Society* Vol 7, No 3 (1942) 25-31.
Porritt, Jonathon. *Seeing Green*. Oxford: Blackwell, 1984.
Pusey, Edward. *The Dangers of Riches*. Oxford: J. H. Parker, 1850.
Rahula, Walpola. *What the Buddha Taught*. Bedford: Gordon Fraser, 1967.
Reardon, Bernard M. G. *Religious Thought in the Victorian Age*. New York: Longmans, 1971.
Reckitt, M. B. "A Report of the Anglo-Catholic Summer School." *The Commonwealth* (August 1925) 248.

Reckitt, Maurice B. With C. E. Bechhofer. *As It Happened*. London: Faber and Faber, 1941.
———. *Maurice to Temple*. London: Faber and Faber, 1947.
———. *The Meaning of National Guilds*. London: Cecil Palmer, 1920.
———. *P.E.T. Widdrington*. London: SPCK, 1961.
———. "Two Views of an Election." *The Commonwealth* Vol 30 No 355 (August 1925) 248.
———. "A Word for the Month: Some Thoughts After the Strike." *The Commonwealth* (June 1926).
Report of the Anglo-Catholic Congress. London: SPCK, 1920, 1923, 1927.
"Report of the Christendom Conference." *Christendom* (June 1936) 131.
Richardson, David Bonner. *Berdyaev's Philosophy of History*. The Hague: Martinus Hijhoff, 1968.
Ritchie, A. D. "The Christian Religion and Contemporary Thought." *The Modern Churchman* (September 1950) 203.
Rupp, E. G. "Luther: The Catholic Caricature." *Theology* (October 1949) 197-204.
———. *Martin Luther, Hitler's Cause or Cure? In reply to P. R. Weiner*. London: Lutterworth, 1945.
Schumpeter, Joseph. *Capitalism, Socialism and Democracy*. London: Allen and Unwin, 1943.
Scott, Nathan A. *Reinhold Niebuhr*. Minneapolis: University of Minnesota Press, 1963.
Scruton, Roger. *The Meaning of Conservatism*. London: Macmillan, 1980.
Smith, Brooke Williams. *Jacques Maritain Antimodern or Ultramodern? An Historical Analysis of His Critics, His Thought, and His Life*. New York: Elsevier, 1976.
Stanley, J. M. *Church and the World: A Critical Evaluation of the Corpus Christianum approach in the Thought of John Baille, V. A. Demant, and T. S. Eliot*. PhD diss., Columbia University, 1966.
Stone, Ronald H. *Reinhold Niebuhr: Prophet to Politicians* Nashville: Abingdon, 1972.
Stout, Jeffrey. *Ethics After Babel*. Boston: Beacon, 1988.
Suggatt, Alan. *William Temple and Christian Social Ethics Today*. Edinburgh: T. & T. Clark, 1987.
Surin, Kenneth, ed. *Christ, Ethics and Tragedy*. Cambridge: Cambridge University Press, 1989.
Tawney, R. H. "A Giant In Decline." In *The Observer* (July 16, 1950).
———. *Religion and the Rise of Capitalism*. London: Penguin, 1938.
Taylor, A. J. P. *The Origins of the Second World War*. London: Hamish Hamilton, 1961.
Taylor, M. *The Christian Social Thinking of V. A. Demant*. Unpublished STM Thesis, New York Theological Seminary, 1959–60.
Temple, William. *Citizen and Churchman*. London: Eyre and Spottiswoode, 1941.
———. *Essays on Christian Politics and Kindred Subjects*. London: Longmans, Green, 1927
———. *Malvern 1941*. Convened by Temple. London: Longmans, 1941.
———. *Religious Experience and Other Essays and Addresses*. Edinburgh: T. & T. Clark, 1958.
———. *Thoughts in War Time*. London: Macmillan, 1940.
Vidler, Alec R. *Scenes from a Clerical Life*. London: Collins, 1977.
———. *God's Judgement on Europe*. London: Longmans, 1940.

Ward, J. S. K. "Christian Ethics." In *Keeping the Faith*, edited by G. Wainwright. Philadelphia: Fortress, 1988.

Waterman, A. M. C. "Denys Munby on Economics and Christianity." *Theology* (March 1990) 108-116.

Weiner, Peter F. *Martin Luther: Hitler's Spiritual Ancestor*. London: Hutchinson, 1945.

Wilson, Bryan, ed. *Rationality*. Oxford: Blackwells, 1970.

———. "Secularisation." In *The Encyclopedia of Religion* edited by Mircea Eliade. New York: Macmillan, 1987.

Wright, A. W. *G. D. H. Cole and Socialist Democracy*. Oxford: Clarendon, 1979.

Bibliography of the Writings of V. A. Demant

Some of the best-known articles are reprinted several times. In such cases the article is listed in the most accessible source. The material is listed in order of publication.

AUTHORED BOOKS AND BOOKLETS

Demant, Vigo Auguste. *The Miners Distress and the Coal Problem*. London: SCM, 1929.
———. *This Unemployment: Disaster or Opportunity*. London: SCM, 1931.
———. *God, Man and Society*. London: SCM, 1933.
———. *Christian Polity*. London: Faber and Faber, 1936.
———. *The Christian Doctrine of Human Solidarity*. London: SPCK, 1936.
———. *How to Prevent the Next War*. London: York Social Credit Conference, 1937.
———. *The Religious Prospect*. London: Muller, 1939.
———. *What is Happening to Us?* Broadcast talks. London: Dacre, 1943.
———. *Theology of Society*. London: Faber and Faber, 1947.
———. *The Responsibility and Scope of Pastoral Theology Today*. Oxford: Clarendon, 1950.
———. *Religion and the Decline of Capitalism*. London: Faber and Faber, 1952.
———. *The Elements of Christianity*. Cambridge: Cambridge University Press, 1955.
———. *A Two-Way Religion*. London: Mowbray, 1957.
———. *You and Your Neighbour*. London: SPCK, 1957.
———. *Christian Sex Ethics*. London: Hodder and Stoughton, 1963.
———. *The Idea of a Natural Order*. Philadelphia: Fortress, 1966.
———. *Why the Christian Priesthood is Male*. London: Church Literature Association, 1966.

EDITOR AND CONTRIBUTOR

Porter, Alan, and V. A. Demant, eds. *Coal: A Challenge to the National Conscience*. London: L. & Virginia Woolf, 1927.

Demant, Vigo Auguste, ed. *The Just Price*. London: Student Christian Movement, 1930.
———, ed. *Faith That Illuminates*. London: Centenary, 1935.
———, ed. *Our Culture: Its Christian Roots and Present Crisis*. London: SPCK, 1974.
———, ed. *Thy Household the Church. Proposals for Government and Order in the Church of England. By a Group of the Clergy, Etc.* Dacre: Westminster [London], 1943.

CONTRIBUTOR ONLY

Delahaye, James Viner, ed. *Politics: A Discussion of Realities*. London: Daniel, 1929.
Althaus, Paul, ed. *Die Kirche und das Staatsproblem in der Gegenwart*. Frauenfeld: Huber, 1935.
Lothian, Philip Henry Kerr, ed. *The Universal Church and the World of Nations*. London: Allen and Unwin, 1938.
Box, Hubert S, ed. *The Priest As Student*, 339-64. London: Society for Promoting Christian Knowledge, 1939.
Oldham, J. H., ed. *The Church Looks Ahead; Broadcast Talks*. London: Faber and Faber Ltd, 1941.
Malvern, 1941: The Life of the Church and the Order of Society; Being the Proceedings of the Archbishop of York's Conference, 121-49. London: Longmans, Green, 1942.
Reckitt, Maurice B., ed. *Prospect for Christendom; Essays in Catholic Social Reconstruction*. London: Faber and Faber, 1946.
Man in Society. Worcester: Littlebury, 1947.
Williamson, Hugh Ross, ed. *The Arrow and the Sword: An Essay in Detection*. London: Faber & Faber, 1947.
Koestler, Arthur ed. *The Challenge of Our Time*. London: P. Marshall, 1948.
Ideas and Beliefs of the Victorians: An Historic Revaluation of the Victorian Age. London: Sylvan, 1949.
Western Tradition: A Series of Talks Given by the British Broadcasting Corporation. London: Vox Mundi, 1951.
Abbott, Eric Symes, ed. *Catholicity: A Study in the Conflict of Christian Traditions in the West, Being a Report Presented to His Grace the Archbishop of Canterbury*. Westminster [London]: Dacre, 1952.
Difficulties: Questions on Religion with Answers. London: Mowbray, 1958.
Conservative Political Centre (Great Britain), and G. M. Young, ed. *The Good Society Oxford Lectures 1952*. 1953.
"Man and the Social Order." In Wand, J. W. C., W. R. Matthews, V. A. Demant, and Lindsay Dewar. *Christian Belief to-Day*. London: Mowbray, 1952.
Church of England. *The National Church and the Social Order: An Enquiry into the Principles That Have Governed the Attitude For the Anglican Church Towards the State and Secular Order*. Westminster [London]: Church Information Board of the Church Assembly, 1956.
Ramsey, Michael, ed. *Christian Spirituality Today: Essays Contributed to the York Quarterly 1959-60*. London: Faith, 1961.
Reckitt, Maurice B., ed. *P. E. T. Widdrington*. London: SPCK, 1961.

Montefiore, Hugh, and Frank Lake, ed. *We Must Love One Another or Die: Lectures on Love, Sex and Morality Given in Great Saint Mary's Church, Cambridge.* London: Hodder & Stoughton, 1966.

"Sociological Factors in the Determination of Christian Morals." In Irvine, Gerald, ed. *Christianity in Its Social Context,* 109-121. London: SPCK, 1967.

Macquarrie, John, ed. *A Dictionary of Christian Ethics.* London: SCM, 1984.

ARTICLES IN JOURNALS AND PERIODICALS

[Some of these articles, either in part or completely, are reproduced in Demant, V.A. *Theology of Society: More Essays in Christian Polity.* London: Faber and Faber, 1947.]

Christendom

Demant, Vigo Auguste. "The Prospects of Christian Sociology in America." *Christendom* (March 1931) 31.

———. Book Section: "Political Dialectic." *Christendom* (March 1931) 68.

———. Review of *The Fairy Ring of Commerce, Christendom* (March 1931) 73.

———. Book Section: "The Redemption of Class Consciousness." *Christendom* (September 1931) 225.

———. "Studies in Christian Sociology (1) The Doctrine of Creation." *Christendom* (December 1931) 270.

———. Review of *The Psychology of Character, Christendom* (March 1932) 78.

———. "Our Present Problems." *Christendom* (June 1932) 107.

———. "The Philosophic Basis of Christian Sociology." *Christendom* (September 1932) 172.

———. Review of "Money and Prices." by Augustus Baker; and review of *Warning Democracy,* by C. H. Douglas *Christendom* (September 1932).

———. Book Section: "Magnificent Atheism." *Christendom* (December 1932) 299.

———. Review of *Bolshevism: Theory & Practice,* by Waldemar Gretian, *Christendom* (March 1933).

———. Book Section: "Form and Content in Civilisation." *Christendom* (June 1933) 142.

———. Review of *Enquiries into Religion and Culture,* by Christopher Dawson, *Christendom* (September 1933).

———. Review of *Moscow Dialogues,* by Julius Hecker, *Christendom* (December 1933).

———. "The Religion of Church and State." *Christendom* (March 1932) 24.

———. "God as History: A Comment on Gierke and Contemporary Heresy." *Christendom* (December 1934) 255.

———. "Money and Christian Sociology." *Christendom* (September 1935).

———. "Nationalism and Internationalism, *Christendom* (March 1936) 13.

———. Book Section: "Christianity and the Nature of History." *Christendom* (March 1936).

———. "Providence, Progress or Cleopatra's Nose." *Christendom* (March 1936) 63.

———. Book Section: "The Unsolved Problem of the Church." *Christendom* (December 1936).
———. Review of *Wrestlers with Christ*, by Karl Pfleger, *Christendom* (March 1937).
———. "Church, Community and State." *Christendom* (June 1937).
———. "The Philosophy of Church Social Action." *Christendom* (September 1937).
———. "A Theologian on Historical Existence." *Christendom* (December 1937).
———. Book Section: "Valet to the Absolute." *Christendom* (June 1939).
———. Review of *The Catholic Centre*, by El Watkin, *Christendom* (June 1940).
———. Review of *The Mind of the Maker*, by Dorothy L. Sayers, *Christendom* (March 1942).
———. "Europe: Its Predicament and Its Future." *Christendom* (March 1943) 9.
———. "The Theology of Politics." *Christendom* (September 1943) 74.
———. Review of *Distributism and the Liberal Party*, by Richard Rowe, *Christendom* (March 1949).

The New Age

Demant, Vigo Auguste. "Social Credit and Civilisation." *The New Age* (April 24, 1924).
———. "Anthropological Economics. Wealth and Debt 1." *The New Age* (June 10, 1926).
———. "Anthropological Economics. Wealth and Debt 2." *The New Age* (June 17, 1926).
———. "Anthropological Economics. Wealth and Debt 3." *The New Age* (June 24, 1926).
———. "Anthropological Economics. War and Its Motives." *The New Age* (July 1, 1926).
———. "Anthropological Economics. Revolution—Its Cause and Cure." *New Age* (July 22, 1926).
———. "Anthropological Economics. Revolution—Its Cause and Cure 2." *The New Age* (July 29, 1926).
———. "The Tyranny of Tools." *The New Age* (November 11, 1926).
———. "Religion and Economics." *The New Age* (July 3, 1930).

The Church Quarterly Review

Demant, Vigo Auguste. "Idolatry: Its Place and Influence in Religious History." *The Church Quarterly Review* (January 1936) 652.

The Commonwealth

Demant, Vigo Auguste. "The Over-Population Hoax." *The Commonwealth* (August 1926).
——— and M.B. Reckitt, "Two Views of an Election." *The Commonwealth* (April 1929).
Demant, Vigo Auguste. "'Babylon' or Money Power." *The Commonwealth* (July 1929) 140–3.

The L.K.G. Quarterly

Demant, Vigo Auguste. "The Mass and Money." *The L.K.G. Quarterly* (July 1928).

Psyche

Demant, Vigo Auguste. "Gold: an Anthropologist's View of the Economic Problem." *Psyche* (October 1928).

Stockholm International Review for the Social Activities of the Churches

Demant, Vigo Auguste. "Christianity and Property." *Stockholm International Review for the Social Activities of the Churches*, #1 (1930) 221.

———. "The Approach of the English Christian Social Council to the Problem of Industry." *Stockholm International Review for the Social Activities of the Churches*, #2 (1930).

———. "Is modern Civilisation Materialistic?" *Stockholm International Review for the Social Activities of the Churches*, #1 (1931).

The Torch

Demant, Vigo Auguste. "Unemployment as a Problem in Christian Sociology: The Realities of the Problem." *The Torch* (March 1931).

———. "Unemployment as a Problem in Christian Sociology: The Work Complex." *The Torch* (April 1931).

———. "Unemployment as a Problem in Christian Sociology: The Money Question." *The Torch* (May 1931).

Church Times

Demant, Vigo Auguste. "The Economic Paradox." *Church Times* (August 7, 1931) 153.

———. Review of *The Work, Wealth and Happiness of Mankind*, by H. G. Wells. *Church Times* (August 1, 1932) 42–51.

———. Review of *The Revolt of the Masses*, by Ortega Y Gasset. *Church Times* (July 15, 1932) 79.

———. "As An Economist Sees It." *Church Times* (November 4, 1932) 11.

———. Review of *Monarchy or Money Power*, by R. McNair Wilson. *Church Times* (March 17, 1933) 332.

B.B.C. Quarterly

Demant, Vigo Auguste. "The Unintentional Influences of the Wireless." *B.B.C. Quarterly* 3:3 (October 1948).
———. "The Unintentional Influences of Television." *B.B.C. Quarterly* (October 1954) 220–25.

Listener

Demant, Vigo Auguste. "Ethics and the Technical Revolution." *Listener*, June 28, 1951.
———. "Fabian Essays, Old and New." *Listener* (October 16, 1952).
———. "Temptations of Civilisations." *Listener* (November 2, 1950).
———. "The Question of Self-Interest." *Listener* (November 9, 1950).
———. "Mastery and Contemplation." *Listener* (December 1, 1950).

Church Teaching Quarterly

Demant, Vigo Auguste. "The School and the Churches." *Church Teaching Quarterly* (Michaelmas 1953) 61–73.
———. "Kenneth Kirk as Moral Theologian." *Church Teaching Quarterly* (Michaelmas 1957) 423–34.
———. "Mackinnon's Ethics (A Review of his Study in Ethical Theory)." *Church Teaching Quarterly* (January 1959) 85–88.

Church Observer

Demant, Vigo Auguste. "Faith and Morals." *Church Observer* (1953).

Journal of Theological Studies

Demant, Vigo Auguste. Review of *The Elements of Moral Theology*, by R. C. Mortimer. *Journal of Theological Studies* (July–October 1948) 248.
———. Review of *The Protestant Era*, by P. Tillich. *Journal of Theological Studies* (April 1952) 138.
———. Review of *The Self and the Dramas of History*, by Reinhold Niebuhr. *Journal of Theological Studies* (October 1957) 398–401.
———. Review of *Reinhold Niebuhr: His Religious, Social and Political Thought*, by C. W. Kegley and R. W. Bretall. *Journal of Theological Studies* (October 1957) 398–401.
———. Review of *The Realities of Faith*, by B. E. Meland. *Journal of Theological Studies* (April 1964) 217–18.
———. Review of *Loi naturelle et Loi du Christ*, by E. Hamel. *Journal of Theological Studies* (April 1966) 264–65.
———. Review of *The Disinterested Love of God according to Eusebius Amort*, by R. Hindery. *Journal of Theological Studies* (October 1964) 453.

———. Review of *The Just War in Aquinas and Grotius*, by J. D. Tooke. *Journal of Theological Studies* (April 1967) 265–70.
———. Review of *Deeds and Rules in Christian Ethics*, by P. Ramsey. *Journal of Theological Studies* (October 1967) 545–48.
———. Review of *The Ghost Dance: The Origins of Religion*, by W. La Barre. *Journal of Theological Studies* (April 1974) 240–47.
———. Review of *Identity and the Sacred*, by H. Mol, *Journal of Theological Studies* (October 1977) 599–601.
———. Review of *A Persian Stronghold of Zoroastrianism*, by M. Boyce. *Journal of Theological Studies* (January 1978) 394–96.

Theology

Demant, Vigo Auguste. "The Importance of Niebuhr." *Theology* (May 1942) 267–75.
———. "Niebuhr, the Dialectical Moralist." *Theology* (January 1944) 1–9.
———. "The Christendom Trust." *Theology* (July 1971) 296–300.

Frontier

Demant, Vigo Auguste. "Two Kinds of Faith." *Frontier* (March 1960) 41–2.
———. "Faith of T. S. Eliot." *Frontier* (August 1965) 215–18.
———. Review of *In the Shadow of Man*, by J. van Lawick-Goodall. *Frontier* (March 1972).
———. Review of *The Absoluteness of Christianity and the History of Religions* by E. Troeltsch. *Frontier* (August 1972) 183–4.

Journal of Religion

Demant, Vigo Auguste. "Ancient Heresy and Modern Belief." *Journal of Religion* (April 1947) 79-90.

Shakespearian Authorship Review

Demant, Vigo Auguste. "John Thomas Looney." *Shakespearian Authorship Review* (Autumn 1962).

UNPUBLISHED PAPERS CONSULTED

[Currently held with the Demant Family at Headington, Oxford.]

1. Unpublished Gifford Lectureships University of St. Andrews. Subject: The Penumbra of Ethics. Session 1956–57: Series One: Studies in the Natural History of Christianity. Session 1957–58: Series Two: The Moral Career of Christendom.

2. A collection of his Sermons Unpublished, "Not One World But Two."
3. Speech made by Reckitt on Demant's 80th birthday November 6, 1973.
4. "The Work of the Christendom Group in the Field of Business and Economic Thought" on the 18.7.80.
5. "The Chandos Group."
6. Demant correspondence with M. B. Reckitt. [Reckitt Papers held at Sussex University.]

UNPUBLISHED INTERVIEWS

Houlden, Leslie. Interview by Ian Markham. November 10, 1987.
Chadwick, Henry. Interview by Ian Markham. January 11, 1988.
Preston, Ronald. Interview by Ian Markham. February 2, 1988.
Ramsey, Michael. Interview by Ian Markham. March 16, 1988.
Mayhew, Peter. Interview by Ian Markham. March 16, 1988.
Demant, Jocelyn. Interview by Ian Markham. March 17, 1988.
Mrs. V. A. Demant. Interview by Ian Markham. March 17, 1988.
Mascall, E. L. Interview by Ian Markham. June 22, 1988.
Nash, A. Interview by Ian Markham. July 18, 1988.
Louth, A. Interview by Ian Markham. July 19, 1988
Ward, Keith. Interview by Ian Markham. February 11, 1989.
Dunstan, G. Interview by Ian Markham. February 20, 1990.

UNPUBLISHED CORRESPONDENCE

Dilliestone, F. W. to Ian Markham, April 23, 1988.
Nash, A. to Ian Markham, October 19, 1988.
Every, George to Ian Markham, November 21, 1988.
MacIntyre, Alasdair to Ian Markham, October 5, 1989.
MacKinnon, Donald to Ian Markham, February 2, 1990.

Index of Names

Abelard, Peter, 150, 246
Adamthwaite, Anthony P., 35
Adler, Alfred, 257
Aeschylus, 241, 262
Ambrose of Milan, 232, 274
Angela of Foligno, 187
Anselm, 150, 201n2
Anthony of Padua, 222
Aristotle, 109, 118–9n33, 143, 189, 232–33, 249
Arnold, Matthew, 135, 226, 274
Athanasius of Alexandria, 222
Augustine, 45, 58, 60, 65, 93, 117, 121, 149, 150–52, 158, 182, 186n21, 223, 230–33, 243, 268, 274–78

Bacon, Francis, 76–77, 84–85, 213, 225
Bagehot, Walter, 287
Bailey, Derrick Sherwin, 186
Baille, D.M., 155–56
Barth, Karl, viii, 18, 43n5, 46–47, 182–83, 247n24
Beauvoir, Simone de, 187
Belloc, Hilaire, 14
Berdyaev, Nikolai Aleksandrovic, 17–19, 163–64, 178, 227–28, 237n24–238, 258, 271, 282, 294n6
Berlin, Isaiah, 116
Bernard of Clairveau, 158, 187–8n23, 234nn13–14
Bertholet, Alfred, 188n24
Blake, William, 81, 138, 215
Boethius, 173n15

Bonhoeffer, Dietrich, 47, 111, 138
Boorstin, Daniel Joseph, 266n20
Borne, Etienne, 273n13, 278
Bouyer, Louis, 222
Boyd, Andrew, 92n29
Bradwardine, Thomas, 155
Brown, Norman O., 98
Brunner, Emil, 18, 32, 46
Bryce, James, 230n5
Buber, Martin, 179, 184–85, 295
Bultmann, Rudolf, 128–29, 139, 148, 222
Burckhardt, Jacob, 162–63
Burke, Edmund, 5, 226
Bury, J. B., 125
Butler, Joseph, 93
Butterfield, Herbert, 157, 203

Calvin, Jean, 98, 109, 159, 236–37, 244–47, 275–77
Cassian, John, 222
Cataldo, P. J., 16n33
Chadwick, Henry, 6n4, 8, 41n1
Chadwick, Owen, 35, 222
Chalmers, Thomas, 234
Charlemagne, 168, 239
Chateaubriand, François-René de, 226
Chenu, Marie-Dominique, 278
Chesterton, G. K., 9–14, 184
Cicero, Marcus Tullius, 232, 242
Clement of Rome, 230–32, 274n16
Cochrane, Charles Norris, 221–2n13
Cohn, Norman, 222
Coleridge, Samuel Taylor, 84, 115, 226, 240

340 INDEX OF NAMES

Collingwood, Robin George, 17, 19, 121, 161, 241
Comte, Auguste, 4, 90, 226, 252–53
Confucius, 190, 191, 206
Cooper, John W., 15n31, 267
Cox, Harold, 27
Cromwell, Oliver, 266
Cross, F. L., 65
Cudworth, Ralph, 186
Cullmann, Oscar, 171–72
Cupitt, Don, 42n2

D'Entreves, Alessandro Passerin. P., 243, 247–8n31, 306–7n38
Daking, D. C., 88n23
Dante, 158, 173, 224, 232, 242, 254
David-Neel, Alexandra, 126n10
Dawson, Christopher, 15–19, 40, 92, 163, 205n11, 207n20, 208n26, 213, 226, 266n19, 282, 286, 304
De Grazia, Sebastian, 262n13, 275n21
Descartes, René, 29, 43, 85, 213, 217
Dix, Gregory, 209–10
Dodds, Eric Robertson, 118, 129n19, 130n21
Douglas, Major C. H., 5–6, 13–14, 21–28
Douglas, Mary, 237–38
Drucker, Peter F., 289
Dryden, John, 78–79, 84
Durkheim, Kenneth, 286

Eckhardt, Meister, 189
Edwards, David L., 53n39, 316n28
Eliade, Mircea, 89n27, 95n36, 168, 273n12
Eliot, T. S., 6, 15, 34–37, 40, 50, 63, 258, 316
Emerson, Ralph Waldo, 83, 176
Emmet, Dorothy M., 237n24, 266n17
Engels, Friedrich, 116, 278
Eriugena, John Scotus, 124, 178
Eusebius of Caesarea, 223
Evans-Pritchard, Edward Evan, 87n21, 90n28
Evans, Christopher, 53n39

Fichte, J. G., 43, 152–53

Figgis, John Neville, 260
Forsyth, Peter Taylor, 155, 218
Foster, Michael, 8
Francis of Assisi, 163, 223–24
Francis of Sales, 234
Frankfort, Henri, 147, 160, 121, 205, 212n36, 304
Frazer, James George, 86, 101, 217, 258
Freeman, Edward Augustus, 203
Freud, Sigmund, 88, 152n34, 195, 240, 298
Fuller, Reginald Horace, 140n17, 170n5

Gabor, Dennis, 270n4, 279
Gaitskell, H., 23
Gavin, Frank, 275
Gebhard, Frei, 177n3
Geer, Walter, 153n39
Gifford, Adam Lord, 75–76, 91
Goethe, Johann Wolfgang, 82–83, 152–53, 195, 226, 267
Gore, Charles, 4, 9, 11–12
Gore, Charles, 4, 9, 11–12, 242
Gregory of Nyssa, 178
Guénon, René, 124n5, 189n25

Haas, William S., 129–30, 169n3
Halévy, Elie, 114n19
Harnack, Adolph von, 222
Hartmann, Nicolai, 143–44
Hastings, Adrian, 10–11
Hegel, Georg Wilhelm Friedrich, 29, 109, 153, 225, 245–46, 248n33, 267, 311
Hitler, Adolf, 9, 29–30, 34–35, 38, 64n82, 98, 153, 248, 266
Hobbes, Thomas, 241n1, 245–46, 286, 309
Hobhouse, Leonard Trelawny, 215
Hodges, H. A., 34, 122, 201
Holland, Scott, 11
Hooker, Richard, 109, 231, 236, 250, 231n7
Hugh of Victor, 151, 243
Hughes, Gerald J., 64n84
Hulme, T. E., 65

Hume, David, 78, 114, 146, 216, 247
Huxley, Aldous, 94–95, 115, 124, 160, 179, 270–71
Hyde, Lawrence, 176–77

Isidore of Seville, 243

Jacobi, Jolande, 178n3
James, William, 87–88, 203, 215
Jaspers, Karl, 164, 192n1, 206–7, 227, 282
Jenks, Edward, 260–61
Jerome, 230
Jerome, Jerome K., 269n2
Joachim of Fiore (or Flora), 222–23
John of Olivi, 225
Jones, William, 87
Jouvenel, Bertrand de, 241, 288–89
Julian of Norwich, 180–82
Julius Caesar, 231, 266
Jung, Carl Gustav, 88–89, 177, 178n3, 294

Kant, Immanuel, 43, 80, 93, 119n33, 135, 142–44, 234–35
Keble, John 9
Kenyon, Ruth, 11
Keynes, John Maynard, 22, 27–28, 110–11, 270, 272, 312
Kierkegaard, Søren, 204n7, 258, 267
Kingsley, 9
Kitto, H. D. F., 259
Knight, Margaret, 106
Knox, John, 234
Kojecky, Roger, 6n3, 34n1, 36, 39n17–40

Lactantius, Caecilius Firmianus Lucius, 230
Lamennais, Félicité Robert de, 226
Lampert, Evgueny, 18
Lang, Andrew, 91, 204n8, 303
Law, William, 81
Lawrence, D. H., 184, 195, 252
Leibniz, Gottfried Wilhelm, 225, 246
Lessing, Gotthold Ephraim, 83, 137
Levy, G. Rachel, 237n24, 258–59

Lewis, C. S., 22n8, 135, 137n2, 240, 247, 295
Lewis, Hywel David, 108, 119n33
Lewis, John, 22n8
Lilburne, John, 251
Lloyd, Roger, 10
Llull, Ramon, 187
Locke, John, 159, 245–47, 250–51, 309
Long, Haniel, 290n16
Lovejoy, Arthur, O., 85–86
Löwith, Karl, 267n21
Ludlow, John, 9
Luther, Martin, 9, 29–30, 94, 150, 237, 246–47, 275

MacIver, Robert M., 204n10
Mackinnon, Donald MacKenzie, 46–47, 237n24, 238n25
Macquarrie, John, 17n38
Mairet, Philip, 6, 13, 37, 253
Maistre, Joseph de, 90, 226
Mannheim, Karl, 34, 36, 119n33, 284–85
Maritain, Jacques, 15, 19, 29–30
Martin, David, 48,
Marx, Karl, 42, 48, 70, 90, 97, 109, 114–16, 125, 127, 158, 194, 226, 240, 267, 278, 288, 297, 311, 316
Matthew, Arnold, 135, 226, 274
Matthews, W. R., 28n22
Maurice, Frederick Denison, 3, 9–10, 171, 237n22
Maximus the Confessor, 178, 278
Mayhew, Peter, 4–8, 13n26, 22n7, 28n20, 48n25, 63
Mayo, Elton, 286–87
Mazzini, Giuseppe, 226
Milbank, John, vii-viii
Mill, James, 114
Mill, John Stewart, 109, 241, 291
Mink, Louis O., 17n39
Molinos, Miguel de, 151
Montesqueue, 251
Munby, Denys L., 6, 21–22, 47–48
Murray, Gilbert, 206, 211n33

Nash, Arnold, 48

INDEX OF NAMES

Newman, John Henry, 9, 130, 151, 214
Newton, Isaac, 81
Nicholas of Cusa, 185n15, 189
Nicholson, Harold, 203
Niebuhr, Reinhold, viii, 6, 8, 31, 34, 40, 63, 171, 204n7, 253n11, 284n2, 291
Nietzsche, Friedrich, 90, 109, 115, 135, 152, 153n37, 195, 226, 240, 258, 267
Nock, Albert Jay, 226n21
Noel, Conrad, 11
Norman, Edward R., 21, 41, 48–50, 56n54, 58n62, 98, 222

Oberman, Heiko Augustinus, 155
Ockham (or Occam), William of, 150, 246–47
Oldham, Joseph Houldsworth, 35–39, 203n6, 273
Oliver, John, 10n17, 12, 13n26, 22–23
Origen, 178, 186
Otto, Rudolf, 95n36, 139, 247

Paley, William, 78
Parkyns, Mansfield, 279
Pascal, Blaise, 80, 150, 247n26, 281
Peart-Binns, John S., 12n24, 13n26
Peck, W. G., 28
Pelagius, 151–52
Penty, A. J., 20, 24
Pierce, C. A., 214
Plato, 59–60, 97, 118, 123–26, 143, 148, 161, 189–91, 207, 209, 232, 253–54, 262, 307
Polanyi, Michael, 107–8, 111–12, 286
Pope, Alexander, 265
Pope, Pius XII, 35–36
Pound, Roscoe, 242n4
Preston, Ronald H., 6–7, 13n26, 47, 49n28, 63–64, 313
Pufendorf, Samuel von, 246
Pusey, Edward, 9

Ramsey, Michael, 8–9, 171n11
Reckitt, Maurice. B., vii, 5–7, 10–14, 20–21, 24–27, 30–33, 37–39

Ritchie, A. D., 109
Ritchie, David George, 241, 247
Rivers, W. H., 202
Roberts, Richard, 46
Robespierre, Maximilien, 78
Rousseau, Jean-Jacques, 29, 79–80, 84, 98, 107, 225, 245–51, 267–68, 286, 311
Rupp, Ernest Gordon, 30
Russell, Bertrand, 110, 119n33, 217, 252, 296

Sainsbury, Geoffrey, 176–77
Samardu, 204n7
Sanderson, Robert, 236, 250
Saurat, M. Denis, 66, 117, 259n4
Schleiermacher, Friedrich, 96
Schuon, Frithjof, 95
Schweitzer, Albert, 131–32, 170n5
Scotus, John Duns, 150–51, 247
Scruton, Roger, 60
Shakespeare, William, 8m 265n15
Sharp, D. E., 150n24
Smith, Adam, 278
Smith, Wilfred Cantwell, 93
Sophocles, 211, 241
Spencer, Herbert, 14, 204n10, 251, 267
Spinoza, Baruch, 76, 143, 213
Sprat, Thomas, 225
Stanley, John Mack, 32n34, 41, 44, 51n33, 53, 61n73
Steiner, Rudolf, 253
Stephen, Leslie, 114, 213, 241
Stout, Jeffrey, 309n15
Strachey, Marjorie, 222
Surin, Kenneth, 46n19
Swann, N. Egerton, 6, 11, 13
Sweitzer, Albert, 131–32, 170n 5

Taubes, Jacob, 222
Tawney, R. H., 34–35, 277
Taylor, Alfred Edward, 92, 160, 211n33, 215n48
Taylor, Jeremy, 186, n20, 231, 236–37, 250
Taylor, Michael, 41, 44, 51, 63, 311
Temple, William, 10, 28, 30–31, 35–40

INDEX OF NAMES

Teresa of Ávila, 187
Tertullian, 204n7, 221, 230, 273
Thibon, Gustave, 109
Thomas Aquinas, 15, 94, 149, 231, 234, 247, 249
Thornton, Lionel Spencer, 11–12, 186
Thornton, Martin, 218–19
Tillich, Paul, 138, 294
Tillotson, John, 213
Tindal, Matthew, 77–78
Toynbee, Arnold J., 94, 206n17–209, 226
Trilling, Lionel, 267n21
Troeltsch, Ernst, 84, 95n37, 229–30, 243, 252, 273
Twain, Mark, 235

Vidler, Alec R., 34, 38, 39n15
Voltaire, 78, 84, 266
Vonier, Dom Abbot, 180

Waley, Arthur, 190n27
Ward, J. S. Keith, 306–8
Webb, Clement Charles Julian, 241
Weber, Alfred, 207n19
Weber, Max, 96, 100, 277
Weiner, Peter F., 29–30
Wesley, John, 81, 237, 276
Westermarck, Edward, 204
White, Victor, 89n27, 136, 177n3
Whitehead, A. N., 161, 236
Wicksteed, Philip H., 137n3
Widdrington, P. E. T., 11, 25
Williams, Charles, 141
Williamson, Hugh Ross, 225
Wilson, Bryan, 64n84
Wilson, Monica, 237
Wycliffe, John, 234, 247

Zimmern, Alfred, 211, 262

Index of Subjects

Agape, 175, 231, 292
Alienation, 18, 42–43, 55, 57, 59, 134, 203, 210, 264–65, 294, 298, 304
Anglican, 4, 6–7, 47
Anglo-Catholicism, 4–5, 9–10, 15, 24n14, 47
Anthropology, 3, 5, 48, 51, 59, 64, 86, 91
Asceticism, 154, 209
Atheism, 158

Buddhism, 99, 123, 207–10, 279, 304–5

Calvinism, 159, 275–77
Capitalism, vii, 12, 13n26, 15, 17, 20–26, 218, 256, 287
Christendom, 16, 21, 28, 30, 36, 38–39, 49, 75, 113, 119, 127, 132, 134, 143–44, 144, 148, 157, 160, 163–64, 174–75, 197, 199–203, 212–13, 216, 218–19, 222–23, 227, 230, 238, 253, 255, 272, 277, 280, 282, 292–94, 297, 303, 325
Christendom (Christian sociology journal), x, 5, 6, 11, 16, 25
Christendom Group, the, vii, 3, 7, 11–13, 15, 20–22, 24, 28, 30, 46–48, 63–64
Christian Ethics, viii, 3, 5, 46, 131, 135, 201, 204, 218, 227, 232, 235, 239, 251, 292, 298, 305–6
Christian Social Union (Council), 5, 10–11
Christian Socialist League, 10–11

Christian Sociology, vii, 5, 12, 28, 30–32, 41, 47–51, 56–59, 64n82, 68, 253, 316
Church of England, 3, 9, 22, 276
Collectivism, 14, 21, 71, 119, 307
Communism, 16, 26, 97, 108, 192, 238, 268, 298
Confucianism, 169, 190–91, 206–8
Consumption, 14, 25, 27, 68, 226, 273, 297
Council on the Christian Faith and the Common Life (C.C.F.C.L.), 35–36
Creation, doctrine of, 37, 42–45, 51, 55–59, 76–77, 124, 127–31, 141, 160–62, 168, 175, 178, 181–85, 212, 250,
Creator, 18, 42, 44, 51, 54, 80, 124, 128–30, 154, 174, 181, 183, 219, 241, 278, 282–83
Crucifixion, doctrine of the, 46, 224
Deism, 76–81
Democracy, 16, 107, 253, 256, 260, 288
Determinism, 62, 97, 116, 142, 144–46, 152–53, 264, 281, 294
Distributism (Distributist League), 12, 14
Dualism, 129, 131, 137, 165, 176, 225

Eastern Religion, 89, 100, 144, 160, 169, 192, 194, 210, 240, 304–5, 315
Economic Nationalism, 25

345

INDEX OF SUBJECTS

Economics, vii, 8–11, 17, 20–29, 32–35, 48–49, 53–56, 62–69, 86, 96–97, 110, 119, 153, 192, 201–4, 208, 218, 238, 259–61, 269–70, 277–79, 284–88, 292, 295, 299, 308–16
Empirical world, 58, 61n72, 88, 99–100, 169, 193
Enlightenment, 15, 29–30, 29, 76–83, 86, 90–101, 107, 143, 214–15, 245
Eros, 175, 177
Eschatology, 171, 222–23, 225, 229
Eternal God, 18, 42, 123
Eternal law, 207, 249
Eternal life, 43, 57, 167, 171
Eternal reality/world, 42, 45, 53, 55, 123 158, 164, 168, 207
Evolutionary Naturalism, 114–15
Existentialism, 17–18, 145, 258, 292

Fall, the, 112, 124, 131, 141, 155–56, 160, 183–85, 206, 213, 250, 279, 283, 306
Fascism, 16, 153n37
Fatalism, 33
Feudalism, 261, 296, 308
Freedom, 14–15, 37, 52–55, 59, 118, 125, 135, 142–55, 161, 202–3, 208n25, 212, 218, 231, 236–37, 248, 250, 254, 256n14, 283, 286–87, 293, 297–98, 306

Gender, 165, 174–83, 187–88, 227, 190
General Strike, 5, 12–13
Globalization, vii-viii, 35
Grace (divine grace), 56, 59, 68–69, 77, 139, 148, 152, 159, 183, 186, 236, 239, 250, 277
Great Depression, 15
Guild Socialism, 12, 15, 19–21, 24, 26

Hammurabi, Code of, 205
Heresy, 10, 43, 100, 128, 159
Hinduism, 87, 89, 95, 99, 160, 168, 188–89, 207, 210, 305
Humanism, 18, 107, 266–67, 278, 292

Humanism, ethical, 107
Humanity, 18, 29, 31, 48n27, 51–59, 65, 70, 97, 135, 178, 183, 209, 213, 226, 248, 252–53, 261, 264, 304, 307, 311

Idealism, 100, 127, 195
Incarnation, doctrine of the, 41, 46–47, 128, 168–69, 172–73, 186, 212, 218, 223, 245
Individualism, 12, 14, 29, 260, 307, 310
Industrialism, 24, 114, 127, 153, 270, 288
Islam, 95, 207–10, 304–5

Jesus (Christ), 15n35, 46, 99, 132, 167–68, 170, 172, 181, 186, 188, 209–10, 221, 282
Judaism, 81, 100, 121, 128, 131, 165, 178–79, 189, 194, 199, 208–11, 215, 219, 222, 249, 305

Koinonia, 186

Labour Party, 10–11, 39, 49
League of Nations, 24–27
Liberalism, 5, 35, 80, 218, 252, 298
Lutheranism, 29, 275

Manichaean dualism, 225
Marriage, 64, 166, 175, 183–90, 247, 254, 257, 277, 284, 308, 314–15
Marxism, 114, 125, 194, 297, 316
Materialism, 195, 206
Medieval Europe, 261, 308
Medieval period, vii, 9, 11, 15–16, 20, 24, 28–30, 48, 81, 94, 97, 126, 150, 201n2, 217, 229, 236, 248, 261, 275, 308
Middle Ages, 18–20, 30–32, 65, 100, 144, 152, 175, 201n2–202, 214, 222, 228, 234, 253, 255–56, 260–61, 307
Moot Group, 34–40
Moralism, 21, 92, 109–11, 120, 135, 137–38, 211, 215, 233, 236, 242, 264, 267, 271

INDEX OF SUBJECTS

Natural Law, vii, 29, 31, 35, 41, 44–51, 57, 63–64, 135, 153, 236, 240–53, 303–9, 316–17
Natural Law theology/religion, 44, 47, 51, 75–85, 92–93, 96, 101, 213–16, 268
Natural Order, 31, 54n45, 56–70, 252n9
Nazism, 38–39, 43, 111, 127, 226
Neo-platonic, 95
Neo-Thomism, (Thomism), 15, 46, 229
New Testament, 32, 77, 93, 121, 128n15, 131, 139–40, 147, 167, 172, 209, 214, 220, 276
Nirvana, 168

Old Testament, 128o9, 139, 147, 211–12, 218–20, 293
Orthodoxy, vii, 27, 65n86, 137
Oxford, 3–5, 7–8, 17, 20, 35, 39, 91, 150n24

Parliament, 14, 251, 253, 260
Platonism, 42, 95, 113, 168, 186, 221
Polygamy, 64, 308
Post-modernity, vii
Protestantism, 10, 12, 41, 43, 45, 60, 63n81, 94–95, 113n17, 244–45, 266, 275
Psychedelic Drugs, 98

Quietist Movement, 151

Rationalism, 100, 114, 118, 127, 236, 252, 307
Redemption, 45, 56–57, 60, 154, 171, 181–82, 215, 297
Reformation, the, 29, 30, 45, 94, 144, 159, 237, 247, 275, 312
Reformers, the, 29, 155, 244, 247, 264, 311
Reform, social, 120, 127, 132, 217–18, 264–66,
Relativism, 17, 60n68, 251n4
Religious Experience, 45, 81, 87–88

Renaissance, the, 65, 89, 225, 228, 237, 256n14
Renaissance, Post-, 71, 192, 225
Renaissance, Pre, 89
Resurrection, doctrine of the, 46, 170, 172, 282
Revealed Theology, 75–76, 92–93
Revelation, 38, 44, 56, 76–81, 92, 95, 99, 108n7, 112, 129, 147, 161, 171–72, 180, 185, 194, 212, 236, 241, 249, 251, 258, 303–4
Revolution, American, 247–48
Revolution, French, 78, 225, 247–48, 256, 258, 287
Revolution, Indian, 256
Roman Catholic Church, x, 4–5, 9–12, 15, 19, 30, 43, 44–46, 49n28, 95, 113n17, 174, 306
Roman Empire, 230, 243n8, 255, 266
Romanticism, 85–86, 119, 252n9, 307

Schizophrenia, 121
Scripture, 76–77, 84, 88, 184, 186, 214–15, 250
Secular Society, 35, 39
Secularism, 39, 67–68, 128, 158–59, 163–65
Secularization, 35, 37–39, 102
Sexuality, 51, 53, 99, 174–75, 184, 234, 306, 314, 315
Sexuality, homo-, 7, 175, 306, 308
Sin, 26, 38, 44–45, 49, 52–61, 65–68, 117, 131, 139, 144, 154, 168n2, 183, 219, 229, 231–35, 243n9, 282–83, 294–95
Sin, original, 54, 65, 138, 200, 274
Social Credit, vii, 5–6, 9, 12–14, 19–28, 33, 253, 313
Socialism, 10, 12, 15–16, 19–21, 24, 26, 30, 108, 125, 226, 258
Socialism, National, 30, 108, 125
Sociology, 30–31, 47–48, 90, 253, 258
Sociology of religion, 48, 90
Sociology, Christian, vii, 5, 12, 28, 30–32, 41, 47–51, 56–59, 64n82, 68, 253, 316
Stock market crash, 28
Subjectivism, 42, 88

Suicide, 8
Supernatural, 56–59, 63, 75, 78–82, 101, 132, 158, 162, 165, 227, 229, 304

Technology, 18, 24, 153, 164, 271
Theism, 91, 158
Theism, mono-, 84, 147, 212
Theism, pan-, 143
Theological Liberalism, 5
Totalitarianism, 29, 32, 35, 37, 62, 67, 71, 105, 107, 119, 162, 239, 248, 252, 262, 268, 286, 307
Tractarians, 3, 9–10
Trade Unions, 12, 20–21, 60, 202, 260, 264
Transcendence, 54, 83, 128, 159, 161, 192, 208, 282
Trinity, doctrine of the, 41, 46, 94, 174, 180–81, 186, 188

Tudor, 237

Undated Salvation, doctrine of, 33
Unitarianism, 4, 41, 163
Utilitarianism, 29, 114–15, 256, 297, 316

Voluntarism, 116, 150–52, 244–47

Wall Street, 15
Western civilization, 35, 38, 175, 226
Western Ethics, 135
Western religion, 89, 92, 94, 97, 99–100, 191
World Council of Churches, 112
World War I, 10, 35, 266
World War II, 6–7, 9, 39

Zoroastrianism, 129, 199, 207

www.ingramcontent.com/pod-product-compliance
Lightning Source LLC
Chambersburg PA
CBHW020109010526
44115CB00008B/754